MW01485126

THE
HISTORY
OF THE
FITZHUGH
FAMILY

IN TWO VOLUMES

by Henry A. Fitzhugh & Terrick V.H. FitzHugh

VOLUME THE FIRST:
TO 1639 AD

FITZHUGH
THE STORY OF A
FAMILY THROUGH
SIX CENTURIES
by
Terrick V. H. FitzHugh

VOLUME THE SECOND:
FROM 1614 TO 1986

THE HISTORY
OF OUR
FITZHUGH FAMILY
by
Henry A. Fitzhugh

FITZHUGH

The Story of a Family

through

Six Centuries

by

Terrick V. H. FitzHugh

AuthorHouse™
1663 Liberty Drive, Suite 200
Bloomington, IN 47403
www.authorhouse.com
Phone: 1-800-839-8640

AuthorHouse™ UK Ltd.
500 Avebury Boulevard
Central Milton Keynes, MK9 2BE
www.authorhouse.co.uk
Phone: 08001974150

First published by AuthorHouse 1/11/2007

ISBN: 978-1-4259-7829-7 (sc)
ISBN: 978-1-4259-7830-3 (hc)

Printed in the United States of America
Bloomington, Indiana

This book is printed on acid-free paper.

T he retrieving of these forgotten things
from oblivion in some sort resembles the art
of a conjuror, who makes those walk and appear
that have lain in their graves many hundreds of
years, and represents, as it were to the eye,
the places, the customs and fashions that were of
old times.

John Aubrey (1626-97)

CONTENTS

Chapters

Figures & Illustrations

CHAPTER ONE

OLD UNHAPPY, FAR-OFF THINGS

"Loke that thou ne slee non man
Ne do non foly with non woman.
Gey, gey, gey, gey,
Think on dredful domes day!"

In mediaeval England a minstrel sang that song. If he had trolled his warning to really attentive listeners in the houses of the north Bedfordshire gentry, the events there of Tuesday, 24th July, 1358 might never have happened. In that case lives would have been lengthened, but only to sink into oblivion. Indeed, three generations of Fitzhughs *Tuesday, 24th* would now still lie unknown behind the dark *July, 1358* curtains of the past. That murder will out is true in more senses than one. Six centuries ago it was murder that caused lawyers' and officials' clerks to set quills to parchment and to file away their writings in royal and legal archives. There they lay until, generations later, they were unrolled to reward the persistence of the family historian.

The evidence of the documents is brief. What occurred that day is clear in outline; what caused it is sufficiently obvious; but the details need to be pieced together from inferences and implications. What follows is an attempted reconstruction of the happenings at the Fitzhugh home on that distant summer day.

John Fitzhugh must have been away from the house when the train of events began. Perhaps he was making the daily round of his farm. Certainly he was mounted, or his horse would not have

CHAPTER ONE

been saddled and ready for the urgent use to which it was put so soon after his return. As he rode, the gently undulating Bedfordshire countryside was stretched around him, heavy with the foliage of late July. The wheat must have been standing green and tall; and swathes of cut grass would be striping the meadows along Beggary Brook because in a week's time it would be Lammas. By then the hay ought all to be in and the sheep moved to pasture in the meads; but John was doubtless facing the problem that troubled cultivators of the land all over England; the labour needed for haymaking, ploughing and sowing was scarce and dear and had been so throughout the decade. Nine years earlier, in what was then called "the time of the mortality" and nowadays the Black Death, the pestilence had killed one man and woman in every three; and since then life had never been the same. The sudden disastrous fall in the population had driven wages up and the prices of grain and wool down, and the two Statutes of Labourers which had fixed maximum wages by law were constantly evaded.

For the Fitzhughs and their neighbours the chief source of ready money was the grain they took to the market two miles away at St Neots eked out by the wool from their sheep. The north Bedfordshire flocks were not large, but their fine wool was in demand by Flemish weavers, and it could be economically transported down the River Ouse to Lynn for export to the Low Countries.[1]

In the plague year of 1349, John had been a youth; now he was a grown man, lately married, and freeholder of the Beggary property that his father, William, had conveyed to him and his wife by charter.[2] It comprised a hundred acres of arable land, six acres of permanent pasture, and three of meadow.[3] It lay in the 'vill' of Wyboston within the parish of Eaton, later known as Eaton Socon. His father's intention in enfeoffing him and his wife jointly had been to avoid what would otherwise happen if John were to die before any son of his could come of age, *The family property at Beggary, Bedfordshire* which was that during the boy's minority the profits from the farm would go to the family's feudal lord, a situation often harmful to an estate and to the heir's future. Joint tenure by husband and wife at least gave the land a double chance of descending direct to an adult heir. However, so far the couple were childless.

OLD UNHAPPY, FAR-OFF THINGS

The land granted to John was part of a manor[*] that William Fitzhugh held of the Priory of St Neots. In documents from the Middle Ages down to the 16th century it is sometimes called Beggary, sometimes Goodwick and sometimes Goodwick alias Beggary, from two adjacent farms that still exist southwest of Eaton Socon village. Here we will use the name Beggary-cum-Goodwick when we refer to the manor as a whole to distinguish it from either of its parts. In Doomsday Book 1087, the property is described as comprising two hides and half a virgate of land with woodland for 100 swine, which means that, apart from the woodland, it contained about 255 acres of arable, meadow and pasture. At the Conquest, King William had rewarded his prominent follower and kinsman, Richard Fitzgilbert with the Honour of Clare and 175 other lordships in various parts of England. Among them were Beggary-cum-Goodwick and other manors in the neighbourhood.[4] This powerful Norman emptied the Priory of St Neots of its English monks and filled it with French Benedictines from the great Abbey of Bec in Normandy, of which it became a cell. For its support, he and his wife Rose bestowed lands upon it, including Beggary-cum-Goodwick in 'frank almoign,' free alms. This meant that in perpetuity the only services in respect of that manor that were due from the black-robed brethren to their feudal overlords the de Clares would be those of prayer for the souls of the founders and their descendants. The monastery was thus able to retain for itself the full service due from the tenants of the manor, who, by the early 13th century and perhaps earlier, were the Fitzhugh family.[5]

In the hierarchical system of feudalism all the land of England was owned by the King, and his subjects held their estates hereditarily either from him or as sub-tenants; so the de Clares held Beggary-cum-Goodwick of the King as tenants-in-chief; the Priory held it of the de Clares as mesne (middle) tenant; and the Fitzhughs held it of the Priory as terre tenants, the ones actually occupying the land.

Manorial lords and freeholders were the backbone of England's administrative system. John was one of the 'lawful and

---

[*] An Appendix to this Volume has been added with a map showing the boundaries of the Manor and aerial photographs showing part of the ancient moat. – HAF.

discreet men' on whom the court of Barford Hundred (a subdivision of the county) relied in administering the area and in dealing with civil disputes and local crime[6] and only recently his sworn statement had been carried to Westminster Hall in London in a rent dispute between the priories of Newnham and Merton.[7]

As John rode homewards, he could see, on the crest of a slight rise, his house rising above the wall that surrounded its courtyard. Around the wall lay the rectangular moat[8] that served the purposes of draining the site, keeping out intruders and providing the family's water supply. Though this, the earliest-known home of the Fitzhughs, was a modest enough place, it was certainly not so humble as its name suggests. "Beggary," guesses the English Place-Name Society,[9] "land so poor that its tenants must always be beggars." It is not surprising that as time went on the alternative name of Goodwick ('Godiva's dairy farm') became the more popular.

The house to which John was returning no longer exists; on its site stands a 16th or 17th century farmhouse with its half-timbering covered by later plaster and still surrounded on all but the road side by the moat. In the 14th century, a small manor house, such as that at Beggary, was a timber-framed, thatched building, most of which was made up of one large living room called the hall with a floor of rammed earth or chalk strewn with rushes or straw, and the rafters of the roof formed its ceiling. *John's & Elizabeth's house* Heating was from an open fire on a central hearth from which the smoke rose to the roof and made its way out through a vent in the thatch. Flue-boards may have made a simple chimney. The furniture consisted of a number of trestle tables and benches. The whole household ate in the hall, including at harvest time all the cottagers of the manor whose feudal duty it was to help get in the crop of the lord's demesne land. The private rooms of the house, called chambers, would probably be on the ground floor, but there may have been one or two to form an upper floor. They too were sparsely furnished, each with a trestle table and bench. The beds may well have been mere straw-filled berths or bunks. The food was cooked in a kitchen which, because of the fire risk, was often a separate building or sometimes the lower end of the hall. The courtyard that surrounded the house would also take in a bakehouse, barns, a maltkiln and a malthouse.

John's riding horse and his father's are likely to have been the only horses on the manor. The drawing of the waggons and the ploughing of the fields was done by oxen. Each daily round, indoors and out, went on from sunrise to sunset; torches were ineffectual and fire hazards, so once darkness set in little could be done but sup and chat and perhaps listen to an itinerant minstrel and then retire to bed.

Whether John's mood was as sunny as the season one may perhaps doubt. Possibly he already had reason to feel unhappy about his young wife. Eighteen-year-old Elizabeth Fitzhugh was the daughter and co-heiress of the late Nicholas Gamage of Wezebury in Gloucestershire.[10] In the normal way, she and John were unlikely ever to have met, across half the breadth of England, but both her parents had perished in the plague year,[11] and she had been taken in, at the age of seven, by her adult half-brother, Thomas Wauton, a son of her mother's first marriage,[12] who was lord of the manor of Basmead in Eaton parish and so a near neighbour of the Fitzhughs.

John comes home unexpectedly...

John rode over the bridge into his courtyard. Dismounting, he threw the rein to his servant Piers. What happened next is known only from the brief record of the next County Assizes,[13] but the charges made there and tacitly admitted imply something like the following.

Leaving his horse with Piers, John entered the house. There he found Elizabeth in company with young Richard Stocker, the son of a neighbour in circumstances that left no doubt as to their relationship. Out in the courtyard, it was probably John who drew his weapon first; a dagger was the one most commonly carried. Stocker defended himself and, in the fight that followed, struck the cuckolded husband a mortal wound. Then he seized John's horse with the intention of making a speedy escape. Piers tried to prevent him and was struck down like his master. Seeing her lover about to make off, Elizabeth cried out to him not to leave her behind. He

...and catches Elizabeth in flagrante.

John is murdered. Elizabeth and her lover escape.

pulled her up on the crupper, clapped heels to the horse's flanks and galloped out of the courtyard, making for the woods. The horrified houses-servants took up master and man, both either dead or dying.

The hue and cry were raised, but on horseback the couple were able to outride pursuit; and when the County Assize met they were still at large and in hiding.[14] A grand jury of reputable neighbours indicted both of them for double murder *Richard and* and also charged them with the theft of the horse, *Elizabeth are* worth 16s, and of its saddle, 6s 8d.[15] A further *charged* charge against Stocker was the abduction of Elizabeth. As the accused could not be produced in court to stand their trial, the goods and chattels of both were adjudged forfeit to the Crown. It was ordered that their presence be *John is dead, so* demanded at five successive courts if necessary, *Beggary is forfeit* and that if they were then still absent they be declared outlaws and any lands they held be forfeit to the Crown for a year and a day and then revert to the superior lord. As John was dead, the tenure of Beggary had passed automatically, by the terms of his father's charter, to Elizabeth and the land was therefore liable to the forfeiture. Its superior lord was Father Pierre, the French Prior of St Neots.

The months passed; the couple successfully remained at large and so they were outlawed and became in the eyes of the law little better than wolves. Once caught they could be judicially hanged without further trial. However, fortune favoured them. In the following year, King Edward III commenced preparations for a fresh campaign against the French, intending to march on Rheims and have himself crowned in the cathedral of that city as rightful King of France. Among other measures to bring his forces up to the necessary strength he proclaimed an amnesty for all felons who *But Elizabeth* would enlist and render satisfactory service in the *and Richard* campaign. Richard Stocker seized this *escape* opportunity and joined the retinue raised by the *punishment* Bedfordshire magnate, Roger de Beauchamp. At first sight this looks as though he left Elizabeth to endure her outlawry alone, but it is possible that the couple had already taken steps to evade its worst pains. If they had been able to reach a church of sanctuary, they would have been allowed to 'abjure the realm of England' and walk, barefoot, penniless, white-robed and carrying crosses, to a seaport and exile; so they may have been already at Calais when King Edward and his army landed there in October.

As the war turned out, the King failed to capture Rheims and abandoned temporarily his claim to the French throne, but his campaign did have the effect of freeing his continental dominions from the overlordship of the French King. He returned to Westminster at the end of May 1360 and, a few days later, granted Stocker and others their promised pardons.[16] There is no mention that Elizabeth's sentence was ever remitted; nevertheless she managed to live on for many years, as outlaws often did.

The decision of the Bedfordshire Assize Court had made Beggary forfeit to the Crown for a year and a day, after which it was to revert to the Prior of St Neots, who would be free to put in a new tenant of his own choice. In the meantime, the land had to be cultivated; so John Fitzhugh's younger brother, Richard, who but for the forfeiture would have been next heir to the childless Elizabeth,[17] applied for the tenure for the time being and received an Exchequer grant of it, one-tenth of a knight's fee, for as long as the land should remain in the King's hands. However, at that time the Priory of St Neots was in an unusual situation. Ecclesiastically, as has been said, it was subordinate to the Abbey of Bec in Normandy. Its Priors were appointed by the Norman Abbot, always by promoting his own French monks; and the Priory paid the Abbey annual dues in coin of the English realm. However, King Edward, being at war with the King of France, had appropriated St Neots and all similarly situated English priories for the duration of hostilities, together with their manors, granges and dues; so when Beggary fell doubly into his hands through the forfeiture, his royal grip was not easily loosened. The Prior, in claiming recovery at the end of the year and a day, was unable to call on the support of abbatial influence; and in fact the forfeiture stretched out for as long as Elizabeth remained alive, and that was another fifteen years. She died in 1374,[18] where and in what *After twenty five years, Richard gains title to Beggary* circumstances we do not know. Then, William being dead, Richard put in his claim for the land as next heir to his father, but the law's consideration of the claim dragged on through another nine years.

CHAPTER ONE

Eventually, in 1383, when he was in his forties, he achieved from the King's sub-escheator the recognition he sought, his hereditary right to the tenure, and thereafter held it by homage and fealty and the service of 20s a year.[19]

It is to the passion and blood of that unhappy July day that we owe our knowledge of the family in the 14th century. Were it not for the steps taken, first by the law to punish the crime, then by the murderer to evade his punishment, and finally by Richard Fitzhugh to recover half his inheritance, we should have no more than brief glimpses of the family, living in north Bedfordshire and carrying out the responsibilities of their position. As it is, we can identify and connect three generations and confirm their tenure of a manor that was to continue in the family for another two hundred years.

.oOo.

References

1	C.F. Tebbutt, *St Neots in Retrospect.*
2	Inquisition post mortem, Edw III, f. 237, no. 25.
3	Calendar of Close Rolls, 1369-74, p.417.
4	Victoria History of Bedfordshire.
5	History of St Neots, Huntingdonshire.
6	Assize Roll 32, Bedfordshire, 31-33 Edw III, 143.
7	Cartulary of Newnham Priory (Beds Hist Rec Soc, 43)
8	Victoria History of Bedfordshire.
9	Place-Names of Beds & Hunts.
10	Cal of Inq, Vol I, Edw III, p.337.
11	Inq p.m., Glos, Edw I-III, pt 5.
12	Cal of Inq, Vol I, Edw III.
13	Assize Roll 32, Beds, 31-33 Edw III, 152.
14	*Ibid.*
15	Cal of Inq p.m., Vol XIV, 48-51 Edw III.
16	Cal of Patent Rolls, Vol XI.
17	Cal of Close Rolls, 6 Ric II, pt ii.
18	*Ibid.*
19	Cal of Inq p.m., Vol XIV, 48-51 Edw III.

CHAPTER TWO

THE MISTS OF TIME

Entia non sunt multiplicanda, praeter necessitatem.
(Things not known to exist should not, unless it is
absolutely necessary, be postulated as existing.)
William of Occam, c.1300-1349

The documents to which the affray at Beggary gave rise revealed the name not only of John's and Richard's father but also of their grandfather, Richard Fitzhugh[1] for whom earlier evidence is also available. In 1309 he, together with a William Fitzhugh and twenty-three other men of the hundred *John's &* of Barford, were elected as collectors of a tax to aid *Richard's* King Edward II in his war against Robert the Bruce of *forebears* Scotland.[2] They assessed and gathered in a twenty-fifth of the value of the neighbourhood's sheep, cattle and crops. Richard himself was assessed at 7s 0 ¾d; and William, perhaps his younger brother, at 2s 0 ½d in the next parish.

Earlier than Richard, the family lineage becomes a matter of speculation and deduction. Every genealogist hopes, nearly always in vain, to trace back to the ancestor from whom his family surname derives, the man whose christian name or occupation, place of origin or personal characteristic has been handed down the ages by his male-line descendants as the mark of their common blood. In the case of the Fitzhughs, their surname identifies the family-founding ancestor as a man of the middle ages called Hugh.

Heritable surnames were first brought into England by the captains of the Conqueror's army; but it was not until a hundred years later that it became at all common for a whole family to inherit the same name; and then, over the 13th and 14th centuries, the custom slowly spread, from the upper classes to the lower and from the south of England to the north. In the county of Bedford, families of the gentry were already passing down heritable family names in the early 13th century.

Patronymic surnames, such as Fitzhugh, present difficulties to anyone trying to decide whether, in any given document, they were intended as family names or as purely personal cognomens. In the Latin records of the period, "Ricardus filius

The origin of the   Hugonis" can be translated as either "Richard
Fitzhugh surname   son of Hugh," "Richard Fitzhugh" or "Richard

Hughson;" so it is hard to tell whether that Richard was actually the son of Hugh or whether Hugh was some earlier forebear whose name, either prefixed by Norman 'Fitz' or suffixed by Anglo-Saxon '-son,' had become an hereditary surname. The records were written, not by our ancestors themselves, but by clerks who may have had little or no personal acquaintance with them and who surnamed them according to their own ideas. So in one document a man may be described as the son of his father, e.g. John Robertson; in another by his occupation, John Mercer; in a third by the place where he then or formerly lived, John Walton; and in yet another by some personal characteristic, John Short; though all the time his friends and neighbours habitually called him by some older surname that had become hereditary in his family. As already mentioned, we know of this happening in the case of William Fitzhugh, who was sometimes more conveniently known as William Fitzrichard, i.e. as the son of his father. It is this fluidity of nomenclature in the 13th and 14th centuries that gives us some trouble in identifying Richard's father.

In a document of 1317,[3] eight years after Richard had been Subsidy collector in the hundred, a woman confirmed lands in Eaton to a subtenant. She is described as "Joan, the widow of Richard son of Roger de Beggary." Can it be that Joan's late husband was the same man as our Richard Fitzhugh but identified in this document by the name of his actual father, Roger? If so, that record adds the name of one more ancestor to our family tree. The *Victoria History of Bedfordshire,* referring to this Richard and Roger, says "There is no evidence to connect them with the family of Fitzhugh." Certainly there is no explicit evidence, but when their personal names, their property and the office performed by them (or him) are considered together, there is implicit evidence that does more than just connect Richard son of Roger with the Fitzhughs.

The preposition 'de' before a surname could mean either 'of' or 'from'; more frequently the latter. A John de Eaton would usually be a man born in Eaton who settled elsewhere among new neighbours who distinguished him from their other Johns by surnaming him with his place of origin. A man named after a manor or sizable freehold in which he was still living might be called 'of' it, but he would be so named only if he were a member of the owning family. In the case of Richard and Roger de Beggary there can be no question of the 'de' meaning 'from', because the widow of the son still held land in the parish after his death. So they were 'of' Beggary, members of the manorial family; but we know who held Beggary at that time, the Fitzhughs. This makes Richard son of Roger look very like the same man as Richard Fitzhugh; but there is other and stronger evidence of identification.

In the Subsidy Rolls of both 1297[4] and 1303[5] the name Richard son of Roger appears. In the former year he is one of the two Subsidy collectors for Wyboston and Beggary (significantly the other collector is the lord of Wyboston manor), and in the latter year one of the twelve collectors for the hundred of Barford - as Richard Fitzhugh was in 1309. So we have the following data:

    1297:   Richard son of Roger, collector.
    1303:   Richard son of Roger, collector.
    1309:   Richard Fitzhugh, collector.
    1317:   Richard son of Roger already dead.

It is noticeable that whenever Richard son of Roger is listed in the Subsidy Rolls there is no mention of Richard Fitzhugh and vice versa.

If we knew that Richard son of Roger was still alive in 1309, then the two names would certainly overlap in time, and as both men were 'of' the same manor and performing the same tax-collecting function the conclusion that they were the same man would be inescapable. And there is indirect evidence to this effect. If, in 1309, Joan, wife of Richard son of Roger, was already a widow, she would have been assessed in that year for tax on the lands she held (as mentioned in 1317); but her name does not appear in the subsidy though those of other independent women do. This implies that her husband was still alive and listed on the Roll; and in that year the collector is shown as Richard Fitzhugh. So there was only one Richard but known by two surnames, one of them his patronymic and the other his hereditary family name; and this means that his father's name was Roger, because there is other evidence that Fitzhughs, under that name, held Beggary from the early 13th century.

A Foot of Fines of 1241 shows an earlier 'Ricardus filius Hugonis' holding and subinfeuding land in Beggary to a certain William Pewdy. The process takes the form, necessary under the land laws of that time, of a collusive law suit. In the Calendar it reads:

"Newport Pagnell. Morrow of Hilary (14th January 1241). William Pewdi' against Richard son of Hugh, whom William son of Hugh, Hugh le Blund and Jowet his wife called to warranty and who warranted to them, land in Beggary. Assize of mort d'ancestor."

The final agreement was:

"Right of William (Pewdi'), to be held of Richard and his heirs paying therefor yearly two shillings and three hens and one cock at Christmas by two men, who shall eat that day with the said Richard, and likewise finding a man in autumn to reap the corn of Richard and his heirs, for all service."[6]

The meaning of the warranty is that various members of the same family, having rights or potential rights in the land, were associating themselves with the agreement to guarantee to William Pewdy that his tenure of the land would not thereafter be disputed. The note 'Assize of mort d'ancestor' means that William Pewdy was bringing his action on the grounds that his family had held the land before him.

William son of Hugh must have been Richard's brother or, less likely at that early date, his son already using an hereditary surname. Who then were Hugh le Blund (the heir) and Jowet his wife? From a Curia Regis record of 1223 dealing with land in Wyboston, we know that Richard's mother was Joyce.[7] As his father was not named in the case, he can be presumed to be dead, in which case Hugh le Blund cannot have been his father. It therefore seems likely that Jowet was either Richard's sister or daughter, because in either relationship she might in certain eventualities have inherited a right to the land. We are left with the question: was Richard's father called Hugh or does the family founder lie still further back? At that early date in surname history it is almost certain that "filius Hugonis" did mean "son of Hugh" because Richard's father cannot have been born later than about 1175; so we can draw up a pedigree of the family in the 13th and 14th centuries though with the earlier part only tentative:

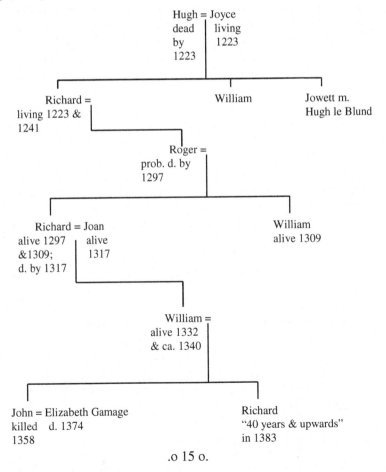

CHAPTER TWO

Though the word 'fiz' was Norman French (the 't' became inserted in England to give effect to the continental pronunciation of 'z'), it is not safe to assume that the Fitzhughs' earliest English ancestor was a follower of the Conqueror, either at Hastings or after a safe interval, because in the 13th century the English gentry, whether of Norman or Saxon descent, still spoke the language of the ruling race.

The date of the Conquest is another dream goal of the ambitious genealogist but one only achievable by hopping from family to family through female lines of descent. Though it is possible in that way to trace <u>ancestry</u> back to 1066, indeed to the Conqueror himself, the same is not true of <u>families</u>. It is thought that all possible male-line descents from the time of the Conquest have already been traced. This is because the surviving records of that period refer only to men and their families who were rewarded by the Conqueror with earldoms, baronies and major grants of land. Doomsday Book does mention lesser men, but their sons and grandsons are lost to us. So we cannot hope to reach further back than our 12th century Hugh. Even as early as 1291, royal officials realised the impossibility of finding documentary evidence for claims to entitlements originating before the death of King Henry II in 1189; so they accepted them on the grounds that they had existed from "time whereof the memory of man runneth not to the contrary," usually shortened to "time immemorial." So we must take satisfaction that our Fitzhugh line also reaches back, though with some tentatively, into the acknowledged impenetrability of that age of antiquity.

The earliest known documentary evidence for the Fitzhugh coat of arms is of the year 1566,[8] but the description of it then given in the records of the College of Arms implies that it was borne by our ancestors from at least eighty years earlier and almost certainly longer. Indeed there is reason to suspect that Richard, brother of the murdered John, was armigerous. At that period most *The Fitzhugh* families adopted armorial bearings on their own *Coat of Arms* initiative as there was not yet any fully effective control to prevent misuse or duplication. It was not until over a hundred years later, after the King's Heralds had been incorporated into the College of Arms, that they were able to take firm steps to maintain the prestige of coat armour by covering the country with tours of inspection, examining claims to arms and either confirming or disallowing them. On the first Herald's Visitation of Bedfordshire in 1566, Clarenceux, King of Arms for England south of the River Trent, confirmed to the Fitzhughs the arms they were using, namely: *'Ermine, on a chief gules three martlets or'*, which means a white shield sprinkled with ermine tails, except that the top one-third of the area was red with three golden martlets on it. And Clarenceux did more than that; he also confirmed that their arms were quartered with the arms: *'Argent, three chevrons sable, each charged with a bezant'*, which means a white (not silver) shield with three black chevrons one above the other, each bearing a golden orb. Unfortunately neither Clarenceux nor the Fitzhughs he discussed the matter with seem to have known to what family those quartered arms belonged. Quartering is an heraldic record of an ancestral marriage with an heiress - not a rich bride but one without surviving brothers so that she was the last of her line. The grandfather of the Nicholas Fitzhugh with whom Clarenceux dealt had married an heiress in about 1475, but Nicholas would have known if the arms had been of her family; so the union recorded by the quartering must have been in some earlier generation. Three and a half centuries after the Visitation, my father and uncle asked the Clarenceux of their day to identify the arms, but the King of Arms was only able to say that it was "either Colville or Malabassel."

A fine-sounding name, Malabassel, with a hint of wickedness in it. I did my best to trace a link between the family and the Fitzhughs but no sign could I find of them anywhere within mating distance of Beggary. But with Colvilles it was just the reverse. Directly I stepped, metaphorically speaking, over the Beggary boundary, I bumped into them. In the year when John Fitzhugh was murdered at Beggary, the adjoining manor of Eaton was held by a Sir William Colville in right of his wife Joan,[9] and his tenure of it continued only until her death in 1390, when the manor reverted to its hereditary tenants, the family of Joan's first husband, John Engayne. There is no evidence that Richard Fitzhugh married Sir William's daughter or indeed that he ever had a daughter, but the combination of Clarenceux's statement and the very close proximity of the two families during that one generation do present a choice of probabilities. Either such a union did take place or there were two coincidental relationships between the Fitzhughs and Colvilles, one as next neighbours and the other as in-laws.

On coats of arms, martlets are usually drawn by modern artists with the forked tails of swallows, but in mediaeval emblazons they are shown with spatulate tails because 'martlet' was the old name for the swift.[10] The heraldic birds have feathery legs but are footless because the feet of swifts are so undersized that they are unsuited, and seldom used for perching or walking. It seems odd, at first thought, that such an inoffensive, familiar creature of the English countryside ever became a popular heraldic charge in an age when a shield of arms was a piece of military accoutrement. Lions yes, leopards, griffins and eagles, all very virile and fear-inspiring; but the outstanding characteristic of the swift is speed in flight! Enquiry on this point to the Heraldry Society shows that no research has been carried out into the origin of this ancient and frequently chosen heraldic charge; so the following is put forward as a suggestion in the hope that it may one day be either confirmed or corrected.

In the middle ages, knights and esquires selecting a design for their coats of arms often chose charges from the shields of their feudal overlords in graceful acknowledgement of their vassalage. The Fitzhughs held Beggary-cum-Goodwick of the Priory of St Neots, a religious body not known to have had arms of its own; but martlets have always had strong associations with the church. In an account of their nesting habits as late as 1778, the naturalist Gilbert White, clearly with this tradition in mind, commented on the fact that the swifts of Selborne "though they do not all build in the church, yet so frequently haunt it and play and rendezvous around it;"[11] and nearly two hundred years earlier Shakespeare made Banquo[12] speak of "the temple-haunting martlet." The revered King Edward the Confessor, who lived and died before the dawn of heraldry, was posthumously made both saint and armiger. The blazon chosen for him was based upon a penny of his reign that bore a cross between five doves and the heraldic translation thought appropriate was *"a cross patonce between five martlets or."*[13] As the church was, under the King, the largest landholder, the frequent choice of this unwarlike bird as an heraldic charge would no longer be surprising if it was found to be owing to the feudal influence mentioned.

.oOo.

References

1 Cal. of Patent Rolls, Vol xi.
2 Subsidy of 3 Edw II, 1309-10 (Beds. Hist. Rec. Soc.)
3 Harleian Charter 45, cited in Victoria History of Bedfordshire.
4 The Taxation of 1298 (Beds. Hist. Rec. Soc., 39)
5 Feudal aids, Beds.
6 Cal. of Foot of Fines for Beds. (Beds. Hist. Rec. Soc, 6)
7 Curia Regis Rolls, Hen III, m. 10d.
8 Visitation of Beds., Harliean Society, 19.
9 Chan. Inq. p.m., 44 Edw III (2nd nos.), no. 26, cited by Vict. Co. Hist. Beds, Vol ii.
10 Oxford English Dictionary.
11 Gilbert White, *Natural History of Selbourne*, Ch. 21 & 29.
12 Shakespeare, *Macbeth*, i,vi.
13 A.G. Fox-Davies, revised by J.P. Brooke-Little, *A Complete Guide to Heraldry*, Ch.14.

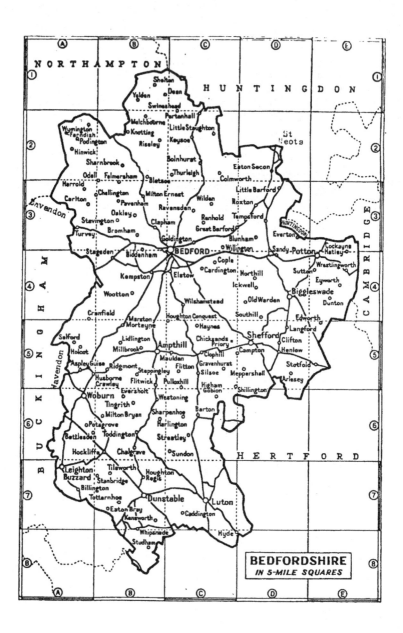

NORTHAMPTON

HUNTINGDON

CAMBRIDGE

BUCKINGHAM

HERTFORD

BEDFORDSHIRE
IN 5-MILE SQUARES

.o 20 o.

CHAPTER THREE

THE END OF OUR DARK AGES

Oure life shall passe away as the trace of a cloud, and
come to naught as the myst that is dryven awaye with
the beames of the Sonne and put down with the heate
thereof. Our name also shal be forgotten by litle and
litle, and no man shal have oure workes in remembraunce...

Soch things do the ungodly ymagin, and go astraye.

Miles Coverdale, 1488-1568
The Boke of Wysdome

The mists of time are not of uniform density. When we
emerge from the 1300s, where we have been enjoying
comparatively good visibility, considering the distance, we run into
a thick patch of ground-mist. Following Richard Fitzhugh are three
generations of shadowy figures who are glimpsed momentarily and
then lost sight of. Indeed we can assume three generations only
because to fit in more or fewer would be Procrustean. In 1437, at an
escheator's Inquisition Post Mortem held at Bedford, a William
Fitzhugh was one of a 12-man jury comprised of men recognisably
from Barford Hundred.[1] Seventeen years later we come upon
William Fitzhugh, this time explicitly "of Beggary, gentleman,"
who had charged one of his neighbours, John Laurence of
Wyboston, with rustling his cattle, in which accusation he was
joined by John Baker, husbandman, also of Beggary. Laurence had
evaded capture for some time but at last, in 1454, gave himself up
at the Fleet Prison in London.[2] And that, disappointingly, is all that
is known of that interesting episode. Because William was "of
Beggary" he was almost certainly the grandfather of the next
Fitzhugh to appear by name, one Thomas, who will have been born

at about that date. With this infant we step at last onto a firmly marked trail. We meet him occasionally during his long life, and we know a great deal more about his sons and his descendants from then on.

Thomas lived through the Wars of the Roses, but that struggle, for all its ferocity, did not greatly upset the lives of those minor gentry who, like the Fitzhughs, held their lands not of a baronial partisan but of a peaceable religious house. Late in the

Thomas Fitzhugh marries Christine Maidbury during the Wars of the Roses

reign of the Yorkist Edward IV, Thomas married Christine, one of the three daughters and co-heirs of William Maidbury,[3] lord of the manor of Maidbury in the parishes of Elstow and Wilshamstead, two miles south of Bedford; and, among other children, they had three sons, Richard, born about 1480,[4] Thomas some eighteen months later and William, our ancestor, in 1483-4.[5] Our authority for the parent-sons relationship is a pedigree supplied to the heralds at the 1634 Visitation of Oxfordshire. That is a late and secondary source, but as the brothers between them inherited all the properties of both Thomas Fitzhugh and the Maidburys and the two Thomases were long known as Thomas the elder and Thomas the younger, there is little reason to doubt it. Indirect evidence also indicates that Thomas the elder had three daughters. One married John Stocker[6] of Wyboston, thus finally healing the great scar on the families' neighbourly relationship; and the others married men called Watson[7] and Houghton.[8]

In due course Christine's father died, and one-third of his estate came to Thomas in right of his wife, since married women could not normally hold land. It consisted not only of the manor of Maidbury but also of a house and land in the parish of Wavendon,[9] just over the county border in Buckinghamshire. The other co-beneficiaries were a man called Lawe and a William Smith, husbands of Christine's sisters Joan and Alice Maidbury.[10] At this time another Wavendon man, Thomas Lowe, married a Fitzhugh girl, probably sister of Thomas the elder. Her Christian name is unknown but her family bore our arms.[11] Spelling being what it was at that period, Lawe and Lowe, both of Wavendon, are quite likely to have been of the same family.

Apart from a single mention of a William Fitzhugh, late of Ampthill,[12] the only other 15th century Bedfordshire Fitzhughs whose names have come down to us are a William Fitzhugh who was Mayor of Bedford in 1487 and another William closely associated with him and so probably his son.[13] The elder could, from his date, have been a younger brother of Thomas's father sent to the county town to be apprenticed to a burgess, in time becoming a burgess himself and eventually, at the age of about 60, Mayor. There is no sign of his line having continued for more than one generation.

Life for the family changed slowly. Their feudal landlords, the successive Priors of St Neots, ceased to be Frenchmen. In 1409 King Henry IV ended the subordination of the Priory to the Norman Abbey. All but two of the French monks were sent back to Bec. At that time, the Friar happened, exceptionally, to be an Englishman, but it was ruled that from then on all his successors and indeed all the inmates of the monastery were to be natives of the realm. This politically motivated change did not turn out all for the good. Thirteen years later, the Bishop of Lincoln had reason to censure the then Prior for his conduct of the house; and by 1439 conditions were the talk of the neighbourhood. The Priory was in debt, and the local lay people of the district who worked for it in one capacity or another were not being paid. The church was in such a state of disrepair that in the choir in rainy weather one could not keep a book open. Lay people wandered in and out at will and even ate with the monks. The Prior was accused of having paid an Eaton man to help him get elected; and both he and one of the brothers were charged with adultery with two local married women. The monastic ideals of the high Middle Ages were indeed in deep decay; but in Wyboston in 1476 a chantry chapel was erected, dedicated to Saints Mary, James and Christopher. This was the pious foundation of one of the Stocker family of Beggary. William Stocker, a younger son, had been apprenticed to a freeman of the Drapers' Company in London, had prospered there, fought for King Edward IV in the dynastic wars and been knighted on the field of battle at Tewkesbury. After founding the chantry in his home village, he crowned his career in 1484 by becoming Lord Mayor of London, only to die a few days later of the sweating sickness. His chapel and chaplain, intended for prayers for the souls of Stockers past and to come, proved a boon, not only to the villagers of Wyboston but also to those of the neighbouring village of Chawston when winter floods cut them off from attendance at their own church.

The wool from sheep on the Eaton pastures continued to be floated down the Ouse for export to the continent, but a wool market of even greater potentialities was developing at home from the increasing manufacture of English cloth.

At the manor house, the hall was by this time probably no more than a dining-room, while a new room called the parlour, either taken out of the hall or built onto it, took over as the chief living-room, in which painted wall-hangings enhanced its air of comfort. More, or perhaps the whole, of the hall would be now ceiled over by floors inserted to form additional upper chambers, and these would make a chimney-stack necessary. In spite of all these improvements, the family home still suffered from damp, as moated houses always did.

It was becoming the custom for the youthful sons of landowners to be trained in a knowledge of the law even though they had no intention of taking it up professionally. Their fathers considered it likely to be useful to the family in the maintenance of their rights of ownership. The notorious litigiousness of the 16th century may well have been in some part due to there being so many private persons who, when in dispute with their neighbours, felt confident, rightly or wrongly, in their powers of making their cases good in a court of law. Thomas kept his heir at home to learn and help in the day-to-day running *Thomas sends his son Thomas into the Law* of his properties, but he sent his teen-age second son Thomas to London to study to become a lawyer. The institutions for teaching law were the four Inns of Court and their eight satellite Inns of Chancery. The training at the latter brought the student up to a qualification for an attorney or solicitor, but if the young man had higher ambitions or his father a deeper purse, he would then go on to the parent Inn of Court to learn advocacy and become a barrister. Thomas must have gone to either New Inn or Strand (also known as Chester) Inn, both satellites of the Middle Temple, where he would pursue his studies for several years in the company of another three dozen or so young men from different parts of England.

Meanwhile, at home, Thomas the elder in 1503 was helping one of his neighbours, Robert Blackwell, who lived in Wyboston at a house called The Fortie, to surmount a family difficulty. It was a question of getting round the current law governing the passing of real estate at its holder's death. In the Middle Ages the holding of land by knight service had been the basis of the whole feudal system, and, when a freeholding tenant died, he had no power to bequeath his land to whomever he wished, as he could with his personal property. By the Common Law it had to descend undivided to his heir. This left little means of providing for younger sons, and by the beginning of the 16th century such a limitation was largely out of date as the feudal system was all but a thing of the past; so lawyers had devised a detour around the law. The landowner, while living, could convey his property to trustees on the condition that they would hold it according to his will ('will' being the current word for 'wish'), which normally meant for his own continued use. Then, on the approach of death, he would express, in writing, a new, and last, will telling the trustees for whose use they were to hold it or to whom they were to hand it over after he was dead. At this period a Last Will and a Testament, later combined in one document, were two separate legal instruments the latter valid only for the disposal of personal property.

This Robert Blackwell of the Fortie was at that time a married Officer of the King's Receipt on the staff of the Court of the Exchequer. He was purchasing a messuage (house together with grounds, outhouses, etc.), a toft (cottage site plot) and six acres of arable land in the open fields of Eaton Manor; but he wanted them conveyed, not to him but to trustees for the use of himself, his heirs and assigns; and the men he was asking to accept this trust were his brother William, priest of a Huntingdonshire parish, a colleague in the Exchequer called John Castell, and his neighbour Thomas Fitzhugh. They accepted and carried out this salutary process, thus enabling Robert to make better provision for his younger children.[14]

Two years later, on 1st July 1505, Thomas the younger, having passed out of his Inn of Chancery, was admitted to the Middle Temple.[15] There his father was not only put to greater expense in supporting him - at least £28 a year - but was also expected to provide him with a servant. Learning advocacy was a keen test of the students' wits. For them the Summer and Lent Vacations between the law terms were the busiest and most interesting times of the year. It was then that Thomas, among about two hundred other juniors, called Inner-Barristers, attended, as audience and learners, criticisms of parliamentary statutes and

FITZHUGHS OF THE 15th CENTURY

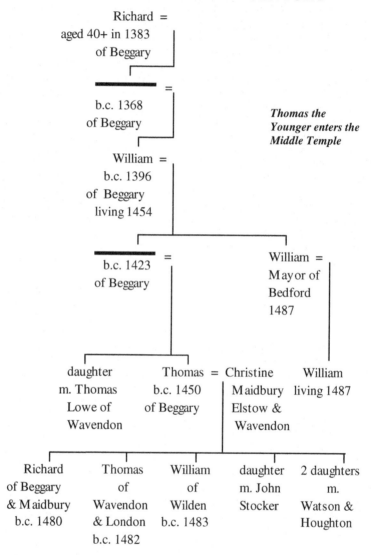

Richard =
aged 40+ in 1383
of Beggary

b.c. 1368
of Beggary
=

*Thomas the
Younger enters the
Middle Temple*

William =
b.c. 1396
of Beggary
living 1454

b.c. 1423
of Beggary
=

William =
Mayor of
Bedford
1487

daughter
m. Thomas
Lowe of
Wavendon

Thomas =
b.c. 1450
of Beggary

Christine
Maidbury
Elstow &
Wavendon

William
living 1487

Richard
of Beggary
& Maidbury
b.c. 1480

Thomas
of
Wavendon
& London
b.c. 1482

William
of
Wilden
b.c. 1483

daughter
m. John
Stocker

2 daughters
m.
Watson &
Houghton

doubtful legal judgments propounded in hall as exercises by the seniors, or Utter-Barristers, and also the mock trials performed by the latter, all in the presence of the Benchers and under the direction of the Reader, a lawyer appointed half-annually to select and supervise these exercises. The pleading and arguing in these trials or Moots had all to be carried on in Norman-French, but the comments upon them by the Benchers were fortunately made in English. Here, as at his Inn of Chancery, Thomas also studied history and the social arts of music, singing and dancing. Twice during his first two years at the Middle Temple studies were suspended owing to epidemics, first the sweating sickness and second the plague, but he seems to have lost little time in being called by the Reader to the grade of Utter Barrister, a qualification that a man had to hold for several years before he was allowed to plead in the courts, either at Assizes or at Westminster Hall.

At about the same time as Thomas was entering the Middle Temple, his younger brother William got married,[16] though he was no older than twenty-three, an early age for a third son with his way still to make. His bride was a young girl called Catherine Bill whose late father had been a draper at Ashwell in

Our Ancestor
William marries
Catherine Bill

Hertfordshire. She can have brought little into the marriage in the way of dower for she had seven brothers and sisters. Apparently there was no marital home for them on the Fitzhugh properties, so they set up house in the neighbouring parish of Colmworth.[17] There is a suspicion of a rift between Thomas the elder and his youngest son, which may have been caused by the father considering his marriage unsuitable. However, the couple themselves seem to have been happy enough. They began to raise what was to become an exceptionally large family even by the standards of the time.

Thomas's second son and namesake must have been a source of parental pride. After passing out of the Middle Temple and a very short practice as barrister in the courts, he was elevated to the bench as Justice of Assize on the Western Circuit.[18] The Assizes were courts of law held in each county several times a year before judges trained in the Common Law and appointed from Westminster. The country was divided into seven circuits, and four judges were allotted to each. In general they dealt with cases more serious than those brought before the Quarter Sessions, including all charges of felony and treason. They also tried all the prisoners currently in the county gaols. The Western Circuit was somewhat misleadingly named since it covered the counties of the south-west: Southampton (now called Hampshire), Wiltshire, Somerset, Dorset, Devon and Cornwall. From 1511 Thomas toured them on horseback in company with three senior members *Thomas becomes* of the Middle Temple, Richard Elyot and his son *a Circuit Judge* Thomas, of Somerset, and a Devonshire man, Lewis Pollard. The younger Elyot, a man of many interests and talents, officiated as Clerk of the Circuit. Together they listened attentively to charges and evidence spoken in all the variety of accents, burrs and local idioms of the six counties through which they travelled. No wonder that Thomas Elyot, when he came to write his book, *The Governour*, on education, raised the notion of a 'correct' way of speaking English, 'clean, polite, and articularly pronounced.'

In the second year of Thomas's judgeship, Henry VIII, with the encouragement of the Pope and the assistance of the King of Spain, renewed the hereditary claim of English monarchs to the throne of France and declared war on King Louis. His first efforts on land and sea were unfortunate, and early in the following year King Ferdinand let him down by making a separate peace. However, Parliament had granted the funds and the Pope was still encouraging his cause, so Henry planned an invasion at Calais to be led by himself in person. Among his subjects called upon to provide a contingent of forces was a neighbour of the Fitzhughs, one George Harvey of Thurleigh. Harvey was a wealthy man, owning lands not only in Bedfordshire and Buckinghamshire, of which counties he had been Sheriff in 1508, but also in the counties of Oxford, Hertford and Huntingdon; so before exposing his life to the perils of war he was anxious to settle the devolment of his estates. His wife Elizabeth had presented him with a son and daughter, Nicholas and Elizabeth, and these children he was planning to disinherit. To ensure that his intention could not be frustrated after his death, he called together six of his trusted friends, of whom Thomas the elder was one and Walter Luke of Cople, a lawyer, another, and confided to them a family secret. He was convinced, and gave reasons for his conviction, that Nicholas and Elizabeth were not really his children, his wife being, as one of the friends expressed it later, 'very light of her conversation.' And that was not all. He had a cousin Margaret, married to a certain William Smart and mother of a little boy called Gerard; but, he assured them, that boy, though born in wedlock, was not Smart's son but begotten by him, George Harvey (no mention apparently of lightness of conversation), and it was to Gerard and to no one else that he intended to leave all his estates.[19]

For Harvey to enfeoff trustees with his lands, as Blackwell had done, so that he could direct them by his Last Will to Gerard, to the total disinheritance of both his legitimate children, was not likely to be sufficient. Such a will might be upset in a court of equity on a plea from his widow; so he appealed for the advice and co-operation of his friends in carrying out another legal device, one sometimes used for breaking entails, called 'suffering a Recovery.' In the light of all he had told them, his friends agreed to this proposal, and together they entered a claim in the Court of Common Pleas to all the Harvey estates on their own behalf. The grounds they put forward were as outrageous as the claim itself. Harvey, they declared, had come into possession of them only after a certain (entirely fictitious but legally familiar) Hugh Hunt had dispossessed

Thomas helps a friend to disinherit a natural son and leave all to an illegitimate son

them, the claimants, of the said lands. Harvey played his role in this piece of make-believe by bringing into court a third person who was said to have assured him of his title and was therefore bound to defend Harvey's claim in his stead. The claimants prayed the judges for permission to confer privately with this person; but when the court reassembled, the vouchee, as he was called, failed to reappear. Judgement was therefore given, in default, to the plaintiffs. After the success of this ploy, the 'dispossessed' owner, his mind at rest, sailed off to France, was present at the Battle of the Spurs and took part in the sieges of Therouanne and Tourney, at the latter of which he was knighted by the King, thus winding up, both for him and his sovereign, a highly successful campaign. Harvey and the 'recoverers' had of course a private contract that the latter were only holding the lands to Harvey's own use.

Thomas the younger's tours of the south-western county towns gave him little time to get home, so it was probably before taking up his judgeship that he married a young woman of his own parish. His father-in-law, Sir Thomas Wauton, now died, and as he had no son to carry on his family's ancient tenure of Basmead, he left his two daughters as his co-heirs. One of them, Cicely, had married Walter Luke's son Nicholas and the other, whose name has not come down to us, was Thomas's wife.[20] Her share of the Wauton estate consisted of a messuage with lands in Honeydon, called Wautons, and another at Toddeston in Huntingdonshire. Thomas was soon at loggerheads with his mother-in-law, Anne Wauton, about them. She refused to give up the title deeds to the properties, having probably a life interest, and for that he laid a Complaint against her in the Court of Chancery.[21] As the case was not pursued, the threat of it seems to have been sufficient for the purpose.

After riding the Western Circuit for seven years, Thomas in 1518[22] obtained a transfer to his own part of the country and worked the Norfolk Circuit, which covered Norfolk, Suffolk, Cambridgeshire, Huntingdonshire and his home counties of Bedfordshire and Buckinghamshire. On his Commission of Gaol Delivery he now tried prisoners from the gaols of Aylesbury, Ipswich and Bury St Edmunds and the castles of Bedford, Norwich, Cambridge and Huntingdon. Besides all his official duties he was, as a lawyer, much in demand among neighbours and friends as executor of their testaments, trustee of their last wills and counsel in their lawsuits. Newnham Priory paid him a regular retainer[23] and so did the Priory of Bushmead.[24]

In 1520 Sir George Harvey, perhaps not feeling too well, thought it wise to make his testament and last will. By the former, however it was made, he could not prevent one-third of his personal goods from devolving upon his widow and a further third from going to the children borne by her, but what concerned him more was his last will. He called in two lawyers, Walter Luke and Thomas Fitzhugh the younger, to give him professional advice. He was 'divers and sundry times accounsell' with them, and together they produced a document expressing to his trustees the wish that two of his properties should go to Margaret Smart for life and, after her death, to her son. The rest were to remain in the hands of the trustees for the next fifteen years and then devolve upon Gerard Smart absolutely. To Thomas, his legal adviser, he left a retaining fee of 6s 8d a year for life 'to the intent that he shall give counsel to mine executors for the true performance of this my last will when he at any time hereafter shall be by them required.'[25] Perhaps it was for a further assurance that he left money to have Gerard 'set in an Inn of Court to learn the Common Law.' Sir George recovered his health and lived on for nearly two years, but when he died his son-in-law Edward Wauton, Elizabeth's husband, obtained possession of the title deeds, her brother having died, and actually sold some of the Harvey lands; so the condition attached to Thomas's legacy was no sinecure. His father and his fellow trustees were obliged to bring an action in Chancery against not only the Wautons but also the purchasers of the land in order to defend the wishes of the deceased Sir George, and in this they were successful.[26]

In 1523 and again in the following year, Thomas the younger was made a member of the Lay Subsidy Commission for collecting the King's taxes in the county of Bedford[27] and in 1524 he was appointed Steward of the Middle Temple for Christmas, though he declined that position.[28] In the following February the Benchers elected him Reader for the Lent Vacation.[29] The grounds for appointment to this post were the appointee's 'knowledge, gifts of utterance, discretion and ability to maintain his countenance.' It was the Reader who directed the students' studies by selecting the parliamentary Acts and judicial verdicts for them to discuss, devising the imaginary lawsuits to be disputed and supervising the carrying out of these exercises in *Thomas is elected Reader of the Middle Temple* advocacy. The appointment was a considerable honour and carried with it a place on the Middle Temple Bench for life, but it was also a considerable expense. The Reader was expected to dispense a generous hospitality during the weeks of his office, culminating in a final feast. On all these occasions venison was the customary viand, and although some entertainment expense was recoverable - in the following reign twelve buck were considered an adequate allowance - it was always expected that the Reader would exceed this minimum. For financial reasons many chosen Readers were obliged to decline the honour, and so did Thomas, preferring to pay the customary fine.[30]

In 1520 Robert Blackwell had died. He left two sons, George and Henry, three daughters, Barbara, Alice and Jane, and his second wife Joan.[31] By then or soon after, Thomas the younger had been bereaved, his wife dying without having borne him any children to welcome him home from his circuit tours. Though Robert himself had spent much of his time in London, the Blackwell and Fitzhugh families had long been neighbours and friends, so what could be more suitable than a match between Thomas and Joan? And so it came about.[32] To her second husband Joan brought more or less intact the household stuff she had taken into her first marriage: all the hangings of parlour and chamber, with all the bedding, blankets, counterpanes, mattresses, featherbeds, pillows, napery and kitchen and buttery equipment.[33] But the Blackwells were a deeply religious family. Robert and his first wife had been lay brother and sister of the monastery of West Smithfield in London; their daughter Alice was a nun; and Robert's brother a priest; so Joan found a very different atmosphere in her new home, for Thomas was worldly and acquisitive and little interested in religion.[34] There was also another change. The new wife bore a name that was now out of fashion. Joan was thought all right for the lower orders but had lately been replaced in polite society by Jane.[35] Thomas preferred Jane and always referred to his wife by that name.[36]

Thomas the elder was now in his seventies. During the last years of his life he busied himself with buying out the survivors and descendants of the heirs to the Maidbury family's estate.[37] The properties in Elstow, Wavendon, Aspley Guise, Cotton, Cardington, Fenlake, Harrowden and *Thomas dies, and* Wilshamstead all passed into his hands. *William is* Never before had the Fitzhughs owned so *disinherited, at least* great an area of land. He died about 1526 *for a while* and unfortunately no will survives to show what his plans were for his several properties, but we may deduce them from the actual distribution, which was somewhat unusual. Richard the heir, as was natural, inherited the Beggary-cum-Goodwick manor, and Thomas received Wavendon, Aspley Guise and some parcels of land in Eaton. One would therefore expect that Maidbury manor would go to William, but it did not; it was added to Richard's portion. As concerns land, William seems to have been left nothing. It was only at the end of his life that our ancestor came into a share of the family property.

.oOo.

CHAPTER THREE

References

1	Chan. I.P.M. File 79/3, Beds CRO.
2	Cal of Pat Rolls, Hen VI, 1452-61.
3	De Banco Rolls (129), 4 Hen VII, m 530d.
4	Cal of Pat Rolls, Edw VII, Vol 5.
5	Exemplifications of Depositions, Beds CRO.
6	Will of Thomas Fitzhugh, PCC 26 Powell.
7	*Ibid.*
8	Register of Bishop Goodrich of Ely.
9	Cert of Musters for Bucks, 1522.
10	De Banco Rolls, (129), 4 Hen VII, m 530d.
11	Visitation of Buckinghamshire, 1634.
12	Cal of Pat Rolls, Edw IV.
13	DDX 67/71, Beds CRO.
14	CRT 64, Beds CRO.
15	Middle Temple Records.
16	Will of John Pooley, Beds Notes & Queries.
17	Beds Subsidy Rolls, 26 Hen VIII 71/118.
18	Letters & Papers of Reign of Hen VIII.
19	Early Chan Proc C/1/556/1; An Ancestral Scandal, *The Ancestor*, Vol. 5.
20	VCH Beds.
21	Early Chan Proc 134/68.
22	Letters & Papers of Reign of Hen VIII, Vol 2.
23	Two Monastic Account Rolls, Beds. Hist. Rec. Soc.
24	Subsidy in Lincoln Diocese, 1526.
25	Will of Sir Geo Harvey, PCC 3 Ayloffe.
26	Early Chan Proc C/1/556/1; W.M.Harvey: The Hundred of Willey.
27	Letters & Papers of Reign of Hen VIII, Vols 3 & 4.
28	Middle Temple Records.
29	*Ibid.*
30	Middle Temple Bench Book.
31	Will of Robert Blackwell, PCC 29 Ayloffe.
32	Will of Thomas Fitzhugh, PCC 26 Powell.
33	Will of Robert Blackwell, PCC 29 Ayloffe.
34	Will of Thomas Fitzhugh, PCC 26 Powell.
35	*Oxford Dictionary of English Christian Names.*
36	Will of Thomas Fitzhugh, PCC 26 Powell.
37	Cal of Foot of Fines, Hen VIII.

Thomas Fitzhugh = Christine Maidbury
b. ca. 1450   m. ca. 1478
Of Beggary, Maidbury
and Wavendon
d. ca. 1526

---- 1st = Thomas = 2nd Jane
Wauton   b. ca. 1482   widow of
         Of   Robert Blackwell
         Wavendon   m. after 1520
         & London
         dsp. May 12, 1552

William = Catherine   William =
b. ca. 1483   Bill   b. ca. 1483
Of   m. ca. 1506   Of
Wilden   living 1546   Wilden
d. ca. 1560   d. ca. 1560

3 Daughters
who m.
John Stocker
---- Watson
----Houghton

Richard = --------
of Goodwick and
Maidbury
b. ca. 1480
d. 1553-6

Nicholas
m. 1st 1552
Grace Stokes
m. 2nd 1570
Agnes Smith
Of Wilden
bur. July 3,
1575.

Agnes m. 2nd
Robert Carter
Nov. 26, 1576

Thomas
d. before
1566

John
Of Great
Barford
m.
Amy Negus
bur. Sept. 24,
1579
She m. 2nd
Wm. Negus
and d. 1626

Mary
m.
Thomas
Nokes

Cicely
......
Jane
......
Anne
d. Feb. 2,
1608 umm
Bridget
bur. Dec. 18,
1545, unm.

Robert
b. ca. 1527
Of
Wavendon
m. ca. 1558
Elizabeth
Bury
d. Feb. 3,
1609
She d. Sept.
17, 1612

William
living
1568

Richard
m. Frances Wyatt
m. 2nd
Ed. Bridges
d. Nov. 3, 1557

Nicholas
d. ca. 1581

Christine
m. --- Townsend

Alice
m. George Bowles

.o 35 o.

CHAPTER FOUR

THE ANXIOUS YEARS

"It was merry in England afore the New Learning came up. Yea, I would all things were as hath been in times past."

Thomas Howard, Duke of Norfolk (1473-1554)

By his death old Thomas was spared the monstrous brood of troubles with which the times were then pregnant. Their seeds had lain latent in England ever since John Wycliffe, over a century before, had striven to free the Christian faith from the accretions, complexities and corruptions acquired in the Church's centuries of power over the European mind. The stronghold that Wycliffe's itinerant preachers had failed to shake had now been undermined by a technological development made in Thomas's lifetime, the invention of printing by movable metal type cast from matrices. Books, previously an expensive luxury for the rich, had been transformed into a medium of widespread information and opinion. Hitherto the motive to acquire literacy had been confined to those who would need to work with the written word, but now education, both in schools and at home, had received a powerful stimulus; and no subject of reading was of greater interest than religion. Wycliffe's mediaeval themes, enriched by the development of classical studies, were elaborated in the rational and articulate Latin works of men like Erasmus of Rotterdam. From printing presses in Venice, Paris, London, Basle and elsewhere, they circulated widely among educated and influential people throughout Europe, including members of the English royal court. What they expounded was called the New Learning, which, though loyally Catholic, depreciated respect for images, relics, indulgences, dogma and superstitions. For some, inevitably, it did not go far enough; in Germany and in Switzerland, Luther, Zwingli and others had advanced to the heresy of calling for personal experience of God; and already German princes were defying Bulls issued by the Pope in Rome. However, all that was abroad; in England religious life was quiet and orthodox. King Henry himself became the author of a book dedicated to Pope Leo X, called *The Assertion of the Seven Sacraments*, in which he defended the Church from the attacks of Luther, and for which he proudly accepted as thanks the Papal title of 'Defender of the Faith.' But the worm was in the bud; King Henry had no male heir, and Queen Katherine was now unlikely to give him one. In 1527 he dispatched Cardinal Wolsey to Rome to consult the Pope about the possibility of a divorce.

Richard Fitzhugh was now lord of his ancestors' manor, but, understandably, he changed the name of the old house from Beggary to Goodwick after another property within the manor.[1] His other manor, the 420 acres at Maidbury, he probably placed in the charge of his married son and heir, Richard. There the young man had their feudal superior, Dame Elizabeth Bonville, right on his doorstep. She ruled over the Abbey of Elstow, the religious house in which Jane Fitzhugh's stepdaughter, Alice Blackwell, was one of the inmates.[2]

Thomas and Jane settled into their new home at Wavendon in Buckinghamshire. The district was widely known in southern England for its deposits of fuller's earth, which was a valuable cleansing medium for woollen cloth, and the local landscape was scarred with the pits from which it was extracted. One of Thomas's neighbours there, Lawrence Maidbury, a cousin on his mother's side, had an interest in several pits, and Thomas himself owned one in neighbouring Aspley Guise.[3] Today Wavendon parish has a reputation for pillow-lace making, a skill said to have been introduced there at this period. Besides his new home, Thomas retained his property in Eaton parish and even acquired two more messuages there with 127 acres of arable, meadow, pasture and wood stretching into Wyboston and Roxton,[4] and it was not long before he extended his property interests to Bedford town where, in 1528, he purchased yet another house, garden and orchard in the parish of St Mary the Virgin.[5] At that period land was still almost the only form of capital.

William and Catherine lived on at Colmworth. They had now produced a family of fifteen or sixteen children.[6] Several had died young, but they still had five boys William, Thomas, Nicholas, John, and Robert, and five girls, Mary, Cicely, Jane, Anne[7] and Bridget.[8] The present baby of the family, only months old, was Robert, and he was to be their last.

After their father's death, one of the first acts of the three brothers was to make a joint approach to the Prior of Barnwell, who was patron of the living of Caldecott, and to purchase from him the right to appoint a parson there of their own choosing when the benefice next fell vacant.[9] The only motive for obtaining an advowson for a single occasion, unless for one's own parish, was to obtain a living for a young clerical relative, and Caldecott was intended for Father Thomas Houghton, who must have been a sister's son. As the brothers were all now middle-aged and the living might not fall vacant for some time, obtaining the concession jointly was a precaution against any two of them not living to fulfil their intention.

In 1529 Thomas, in addition to his work as Justice of Assize, was appointed a Justice of the Peace for Bedfordshire.[10] Henry VIII found these magistrates a cheap and convenient instrument for operating the counties' legal and administrative affairs. Because they were virtually unpaid, they were selected from knights and gentry holding land to a minimum value of £20 per annum. A justice of the peace was an altogether different functionary from a justice of assize. The latter toured several counties trying cases as an impartial outsider and disqualified from occupying the bench in his own county, whereas the former was an official on whom the Crown relied for his local knowledge. His jurisdiction was confined to his own county and his influence to the part of it in which he lived. As all the justices were members of the local gentry, they were on terms of more than mere acquaintance with one another. In Bedfordshire, Walter Luke was the father of Thomas's brother-in-law; Simon Fitz was his close neighbour at Aspley Guise; Sir Michael Fisher and Sir John St John had been friends of the family for years; and Sir Robert Brudenell and Sir Richard Broke shared the assize bench with him. They, or rather some of them, sat together on the bench, usually at Bedford, every Epiphany, Easter, Midsummer and Michaelmas in a Court of

Quarter Sessions; and, between times, two or more of them might meet together in Special Sessions for particular purposes or in Petty Sessions for particular districts. At the local level it was the village constable and his assistant the headborough who made the justices' powers effective. These humble unpaid officials whom, later in the century, Shakespeare poked fun at as Dogberry and Verges, were responsible to the JPs for law and order and a number of administrative functions. At quarter Sessions the proceedings included not only judicial cases but also the business of administering the county. The Court was the forerunner of our present county council.

In the same year, 1529, the King's moves towards a divorce were proceeding indecisively. Cardinal Campeggio came from Rome to hold a court with Cardinal Wolsey on the validity of the King's marriage to his brother's widow but finally could do no more than decide to refer the matter to the Pope, because they knew that the influence of *Religious ferment in England, and its effect on the Fitzhugh family* Katherine's nephew, the Emperor Charles V, with the Vatican was too powerful for there to be any prospect of an annulment. Also Wolsey had secretly turned against the undertaking because Anne Boleyn, the lady whom Henry had clearly chosen as Katherine's successor, had become one of the court's keenest followers of the New Learning. His defection was discovered by the King and he was dismissed to a castle in Yorkshire.

All the time among ordinary people, religious tensions were becoming more open and more complex. Many tenets of the faith were being questioned, and the people's desire to read the Bible for themselves, which would have meant a translation from the Latin, was becoming a clamour. One summer Sunday that year in Colmworth Church, William and Catherine, standing separated on opposite sides of the nave, each among their own sex, heard the rector read a royal proclamation against heretical books printed abroad and imported into the country. From the pulpit four were named and banned as containing "pestiferous errors and blasphemies." One of them, *The Supplication of Beggars*, was a satire on the clergys portraying "the bishops, abbots, priors deacons archdeacons, suffragans, priests, monks, canons, friars, pardoners and summoners" as "puissant and counterfeit holy and idle beggars and vagabonds," who had "gotten into their hands more than a third part of all the realm. The goodliest lordships, manors, lands and territories are theirs," a statement that the Fitzhughs, if they ever read it, are unlikely to have thought erroneous, since most of their lands were held of religious houses. Anyone in the parish who possessed any of these books was commanded to hand them in to the rector or the curate or else to the bishop within fifteen days. After that, anyone found owning one would be taken before the King's Council. William may well have wondered whether the order would affect his brother Thomas. He knew he had a collection of books; but his wife Joan - sorry, Jane - would never approve errors or blasphemies. The proclamation went on to announce that an English translation of the Bible had been decided against. "Considering the malignity of the present time, a translation into English would tend to the increase of error. It is therefore more expedient that the people have the Scripture expounded to them by preachers as heretofore." It did however add that when times were more settled, the matter might be reconsidered.

In Christendom generally, the times were not in process of settlement. In Germany the reformation movement was growing in strength. An 'Appellation and Protestation' had been published by a number of Lutheran cities and princes, which had earned them the nickname of 'Protestants.' In England, Wolsey was charged with treason and died on his way to the Tower. The Chancellorship went for the first time to a layman, Sir Thomas More, who was one of the leading 'maintainers of the Gospel' as the followers of the New Learning called themselves. In July of the following year, 1531, Queen Katherine was sent into Bedfordshire, banished from court by the King, to live at the royal estate of Ampthill. It happened in that same month that Thomas and Jane heard the astonishing news from the nunnery at Elstow that Alice had been threatened with excommunication by the Bishop of Lincoln.

All bishops made periodical visitations of the religious houses in their dioceses either in person or by deputy. Elstow was a fashionable convent, and on an inspection there Dr Rayne, vicar-general and chancellor of the Bishop, was taken aback to find that the ladies were in the habit of giving parties to entertain their friends and relations in the neighbourhood. At the same time he noted that the entrances to the chancel of the Abbey church were "not properly constructed." As the chancel was the part of the church exclusively for the nuns, this presumably meant that he suspected them of allowing the lay congregation access to it. He issued orders that both these derelictions were to be corrected, but on his next visitation he found that his instructions had been entirely disregarded. He had therefore pronounced the Abbess, Dame Elizabeth, to be contumacious, negligent, disobedient and lacking in respect for his injunctions and suspended her from entering the church and from the performance of divine service. The Prioress, Dame Anne Wake - all nuns were called Dame - who was responsible for the structure of the Abbey was stripped of her office, and the sacrist suspended. In place of Dame Anne he appointed Ellen Snowe to be Prioress. However, the nuns were not prepared to accept her. At their next meeting in the Chapter House they walked out on the Abbess, ignoring her order to stay where they were. On this insubordination being reported, the chancellor came again and interrogated the inmates. Dame Maud Shelton, the Sub-Prioress, when asked why she had walked out, answered in Latin that it had been "for a necessary cause of her body" and that she had not known about the others leaving until she had seen them in the dorter (dormitory). But the other nuns replied roundly in English. Margaret Nicolson said she had quitted the Chapter because she "would not consent that my lady Snowe should be Prioress"; no, no one had instigated her to leave; yes, the Abbess had commanded her to tarry; no, they had not followed the lead of the Sub-Prioress. Barbara Grey said the new Prioress "makes every fault a deadly sin." When Alice's turn came, she too declared she had left "because the old Prioress was put out of her office," but she also pointed out the principle behind their protest: "After their custom and their rule of St Bennet, the Prioress should have been elected by the Abbess and the convent and not by my lord"; and others supported her. This was throwing the blame onto the chancellor, a challenge to episcopal authority.

For over three weeks they awaited the consequences of their temerity. Then, on 20th July, the Bishop came down in person and, presiding in the Chapter House, admonished them all. He ordered them on pain of excommunication to accept Dame Ellen Snowe as Prioress in seemly manner and to obey her as they had her predecessors in accordance with the rule of St Benedict. He pardoned the Abbess but declared the former Prioress ineligible for the office in perpetuity. His threat was of course more than sufficient to quell the little revolt.[11]

In London, the drama that was eventually to involve the consciences of all the people of England, and the lives of many of them, was drawing to a crisis. Pope Clement ordered the King back to his wife, and when a preacher in St Paul's Cathedral spoke in favour of a divorce, a woman in the congregation shouted that he lied and that the King was violating the sanctity of marriage. On one occasion Anne Boleyn had to flee from a furious crowd of women. But Henry replied to the Pope's attack by marrying her and by forcing an Act through Parliament declaring himself, a layman, Supreme Head of the Church of England, a step that would have been unthinkable thirty years before. All through the summer royal commissioners went around the country administering the oaths of abjuration of the Pope's authority and recognition of the validity of the King's new marriage. Those who refused were declared guilty of treason and were sentenced to be hung, drawn and quartered. Hundreds died. Some towns witnessed an execution nearly every week throughout the following year. Three priors of the great Charterhouse monastery in London suffered this death. Sentences on John Fisher, Bishop of Rochester, and Sir Thomas More were commuted to beheading, and More's head was impaled on London Bridge. As a further anti-papal step, Coverdale's English Bible was allowed to be printed, but when a group of Anabaptists arrived from Holland, thinking that England must be safe for them, they were burnt at the stake. From then on, no one could be sure from day to day which thoughts were orthodox, which heretical and which treasonable. Loyalty to the Pope was consistently treason, but the rites of the traditional Catholic Church alternated between favour and condemnation. To support Luther was flat heresy, but many liberal opinions from the New Learning were acceptable today and tomorrow a burning matter.

The people of Bedfordshire took the oaths quietly whatever their private opinions and were spared the gruesome sights that became common elsewhere. They were more nearly concerned with the failure of their crops after the miserably wet summer. The saying went round that it had never stopped raining since Sir Thomas More was executed. For most, a fairly normal life went on; even the monasteries, symbols of the old religion, continued to exercise their influence on the social and economic life of their neighbourhoods, serving as inns and banks and poor relief centres and employing the country gentry as land agents, farmers and surveyors. William Fitzhugh himself added to his income by auditing the annual accounts of Bushmead *The Fitzhughs* Priory, a small house of Augustinian canons in *profit from* the parish of Eaton, a job that brought him a fee *Church turmoil* of £1 6s 8d a year. His brother Thomas had the more arduous and lucrative task of supervising the annual collection of rents for the same house[12] and was also sub-steward of St Neot's Priory.[13] But early in 1535 clouds began to threaten the continuance of this type of work, though, for William at least, their immediate effect was greatly to increase it.

The King was moving to divert into his own coffers the ecclesiastical revenues that hitherto had flowed to Rome. He began by ordering an account to be taken of the two forms of papal tribute payable by all parish priests and higher dignitaries, namely First Fruits, representing their first full year's income from a benefice, and Tenths of Spiritualities, which were ten per cent of incomes from tithes, offerings, glebe and land held in free alms. In every county, commissioners were appointed to inquire the amounts of the payments, and William was made one of the four auditors of the assessments in Bedfordshire.[14] Close on the heels of this investigation, Thomas Cromwell, the King's Secretary and his Vicar-General for Church affairs, empowered the same commissioners to assess the capital value of all property owned by churches and religious houses; and for this inquiry too William was appointed auditor in Bedfordshire, which put his ability with accounts under heavy demand for a considerable part of that year.[15] However, the task was accomplished with surprising rapidity. Within seven months a mammoth report, known as the Valor Ecclesiasticus, was compiled for the whole country. The property valuation was secretly intended to form the basis for Cromwell's planned attack on the wealth of the monasteries. At each religious house, the apprehensive inmates faced no less than 86 questions on the details of their way of life, a questionnaire drawn up to bring to light scandals that could be used as propaganda against the monastic life itself and so prepare the mind of the country for its abolition. In one Bedfordshire nunnery, not Elstow, the commissioners did discover two of the inmates to be pregnant. Working on public opinion from another angle, Archbishop Cranmer assured a congregation at Paul's Cross that if the abbeys went down, the King would never want taxes again.

The axe fell the following year; for Queen Anne, victim of dubious charges by Catholic enemies, at the Tower; for the smaller monasteries, in Parliament, where the Act of Dissolution was passed on them for "manifest sin, vicious, carnal and abominable living." The larger monasteries were not attacked - they were even praised - because many of their abbots sat in Parliament and would have resisted any such attempt. A new department of state was created, the Court of Augmentations, to carry out the dissolution and administer the wealth that was to accrue to the King. St Neot's and Elstow, their income being more than £200 a year, were classed as large and escaped; Bushmead was small and condemned. Men came and took away the plate and the lead from the roof, and soon afterwards the property was sold to Sir William Gascoigne. The actual breaking up of nearly 400 organisations took time, but in the diocese of Lincoln the business was pressed forward. The Bishop, John Longland, was a keen supporter of the supremacy and the dissolution although conservative on the question of church rites and ceremonies. His diocese, one of the largest in the country, covered five and a half counties, including Bedfordshire. In his own shire his vigour caused a reaction that developed into a popular revolt. The leaders demanded a halt to the dissolution and the dismissal of the "heretical" bishops, and they added a number of secular grievances, the enclosure of the common lands, the raising of rents and the recently passed Statute of Uses. This last was of concern to all landholders; it made illegal the process by which the Fitzhughs had helped Robert Blackwell and George Harvey to bequeath their lands in their last wills. The rebels occupied the city of Lincoln but failed to spread the revolt to the rest of the diocese. The rising was put down with false promises but soon broke out more fiercely in Yorkshire with a demand for the restoration of the papal authority. The rebels called themselves Pilgrims and their movement the Pilgrimage of Grace. It took the advance of a royal army and more false promises to defeat it. The rising showed how strongly the conservative north felt for its age-old faith. In the south the New Learning was more widespread; loyalty to the Roman pontiff still burned in the hearts of individuals and families but not in communities. The King was still popular, and bonfires burned in nearly every town and village to celebrate with him the birth, on 12th October 1537, of a son and heir.

The failure of the Pilgrimage led to nearly 200 executions including some of abbots and priors, and it opened the way to the dissolution, always intended, of the larger monasteries. Another round of commissioners' visitations of them began, and at these a written form of surrender was presented to each community and in most cases accepted. However, at the Abbey at Woburn, a parish adjacent to Wavendon, Abbot Robert Hobbes had been shamed by the staunchness of the northern abbots and the Charterhouse priors. Although earlier he had taken the oaths required, he now spoke his true mind. "It is an unmerciful thing," he protested, "thus to put down the houses of God and expulse the inhabitants from their living, yea and many one from their life too." But in the ears of the authorities this was a venial offence compared with what he went on to declare. "The Bishop of Rome's authority is good and lawful within this realm according to the old trade, and that is the true way; and the contrary, of the King's part, but usurpation deceived by flattery and adulation." and not only that. "It is a marvellous thing that the King's Grace could not be contented with that noble queen, his very true and undoubted wife, Queen Katherine." And in these treasonable sentiments he was supported by his sub-prior and sexton.

Their statements were in due course reported to Westminster, and in the following May, nine commissioners were appointed to try them for their lives at Abbots Woburn, and one of them was Thomas Fitzhugh. The others too were all Bedfordshire men: Lord Bray, Lord Mordaunt, Walter Luke, now a serjeant-at-law *Thomas sits in judgement on religious rebels* and a knight, Sir William Parr, Sir William Gascoigne, Sir John St John, John Williams and John Gostwick. The Sheriff of the county was ordered to bring before them from every hundred twenty-four men "as well knights as other good and lawful men" and from the body of the county another twenty-four "of the most discreet and sufficient persons by whom the truth of the matter would best be known."

On Friday in Whit week, 14th June 1538, the trial took place. The Abbot was charged on two counts under the Supremacy and Succession Acts. Several of the nine judges must have known the chief prisoner personally. Thomas, who lived only two or three miles away, certainly did. As long before as 1521 he and the Abbot had co-operated as joint overseers of the will of John Richardson of Wavendon. At least his friends were spared the painful task of deciding as to his guilt or innocence. Hobbes confessed his guilt on both counts, and the sentence was mandatory. The Abbot was "to be taken to the prison whence he had come and be drawn through the midst of the town of Woburn to the gallows." Tradition, for what it is worth, identifies the spot as an ancient oak in the park of the present ducal Abbey. He was there to be "hanged and, while living, thrown to the ground and his bowels taken out and burned and his head cut off and his body divided into four quarters." The sub-prior and the sexton were condemned to the same fate. The quarters of their bodies were to be set where the King should appoint.[16]

In a circular to the justices of the peace, the King now reminded them of their duty under the Act against Papal Authority. "Divers seditious and contentious persons, being imps of the Bishop of Rome and his See and in heart members of his pretended monarchy, do in corners, as they dare, whisper, preach and persuade and instil into the ears and heads of the poor, simple and unlettered people the continuance of the Bishop's feigned authority. Every such person, their aiders, abettors, maintainers, concealers and every of them shall incur the penalties, pains and forfeitures ordained." The circular can only have sharpened in Thomas an anxiety already nagging, because among the "privy maintainers of the papistical faction" was his brother, and he himself was his "concealer." Richard and his sons held steadfastly to the old faith.[17] Their family lived quietly, but at any moment unguarded words could become the subject of local gossip and unfriendly report. For the unfortunate Thomas, who did not share Richard's beliefs or know from day to day how careful he was, the worry was probably greater than for the household at Goodwick. Nor was he the only JP in this predicament. Some others certainly had relations, friends or neighbours with unlawful opinions and who were yet law-abiding

The family sticks to the old Faith

subjects of the King. The only convincing excuse for failing to report pockets of dissent was not to know about them, so a trend commenced for JPs to spend as much time as they could away from their county. The wealthier of them frequented London where they had town houses.

Thomas buys tenements in London

Thomas, though by now the most prosperous of the three brothers, was far from being among the wealthier justices, and it is unlikely that he had indulged in the luxury of a London residence, so it was probably not till he now found it useful that he acquired a property in the London parish of St Sepulchre consisting of two tenements and a garden in Charterhouse Lane,[18] a street that ran along the outer wall of the Carthusian monastery, of whom the property was held. Once there, he also bought, as an investment, two tenements in the parish of St Clement, just outside the City gate at Temple Bar.[19]

It was in the same year, 1538, that the Fitzhugh brothers were at last able to present their nephew, Thomas Houghton, to the vacant living of Caldecott.[20] He came in at an historic time, just as it was ordained that every church in the country should acquire a copy of Coverdale's English Bible and have the lessons read from it. Noblemen, gentlemen and merchants were also permitted to read the Bible within their own families, but not husbandmen, journeymen, apprentices or women. This was an important step forward for the maintainers of the Gospel; but if changes now seemed to them to be proceeding smoothly in England and resistance simmering ineffectively beneath the surface, on

The Fitzhughs install a nephew into a Church living

the continent English emigrants became more strenuously active against their heretical King. Cardinal Pole, Papal Legate and a relative of King Henry, accepted a mission from Pope Paul III to form a league of Christian princes against England, and with that aim made his way to the courts of Paris and Madrid. The Kings of France and Spain patched up their differences, and to Henry a joint attack from across the Channel seemed an imminent threat. A royal order went out to all county sheriffs to summon musters of the militia, the stand-by force for local defence to which all able-bodied men below the rank of baron and between the ages of 16 and 60 were liable to be called up in case of emergency, bringing arms and armour according to their status and means. Thomas Fitzhugh was appointed one of the commissioners for carrying out the order in Barford hundred. These musters were displays held at irregular intervals and in times of danger, of what force was available. They were made public holidays, usually as a prolongation of a church festival and so were also something of a social occasion, a district gathering of neighbours. On Easter Tuesday 1539 the yokels of Eaton and Wyboston joined the other men of the hundred at a wide open space, probably at Barford, carrying what weapons they owned - or were supposed to own, for borrowing was a common but illegal practice. Eaton produced a contingent of sixteen archers and twenty billmen; and Wyboston six archers and ten billmen. The archers carried longbows, the crossbow being an inferior French weapon; and the bill was a long staff mounted with a *The Protestant Realm is threatened by Catholic invasion, and the Fitzhughs help raise the Militia* metal spike, another at right-angles to it, and a curved blade for hooking enemy cavalrymen off their horses. The gentry, who came with their swords, were also required to supply armour for a certain number or fraction of men, a cause of much preliminary scouring and sanding by the household servants. From Eaton, William Wyat came with one complete suit; William Fitzhugh, now living at Bushmead, joined with John Knight to produce equipment for one man between them. This consisted of a coat of plated armour, a bill or halberd, a longbow and a steel helmet. Had Catherine and Mistress Knight been given to wearing velvet kirtles or silk petticoats, as fortunately they were not, then William and his neighbour would, under the sumptuary laws, have had to provide also a light horse properly equipped. Four other residents shared the fitting out of a third man; and the village itself and its hamlets provided the 'harness' for two more from the stock usually kept locked up in the church. From Wyboston, Richard Fitzhugh brought a complete suit of armour, as did John Stocker and Henry Blakebill; and the village constable came with one more from the public stock. The commissioners assessed their own liabilities, and Thomas provided armour for two men.[21] While the officials carried out the purposes of the muster, the inspection and recording of each contingent followed by the drilling of the combined force of each arm in the handling of their weapon, a good time was had by all not momently involved, much ale was consumed, and Pole's efforts to bring the combined forces of France and Spain against his native country came to nothing, the good cardinal himself narrowly escaping assassination. The arms and armour were stacked away to rust until another day.

That year the last of the monasteries was closed down. The bells that had sounded across the countryside at the canonical hours were heard no more. The prayers on which *The Monasteries are closed. Alice is expelled.* their founders and benefactors had relied for the welfare of their souls in purgatory no longer rose to heaven. Alice Blackwell, in secular clothes and provided with money for current expenses, walked out of her Abbey to face life in the outside world on her pension of 53s 4d. The Abbess and some of the ladies went to live at Bedford, but Alice and a few others settled in Elstow village, where they probably continued to live together and give parties.[22] They had been released from all their vows except that of chastity, and even that was lifted in the following reign; but Alice never married.

The monasteries' lay employees also received pensions. Thomas, for the loss of his sub-stewardship at St Neot's, was granted £1 6s 8d per annum.[23] As soon as the inmates of a religious house moved out, the Augmentation men had to clear the premises promptly or they might be looted by the poor of the locality. As soon as the Charterhouse was suppressed in November 1538, Thomas obtained a permit to remove a whole cell of panelling, and when he went to collect it, showing the official in charge a gold ring belonging to Master Richard Cromwell as his authority, the King's gardener was there taking delivery of the best bay trees and grafts of rosemary, and others were being carted away by Cromwell's own gardener.[24] This Richard Cromwell was a Welshman originally named Williams, who worked closely with his uncle Thomas Cromwell, the King's Secretary and Vicar-General, and had adopted his surname. He was a favourite with the King and survived his uncle's downfall. *The Fitzhughs begin buying Church lands* Soon after this he was knighted and acquired the site of St Neot's Priory and its neighbouring lands, a large portion of which, 'the holmes, lands, tenements, meadows and pastures in Berkford (now Little Barford), Tempsford, Roxton and Wyboston' he then sold off to the ever acquisitive Thomas Fitzhugh.[25] A little before that major purchase,

Thomas had also enlarged his property at Wavendon by buying from Alice Stratton and her sons Thomas and William a messuage with 40 acres of land, 36 of them in Wavendon and the remainder in Aspley Guise, a transaction that was to cause much worry in the family in years to come.[26] Thomas's relative prosperity at this time is to some extent reflected in the taxes he paid, 40s compared with Richard's 26s 8d and William's 10s.

In 1539 the King had executed Thomas Cromwell and now he suffered a reaction against that minister's pro-Protestant policies. He forced through Parliament an Act of Six Articles laying it down that in the sacrament of the mass the bread and wine became the actual and not the symbolic body and blood of Christ; that priests must not marry; that private masses should be continued and auricular confession obligatory; and that priests were capable of granting absolution of sins. Anyone who denied the first Article and those who preached against the Articles as a whole were to be burnt as heretics; first offenders against the other Articles were to be treated as felons, and second offenders burnt. Many maintainers of the Gospel now suffered death for their beliefs including several judges, but Thomas evidently trimmed his sails, William conformed along with the great majority of the congregation, and Richard must have welcomed the backward turn of events.

.oOo.

CHAPTER FOUR

References

1   PCC 9 Chayney, Will of Richard Fitzhugh.

2   Lincs Rec Soc, Vol 37, Diocesan Visitations.

3   PCC 26 Powell, Will of Thomas Fitzhugh.

4   Foot of Fines, Divers Counties, 1527; Foot of Fines Beds, bdle 1, file 2.

5   Foot of Fines, Beds, bdle 1, file 2, Mich.

6   Star Chamber Proc, STAC.8/108/1.

7   Harleian Soc, Vol 19, Visitation of Beds.

8   Registers of Wilden Parish.

9   Ely Episcopal Registers.

10   Letters & Papers, Henry VIII, Vol 4.

11   Lincs Rec Soc, Vol 37, Diocesan Visitations.

12   *Cartulary of Bushmead Priory*, Beds Hist Rec Soc, Vol 22.

13   *History & Antiquities of Eynesbury & St Neot's*.

14   I.D. Parry, *Select Illustrations History & Topography of Bedfordshire*.

15   Letters & Papers, Henry VIII, Vol 8.

16   Transact of Roy Hist Soc, 4th Series, Vol 16.

17   PCC 9 Chayney, Will of Richard Fitzhugh; Cal of MSS of Marquess of Salisbury, Recusants at Liberty.

18   Letters & Papers, Henry VIII, Vol 15; Court of Wards 6/83.

19   PCC 26 Powell, Will of Thomas Fitzhugh.

20   Ely Episcopal Registers.

21   Beds Muster Cert, E.101/59/6.

22   Report on Former Monks & Nuns, E.101/76/26.

23   Lincs Rec Soc, Vol 53, State of Ex-Religious in the Diocese.

24   Letters & Papers, Henry VIII, Vol 13.

25   PCC 26 Powell, Will of Thomas Fitzhugh.

26   Court of Star Chamber, STAC.5/B20/31 & B82/8.

CHAPTER FIVE

SIMPLE SIMON

Tis bad enough in man or woman
To steal a goose off the common
But surely he's without excuse
Who steals the common from the goose.
Anon.

Biographies of famous people are expected to reveal their subjects' activities in some detail, since they are normally based on a considerable stock of documentary evidence, but the lives of ordinary private people do not raise the same expectations, so readers of this history are likely to raise their eyebrows when they come to episodes described in a degree of detail extending even to the reporting of conversations carried on four centuries ago. They could hardly avoid concluding that the family chronicles were now degenerating into historical fiction. But that is not so, neither in this chapter nor in any other. In cases of such detailed narrative, the sources given in footnotes will usually be records of the central law courts, which are a treasure house not only of accusations, rebuttals and excuses that are a revelation in themselves, but also of evidence by witnesses that throws rays of light upon the characters and everyday lives of ordinary people long ago. I well remember the first time I delved into them and read with amazement and delight the intimate detail with which domestic occurrences in a Fitzhugh home during the winter of 1609 were related by members of the family, their servants, friends and neighbours. I felt like Howard Carter when he first made a hole in the wall of Tutankhamun's tomb to shine a torch through. Lord Carnarvon, behind him, asked what he could see, and he replied: "Wonderful things!"

From 1540 onwards, manors and freeholds at the disposal of the Court of Augmentations were on offer and were snapped up by all who could afford them. Because of the great quantity on the market, prices were not high. New men acquired manorial status; wealthy men added to their landed possessions. Farming was undergoing great improvements. Apart from the incentive to turn arable land over to pasture for flocks, the communal cultivation of fields in strips was now seen as a hindrance to efficient production. The knowledge of agriculture was no longer limited to local experience; publications on the science were available, such as Fitzherbert's popular *Book of Husbandry*. The first of the family to enter the royal land market was, *William buys up more* surprisingly, William, but he did so in *Church land* collaboration with his wealthy friend Sir John St John, whose influence was perhaps necessary to obtain the grant and who probably acquired the major share. The Bedfordshire properties that attracted them had belonged to the Priory of Chicksands. They included the manor of Keysoe, a grange in Keysoe parish and pasture land stretching through Keysoe, Riseley and Little Staughton. They bought them for £305 2s 6 ¾d and also about 24 acres, called Bateman's, partly in Keysoe and partly in Pertenhall, that had belonged to the nunnery of Harrold.[1] Thomas soon followed his brother and, in 1542, bought from the Court of Augmentations a lease of the manor of Gamlingay in Cambridgeshire.[2]

It was the practice of owners of widely separated manors to appoint one of the gentry of the neighbourhood, preferably with legal knowledge, to deputise for them in the capacity of steward, and now the demand for such services was greatly increased. Thomas took on the stewardship of Sir John St John's new manor of Abbots Ripton in Huntingdonshire, which had belonged to Ramsay Abbey. Over the last few years, rapid inflation, caused by debasement of the coinage, had made the customary payments by manorial tenants to their landlords altogether uneconomic, and Sir John looked to Thomas to achieve a more satisfactory return on his investment. He went to work and succeeded in persuading the villagers to relinquish their copyhold tenures and accept leases for terms of years. The leases he then granted them were for short periods so that it was not long before they found themselves faced with rent increases. They were outraged, and were not the only ones. "Consider you," cried one published protest, "what a wickedness is commonly used through the realm unpunished in the inordinate enhancing of rents and taking of unreasonable fines, and by them specially to whom the King hath given and sold the lands of those imps of Anti-Christ, abbeys and nunneries. But for the faith's sake, it had been more profitable for the commonwealth that they had remained still in their hands; they never enhanced their lands nor took so cruel fines as do our temporal tyrants."

The villagers took their lord to court at Westminster. They claimed that his steward had tricked them by telling them that "copyholds were always voidable at the will of the lord," which was false because copyholds were for life and though, on a copyholder's death, his heir had to pay a fine to the lord to succeed to his holding, in most manors his right of succession was secured by customary law. As a general statement, Thomas's assertion would certainly have been incorrect but he is more likely to have been referring to their particular tenures, because the defence that St John put forward was that the plaintiffs' copyholds had not existed from "time out of mind" as was necessary to their full validity, but had been created only twenty years before. The villagers retorted that they had not disclosed the origins of their holdings to the steward, but the manor court rolls would have been available to him, indeed were probably in his keeping.[3] Thomas himself was not called upon to give evidence. In fact, by the time the case came to court he was no longer steward of the manor, perhaps because in 1543 he had been appointed Clerk of the Assizes and Gaol Delivery, which made him the justice in charge of his circuit, a post that involved a great deal of extra work.[4]

Soon after William acquired the Keysoe sheep pastures, he moved house to the nearby parish of Wilden,[5] where he took over two messuages and 200 acres of arable, meadow and pasture from a couple called William and Margery Rawlyn who seem to have been in financial difficulties. In return for loans of money, cattle and corn for another of their properties they allowed him the use and profits of the land until the loans were repaid.[6] It was an unbusinesslike arrangement.

Wilden village, grouped around its church, stood in a pleasant dell with a brook flowing alongside the roadway down to its junction with the Ouse. The manorial jurisdiction belonged to the Lucy family, but much of the land had lately changed hands from the dissolved religious houses of Warden, Bushmead and Caldwell. Whether William's house was Sewick End, Smartwick, East End, Church End Farm, Overwick, Hudwick, Lamarestwick or Redwick we do not know, but the derivation of so many placenames ending in 'wick' identifies the area as good dairy-farming land with lush meadows. Once settled there, William sold the 12 acres that were his share of the Bateman's property. He and his wife Catherine were now in their sixties. They had fifteen or sixteen children,[7] some of whom had died young, and not long after their move they buried one of their unmarried daughters, Bridget, in Wilden churchyard.[8] At this time, 1544, the survival of the Fitzhugh family seemed likely to rest solely with Richard's descendants, because Thomas and Jane had no children, and of William's five surviving sons not one was married, although the elder two must have been approaching middle age. Only Richard's heir, Richard, had a wife, and she had just presented him with a son, yet another Richard.

In the spring of that year King Henry was again at war with France and planning an invasion near Calais. Among other men of substance, Thomas was called upon to provide and equip men to join the army, in his case two billmen. Then in October his neighbour Simon Fitz of Aspley Guise died. In his will he appointed his son-in-law William Richardson, husband of his daughter Alice, and his friend Thomas Fitzhugh to be his executors.[9] Fitz had been a man of considerable possessions, which he wished to divide between his two sons, William and Simon. To the former he had already made over properties in several Bedfordshire parishes and had covenanted to leave him worth another 300 marks (£200) in goods and cattle at his death. In his will he left his younger son Simon his manors of Blundells and Bilkmore and, after his wife's death, the manor of Aspley Guise and land in Birchmoor. To his four daughters he left money. By his will he also revoked his covenant with his son William on the grounds that he had built him a house at Pulloxhill and left uncut the woods there.[10] At first the executors had no trouble, but in the following year William Fitz died childless, and his wife Marcy took another husband, a man named Edward Warton. This couple lodged a claim against the executors for the value of the 300 marks covenanted to William. The defence of Thomas and Richardson was that Fitz had known that his will could not be carried out if the value of 300 marks had had to go to William, and that William, before his father's death, had formally released him and his executors from the covenant; also that, after his father's death, William Fitz himself had made no claim. The Wartons came back with a charge that the executors had obtained the release by craft and subtlety, that the house had already been built before the covenant was made, and that, even with the unlopped woods, it was worth less than 300 marks.[11] There is no record of the result of the suit, but since the release from the covenant was admitted, it seems unlikely that it had any success.

Unfortunately this was only the beginning of Thomas's involvement with the Fitz family. Something far more serious was to follow. It evolved out of a matter of little importance that had nothing to do with him, concerning some furniture and household articles belonging to the late Simon Fitz. Alice, Simon's widow, leased the manor house at Aspley Guise, called Aspley Hall, to a tenant for the duration of her own life. Some of the contents were still in the house, and the tenant asked for them to be left there, promising to give them up on request. Soon afterwards the lease of the house changed hands, so Richardson, as co-executor, sent his bailiff to collect his late father-in-law's things and store them in a loft over his malthouse. However, at the new tenants' request, some articles, were still allowed to remain in the house. Unfortunately the lease passed once again and came into the hands of a man named Forster, who had lately acquired by marriage the manor of Salford, just north of Aspley Guise.

Thomas Forster lived a highly irregular family life. His second wife, Elizabeth Pedder, widow, of Salford, had a niece Blanche and a daughter Anne; Forster seduced them both, and his association with Anne became a continuous one.[12] When old Fitz's younger son Simon came into the reversion of both his father's and his brother's lands, he became an object of particular interest to Forster. Young Simon was a sufferer from the ague (malaria), which was common in England at that time and which made him subject to recurrent painful fits, of which severe shivering and vomiting were the outward signs. He was also of limited intelligence, which made him easy prey for a schemer. Forster inveigled him into marriage with his mistress Anne, "giving little or nothing with her," and took him to live in his own household at Salford. Having acquired the lease of Aspley Hall, he put in a housekeeper, and hearing that some of the Fitz furniture had been removed, he sent a raiding party to break into Richardson's malthouse loft and take the things stored there back to the Hall. When Richardson demanded their return, he refused to give them up.[13]

That was at the end of November 1544. In the months that followed, the war with France called for more recruits, so the justices of the peace in every county were empowered to offer commissions in the army to suitable volunteers. At a sessions of Bedfordshire justices on 5th August, an application from Thomas Forster was considered and must have been welcomed by at least one of the JPs, Thomas Fitzhugh. They appointed Forster Captain of 100 men and ordered him to report at once to London. He departed taking his eldest son George and some friends with him. When George arrived back at Salford on the 9th he found his stepmother Elizabeth in conversation with Simon Fitz and William Richardson and in their hearing he told her that his father was expecting, if the wind was favourable, to be sailing for Boulogne that very day.[14]

With Forster now well out of the way, the local situation changed. Simon had realised that his stepfather-in-law was making use of him and went to call on his brother-in-law. He found Richardson in one of his barns and suggested that he should go with him to Aspley Hall to recover the disputed articles. Richardson approved and took two of his men with him. The housekeeper let them in and they removed some of the furniture and restored it to Richardson's loft. Two days later, Simon transferred more things, and Richardson sent for the village constable to view them and hear of the orderly manner in which they had been removed, but that official dared not come for fear of Forster's displeasure.[15]

After this act of defiance Simon did not return to Salford but was taken in by the Richardsons at Wavendon. When his wife called to see him, she was turned away, so she went to occupy Aspley Hall to prevent further removals; but about a fortnight later she arrived at her mother's, crying and complaining that Richardson and Simon had broken in and taken more things and that Simon had told her he was planning to sell his lands and take her away somewhere out of the district. Elizabeth asked who had put him up to this, and she said: "Mr Fitzhugh and William Richardson." So Elizabeth, taking a servant with her but leaving Anne at Salford, went to Aspley to investigate. Finding that more things had indeed been removed and encountering Simon, she said to him:

"Son, your wife telleth me that you will sell your lands and your goods and will steal her away without our consent and will go out of this country forty miles hence to receive £60 in part payment of the sale of your lands."

He confirmed it and asked who could prevent him.

"Son Fitz, I beshrew them that gave you such counsel for they care little for your wealth [welfare]. But, with the love of God, I will let you of [prevent you from] that purpose, for here you have your wife with child, and you are both young and like to have more; and I had rather keep you with somewhat than with nothing."

And she told him he was not to go until he could take her husband's advice. By this time Simon was beginning to shiver, so she took him back with her to Salford, put him into a spare bedchamber and told him to go to bed and stay there all next day. Simon was once more under the Forster wing.

On the following Saturday three men rode up to the Salford manor house. They were William Richardson, the Under Sheriff of the county and a justice of the peace. When Mistress Forster received them, the Under Sheriff said they had come thither to take a prisoner. She replied that there was no one in her house for them to take that she knew. On which the Sheriff said: "Let us make no more to-do, but let us do that thing that we came to do." She asked what that was, and he said it was such a thing that she and all her friends could not help. After which beating about the bush, he took out a box containing a large seal and demanded the presence of the village constable; but the JP said: "Let us go speak with Fitz first." Richardson, who knew what Simon's attacks were like and perhaps noting recent signs of one, said that Fitz would be past speaking to, he had cast his gall all round the house. At this remark Elizabeth lost her temper and cried: "I trust to see thee hanged for breaking of my house." To which he could find no better retort than: "I trust to see thee hanged." As they were intent on seeing Simon, she hurried upstairs to him and told him to move into her bedchamber because the one he was in was "not dressed." The three men went to see Simon in her room, shut the door in her face and would not let anyone hear what was being said. Eventually the Under Sheriff and Richardson emerged and quitted the house, leaving Simon still shut up with the justice.

They rode off to Wavendon to consult with Thomas Fitzhugh who was behind all this attempt at a bogus arrest. The fact was that Simon's intention to sell his lands was not just a course of action that Thomas and Richardson had advised; it was they who were to be the purchasers, and now they needed Simon to carry out the sale. The 'arrest' by the Under Sheriff was a ruse to recover him from Mistress Forster, and it had been bungled by officials all too aware of the weakness of their position. After reporting at Wavendon their lack of progress, the couple turned back to Salford, but this time Thomas went with them. They arrived at the manor about three or four hours after they had left it. Thomas took charge right away. He ordered a servant to bid Simon come down to them. When the young man descended, Thomas asked him how he was, and he replied: "Sick of an ague." Thomas asked how his mother-in-law was treating him and whether she gave him enough to eat and drink, and he said he was being well treated and had good meat and drink dressed for him. Did she give him gentle words, or no? Yes, she handled him very gently. Then Thomas asked why she kept him there, and he said it was because he had taken his gear out of her house at Aspley. Was there anything else she accused him of? Yes, he had removed some deeds. "That," commented Thomas, "was not well done." He asked if anything more had been taken, and Simon admitted having taken some silk and gold, and when asked its value he put it at £10. At this, Thomas said: "I am sorry for you, for that is a felony."

Thomas connives at and benefits from the swindle of a neighbour

He turned to the Under Sheriff and said: "Writ now!" And to Simon: "Master Fitz, you must go under bail to appear on the law day. Your brother Richardson shall be your surety to bring you in on the law day." So they took him back to Richardson's house at Wavendon. The charge, of course, was not pressed, but Simon remained with the Richardsons and shortly afterwards sold to Thomas Fitzhugh and William Richardson and their heirs forever the reversion of all his lands in return for a rent to him and the heirs of his body of £50 per annum,[16] and Thomas caused a copy of the agreement, dated 12th September 1545, to be enrolled for permanent record in the Court of Common Pleas.[17] In this case the goose from whom the land was stolen was a human one.

At Christmas time there was another break-in and removal of chattels from Aspley Hall. Anne Fitz and her mother sent for the village constable to view the damage to the door and the coffers that had been rifled. They then got him and two local men to take an inventory of all that remained in the house in case of further 'robberies.' Anne Fitz handed the completed list to the constable for safe keeping, asked her mother to look after the house, and rode away on a visit to someone in Northamptonshire. Whether she was still pregnant seems doubtful; certainly no child was born to her and Simon.

Early in February, word of the making of the inventory came to the ears of Thomas Fitzhugh. He sent for the Aspley constable, questioned him about it and asked him for the document. The man demurred. As constable he was directly subject to the authority of the justice of the peace, but he felt that looking after mistress Fitz's inventory was a private service. However, Thomas threatened to "send him up to London" for disobedience, so he submitted and fetched the inventory for him to look at; and then Thomas refused to part with it.[18]

It began to be gossiped in the district that Simon Fitz, heir of the late wealthy landowner, was in rags and that William and Alice Richardson were making him work for his keep by doing all sorts of menial jobs, including "the vile office of beating of hemp." Shortly after this, his mother Alice Fitz died, which meant that old Simon's lands in Aspley Guise reverted, under the terms of his will, to Simon the younger, and also that Alice's lifetime lease of the Hall expired; but Mistress Forster refused to move out. Simon - or Thomas Fitzhugh in Simon's name - obtained a court order directing her to vacate the premises, but it was not until the Under Sheriff intervened officially that she was turned out and possession of the house handed over to Simon.

Whether Richardson would have allowed Simon the independence of occupying the Hall is very doubtful, but by now the young man was in too poor a state of health to be on his own.

CHAPTER FIVE

The discovery of quinine as a treatment for ague being still a century away, the continual unrelieved attacks that enlarged the spleen and liver had undermined his constitution. Despite the rumours about their treatment of him, William and Alice Richardson were employing two women from the village to look after him. One day in April, as he was lying in bed, he said to his attendant:

"I would that my mother[-in-law] would come unto me, for she is a good woman and she loveth to cherish sick folk, and she can dress them meat and drink very well. But if I might speak with her a small season, I should do well enough. If I might but see her, I should be whole. but I pray you, Goodwife Charge, do not speak to my sister what I say."

Moved by this, the woman returned to her cottage without saying anything to Alice Richardson. There she found her husband in company with a servant of the Forsters and told them what Simon had said. After discussing the situation, they went to consult Simon's ghostly father, his confessor, the curate of the parish; and the priest went to call on the sick man. After talking to him he came to the conclusion that Elizabeth should be told, but as he was leaving the house, Alice Richardson, who had overheard their conversation, plucked him by the sleeve and said: "Sir Richard ['Sir' was a courtesy title for clergymen], I advise you to take further counsel before you do send for mistress Forster, or else you will be sorry." But the curate was not to be deterred; so, as her husband was out, Alice sent an anxious appeal to Thomas Fitzhugh. His house was quite near but there was some delay in contacting him. As soon as he heard what was afoot, the sixty-two year old judge came hurrying over. He at once tackled Simon.

"I hear you have sent for your mother-in-law," he said.

Simon did not dare do anything but deny it.

"Look that you keep you there in that mind," stressed Thomas; and he was about to leave, when Alice, who had probably been keeping watch from an upper window, cried in alarm:

"Mistress Forster is coming! She would come in whether I would or no. I pray you be good master to me, or else I am undone!"

Thomas ordered her to bar both the house door and the one leading from the hall to the room where Simon lay attended by the two women, and he went out to meet Elizabeth Forster as she was about to enter the yard.

"Ah, Mistress," he greeted her, "Do you come to help Simon Fitz away?"

She said she came for no such purpose. They fell into an abusive argument, in the course of which [according to her servant] Thomas bade her give up the chalice and vestments that had been recently stolen from Milton church, an alleged reference that will be explained later. Their raised voices became audible in Simon's room.

"What noise is that?" he asked. "Is my mother come?"

The two women said No, not daring to do otherwise, but Simon understood.

"Good Lord, have mercy upon me" he cried. "Goodwife Charge, is not this a piteous tale, that when a man's good friends be come and may not appear with him!"

And he turned over on his side and at midday he died without saying another word. Elizabeth Forster, finding the door bolted against her, returned home without having seen him.

When Simon's sisters, other than Alice Richardson, heard the news of his death childless and intestate, they assumed that the four of them were his co-heirs and so went *Thomas compounds the swindle* about claiming the family lands, only to find that their brother-in-law and his friend had bought them all at a price that, because Simon had died childless within a year of the sale, amounted to only a single half-year's payment of the agreed rent.[19] They and their husbands immediately instituted a suit in Chancery against William Richardson and Thomas Fitzhugh on the grounds that Simon had had no learned counsel with him to peruse the conveyance deed, that the defendants were "witty and wise men" and "learned in the laws," whereas their brother had been "a person of small wit and less discretion" who had been unable to discern "their great abusion and feigned friendship towards him," as was proved by the rent he had agreed to, which was £30 a year less than the lands were worth and did not amount to a ten-year purchase. The defendants denied any covin or fraud, saying that the feoffment had been made purely out of Simon's good will and benevolence in discharge of certain bonds in which he was bound to Richardson and "in consideration of such friendship, favour and kindness as Simon had at all times found at their hands"; nor, they maintained, was he a man of such simplicity as was alleged.[20]

In September the Court of Chancery issued an order to Thomas Fitzhugh and Richardson declaring that they had "unlawfully disturbed the lawful possession of the premises by colour of a certain feoffment fraudulently fabricated to the hurt of Simon Fitz the younger, who was a person without experience." The order pointed out several deficiencies in the conveyance, such as that there was no written evidence of any consideration, any down payment, having been made; there had been no livery of seisin; and the tenants of the land had never transferred their homage or service to the two purchasers. Livery of seisin was an ancient formality for transferring the possession of land. The contracting parties had to meet on the property in the presence of witnesses so that the vendor could hand the purchaser a symbolic clod of earth and the twig of a tree or, if a house was involved, the ring of the door that enabled the latch to be lifted. A note that this delivery had taken place had to be written on the back of the conveyance deed. The omission of this procedure by Thomas, who was not only a lawyer but a constant purchaser of real estate, could not be put down to ignorance. It was clearly in order to frustrate the purpose it was meant to serve, namely to make the change of ownership public.

The Chancery order continued: "In this regard we provide indemnity (as equity requires) by your contributing willingly towards our action of relief under penalty of £300 of your lands and chattels and anything of yours." The action of relief was to be that

But Thomas is brought to book over the affair the defendants must permit the plaintiffs to enter into the lands and occupy them in shares with them until the matter was settled.[21] It was eventually concluded that their four learned counsel should confer in order to recommend an agreed settlement. This they did, and on 13th May 1547 it was decreed that all the lands of Simon Fitz should be divided into two equal parts by the learned counsel. The parts should be named on separate pieces of paper and be drawn by lot out of a cap. The three plaintiff sisters and their husbands should draw half the total properties between them, and William and Alice Richardson and

Thomas Fitzhugh should draw the other half in equal third parts. This was decreed "in consideration that all variances and debates may cease and that perfect love and amity may hereafter grow betwixt all the said parties."[22]

During this time the health of King Henry had been declining. He had patched up a peace with the King of France. Boulogne was to continue to be occupied by the English while a price was paid in instalments for its redemption by the French. The bulk of the English army was withdrawn and disbanded. On 28th January 1547 the King died. On the throne he was succeeded by his nine-year-old son Edward, but in power by a Council he had appointed to protect him. For all his catholicism of recent years, Henry had chosen men mainly of the new faith to guide the country after his death. The Duke of Somerset, who headed the Council as Protector, was a man of liberal views and character. Under him the Act of Six Articles, the Treason Act and the Heresy Act were all repealed to the great relief of the English people; and absentee justices of the peace were ordered back to their dwelling-houses in their counties.

With the demobilisation of the army, Thomas Forster returned home, and he at once put forward a claim for possession of the Aspley Guise property from which his wife had been evicted. In spite of the elder Simon's will leaving the reversion of the property to young Simon, Forster now claimed that in fact the old man had already given it away to his elder son William and his wife Marcy on their wedding day and that William had later sold it to him, and he produced witnesses who gave circumstantial evidence of both transactions.[23] Perhaps in exasperation at this claim, Thomas Fitzhugh expressed his feelings about Forster in public at a sessions of the peace, saying that in every village within ten miles around Salford there were two or three people who went in dread of their lives because of Forster and his servants. This statement was reported to Forster and he brought a comprehensive Bill of Complaint in the Court of Chancery against Thomas Fitzhugh, William Richardson and others for "injuries, wrongs and defamation," among which injuries, or possibly wrongs, he included his dispossession of Aspley Guise.

His Bill was deficient, and the Court directed him to put in a new one and to allow the defendants to enjoy the disputed lands peaceably until the matter be determined. Thomas, however, was ordered to make Answer to the first Bill. This was in January 1548. In April a day was appointed for Forster to reply to the Answer; in June a day was fixed for the hearing; and in the meantime depositions were to be taken from witnesses. In November all the depositions were ordered to be frustrated because Forster had not yet put in his new Bill. And that was to be the continuous story of the action. From time to time hearings were fixed "at the peril of the plaintiff," but after three years of inaction the suit petered out.[24] As it never came to court, the Bill and Answer were not kept, but the depositions on Forster's behalf were filed separately and survived. It is they that tell us of the goings-on around the unfortunate Simon. They paint an unfavourable picture of Thomas Fitzhugh, as they were intended to do. They also give glowing character references for Forster. Most plaintiffs' cases look very convincing until the defence is heard, and we have no witnesses on Thomas's side. Forster was certainly not the exemplary character he tried to make out. Later on, even his wife Elizabeth left the marital home because she went in fear of her life from him.

One accusation made by Forster has not been mentioned. He produced depositions from four people who said they had heard from one Isabel Wright, widow, of no mentioned abode, that Thomas Fitzhugh had tried to get her to confess to taking a chalice and vestments that had recently been stolen from the church at Milton[25] (really by some Protestant extremist) and to say that she had handed them over in a bag to Elizabeth Forster. Thomas was alleged to have promised that if she did so she should lack nothing and "the Friday [fast day] should be worth the Sunday" but that if she did not he would have her sent to Bedford gaol, there to be either hanged or burned.[26] Why was this evidence only hearsay? Was it likely the woman could be persuaded to say what would almost certainly bring her to hanging or burning? As she was said to have refused, why were the deponents unable to allege that the threat was carried out?

In the second year of Edward's reign, a general pardon was offered, to those who would apply for it, for all offences committed in the late King's reign other than a few specific cases. The applicants seem to have been largely those who had tried to follow the fluctuations of Henry's policies and who feared that future changes might find them, retrospectively, to have been out of step. Somerset even put in his own application. Archbishop Cranmer and the Mayor and Commonalty of London followed suit. Among the rest were several Bedfordshire men, including Sir Michael Fisher, two of the Gostwicks and our Thomas Fitzhugh 'of Wavendon and London.'[27] One wonders what offence or offences he had in mind. At that time he was in good official standing, having had the justiceship of the peace for Huntingdonshire added to his responsibilities.[28]

On Whit Sunday in the following year the members of the family in their several churches had to find their way through services conducted from a new prayer book, written largely by Archbishop Cranmer himself. To ensure uniformity in the new official faith, its use was to be common throughout the whole country, replacing the four forms of service hitherto in use in different dioceses. Three years later it was revised, when it omitted, among other changes, the commemoration of the Virgin Mary. England had become a Protestant nation.

By this time Thomas was nearly seventy. In June 1551 he set down his wishes for the disposal of his property after his death. Popular indignation had brought about the repeal of that Act of Parliament against last wills, so he was able to distribute the scattered pieces of real estate in which he had invested his legal fees, and which would otherwise all have gone to his elder brother Richard. He commended his soul only to Almighty God though it was customary to add: "and to Jesus Christ my only Saviour and Redeemer, through whose death and passion I hope to have full and free pardon of all my sins and to inherit everlasting life." He inserted the essential statement that he was "of whole mind and memory," but, as with most septuagenarians, the latter was not what it had been. All his lands he left to his dearly beloved wife Jane for life. After her death, those in Wavendon, Aspley Guise, Wyboston and Eaton, amounting to 500 acres, were to go to his brother William, our ancestor, and his eldest son William; but he excluded Sawtry Holmes, the property he had bought from Sir Richard Cromwell. That he left to his brother Richard on condition that neither he nor his heirs should

Our ancestor William inherits from Thomas

dispute his will. He evidently expected his elder brother to resent the bulk of his lands going to William. If Richard did dispute the will, the Holmes were to be divided between William's sons and daughters. When William and his son came into their portion, they were to covenant to pay each of William's sons and their heirs forever an annuity of 40s. A small item

Thomas redeems himself by leaving property to the poor

excluded from William's portion was a farm, three cottages and land in Eaton left to "my cosyn," i.e. nephew, "Nicholas Fitzhugh and his heirs," a bequest liable to cause a deal of trouble since he was forgetting that both Richard and William had a son living called Nicholas. About his lease of the manor of Gamlingay he was not able to make up his mind at the moment, so he left a space for the legatee's name, and then forgot to fill it in. His houses in Charterhouse Lane were to be sold and the proceeds distributed among the poor, especially to poor prisoners. The property near Temple Bar he left to his wife's stepson, Henry Blackwell, for forty years, during which time he was to take 26s 8d a year for himself out of its profits and pass 86s 8d per annum to a certain Thomas Brown and his wife and to pay for the upbringing of their son, putting him either to school or to an apprenticeship. This family lived at Tempsford in a house belonging to Thomas, so Brown must have been a valued servant, perhaps his clerk.

A year later, and only a few days before his death, Thomas wrote a codicil in which he directed that the land he had, in such doubtful manner, acquired from Simon Fitz and which he called his Sixth Part, was to be sold and the proceeds distributed for specific charitable and parochial purposes by the curate and churchwardens of Wavendon. He had evidently quite forgotten having sold it only a month before.[29] As his property in Bedford town had evidently been disposed of at some time, that left only his title and interest in the manor and farm of Camoys in Eaton parish, and that he left to his nephew John Stocker, his sister's son.

Of his personal property, Jane was to have £33 and all his plate. William's children were to have their choice of his clothes, leaving the rest for "friends where most need is." His books were to be sold except any that his nephew Watson would like to have. Sums of money were left to Alice Blackwell, his male and female servants, his godchildren, every poor householder in Wavendon and

Charterhouse Lane, prisoners in the Marshalsea, King's Bench, Newgate and Ludgate prisons, the high altars of the churches at Eaton, Wavendon and St Sepulchre, London, and to twenty local maidens, 6s 8d each at their marriage. All the residue was to be for "the relief of poor folks and amending of the ways and lanes and streets near adjoining unto my house in Wavendon and within my yards." The only witness to the will was Lawrence Maidbury.[30]

Thomas died on 12th May 1552.[31] His will was proved by Jane and Henry Blackwell and Richard Fitzhugh the younger.[32] In the following January Richard the elder, as "brother and heir" of the deceased, was allowed by the Court of Wards to buy the Charterhouse Lane property,[33] which he passed on to his second son Nicholas.[34] Then followed a high-handed attempt by one of the brothers to seize all the lands that Thomas had left to his wife for life. Jane resisted and would not surrender the title deeds, so her brother-in-law took her to the Court of Chancery for them, claiming that he was lawfully seized of Thomas's lands.[35] Infuriatingly his Bill of Complaint is partly mutilated and his name is missing, but he described himself as "brother and next heir of Thomas Fitzhugh." Richard had already claimed the Charterhouse Lane property in that capacity, and he was the one thought likely to contest the will; but William, as the ultimate beneficiary of the lands in dispute, might perhaps have described himself in the same words. However, there is evidence, from late in the following year, that William's health was by then in no condition for him to take part in a lawsuit, which lessens the likelihood that he was the one who was now suing his sister-in-law. It does not seem that Jane ever put in any Answer to the Bill, so the case must have been settled out of court or dropped. Happily, when she died seven years later, she was still "of Wavendon."

In 1553 the delicate 16-year-old King died and was succeeded by his Catholic sister Mary. Heresy and treason laws came back. The author of the Book of Common Prayer and nearly three hundred men, women and children went to the stake within the next five years, but none in Bedfordshire. There circumspection was still the highest social

State Catholicism returns, and Bedfordshire conforms

virtue. The Bedfordshire man who would suffer more than fines for his faith had not yet been born. For the present, tinker, tailor -, they all conformed.

In the following year, the Rawlyn couple applied for the return of their 200 acres in Wilden. William refused, so they served *William is sued for return of some of the lands, and loses the Case...* a writ on him, claiming also that he was withholding their title deeds.[36] To this he was obliged by law to put in a written Answer within eight days; but it was his youngest son, Robert, now aged 28, who appeared in his stead and stated on oath that his father was unable to make answer because of his "impotency," which presumably meant senility. Accordingly the Court commissioned Sir John St John and Gerard Harvey, the bastard son of Sir George and now a JP, to call on the old man and take his Answer.[37] They visited him and did their best to arrive at his view of the case. Their Answer in his name denied that any more than two messuages and 32 acres of arable, meadow and pasture were involved and maintained that William had purchased them from the Rawlyns by Bargain & Sale in return for money, cattle and grain to the value of £26; that the property had then been in a very bad state; and that the Rawlyns themselves had surrendered the title deeds to him.[38]

The Court appointed commissioners, two for each side, to examine witnesses.[39] Their depositions do not survive, but the result was that the judges found for the Rawlyns since William was not able to produce evidence of the Bargain & Sale. He was ordered to return the property and title deeds to the claimants before the following Michaelmas. The loan repayment due from the Rawlyns was fixed for the same date and the value of it at £16 16s 8d. They were also to reimburse William for what he had spent on improvements.[40] Though William might appear by this to have lost the Wilden property, *...but somehow manages to retain the lands.* that is not what happened. Perhaps the Rawlyns could not raise the cost of the improvements as well as the loan repayment and so agreed to a sale. At any rate William's descendants continued to live at Wilden for generations to come.

The Fitzhughs of that day were of tough enduring stock; William and his brothers, like their father before them, all lived into their seventies. Richard died about 1554-7, but William may have lived until Queen Elizabeth ascended the throne, for which blessing England had to thank a nephew of our ancestress, Catherine Fitzhugh. The grandsons of the draper whose daughter William married had distinguished themselves. William Bill had become Master of Trinity College,

A nephew of ours saves Queen Elizabeth's life

Cambridge, and Dean of Westminster, and his brother Thomas physician to both Henry VIII and Edward VI. In 1549, when the Lady Elizabeth, in her secluded residence at Hatfield House, had fallen seriously ill, Protector Somerset had sent Dr Bill to her; and the future Queen had written him a grateful letter saying that she owed her recovery to him. From doctors' prescriptions of that period, one might think that the princess's strong constitution had more to do with it, but that is what she said. Anyhow, on 17th November 1558, acclaiming a Protestant Queen, William's sons and daughters faced the opening of a new era in English history.

.oOo.

CHAPTER FIVE

References

1	Letters & Papers, Henry VIII, Vol. 15.
2	*Ibid.*, Vol. 17.
3	REQ.2/7/10.
4	Letters & Papers, Henry VIII, Vol. 18.
5	Court Book, Archdeacon of Beds; Wilden Parish Register.
6	Early Chan Proc, C.1/1379/13-15.
7	STAC.8/108/1.
8	Wilden Parish Registers.
9	Letters & Papers, Henry VIII, Vol. 19.
10	Will of Simon Fitz, Beds R. O.
11	REQ.2/10/252.
12	STAC.4/8/44.
13	STAC.2/15/195.
14	STAC.2/15/194.
15	STAC.2/15/195.
16	Early Chan Proc, C.1/1157/34.
17	Common Pleas, Deed Enrolled, Michs, 37 Henry VIII.
18	Town Depositions, C.24/25.
19	Town Depositions, C.24/25.
20	Early Chan Proc, C.1/1157/34-45.
21	Chancery Decrees & Orders, C.33/2.
22	Chan. Decree Roll, C.78/4/38.
23	Town Depositions, C.24/25.
24	Chan Decrees & Orders, C.33/4/65-6/213.
25	STAC. 4/8/44.
26	Town Depositions, C.24/25.
27	Cal of Pat Rolls, Edw VI, Vol. 2.
28	Letters & Papers, Henry VIII, Vol. 20.
29	V.C.H. Beds, Vol. 2,; Comm Pleas, Deeds, Enr, Easter, Edw VI.
30	Will of Thomas Fitzhugh, PCC 26 Powell.
31	Court of Wards, 6/83.
32	Will of Thomas Fitzhugh, PCC 26 Powell.
33	Cal of Pat Rolls, Edw VI, Vol. 5.
34	*Ibid.*
35	Early Chan Proc, 1299, 20.
36	Early Chan Proc, C.1/1379/13.
37	Chan Decrees & Orders, C.33/12.
38	Early Chan Proc, C.1/1379/14.
39	Chan Decrees & Orders, C.33/14/12.
40	Chan Decree Rolls, C.78/9/27.

CHAPTER SIX

OUR ELIZABETHANS

A man shall see, where there is a house full
of children, one or two of the eldest respected
and the youngest made wantons; but, in the
middest, some there are as it were forgotten,
who many times nevertheless prove the best.

Of Parents and Children: Francis Bacon
(1561-1626)

In August 1558 Jane Fitzhugh made her will. She left £10
for a priest "to sing for my soul and my husband's soul and for all
my friends' souls and all Christian souls," but it was a bequest that
must have been frustrated, because she lived on until the following
summer, by which time Protestant Queen Elizabeth had succeeded
Catholic Queen Mary, the Book of Common Prayer was again in
use, and purgatory was finally debarred from official recognition in
England. She left four marks to Alice Blackwell and a number of
articles of household silver, four featherbeds and sums of money to
members of her first husband's family, but nothing to any Fitzhugh
nephews or nieces. The bulk of her personal estate went to her son
(or stepson) Henry Blackwell.[1] Her home and land at Wavendon
passed, in accordance with her late husband's will, to his brother
William, if indeed he had not died shortly before her. Certainly by
1560 it was in the possession of William's eldest son William,
who had also by then increased his stake in the neighbourhood by
acquiring the manor of Paslows from the Stafford family.[2] Paslows
was one of two manors in Wavendon, the other being Wavendon
Manor. William's mansion house stood near the centre of the
village, opposite the church, and was approached by a causeway or
drive raised a little above the surrounding ground to keep it clear
of winter mud.[3]

The Fitzhughs of the generation that now occupied the scene have been set out in the tree on page 35. The second son, Thomas, had died unmarried,[4] so it was the third son, Nicholas, who succeeded his father at Wilden. In fact, owing to the frailty of old William's health in his last years, it was probably Nicholas who finally secured the Wilden property for the family. He was also the first of his generation to get married. His bride was an Essex girl named Grace Stokes, and the wedding was held at her Parish church at White Notley in 1552.[5] That was back in Edward VI's reign and was the first Fitzhugh wedding by the rites of the Book Of Common Prayer. If the bridegroom's old mother was able to be present she must have noticed the difference between the vows now required of her daughter-in-law and the homelier ones she herself had taken nearly half a century before: "to be bonair and buxom in bed and at board till death us do part" - and in that age 'buxom' meant 'compliant.' In the following year Grace returned to her mother, as the custom was, for her first confinement, and at White Notley a son and heir was born, whom they called Nicholas.[6] The marriage continued fruitful; after the son came a daughter and then three more sons,[7] and in time Nicholas was to have, by a second wife,[8] three more daughters.[9] He was to be the progenitor of a line of Fitzhughs who remained at Wilden, with the property getting more and more divided and *The line to the end of the Fitzhugh family in Bedfordshire* subdivided between brothers, until the family disappeared from the parish during the agrarian revolution of the early 18th century, which was unkind to smallholding farmers; but the names of their probable descendants crop up continually in the records of the county until 1903 when the last Bedfordshire Fitzhugh died.

Robert, the youngest son, seemed favoured by fortune. Though in no position to settle much upon a bride, he was able to win the consent of a wealthy man, Richard Bury JP, of Bury Hall, Toddington, to marry his daughter Elizabeth, giving with her a generous dowry.[10] Perhaps Robert had already in mind, and had confided to his prospective father-in-law, an investment for the dowry which satisfied Bury that his daughter would be well provided for, both in marriage and widowhood. At any rate, shortly after the wedding, Robert used his wife's money to buy from his eldest brother William the manor of Paslows and all the lands in Buckinghamshire and Bedfordshire that had come to him from his uncle Thomas.[11]

Why William should have sold not only his birthright but also the manor he had so recently acquired is a mystery. He did not use the proceeds, which must have been considerable, to buy any comparable landed property in the neighbourhood, and yet he did not move far away.[12] Perhaps he put his money into one of the new capital-demanding industries that were being developed in England. Besides the well established manufacture of woollen cloth, the salt-making industry was growing, new ventures for the making of paper, glass, soap and steel were rising in various parts of the country; and, in Bedfordshire itself, brick and tile making was being developed, especially since the Councillors of Bedford had banned thatched roofs from their urban area.

Three of the surviving brothers were now well established, and only the third son, John, was left without material provision. He was put to the malting trade, *Our ancestor John is put into the Malting Trade* perhaps in the employ of a family of maltsters called Negus at Shelton in the north of Bedfordshire. Certainly he both learned their skills and took from them a wife. By the time he was able to marry he was in his forties, but his wife, Amy Negus, was some twenty years his junior.[13] She brought him a farm as her dowry,[14] perhaps at Barford, because it was there that John set up as a maltster on his own.

Malting is the process of producing one of the brewers' essential constituents of ale. The raw material is barley, which John bought from the farms in the neighbourhood. In his malthouse he steeped the grains in water in a great cistern. There they swelled until the corn could be easily pressed from the husks, when it was time to drain the water off. Twenty-four hours later, in the darkness of the malthouse, his man, or men, laid out the grains in heaps on the floor. There, for a fortnight, they grew hot, sweaty and sweet-smelling; then roots began to sprout and rudimentary stems to form within the husks. To control the process the heaps were turned over regularly, and as soon as the grains were loose enough to crumble between finger and thumb and before the stem was able to break out, they were shovelled into a kiln where, over a charcoal fire, they were heated and dried for two days to stop further germination. Then, dry and yellowy-brown, the resulting malt was spread to cool on the maltfloor and was trodden upon to break off the brittle rootlets, which were finally eliminated by winnowing; and then the product was ready for sale. Experience, skill and judgement were required to gauge the times, temperatures and results of these processes, which varied greatly with the weather and the time of year.

Most malt was sold locally, though some did go from Bedfordshire to London. Everywhere the quality and strength of ale were subject to regular strict checks by official ale-conners; and brewers were obliged to produce twelve gallons of ale from a quarter of malt. During John's career, a great change came over English drinking habits following the importation into the country in 1524 of the hop plant and its gradual acceptance. The use of hops in the process of brewing produced a drink called beer, which became popular; but as both ale and beer required malt, the new fashion had no harmful effect on John's business; indeed the increasing prosperity of the country must have ensured his own continued wellbeing.

John and Amy were soon blessed with a daughter, Elizabeth,[15] and over the next ten years four sons, Henry,[16] William, Robert and John,[17] were added to the family. *The last common ancestor of the English and American Fitzhughs* Today we all descend from John and Amy, and it was through two of their sons that all present surviving lines diverged.

Their marriage was in or about 1566, a year marked in Bedfordshire by the visitation of William Harvey, Clarenceux King of Arms, one of the three highest officers of the College of Arms. He came on a mission "to visit the arms and cognizances of Gentry and to reform the same if it were necessary" and armed with powers to deface "all false armory and arms devised without authority." Until the mid years of that century the organisation of the heralds for controlling the use of coat armour had been inadequate to deal with the growing demand for that now time honoured token of gentle status, so that many persons had assumed blazons on their own initiative. Indeed, one of the aims of this first of a number of visitations was to regularise the position of their descendants, provided they were seen to be "men of virtue and repute, worthy to be received among noble gentlemen" and where they were possessed of the minimum property qualification of land in free tenure to the yearly value of £10 or, in movable goods, of £300 sterling. Sir Thomas Wriothesley, Garter King of Arms in Henry VIII's reign, had defined the significance of coat armour as follows:

> "Equity wills, and reason ordains, that men of virtue of noble spirit should be rewarded for their merits and good renown, and not only in their own persons in this brief and transitory mortal life but, after them [that] those who should issue and be procreated of their bodies may be renowned in all places perpetually with others by certain signs and tokens of honour and nobility, to wit, with blazon, helm and crest, so that, by their example, others will be induced to use their days in feats and works of arms, to acquire the renown of ancient nobility in their line and posterity."

News of the imminence of Clarenceux's tour of inspection reached certain members of the gentry in the form of summonses from the bailiffs of the hundreds, acting on orders from the Sheriff of the county, who had selected those who were to be called. In each hundred the King of Arms, accompanied by his scriveners and heraldic artists, set up court at an inn in the chief

The ancient Arms of the Fitzhugh family are re-confirmed in 1566.

town or village, and those named by the Sheriff repaired to him there. Each one was the head of a family: Astry of Harlington, Bury of Toddington, Harvey of Thurleigh, Luke of Cople, Mordaunt of Turvey, St John of Bletsoe and a number of others; but the summons to the Fitzhughs was not addressed to Richard of Wyboston, the head of the family, but to his cousin Nicholas of Wilden,[18] the senior landed proprietor of the junior branch. The reason for this anomaly was probably Richard's adherence to the proscribed Catholic faith. Under Henry VIII, Garter King of Arms had specifically excluded "rebels" from armorial claims. Under Elizabeth, Catholics were tolerated so long as they conducted themselves as loyal subjects and engaged in no opposition to the

Church of England, but they were subjected to certain disabilities: each time they absented themselves from church service they were fined a shilling, and if they balked at taking the oath acknowledging the Queen as head of the Church, they could not become justices of the peace or occupy any official posts. The result was that conscientious objection of this

The Fitzhugh Arms 1566

kind became a cause of nuisance and resentment to a Sheriff who had to rely on the gentry for the carrying out of so many county commissions.

To demonstrate what armorial charges they claimed and to prove that their families had borne them for generations, the men invited ransacked their muniment chests in search of ancient seals, took down dusty shields from their walls, drew up family trees, and carried with them every piece of evidence they could find, because to have their arms disallowed would have been a disgrace no effort was too great to avert. Though Nicholas Fitzhugh seemed to know little about his ancestors, he was successful in satisfying Clarenceux's scrutiny and was one of five men in Barford hundred who received a confirmation of their arms for themselves, their predecessors and descendants. The Stockers had to wait until a second visitation later in the century and even then appear to have been unsuccessful.

The approved arms that Nicholas happily carried back with him to Wilden have already been discussed in Chapter Two. As with the majority of the confirmations, no crest was included. It would not be until the next century that crests were automatically included in grants of arms; so today an heraldic helmet that supports no crest carries its own evidence of antiquity. That same summer, Clarenceux visited Buckinghamshire, and Robert Fitzhugh of Wavendon was named by the Sheriff among those to appear before him. The family's arms of *ermine, on a chief gules three martlets or* were confirmed to him together with the Colville or Malabassel quartering; but the heraldic scrivener, in his notes, wrongly inserted the arms of Robert's wife's family, the Burys, as an additional quartering.[19]

The family's centuries-old tenure of Beggary-cum-Goodwick was now coming to an end. The times were growing difficult for the senior branch. Pope Pius V, after declaring it a mortal sin to attend a Protestant service, issued a Bull in 1570 declaring that Queen Elizabeth, a heretic and bastard, was excommunicated and deposed. Her subjects *The Fitzhughs* were absolved from their allegiance and *leave their* encouraged to rebel. From then on, *ancient manor* assassination plots against Elizabeth, aimed at *of Beggary* putting Mary, Queen of Scots, onto the throne, received papal approval as also did preparations for invasion by Catholic Spain. English Catholics found themselves in the dilemma of being either traitors to their Queen or in disobedience to their Holy Father. In 1572 Richard Fitzhugh sold Beggary-cum-Goodwick.[20] The purchaser was Walter Luke, son of the Nicholas Luke who had been brother-in-law to Thomas Fitzhugh the justice. Richard took his young family into Oxfordshire where he bought the manor of Walcot in the parish of Charlbury.[21] That their religious troubles had anything to do with their uprooting is unlikely. Certainly they did not seek to go where they would not be known as Catholics, because at Charlbury they continued to stay away from church even when the fine was increased to £20 a month.[22] There they remained until 1614 when Roger Fitzhugh, the last of his line, sold Walcot to the ancestor of the Jenkinson Earls of Liverpool.[23]

At the Paslows manor house, the first child to be born to Robert and Elizabeth was a boy, William,[24] and he was followed by three daughters,[25] Mary, born in 1564, Frances and Anne.[26] Sadly the couple lost their only son in childhood, but the three girls were healthy and grew to marriageable age. In families with daughters it was considered proper that they should be wed in order of seniority. Sir Thomas More had been in love with a younger daughter, but he had proposed to and married her eldest sister in order to spare her the social shame of not being first off the shelf. As a father, Robert experienced something of this embarrassment, because his eldest daughter Mary was not sought after by young men. The two younger girls appear to have been more attractive; their suitors lacked the fine sensibilities of the martyred Lord Chancellor; and Robert himself saw no reason to miss opportunities of getting his daughters off his hands. In the summer of 1584, his youngest girl Anne was married to a Buckinghamshire man named Thomas Cranwell,[27] and some four years later a young man came forward for the second daughter Frances. He was one John Fromond,[28] and Robert found that his

Robert has an unattractive daughter, Mary, but he succeeds in marrying her off in a clever property deal. The seeds of downfall are sown.

expectations for his wife's dowry were considerably higher than the modest amount that had been given with Anne; so he promised Frances £400. Soon after this and before he had raised the money, a welcome suitor appeared for his eldest daughter Mary. This was a lawyer of Staple Inn named William Astry, of a cadet branch of the family that held Harlington in Bedfordshire. Robert presented him with a proposition. He offered to settle upon him and Mary the reversion, after the death of himself and his wife, of two-thirds of Paslows Manor, provide board and lodging at the manor house for them, their children, servants and horses, and give them an annual allowance of twenty nobles (£6 13s 4d) for as long as he, Robert, lived; but in return he asked for a down payment of £400. Astry did not jump at this proposal, because Robert insisted on excluding 'impeachment of waste' from his offer regarding the manor, which meant that Astry would have no redress if, when he came into the property, he found that it had been allowed to run to seed. But Robert assured him that the manor was worth £3000 and that he was making the stipulation only because of promises he had already made to his other daughters and their husbands. So Astry accepted, and at last, in 1590, Mary found herself espoused.[29]

Robert fulfilled his part of the bargain by enfeoffing five trustees, consisting of two members of his wife's family, his two other sons-in-law Cranwell and Fromond, and a relation of Astry's, with two thirds of his manor for the use of himself and his wife for life and then of William and Mary and the heirs of their bodies, failing which it was to revert to whomever was then Robert's common law heir or heirs.[30]

After the wedding, William and Mary came to live with her parents at the manor house. At that moment, a lawyer was just what Robert needed in the family, because he was about to be brought before the Court of Star Chamber in an action that might well lead in the end to his having to stand in a pillory with both his ears cut off and his nostrils slit and seared.[31]

The trouble had started five years earlier and involved the forty acres in Wavendon and Aspley Guise that Robert's uncle Thomas had bought from Alice Stratton and her sons Thomas and William. When Thomas Fitzhugh died, the land descended to Robert's eldest brother and had been bought by Robert with all the rest of the inheritance. He had leased it to a tenant and it remained for years in peaceable possession; but when Thomas Stratton died, he left an only child, Elizabeth, married to a man called Thomas Balles and, five years after her father's death, she and her husband suddenly claimed the land on the grounds that her grandmother Alice had had no power to sell it, having had only a life interest. Robert maintained that as Alice had associated both her sons with the sale, it was perfectly legal. The Balles couple sued him at the Bedfordshire Assizes at Ampthill,[32] but Thomas's Bargain & Sale deed was read out and the plaintiffs lost their case. Unfortunately they were undeterred. On their counsel's advice, they leased the land to a tenant and supported him in a suit to eject Robert's own tenant. In June 1589, after being referred from court to court, the case was heard at the Aylesbury Assizes before Mr Justice Perriam. Robert again produced his uncle's deed of Bargain & Sale. Mr Pygott, counsel for the plaintiffs, described it as unworthy to be shown at the Assizes. The judge told the jury to examine it closely, to make sure there had been no erasures, and directed them that: "If the deed be not a good deed, the land is the woman's." But before they left to consider their verdict, he remarked audibly to Elizabeth Balles: "Woman, here will be no land for thee." Not unnaturally the jury decided in Robert's favour, upon which Perriam commented cryptically that the jury had done they knew not what.[33]

Still the couple did not give up. In 1590, in the Court of Star Chamber, they brought against Robert a now and far graver suit. They claimed that the conveyance deed had originally borne no record of livery of seisin on the back and that the endorsement had been added quite recently: in other words, that it was a forgery by Robert, a serious accusation that could lead to a criminal

Robert escapes prosecution and a sentence of mutilation. *a serious charge* Robert, now supported by his son-in-law Astry *of fraud* as his solicitor, denied the charge. The plaintiffs, in their Bill of Complaint, named the purchaser of the land as "one Fitzhugh." This was disingenuous, because they knew that if they gave his full name, he was almost certain to be recognised as the late justice of assize and therefore hardly a man to leave a legal document incomplete. However, Robert did not allow them to get away with it. His witnesses identified the purchaser, particularly remembering that he had been Clerk of the Assizes, and they confirmed that he, and Robert after him, had held the land for years without dispute. The plaintiffs called four witnesses. Two averred that when the deed had been read out at Ampthill, there had been no writing on the back, but that at Aylesbury there had been. A third said he had seen no endorsement at Ampthill but admitted he had not been looking for it. The fourth, one of the jurymen at Aylesbury, confessed that though the judge had directed them to examine the deed carefully, he had not given much attention to it because he had lost his hat.[34] It was of course most unlikely, if there really had been no record of the essential livery of seisin at the time of the Ampthill hearing, that neither the prosecuting counsel nor the judge would have noticed it; and so the case was dismissed.[35] The Balleses at last abandoned their ill-founded claim, but not their attacks on Robert. They brought another suit against him, this time for slander, and he had to instruct Astry to settle the matter for him out of court.[36]

Robert continued to use Astry's legal services in several lawsuits,[37] a form of trouble to which he was particularly liable;

Robert's parsimony leads to friction with Mary and his new son-in-law

but unfortunately the arrangement for the young couple to live with the wife's parents did not work well even from the beginning. Robert was a close man with his money, and when the Astrys first moved in, they were disappointed to find that although they were given a bedroom, they were expected to bring their own bed and bedding. Then, instead of being allowed food, fire, candle, lodging and washing for a maidservant and manservant, and enough hay, provender, grass, litter, stable-room and dressing for two horses, as they had been led to expect, they were provided with only enough for one servant and one horse. The arrangement lasted for four years, during which there was constant bickering between the generations. Robert was a quick-tempered man and, when angry, could be abusive and insulting even to people he respected; and Astry, in the opinion of his brother-in-law Cranwell, was "of a very perverse, unsure, ill-conditioned and most forward and turbulent disposition." He and his father-in-law settled into a steady mutual dislike. At last the young couple decided to move out. They and the parents each called in a friend - man called Edmund Harding for the Fitzhughs, and George Wells, a Wavendon neighbour, for the Astrys - to assess what would be a fair compensation to the latter for the loss of their keep. Their figure of forty marks (£26 12s) was accepted, the a couple set up house about three miles away at Woburn, and Robert told Harding he was glad to be rid of them.[38]

Son-in-law John Fromond died; but his widow Frances soon found a new husband from close at hand. The lord of the manor adjoining Paslows, formerly called Wavendon Manor but now Mordaunt's, was a man named Richard Saunders,[39] who

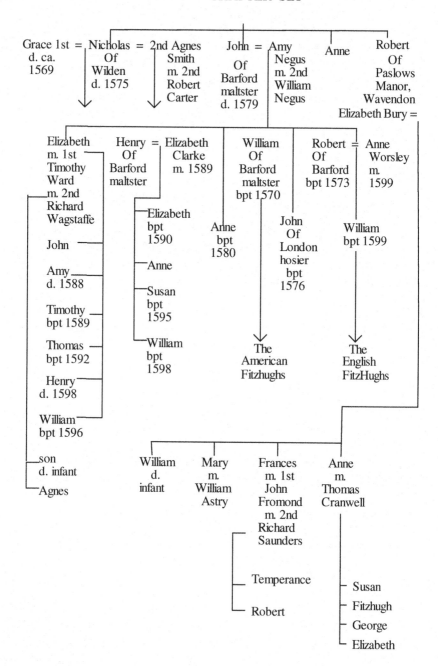

Grace 1st = Nicholas = 2nd Agnes   John = Amy   Anne   Robert
d. ca.   Of   Smith   Of   Negus   Of
1569   Wilden   m. 2nd   Barford   m. 2nd   Paslows
   d. 1575   Robert   maltster   William   Manor,
   Carter   d. 1579   Negus   Wavendon
Elizabeth Bury =

Elizabeth   Henry = Elizabeth   William   Robert = Anne
m. 1st   Of   Clarke   Of   Of   Worsley
Timothy   Barford   m. 1589   Barford   Barford   m.
Ward   maltster   maltster   bpt 1573   1599
m. 2nd   bpt 1570
Richard
Wagstaffe   Elizabeth   Anne   John   William
   bpt   bpt   Of   bpt 1599
John   1590   1580   London
   hosier
Amy   Anne   bpt
d. 1588   1576

Timothy   Susan
bpt 1589   bpt
   1595
Thomas   The   The
bpt 1592   William   American   English
   bpt   Fitzhughs   FitzHughs
Henry   1598
d. 1598

William
bpt 1596

son   William   Mary   Frances   Anne
d. infant   d.   m.   m. 1st   m.
   infant   William   John   Thomas
Agnes   Astry   Fromond   Cranwell
   m. 2nd
   Richard
   Saunders

   Temperance   Susan

   Robert   Fitzhugh

   George

   Elizabeth

THE FAMILY IN THE YEAR 1600

himself had been lately widowed. He and Frances consoled each other, and it was a match that Robert could approve, the groom being a man of ample means. Saunders had had seven children by his first marriage, and his new wife soon added to his family. The Cranwells too had children, and only the Astrys were childless.[40] Robert was bitterly regretting having made over the reversion of two-thirds of his manor to the couple, especially as he became aware that Astry was intent on getting even more into his hands.

The deed of enfeoffment of the trustees had been left in the care of John Fromond, but since his death it had found its way into Robert's hands, and whenever Astry *Conflict develops* queried this he was put off with excuses, *between Robert and* and he heard that Robert was even denying *his son-in-law* its existence. Astry was also worried at the *William Astry* condition of the manor lands. Buildings were being left with their roofs in disrepair, so that their woodwork was rotting. Fences that fell down were neglected so that the cattle were able to strip the coppices; and Robert was cutting trees at unseasonable times and selling off the timber.[41] The fact was that Robert was now over seventy and was unwilling to spend money on property that he expected would all too soon fall into the hands of his detested son-in-law. In considering his death and its consequences, he was aware that if he, the youngest brother, had not bought up the primogenital inheritance of his eldest brother, thus by-passing the prospects of his middle brothers, Nicholas and John, the family lands would by now have passed to his Fitzhugh *Robert plots to* nephews. His eldest brother had been *disinherit Astry* childless, but Nicholas, who had died in 1575,[42] and John, in 1579, had both left sons. Old Robert pondered and planned, turning over in his mind those nephews and his daughters and his sons-in-law.

The death of our ancestor John Fitzhugh in 1579 had occurred during appalling weather in that part of the Ouse valley. Torrential rains and gales continued day after day; the river swelled dangerously, damaging bridges and sweeping over meadows; and, suddenly one night, at St Neots the current overflowed its banks and flooded the streets and houses; swans swam in the market place, and the townspeople left their beds and took to what boats they could reach. There is no report of how the people fared at Barford and the other riverside villages, but when John's condition was critical - "very sick in body" - he was evidently not at home, because after friends had drawn up a short will for him, he asked them "that his seal should be pulled off and brought home," and yet he cannot have been far away because at least one of those gathered at his bedside was a Barford man. If he could not be carried home, his plight must have been both sudden and severe - physical injuries? heart attack? exposure? - so one cannot help wondering whether his condition was brought about by the abnormal situation around him. Certainly one of his first thoughts was to leave a bequest for the repairing of Barford bridge.

The dying man had a family of five children all under thirteen and a wife four months pregnant. After leaving each poor *John, the last* man of Barford a peck of malt and a few *common ancestor* other legacies, he bequeathed one-third of *of the English and* the residue of his estate to his wife Amy *American* and the rest to be divided equally between *Fitzhughs, dies in* his sons, when they reached the age of *1579* twenty, and his daughter at her marriage; but "the part which belongeth to the child my wife goeth with shall be deducted of my wife's part." He asked to be buried within the church of Barford.[43] This was a common request. The site of the church, the holiest of consecrated ground, was usually chosen by the more well-to-do of a parish for their place of burial. He was interred there on the 24th September.[44]

The sixth child, when she made her posthumous appearance in February, was named Anne.[45] By then, one supposes, Amy must have taken over the management of the malting until her sons were old enough to take over from her. Barford was only six miles from Bedford, where she had a cousin, William Negus, who was a maltster and could give her any advice she needed. That she did keep in touch with him is shown by the fact that sooner or later she married him.[46] He was a respected burgess of the town, took his turn at serving the municipal offices and, during the 1590s, came to be twice elected mayor.[47]

The years of Amy's widowhood were anxious ones in the country. It was well known that King Philip of Spain, with the blessing of the Pope, was constructing a great fleet to transport the Duke of Parma's army from the Spanish Netherlands to the invasion of England. From 1583 onwards, the coastal forts were strengthened and the militia forces frequently mustered and trained. Amy's two elder sons, Henry and William, were among those obliged to serve, but Robert was not yet sixteen. Large beacons were erected on hilltops at the most strategic lines of sight and smaller ones elsewhere, sometimes on church towers, to flash the invasion news across the country. In 1588, from March onwards, when the winter weather was past and the danger seemed imminent, watchers were posted at every beacon. The High Constables of the hundreds allocated the watching duties to each village in rotation, and four watchers were chosen from the more well-to-do, reliable parishioners[48] so that at Barford George Fitzgeoffrey at the manor house and Henry Fitzhugh of the malting, the only two householders designated 'gentlemen', and two prosperous 'husbandmen,' Roger Flavell and William Wilshire, were the most likely to be appointed.[49] Two of them had to man the watch by day and two by night. The beacon consisted of a brazier mounted on poles and filled with flammable material. Each watcher had to report for duty armed, in case of attempted sabotage by Catholics, and provided with additional dry wood and candles, and not be accompanied by a dog, which would have been a distraction. A shelter was provided, with an opening towards the next beacon but without seats, in case the watch should fall asleep. The pay, receivable from the churchwardens, was 8d for every twenty-four hours watched.

Our ancestor William joins the defence against the Spanish Armada

On 19th July the Spanish fleet was sighted off the Lizard. The beacons of Cornwall roared into flame, and from high point to high point the message raced east and north across the country; it entered Bedfordshire at Dunstable Beacon.

In this twentieth century it is hard for us to imagine how the Elizabethan leaders of the country roused our ancestors' determination and courage in that national emergency, or indeed what image of their leaders our ancestors' minds were able to form. Today we should all have been able to hear and see the Queen speaking to the troops at Tilbury. She was saying:

CHAPTER SIX

".... I have placed my chiefest strength and safeguard in the loyal hearts and good will of my subjects. I know I have the body of a weak and feeble woman, but I have the heart and stomach of a king, and of a king of England too, and think foul scorn that Parma or Spain, or any prince of Europe, should dare to invade the borders of my realm."

If her words could have been listened to in the draughty shed on the Bedfordshire hilltop, they would have warmed the hearts and stirred the blood of the watchers, and they were men who would not have been as shy as we are today about a lump in the throat and a tear in the eye.

Thanks to the navy under Lord Howard of Effingham and Sir Francis Drake and to a strong southerly gale, the danger was averted. The war with Spain went on but did not greatly affect the lives of ordinary men and women. Henry and William ran the malthouse at Barford, and their younger brother Robert, living in the same Parish, was almost certainly helping them. But the business could not support all the brothers; something different had to be found for the youngest boy, John. So, like the youngest sons of so many English families through the centuries, he was sent off to London to make his living in that Tom Tiddler's ground of opportunities. An essential preliminary to eventually being allowed to set up one's own business in the capital was a seven-year apprenticeship to a freeman of one of the City guilds, and Amy found a member of the Broderers' Company willing to take him.[50] That did not mean that embroidery was to be his occupation; in fact his master was a hosier,[51] but the hosiers had no guild of their own, their mystery being a latecomer among the industries and trades of London, such as those of the Mercers, Goldsmiths, Fishmongers, Merchant Taylors, and Drapers.

In November 1589 Henry married a young woman named Elizabeth Clarke who lived at Henlow,[52] and there, in the following September, under the care of her mother, their first child was born, a girl who was to be the eldest of nine children.[53] But Henry was not the first to have presented Amy with a grandchild; her eldest daughter Elizabeth, married to a Wilden man called Timothy Ward, had had three children, though one of them had died.[54] This Elizabeth seems to have had no lack of admirers around her. When her husband died in 1598, leaving her with four children, another Wilden man, Richard Wagstaffe, married her,[55] and when he died in 1602 leaving her with another child, it was before the first anniversary of his demise that yet another man of the village, John Wilshire, stepped into his shoes.[56]

The last decade of the century saw hard times for the maltster brothers, indeed for almost everyone. In 1594 the English weather entered on a bad period; the crops were poor and consequently prices rose. Barley, which had stood at 12s a quarter in '93, rose to 13s 4d and then even higher. It was the practice for commercial users of grain, such as bakers and maltsters, to buy supplies direct from the growers and to have them delivered to their doors, but soon the shortage became such that the country was threatened with famine, and the Privy Council stepped in with a ban on all direct dealings. At that time the Privy Council performed the executive functions of government that were later taken over by the Cabinet. It was ordered that all sales of grain were to be conducted in the market places, and justices of the peace were to see that churchwardens had priority in buying supplies for their parish poor. Later in the year, barley shot up to 24s a quarter, and it was difficult to procure any, even at that price. In the following year, the weather continuing bad, crops poor and prices high, the Privy Council order was renewed. Even shrewd dealers like William Negus, who had ordered supplies and paid for them in advance when prices were low, found themselves in difficulties with suppliers unable to fulfil their obligations.[57] The weather continued severe for another two years, but at last, in 1598, it took a turn for the better, the harvest was good, and business at the malting picked up.

In the following year, our English branch of the Fitzhughs came within a few days of extinction - not, as might be expected, from an untimely death but an untimely birth. At that period, the twelve days that followed Christmas constituted a holiday of continuous festivity, said to be a survival of the old Roman Saturnalia. Old and young, men, *The English branch narrowly escapes extinction* women and children, gave themselves up to the pleasures of music-making, dancing and singing, hoodman blind, kisses under the mistletoe, hot cockles, mead, ale and decorations with holly, ivy and bays. All very jolly and heart-warming, but in the course of merry-making so prolonged, young blood was sometimes warmed to fervours more tuned to the ancient pagan revels. In the yuletide of 1598-9, Robert Fitzhugh, now aged twenty-five, carried dalliance with a young cousin of the Rector of Wilden, called Anne Worsley, beyond the auspices of mistletoe, so that after Twelfth Night there was much ado for her and her family, and they had no assurance that all was going to end well, because as the anxious months went by, they failed to bring any offer of marriage from Robert. Spring came and passed, summer bloomed and faded, but still Anne had no wedding plans to announce. To the good Rector it must have seemed shamefully certain that his new little kinsman or kinswoman would be recorded in the baptismal register, according to the practice of the day, as: "baseborn son (or daughter) of Anne Worsley." However, at the very last moment, almost certainly under family pressure, for neither love nor conscience can have burgeoned so sluggishly, Robert was brought to the altar in his own parish church. The ceremony was performed on 25th September 1599,[58] and none too soon, because only sixteen days later, on 11th October, the couple were back, at the other end of the church, for the christening ceremony.[59] The wedding had been just in time to ensure our little ancestor William - and hence ourselves his male-line descendants - being registered in the name of Fitzhugh and not Worsley. Good people, the Worsleys, no doubt, but - . Well, you know what I mean.

.oOo.

References

1   PCC 24 Chayney.
2   Foot of Fines, Divers Counties, Easter 2 Eliz.
3   STAC 8/108/1.
4   Visitation of Bedfordshire, 1566.
5   Parish Register of White Notley.
6   *Ibid.*
7   Visitation of Bedfordshire, 1566.
8   Parish Register of Wilden.
9   *Ibid.*
10 STAC.8/108/1.
11 *Ibid.*
12 Foot of Fines, Divers Counties, Hilary 10 Eliz.
13 Archdeaconry of Bedfordshire Wills, Book 16, f. 130.
14 Chancery Proceedings, Series 2, C.3/244/89.
15 Archdeaconry of Bedfordshire Wills, bundle 1626-7/101.
16 *Ibid.*
17 *Ibid.*, and Parish Register of Great Barford.
18 Visitation of Bedfordshire, 1566.
19 Visitation of Buckinghamshire, 1566.
20 Foot of Fines, Beds, Mich. 14-15 Eliz.
21 Cat of Anc Deeds in PRO; Close Roll C.54/1386.
22 Returns of Recusants 28, Dioc. Oxford (Cath Rec Soc).
23 Indent, Jas I, 1613-20, p.66. 16, C.54.
24 Visitation of Buckinghamshire, 1566.
25 B.M. Add MS 43473, Cal.
26 Visitation of Buckinghamshire, 1566.
27 Parish Register of Wavendon.
28 STAC.8/108/1.
29 Chan Proc, Ser 2, C.3/256/4.
30 *Ibid.*
31 STAC.5/B115/13.
32 STAC.5/B20/31.
33 *Ibid.*, Chan Proc, Ser 2, C.3/109/23.
34 STAC.5/B115/13.
35 Chan Proc, Ser 2, C.3/256/4.
36 *Ibid.*
37 *Ibid.*
38 STAC.8/108/1.
39 *Ibid.*
40 *Ibid.*
41 Chan Proc, Ser 2, 3/256/4.
42 Parish Register of Wilden.
43 Archdeaconry of Bedfordshire Wills, Book 16, f. 130.
44 Parish Register of Gt. Barford.
45 *Ibid.*
46 PCC 41 Huddlestone.
47 *Bedfordshire Notes & Queries,* Vols 2 & 3.
48 L. Boynton: *The Elizabeth Militia.*
49 Lay Subsidy Roll, E.179/72/215.
50 PCC 90 Huddlestone.
51 STAC./108/1.
52 Parish Registers of Henlow.
53 *Ibid.*
54 Parish Register of Wilden,; PCC 90 Huddlestone.
55 Parish Register of Wilden.
56 *Ibid.*
57 Chancery Proceedings, Series 2, C.3/244/89.
58 Parish Register of Great Barford.
59 *Ibid.*

CHAPTER SEVEN

"WONDERFUL THINGS!"

"Give me the map there. Know that we have divided
In three our kingdom ...... Our son of Cornwall
And you, our no less loving son of Albany,
We have this hour a constant will to publish
Our daughters' several dowers, that future strife
May be prevented now."
King Lear: William Shakespeare (1564-1616)

In[1] the autumn of 1602 Robert of Paslows resolved to make his will. He sent for a man named Thomas Hill and gave him the information necessary for drawing it up.[2] He said that William Astry could have the remaining third of his manor if he paid £600 to certain named persons. If he did not take up this option, the third was to go to daughter Anne Cranwell for life and then to her son Fitzhugh Cranwell.[3] This boy was Robert's eldest grandson and also his godson, christened Fitzhugh so that, for want of a son, the family name might be carried on as a first name among his daughter's descendants. To a nephew William, his late brother Nicholas's son, who lived in the village, he left a cottage in Wavendon with six acres. A second cottage was to go to his second grandson, two-year-old Robert Saunders; and two messuages in Wavendon to William and Mary Astry. All his lands in Bedfordshire he left to his nephews, John Fitzhugh of Wilden and Henry, William and Robert Fitzhugh of Barford.[4] His personal property he divided between his wife and daughters and his sister Anne who lived with them. He appointed his wife Elizabeth, his daughter Anne, nephew Henry Fitzhugh and old friend Edmund Harding to be executors. When the document was drawn up, he

Our ancestor William and his brothers are willed Robert's property in Bedfordshire

needed witnesses, so he took Hill over to the house where his nephew William lived. They found him in his barn where, with a man called Quaynt, he was threshing corn. Robert asked them to witness his will and said:

"William, I am sorry for one thing."

"What is that, sir?"

"That I have not remembered thee or any of thine."

He was of course pulling his nephew's leg, but Hill evidently thought it unkind.

"Yes, William, he hath" he cried. "He hath dealt very liberally and bountifully with you, for he hath given to you a little cottage and some land to the same."

William and Quaynt witnessed the will by having it read to them and signified accordingly. This was before the time when the law reduced witnessing to a mere vouching for the testator's signature and barred witnesses from being beneficiaries.

But the making of his will did not relieve Robert's anxiety about the fate of his property. He was always worried that Astry might use his legal skill to get round it. After considering one or two of his wife's relations as possible advisers, he *But Robert is determined to disinherit Astry* eventually, in 1605, sent for a lawyer named William Anglesey, who lived at Marston Moretaine. Anglesey was evidently a busy man, and it took two or three messages to get him to Paslows. He found Robert, then approaching eighty, in very good health and was taken by him into an inner parlour. There the old man told him he had matters of great importance and secrecy to impart and asked him to promise never to reveal what he was going to say unless he authorised him to do so. Anglesey cautiously gave his promise "as far as it might stand with the laws of God and were not opposite nor repugnant to the King's Majesty's laws and proceedings." The King's Majesty was now James I, the old Queen having died two years earlier.

Robert then put his hand into a black pouch that hung by his side and took out his will. He explained that he had doubts as to whether it would achieve the effects he wished and asked Anglesey to examine it together with a copy of the earlier indenture conveying two-thirds of his manor to trustees on behalf of the Astrys. Anglesey studied them both and gave it as his opinion that Astry might still obtain free possession of the remaining third, because the requirement of a payment of £600 was not in accord with the terms of the indenture. Robert immediately asked him to use his best skill to prevent something so opposite to his intention, and told him that Astry, with his over-reached (i.e. elastic) conscience - which, he said, would stretch from there to Anglesey's house three miles away - would use his best kind of knavery and devices to defraud his sister-in-law Anne Cranwell and her son and the Fitzhugh nephews of all that he, Robert, was leaving them. He said that if he thought Astry would acquire more of his property than he intended, he would rather set fire to it and burn it all to ashes.

Anglesey wrote into the will, between the lines, some amendments that he thought should assure the third part of the manor to Fitzhugh Cranwell unless he was paid the £600, and would give him also the reversion of the whole manor on the deaths of Astry and his wife, unless they had children, which was now unlikely. Anglesey recommended leaving the Bedfordshire property too to Fitzhugh Cranwell, but the old man replied that that was the ancient inheritance of the Fitzhughs; he had left it between kinsmen of that name, and he would not change his mind for a thousand pounds. He would, he said, never bequeath it away from the

Robert is desperate to leave 'the ancient inheritance of the Fitzhughs' to William and his brothers.

Fitzhughs as long as the Almighty lent him breath. In that case, asked the lawyer, what would remain for Anne Cranwell and her son if Astry did manage to frustrate his intention for the manor? Robert thought about it and said he would as soon trust the devil as Astry, so he would leave Anne and her son all his property in Wavendon not belonging to the manor, except the cottage he had left to William. So Anglesey drew up a codicil revoking the bequests to Robert Saunders and the Astrys in Wavendon and compensating his Saunders grandson with a sum of money. Robert made him promise that, if ever the will and codicil should be suppressed or stolen, he would testify to their having been made.

"For," he said, "I do greatly fear that that devil Astry, with his hellish conscience, and his copesmate George Wells, or some such like, will use some devilish trick and damnable practice to frustrate my true, full and absolute meaning when I shall not [be able to] tell what I say or what I do."

Having read through the amendments and codicil, Robert asked Anglesey to witness them, but he could not because there was no other witness present. So Robert folded the codicil inside the will and took them into an inner chamber. Later he had them witnessed by Thomas Hill and Edmund Harding.

After that day, whenever Robert met Anglesey, he would remind him of his promise. "For," said he, "that knave Astry said he would fain have me dead, and never comes to my house but with his pen and ink at his side, which I greatly fear."

In the next two years Robert lost two close members of his family; first his daughter Frances Saunders and then the last other remaining member of his own generation, his sister Anne. The same years saw his manor house falling into decay. When asked why he did not repair it, he used to say it was good enough, and too good, for him that should come after. Often, when he and Astry met, they were heard quarrelling. What made Astry particularly bitter was the discovery, after he was married, that an *Astry quarrels bitterly* earlier suitor for one of the girls had been *with Robert after* offered by Robert the reversion of the *discovering how* whole manor in return for a down *cheaply Robert had* payment of £200 and had declined it; and *married off Mary.* then he, Astry, had come for Mary and had parted with £400 for only two-thirds. That never ceased to rankle; his father-in-law had made a gull - what we should now call a sucker - of him. The servants at Paslows were often shocked to hear Astry calling their master such names as "rogue," "beggar's brat" and "whore-master" - the last epithet doubtless referring to the large profit he had made out of his daughter - and to see him once even take the old man by the throat. In spite of scenes like these and Astry's actually taking Robert to court over his unpaid legal fees, there never came a complete break between the old couple and their daughter and her husband. Robert often sent them gifts of turkeys, geese and cheeses; and they used to come and stay at the manor house at Christmas time. On one occasion Robert even lent Astry money. The old man's relationship with his youngest daughter Anne Cranwell was very different; he was always glad to see her and her husband and children. In fact, their eldest girl Susan came to live with her grandparents.

As Robert passed into his eighties, people began to notice that he occasionally wandered in his mind. Sometimes he thought he was back in his boyhood homes at Wyboston and Bushmead. A servant who had been with them for years and was now married to a man in the village found that he did not know her; he asked her who she was and where she had come from. Then, at Christmas time 1608, he fell ill and the family did not expect him to recover. Elizabeth had a bed, almost certainly a four-poster with curtains, set up for him in a ground floor room with a fire-place and arranged a roster of people to lie at night on a trundle bed in the same room, so that his needs would always be attended to. As in most houses at that time, the downstairs rooms at Paslows had earthen floors covered with rushes.

Within a day or two the sick man received a visitor. At one time or another he had quarrelled and made it up with most members of his family, but since his daughter Frances had died there had been no balm of fatherly love to heal a breach with his son-in-law Richard Saunders; so now a friend of the latter, Francis Duncombe, perhaps at the prompting of Elizabeth whose cousin he was,[5] thought it important for the Saunders grandchildren that the old man should not die at loggerheads with their father. He brought Richard up to the manor house and left him in the yard while he went in to prepare the way. Soon he came out to say his father-in-law would see him. At the bedside there passed "many kind and good salutations and speeches," which encouraged Duncombe to say: "I hope you forgive your son Saunders."

"Ay," said Robert, "with all my heart; and so, I hope, he will forgive me."

"Ay, God forbid else," responded Richard.

During their conversation Robert talked perfectly rationally, except once, towards the end, when he asked an odd irrelevant question about Stourbridge Fair but then went on immediately to speak sensibly of other matters. As Richard and Duncombe were about to leave, he called for beer to be brought for them.

On the 2nd or 3rd of January an incident happened about which confusing accounts were later given. It seems that Robert told his daughter Anne Cranwell he was anxious to see his will, which was in one of two locked chests in his chamber. Seventeen-year-old Susan, who was with them, said she knew where the keys were, so Anne fetched them and gave them to her father. He handed them back and asked her to get the will out; he had put it under the till of the chest. He said there was money there too, which Anne could have except for 40 marks, which he needed for Astry. Anne opened one of the chests, could not see the will, and had no sooner started searching for it than her mother came in. Seeing documents, money and other things lying on the floor, she was very annoyed, demanded the keys and asked Robert what would be left for her and Saunders's children if he let Anne take all the money. He said there was enough for them in the other chest and asked her to let Anne keep the key as she had always been a dutiful daughter to them, but Elizabeth insisted on having both keys and that the chest should not be searched till Thomas Cranwell could be there. So Anne put everything back and gave up the keys. At that moment Thomas Cranwell arrived with a manservant. Hearing what was happening, he said he would look for the will, whereupon Elizabeth, "for fear to disquiet her husband any further," walked out, taking the keys with her. Later on, when Cranwell and Anne wanted to look for the will, she would not let them.

The news of Robert's illness travelled further afield, and at about Twelfth Tide our ancestor [of the English Branch], Robert junior, now with family responsibilities, turned up at Paslows. He was the old man's nephew and godson and he came to claim an annuity he thought due to him. This was one of 40s a year that his great-uncle Thomas the justice had stipulated in his will was to be paid by his brother William and nephew William to each of the brother's younger sons and their heirs for ever as a condition of their inheriting his Wavendon and Bedfordshire properties. Young Robert considered that this obligation had passed to old Robert when he had bought those properties. However, he was evidently not aware that Thomas in his codicil had cancelled that bequest because by then he had given his nephews something personally; so old Robert answered his nephew's claim by pointing that out. Young Robert said he was only asking for forty shillings a year; to which his uncle replied: "You are better able to live than I. What will you give me?" So the young man returned home readjusting his expectations by 40s per annum.

A day or two later, on 9th January, Robert's friend, sixty-year old Edmund Harding, came from Aspley Guise to see him. He turned the conversation to the subject of his will, and Robert said he had made one but there had been a robbery; he had put the will with some money into a boot, a travelling box, but it had been filched by Astry and now he did not know where it was. Harding went to Elizabeth and asked what her husband meant by saying there had been a robbery. She explained that she herself had gone to the boot and taken out forty marks, twenty of which she had given William Astry as his annuity, and twenty she still had. What she said about the will is not recorded, but Harding went back to Robert and said:

"Sir, I do perceive that you are weak and ill and that your old will is not to be found. Therefore, I pray you, make a new will."

"When would you have me make a new one?"

"Tomorrow morning?" suggested Harding; and he reminded Robert about a local man who had died without leaving a proper will and what a lot of trouble it had caused. So Robert agreed. Harding asked whom he would like to have as witnesses. He chose another old friend, Mr Hughes, the parson of Woughton-on-the-Green, his son-in-law Thomas Cranwell and Harding himself.

Fearing that Astry may have stolen his Will, Robert thinks to make a new one.

When Harding asked who else, he did not name anyone, so Harding suggested George Wells, his neighbour, but Robert would have none of him, saying that neither George Wells nor William Astry should be privy to any will of his. Instead, he chose another Wavendon man, Goodman Thomas Hull who, he said, was an honest man. So Harding went to Elizabeth and asked her to send them invitations for the following morning.

At one point in their conversation, Robert had suddenly asked Harding where he was, and his friend had had to assure him that he was at home, in his own house, in his own bed.

"If you had said," replied the old man, "that I had been in my manor of Paslows, you had said well, for my manor of Paslows reacheth to St Neots and to Barford Bridge."

Next morning Harding arrived, having arranged for a clerk named King to meet him outside the house bringing pen, ink and paper. He found Parson Hughes, Thomas Cranwell and Hull already there, and he asked Robert whether he was ready to have his will drawn up, whereupon the old man flew into a passion.

"Will me no wills!" he shouted. "I have made a will already, but I doubt the knaves have filched it away." He said he had put his money into a boot and it had gone.

Harding calmed him down, and he agreed that everything ought to be put in order, or else Astry would get his whole manor. "That cogging merchant," he said, should have no land of his. So Harding called King into the room and explained to Robert that he was there to take down his instructions. The clerk accordingly wrote out the conventional testamentary preamble: "In the name of God amen"; the name, abode and status of the testator; the statement that he was of sound mind and perfect memory; and the commendation of his soul to Almighty God, etc. That done, Harding asked Robert where he wished to be buried. "In Wavendon church," he said. Next it was customary to deal with charitable bequests. What would he give to the church? Nothing. And though they all urged him to make some donation, he would not budge. The next item was what he would give to the poor. He said they were thieves and robbed him; and no persuasion could move him to leave them more than four shillings at the rate of 1s every three months for one year. Having thus unsatisfactorily covered the charitable bequests traditionally intended for the good of the testator's soul, Harding asked him how he would dispose of his land. Robert answered that he would get on his white gelding and ride home and lie at his manor of Paslows that night. Harding rephrased his question. To whom did he wish to leave the third part of his manor? Robert did not reply, and Harding had to ask him again. Still he gave no answer.

"Mr Fitzhugh," said Harding, "I know that you have conveyed two parts of your manor to Mr Astry."

Robert exclaimed that he had conveyed none of it to Astry; that Astry was a knave and should have no land of his. Harding pressed him to think back, and said that he himself had seen the conveyance deed.

"Belike," retorted Robert, "you know better than I! I tell you, Astry is an arrant knave and shall have no land of mine. Hang him, he shall have none of mine!"

To the witnesses it was now clear that the old man's memory was unfit for proceeding with the will. Harding suggested that they should have a look for the old one; to which Robert replied: "With a good will!" So Mrs Fitzhugh was sent for and asked to bring the keys of the two chests. She brought them but objected that the will had already been searched for by Anne, and she thought her son-in-law Astry ought to be sent for from Woburn. Robert would have none of that, and the men pulled out one of the chests to start the search. However, Elizabeth then invited them to have dinner first. They accepted and took their seats in the hall, but she herself would not sit down but kept going in and out. If she was playing for time to get word to Astry, she was unsuccessful, as he was away in London. However, when the party had almost finished their meal, she came in and said that Robert had changed his mind and did not want them to search for the will. Harding said that in that case they would of course not do so.

After dinner the guests went in to the sick man to say goodbye. Harding mentioned again the trouble that might arise for want of a will and asked whether he would not after all like a search made; and he said he would. So they sent again for Elizabeth to bring the keys. She came but was very unwilling to give them up, until Robert rudely ordered her to do so. One of the chests was opened up, evidently not the one that Anne had started to search because uppermost in it lay a box and inside that, among other documents, Parson Hughes quickly found *But instead he reads his old Will; many of the family are unhappy with what they are left.* the will. It was then read out for them all to hear, with Elizabeth muttering disapproval at parts of it, but with Robert making no comment. Then it was wrapped up again and put back in the box and chest, Elizabeth saying to her son-in-law:

"This makes for your turn, son Cranwell, but not for me. But if I had been wise, I might have burned it, for my husband would have had me burn it a great while ago. But lay it in the box again where it was. I will see it forthcoming or else I will bear the blame."

After Harding and Hughes had taken leave of Robert, who informed them that he was going to Stourbridge Fair, they joined the others in the hall, and Elizabeth had beer brought to them. This time she sat down with them.

"I am sorry," she said, "you did search and find the will."

Harding asked her why, but she did not answer. He urged her to keep it safe. "For now you see he is not in case to make a new will. But if he be in case at any time, if you send to me - at any time - I will come and do the best that lies in me for him." He and the rest of the party then took their leave.

Two days later, William Astry arrived from London. Almost at once he heard from the Cranwell children of the reading of the will. Up to that time, expectation in the family seems to have been that Robert might leave his Bedfordshire property to the young Cranwells, so he asked Fitzhugh Cranwell what he had been left. The boy said he knew nothing about it, but Astry did not believe him and said: "You shall eat your part of the land at Wyboston on Good Friday." By which he meant: never. Mrs Fitzhugh heard him and said:

"Ay, son Astry, the land at Wyboston is given to those that I had thought never it should have been given to."

"To whom?"

"To three or four of the Fitzhughs."

Astry pressed her to let him have a look at the will, so she got it out of the chest and showed it to him. He was furious. That the daughters would lose the Bedfordshire lands was one shock, and that he would have to pay yet another £600 for the remaining part of Paslows manor was probably an intentional affront to him.

"Mother," he said, "if this will stand, neither you nor myself nor any of my brother Saunders's children shall have anything, for if there be but six horses, you shall have but two; and if there be nine quarters of corn, you shall have but three. There must be a course taken for this, for this must not stand. This shall not serve their turn."

He then seems to have persuaded Thomas Cranwell that it would be better for both of them if they could prevent the

Bedfordshire property from being left to the nephews. On Sunday the 15th, the two of them went in to Robert and urged him to change his will "to avoid strife." At the time the old man was perfectly rational. He said that any new will he made would please neither of them; he would leave James Smith, a poor fellow living in the house, the first mess of pottage and would insert a clause stipulating that anyone who wrangled about his will should receive nothing. When they had retired, temporarily frustrated, he unburdened himself to a neighbour.

"They say I am mad," he commented bitterly, "and [yet] they lie at me to make a will. But if I do make a will, it shall please none of them at all."

Next day, Mr Harding, who had been out of his house at Aspley Guise, came home to find Astry and Cranwell waiting for him. Astry produced a copy he had made of his father-in-law's will and requested him to read it. He did so and asked what they wanted of him. Astry said:

"I do understand that you can do no more with my father-in-law than any other, and I pray you see if you can persuade him to this." And he produced another form of will, which, Harding noted, differed from the first in omitting certain important clauses, including the bequest of the Bedfordshire property to the Fitzhughs and the third part of the manor to Fitzhugh Cranwell, and also the appointment *Astry produces a new Will to disinherit the Fitzhughs* of Anne Cranwell as an executrix. He told Astry that he had very recently been with Mr Fitzhugh, whose memory he had found very weak, and that he was not prepared to persuade him to wrong anyone of anything.

Astry flew into a rage, swore a great oath, put the draft will between his teeth and tore it. He had known, he told Cranwell bitterly, what Harding's attitude would be. Harding assured him that if he heard that Mr Fitzhugh was once more in perfect memory, then he would come and do any good that he could. With that, the two brothers-in-law went their way.

That was the last occasion on which Astry and Cranwell saw eye to eye. The provisions securing the manor ultimately to Fitzhugh Cranwell brought his father down on the side of Robert's existing will; but Astry continued determined to revoke it. He told

CHAPTER SEVEN

Elizabeth that unless some change was made, she would fall on the alms of the parish. One day when she was with Robert, he saw she was in tears and asked what was the matter. She told him she feared she would be hardly dealt with and barely left when he was gone. "Lament not," he said, "for I will leave thee my goods and my living. Who should have it else? For they shall be beholden to you, and not you to them, for thou hast been a good wife to me and a good woman."

On another occasion she told him that his chest had been rifled by Anne Cranwell and his gold taken out. "You have given her the key, as she saith, and have given her all that you have. And if you have done so, I am undone, being a sick and aged woman."

Exasperated, Robert swore: "By God's blood, it is not so! I have given nothing from thee, neither will I." He assured her she should have all, and the others should be beholden to her. And next morning he wept to the servant attending him, saying he had been told that his daughter Cranwell had taken the key from under his head. This belief made him very bitter against Anne and Thomas until they managed to convince him that the accusation was false. This brought relations between the Cranwells and Elizabeth to straining point. On one occasion Thomas told Robert that his illness was all his wife's fault, adding: "but so you may overlive her, it is no matter whether God or the devil have her." But that did him no good in Robert's eyes.

On the 24th the old man sank into a 'sound', a coma. The family must have thought that now his end was near, but no; after a short time he came round, but he had lost almost all the strength in his arms and legs.

The idea that a sick person might benefit from peace and quiet does not seemed to have occurred to the household. Robert's bedchamber was a popular place of resort, and Robert himself was only moved to protest when the younger Cranwell children became too rowdy. He asked for them to be kept out of his room and taken home because they troubled him. When the boy Fitzhugh came on his departure to ask his blessing, he answered: "With a rope." The boy was always up to mischief, "rigging and breaking into houses and places, searching for money and other things."

The menfolk having failed to persuade Robert to change his will, the women now took the matter in hand. Mary Astry asked her mother for the will, took it to her father and laid it on his bed. Anne Cranwell and her daughter Susan were present, as was another of the many relatives who made up the Paslows household, a forty-year-old niece of Elizabeth's named Elizabeth Rookes, and also a young servant, Bess Walton.

Mary said, "I pray you, tear it, for else it will set us together by the ears."

Anne protested in a whisper: "Sister, do not so, for he is a man without sense."

But her father heard that. He said he was neither mad nor melancholy, and asked: "Where is it? Let me see it."

The document was picked up, not by Mary but by Elizabeth Rookes, and put into his hand. What happened next became a major matter of dispute among the family. Mrs Fitzhugh, Mary, Elizabeth Rookes and Bess Walton all said he took the will and tore it across. His wife even said he had called for it for that purpose, but that differs from Mary Astry's account. Anne and Susan Cranwell *The women, led by Mary Astry, contrive to have the old Will torn up* said that when he was asked to tear it, he did not do so, so Elizabeth Rookes laid her hands on his, on both sides of the will, and guided his hands to tear it; and Anne added that Mary helped her. The Cranwells thought too that, in spite of what Robert had said, he was not in his perfect sense at the time and did not realise what was being torn.

Later that day, Bess Walton was sitting by her master's bedside attending him, when he said to her: "Bess, here is a stir for a will indeed! But wottest thou what? I will make no will, for if my will were made, I think I should not live long after."

The torn will was not thrown away. It came into Astry's hands and he offered it to Thomas Cranwell, but Thomas refused to have anything to do with it. Eventually Elizabeth took it and kept it.

In the new situation created by the women, the two brothers-in-law did combine to assure themselves of at least some of the property that was not part of the demesne. Robert owned a piece of copyhold land and they persuaded him to make it over to a trustee, Thomas Edwyn of Wavendon, to Robert's own use for the remainder of his life and then to his daughters, Mary and Anne.

CHAPTER SEVEN

Then, at the instance of Elizabeth and Anne, they compensated William of Wavendon for the cottage and land he was expecting by the old will which he had witnessed. They arranged for Robert to grant him a 300 year lease of the same property; and Astry had to guide his weak hand in the sealing of it.

Astry however had something more important on foot than these minor measures. He had drawn up, with Elizabeth's approval, a deed making provision for the younger Saunders children, which Anne too thought fair, but *Astry devises* which, in his wording, would have the effect of a *another new* will disposing of all Robert's landed property. *Will, much more* Without telling the Cranwells, he made *favourable to* arrangements to get Robert to seal this in front of *himself* witnesses, but Anne got to hear of it and sent for her husband, who made it plain that he would prevent it. But Astry did not abandon the plan. Just after sunset on the same day, the 28th, he and Mary got themselves ready to go home to Woburn. To Cranwell they said: "Goodnight till tomorrow" and made a show of riding away on their horse. With them out of the way, Cranwell thought nothing more could happen that evening and so himself went off home to Simpson, but his wife remained behind. At nine o'clock a labourer from the village reported for watching with the sick man through the night. When brought to the bed where his master was lying in his doublet, he found he was not recognised. "Comest thou from Wilden?" he was asked. Elizabeth Rookes had to explain that he was George Hill who had married Agnes, their servant. Robert told him to fetch him his gown, saying that they kept him in a corner and would not allow him to go to his house. However, at that moment Mrs Fitzhugh came in and told him he could go home again as they had no need of a watcher that night. As he was walking back in the dark to his cottage, he caught sight of William Astry. That schemer had sent his wife home alone and now, having waited to see Cranwell leave, was walking towards the manor house in company with his friend George Wells. At the gate the couple parted; Astry turned onto the causeway leading to the house and Wells walked on to the village alehouse.

About an hour later, Elizabeth, Astry, Elizabeth Rookes and her brother Francis all assembled in Robert's room. Anne Cranwell was already there but she was fast asleep in a chair "hanging down her head." Had her mother slipped some poppy or mandragora or other drowsy syrup into her ale? Or was it just that she had been up all the night before watching with her father? At any rate, her sleepiness was remarkably convenient, and they did not disturb her. Robert was in one of his rational spells. When a night visitor called at the house and was heard speaking to someone in the hall, the old man remarked: "There's Wells!"

"It is indeed," said Wells coming into the room. Robert asked what he was doing there at that time of night, to which he replied: "I came to see how you do."

"Not well," said Robert and asked him if he had been to bed. Wells said: "No" and Robert remarked: "It is time for good husbands to be abed now." Whereupon Wells asked what time of night he thought it was. Robert said: "About ten or eleven of the clock," and Wells said it was well guessed.

With Robert so much in his right mind and Wells present, Astry said:

"Mother, if you please we will move my father about my sister Saunders's children."

She replied: "Do, if you think good." So Astry turned to Robert and said: "Sir, my mother hath a suit to you."

"What is that?"

Astry produced his document and said: "Sir, my mother and I would entreat you to seal this writing. Seeing it seems you purpose not to make a will, whereby then your land will descend, and thereby my sister Saunders's child shall have a third part with my wife and my sister Cranwell, my mother desires that she and I, or another if you please, may take the profits of his part till Michaelmas after his full age, to make stocks for his younger brothers and sisters."

At that period, the term 'descend', used of land, meant 'pass at death to the common law heir or heirs.' By the common law, a man's heir was his eldest son if he had sons; if not, all his daughters were his equal co-heirs. So if Robert left no will, each of his three daughters would inherit a third part of his land, but as Frances had predeceased him, her portion would all pass to her heir, who was her eldest son Robert, and her younger children would get none of it.

CHAPTER SEVEN

When Astry had finished speaking, Robert said: "I hear your mother say nothing."

Elizabeth, who was sitting at the foot of the bed, rose out of her chair and came and stood beside him. Laying her hand on the coverlet, she said: "Yes, good Master Robert, grant me this suit; I will trouble you with nothing more. It will never be the worse for Robin Saunders, and it will do the younger children good."

Robert took his wife by the hand and held it a good while.

"Nay, if you request it, you should have it as it were a greater matter."

Then Astry read out what he had written. Halfway through the reading, the servant John Heath came into the room. He took in what was happening and then noticed Anne Cranwell asleep in her chair. He moved to wake her, but his mistress and George Wells stood between them. Astry's document went as follows:

"Be it known unto all men by these presents that whereas I, Robert Fitzhugh, of Wavendon in the county of Buckingham, gentleman, am fully determined and resolved that all my messuages, lands, tenements and hereditaments whatsoever, with their appurtenances in Wavendon, Aspley Guise, Wyboston, Eaton Socon, Roxton and Chawston in the counties of Buckingham and Bedford (except those lands and tenements formerly conveyed to my son Astry and his wife and others), ... shall presently after my decease be descendable to my heirs at the common law (vizt) to my daughter Mary Astry, my daughter Anne Cranwell and to the heirs of my daughter Frances Saunders deceased and to their heirs respectively for ever, yet my mind, will and purpose in this behalf is that the issues and profits of that third part of inheritances which shall come to my daughter Frances her heirs shall be taken and received by my loving wife and my son-in-law William Astry ..." And then followed the legal provisions for Frances's younger children, as Astry had described; and the document ended cunningly:

"And my purpose and will is that, if hereafter I make a will, that this my writing be thereto annexed as a codicil. but if I make no will (as I am yet in mind), yet my will and purpose in this behalf is that this my will be inviolably observed. In witness whereof hereunto I have set my hand and seal the 29th day of January A.D. juxta Ecclesiam Anglicanam 1608 [1609 by present reckoning]."[6]

Astry gets Robert to sign As Robert had so little strength, Astry drew his right hand from under the bedclothes. The old man felt for his seal but accidentally knocked it off the bed. So again Astry helped him to seal the deed. It was then folded up for him and he delivered it to his wife and held her hand a good while as he did so.

The names of six people were then added to the document as witnesses. They were Elizabeth and Francis Rookes, George Wells, John Heath and another servant John Farr. The maidservant Bess Walton was listed, but later she said she had not been present.

Earlier that day, a new rector of the parish had 'rung his bell' at Wavendon. He was 33-year-old William Norton, M.A. in succession to Mr Stone, who had resigned after serving the parish for ten years, On the following day, which was Sunday, the young parson came to the manor house to pay a call on his important parishioner. He was received by Astry, who took him to his father-in-law's bedside. Robert bade him welcome, and the young clergyman, somewhat naively, explained that he had thought it his duty to come and visit him; and he asked how he was.

"Sick, as you see," said Robert.

Norton told him he might do well to call upon God, for he alone was able to raise him out of his sickness. The old man said he doubted that he had wearied God Almighty too much already with his prayers.

"God cannot be wearied with praying," said the parson, "but delighteth with the prayers of the faithful."

"God is a good man indeed," said Robert, "but I doubt we shall trouble him too much with our prayers."

"God is not a man," explained Norton, "to be wearied with prayers."

"Belike," suggested Robert, "you have no need of prayers yourself?"

CHAPTER SEVEN

Norton assured him that he had. "And if it please you, Mr Fitzhugh, we will join in prayers with you." He used the plural because the room was, as usual, full of people.

Robert's reply was not intelligible to his visitor, but most of those present burst out laughing. Norton persevered; he asked the sick man whether he thought there was a God or not; to which he answered: "Why not?" Then, did he think that God had power of life and death over him?

"How is that?" asked Robert.

"Do you think," Norton elaborated, "that God hath power to restore your health again if it please him, or to take your life if it please him?"

"Yes," answered Robert, "as he did my cow the last week," referring to a beast that had just died.

"I think that you are far spent," said Norton, "and that long sickness hath taken away your sleep; and want of sleep doth make you talk idly. Therefore, I pray you, call your remembrance to you as well as you can before God hath taken your remembrance quite from you, when you shall not be able to pray."

"I pray you, Master Parson," retorted Robert, "give me leave to let a fart." And he shifted his leg and broke wind.

"Well, sir" exclaimed Norton. "The best thing that I can do for you is to pray for you." And he took his leave.

Speaking to Mrs Fitzhugh and Astry outside, he begged them to revert to the subject of prayer at a moment when the sick man had woken after a good sleep.

When the clergyman had left the sickroom, Robert asked one of his other visitors, a tenant of his called Knight, if that had been their new rector, and he told him it was.

"I am sorry I was so bold with him," said Robert. "I would he were here again. I would have some more talk with him, for I like his talk well."

So Goodman Knight went off to the church, found the Rector in the chancel and told him what Mr Fitzhugh had said. Norton was sceptical about the sick man's ability to take in what he had to say; but later on, he heard that Mr Fitzhugh had been given, all his lifetime, to a profane custom of jesting and scoffing.

During the week that followed, Robert's mind tended to be clearer - perhaps the family was heeding the Rector's words and letting him get more sleep - but his body was failing, and at last, on Friday the 3rd of February, after over a month of sickness and trouble, he died. The funeral was held in Wavendon Church on the following Monday.[7] After it the family mourners gathered together and arranged a day for them, that is, the Astrys, Cranwells, Richard Saunders and three friends and *Robert dies in a* relatives, Parson Hughes, Elizabeth's brother *bad state of Grace* Francis Bury and her cousin Francis Duncombe, to meet at Paslows to discuss Robert's final wishes for the disposal of his estate.

Old Robert Fitzhugh, the last of his generation, was now at rest, but among the younger members of the family, his daughters, his sons-in-law and his nephews of Wilden and Barford, the struggle for possession of the ancestral Bedfordshire lands was only just beginning.

.oOo.

CHAPTER SEVEN

References

1   Terrick FitzHugh wrote to his readers, in a letter dated 27 March, 1982, the following: "From having examined a considerable number of law court records in the course of my researches, I believe that the source of this chapter, a Star Chamber case, is most exceptional in the amount of intimate detail it contains. Every incident, move and gesture described in this chapter is in the original record, and every quoted line of dialogue is word for word evidence. The title of the chapter refers back to the first paragraph of Chapter Five."

2   STAC.8/108/1. The same reference applies to the whole chapter except the footnotes specifically referenced.

3   Chancery Decrees & Orders, C.33/126.

4   *Ibid.*

5   Archdeaconry of Buckinghamshire Wills, 1613-4, f. 31.

6   PCC Dorset.

7   Parish Register of Wavendon.

CHAPTER EIGHT

THE ANCIENT INHERITANCE

Never fortune
Did play a subtler game: the conquered triumphs
The victor has the loss.
Two Noble Kinsmen: John Fletcher (1579-1625)
& Wm. Shakespeare

When the family mourners around Robert's grave arranged to meet at Paslows, they allowed a day or two for the widow and her sons-in-law, William Astry and Thomas Cranwell, to search the house for documents, money and plate, but when they assembled they found that Astry had refused to allow Cranwell to join in the search. The reason he gave was that his counsel, a Mr Edwards, had advised him against it; nevertheless, he said, he had been prepared to let Cranwell search on condition that he first bound himself to accept any award that arbitrators, chosen between them, might make on any disagreement but this Cranwell had refused to do. So it was probably as a result of this that the meeting broke up without any result.[1]

About a month later, the relations and friends met again at Paslows, but by then the widow had obtained a grant from the Prerogative Court of Canterbury to administer her late husband's lands on the terms of the Memorandum that Astry had inveigled the sick old man into sealing. This was to prevent Cranwell or any other disputant from having any *Robert's widow begins to administer Astry's concocted Will* further say in the matter. Nevertheless, the assembled party was allowed at least the appearance of a search of the house. Small sums of money were found in several purses, amounting in all to less than twenty shillings. Parson Hughes noted that the will, which he had seen placed in a box and put into one of Robert's two chests, was no longer there. The box was not in the other chest, and the will was not among the documents it contained, but he was not to know that it had been taken out by Elizabeth twice during Robert's illness, first to show Astry and later to get her husband to tear it up. This second meeting was equally ineffective in turning up anything relevant to Robert's testamentary intentions.[2]

By the contract between father-in-law and son-in-law at Astry's marriage, the young couple were not to come into their two-thirds of Paslows Manor until after Elizabeth's death, and the remaining third was also the widow's for life as her dower,[3] so Astry's memorandum had affected only the distribution of the real estate after her death. Now some other document was needed to govern the disposal of Robert's money, household goods, horses, farm animals and other movable property. To deal with these Astry concocted a nuncupative will. In the absence of a written will, an oral or nuncupative will could be established by a written

*Astry concocts a
further 'oral' Will*

statement signed by a number of people declaring that they had heard words spoken by the deceased signifying his wishes as to the disposal of his property. In this case Astry made use of the reassuring answers given by Robert whenever his wife had reproached him with being about to leave her destitute. He had always said: "I will leave thee my goods and my living. Who should have it else? For thou hast been a good wife to me." Several members of the family and some of the servants had heard him say this, and they now put their hands to a document to that effect, which Astry submitted to the Prerogative Court of Canterbury for probate. Before it could be accepted however, Thomas Cranwell and the Fitzhugh brothers, the old man's nephews, took a step that obliged the Prerogative Court to hold its hand.[4]

Before we start to follow the contention that developed between William Astry and our ancestor, young Robert, and his brothers, we shall need to bring ourselves up to date with what had been happening to them and their families during the last decade of old Robert's life described in the last chapter.

In the year 1600 the three eldest brothers, Henry, William, and Robert, were all in the malting business at Barford; the youngest, John, was a hosier in Southwark and their sister

Elizabeth was Mrs Richard Wagstaff of Wilden.[5] Their mother Amy was living with her second husband, William Negus, also a maltster, in Bedford. Henry and Robert were married, Henry with three children,[6] and Robert with a three-months-old baby son.[7] That this little boy's early arrival had not too drastically upset his mother's family was shown when her kinsman, the Rev. Richard Worsley of Wilden, died within the year and left the young couple several useful additions to their household equipment in the shape of his best cupboard, the bedstead he slept on, a pair of sheets and half a dozen trenchers,[8] the wooden slabs that people used before plates came into use.

During the next few years both Henry and Robert added to their families, but Robert lost his second child, a daughter, before she was two.[9] Then, for some reason, Robert broke off his association with his brothers at Barford and took his wife, son and another infant daughter away to settle in the Lincolnshire wolds at a place called Ashby-by-Partney.[10] What induced him to move so far from the family's customary haunts is not known. Large towns with their prospect of lucrative employment often attracted people from a distance, but Ashby was a mere village. Possibly he had come into a property there from one of his wife's relations. Soon after his departure, his stepfather, William Negus, died at Bedford. He left his wife Amy £400 and £10 a year for life together with a great deal of household furniture and linen. His will made no mention of his malting business, and it seems likely, in the light of later events, that this was covered by the mention of a bond for £400 into which he and his brother Henry Negus had entered with Henry Fitzhugh. Such a large sum can only have concerned business or property, so it seems likely that Henry, being himself a maltster, had bought the reversion of Negus's malting. The £400 due from him was payable to Negus's brother.[11]

Though the bond was described as made only with Henry Fitzhugh, it was Henry's junior partner William who moved

William moves into Bedford and takes over the Malting business to Bedford and took over the malting. He must have lived with his widowed mother, and there a particular bond of affection grew up between them. He became the son on whom, in her old age, she felt she could rely.[12] However, when he met and, in 1608, married Margaret, daughter of Lawrence

Smith of Milton in Buckinghamshire,[13] and started a family, Amy moved out and went to live at Wilden[14] where she could be near her daughter Elizabeth.

William will have already known Bedford well. In ancient times the town had grown up around the track leading to and from the river ford where Beda the Saxon was the first settler. The crossing of the Ouse, still at the same place, was now by means of the Corporation's High Bridge, and from it the High Street carried the life-blood of commerce through the centre of the town. At its northern end it forked into two country roads, of which one led north-eastwards through Barford, Wyboston and Eaton Socon to St Neot's. Near the bridge and to the west of the High Street stood the church of St Paul where Amy worshipped.

Except for being the county town and a chartered borough, Bedford had little to distinguish it. There were no institutions, ecclesiastical, military or industrial, nor any favourable accident of geography to make it a centre of any importance. Even with its charter, the Corporation's Common Council wielded less than its proper powers, many of which still lay with the ancient manorial Court Leet. Bedford's constitution was behind the time, and the leading traders and council men were resentful of it. Throughout William's career there, a struggle was to be waged for the Common Council to free the borough from the vestiges of its feudal past. When success eventually came, the Fitzhughs of the next generation had done their bit towards bringing it about.

William seems to have thrown himself into the life of the town and his new parish with enthusiasm. Already by 1610 he was made churchwarden of St Paul's,[15] though he had been a parishioner there for less than three years. To be allowed to trade in Bedford, he had to acquire the freedom of the borough, which was purchasable by suitable persons, and that for him was only a first step towards becoming eventually approved as a burgess with a seat on the Common Council.[16]

William's home was called the Green House and stood, with his malting, in an extensive 'yard' (a wide term that could

William lives at the 'Green House' in Bedford High Street   mean both yard and garden, but here the latter), which adjoined on its northern boundary the ground of one Thomas

Paradine. His main entrance was on the west side of the High Street, and his back gate gave onto Duck Lane (now Lime Street).[17] Speed's town plan of 1610, which was a copy of one by Christopher Saxton of ten years earlier (see below), shows such a house in the High Street surrounded by unbuilt-up ground just at a spot south of Duck Lane where the above description could place William's house. It does not corroborate a possible alternative site at the north corner of Duck Lane since it shows the High Street there as fully built up.

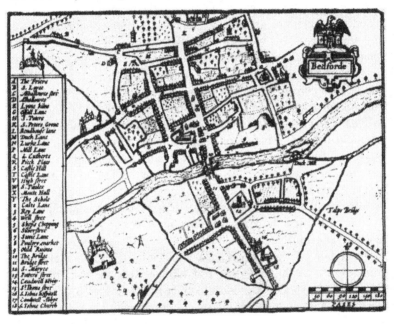

Town Plan of Bedford 1600 – 1610

The youngest of the Fitzhugh brothers, John, who had been sent up to London to seek his fortune, had duly become a freeman of the Broderers' Company but does not seem to have lived a very settled life. He was twenty-nine and unmarried when, at Whitsun 1605, he went to stay in the hall of a lodging-house belonging to a couple called Samuel Ridley and Hester Peltine, and he remained there for a year and nine months without their charging him any rent. By the autumn of 1607 he was living in the parish of

CHAPTER EIGHT

St Olave, Southwark, on the south bank of the Thames.[18] For over a year plague had been rife in the capital. Usually the cold season put an end to it, but it had lasted through the unusually mild winter of 1606-7 and spread throughout the suburbs. Londoners blamed the Corporation of the City for this because they had neglected to close the Southwark theatres, which was a normal precaution. So it was not until the autumn of 1607 that the incidence of the disease began to diminish; but it was then, on 28th October, that John felt impelled to make his will. It cannot have been because he was experiencing the dreaded symptoms - bubonic plague, when fatal, killed very quickly - nor did he seem to be suffering seriously from any other illness; his will, showing wide-ranging thoughtfulness for relations, friends and mere acquaintances, does not give the impression of being the work of a sick man. Perhaps it was that he had been in contact with someone who had later developed the fatal buboes - possibly someone in the house - and realised that he stood in great danger of infection. When anyone contracted the disease, others of his household were shunned and confined to their house. Isolation of this kind could account for John's not having consulted anyone who knew about the drawing up of a will. He omitted the essential requirements of claiming to be of sound mind and even of appointing an executor and having witnesses to the document.

His first thoughts were for the women in his family. To his mother Amy Negus he left £20. About the others he seemed more certain of their whereabouts than of their names. He had some excuse for this. "My sister of Wilden" was the much married Elizabeth, now under her fourth identity as Mrs John Wilshire. The others were his two sisters-in-law, whom he may never have met. He called Henry's wife Elizabeth "my sister of Barford" and Robert's wife Anne "my sister of Lincolnshire." Each was left £5. He made his three brothers residuary legatees. The two married ones, Henry and Robert, were to buy each of their children a present to the value of twenty shillings.[19]

John did keep careful accounts and, in will-making, he referred to his book for people to whom he was in debt and who owed him money. Among the entries was a bet with a friend called Hugh Whittaker, duly witnessed by those then present. The confident odds offered by Hugh were £5 to a shilling (100-1) that John would get married before he did. As John was now expecting to die a bachelor, he considered he was the winner, but in his will he excused his friend the debt of honour except for two shillings. For the accommodation that Ridley and Hester Peltine had allowed him they were to be paid at the 30s per annum rate that they charged to others, but if they did not think that enough then 40s. After dealing with all his debts and dues he cast his thoughts wider. "There is a poor man," he wrote, "which belongs to the King's Bench, which useth to fetch wares of me [and] lost sixpence. Let him have twelve pence for it," and "A young youth let three pence fall into the cellar among the coals. Let him have a groat [4d] for it."[20] Dear John, he would never have become Lord Mayor of London. Two and a half weeks after writing this he was dead, perhaps one of the last victims of that plague visitation, before the severe winter of 1607-8 set in and put an end to it.

John, the youngest brother, dies of the Plague in London

In January of that same winter, at Ashby-by-Partney, Robert's wife gave birth to another daughter, whom they christened Anne.[21] It was at some time after that, perhaps as soon as the better weather set in, that they returned to Barford,[22] probably so that Robert could take the vacant place beside Henry at the family's Malting now that William had gone to look after the business at Bedford.

It was in the following winter of 1608-9 that old Robert Fitzhugh of Paslows Manor died, as described in the last chapter. He had never revealed to his nephews his intention of bequeathing them the lands around Wyboston that were, as he put it, "the ancient inheritance of the Fitzhughs", so they had no particular expectations from his will, especially after his rebuff to young Robert.[23] It was Thomas Cranwell who came and told them what they had been left - a farm house, a cottage, a garden, 100 acres of arable land, 4 acres of meadow, 14 acres of pasture and 1 acre of wood,[24] all worth £40 p.a.[25] - and how they were being cheated of it. Cranwell's son too was being defrauded of half Paslows Manor and other land in Wavendon. So all five of them, Cranwell, the three brothers and their cousin John, Nicholas's son, resolved to join forces to

The Fitzhughs learn to their surprise that they have been left 'the Ancient Inheritance', and that they are being cheated out of it

overturn the Prerogative Court's probate. First they lodged a caveat in the names of Anne Cranwell and Henry Fitzhugh against the nuncupative will.[26] They entered a Bill of Complaint in the Court of Star Chamber against William Astry and George Wells, whom Cranwell considered an abettor, charging them with having created a false will (the Memorandum) for the disposal of the land and a false nuncupative will for Robert's personal effects.[27] The latter would be false if Robert had, as the plaintiffs contended, made a valid written will.

A family coalition takes legal action to thwart Astry's 'oral' Will

In the following month, Astry and Wells put in written answers as required by law. In them, Astry defended what he had done, and Wells denied any part in the matter; he did "much marvel why the complainants should thus deal with this defendant to charge him with such heinous crimes." Counsel on both sides then drew up long lists of questions to be put to witnesses, and the Court appointed commissioners to summon them to a convenient place for examination. Little Brickhill, a few miles south of Wavendon, was the chosen venue, and the commissioners probably took rooms at the village inn for that purpose.[28] Astry and Wells were themselves among those questioned, but they objected, successfully, that that had been illegally done since they were the defendants and had made their case in their Answers. This gave the Fitzhughs' counsel an idea for excluding possibly damaging evidence given by some witnesses for the defence. He revised the Bill of Complaint to include as defendants all the signatories, both to the Memorandum and to the declaration in support of the nuncupative will. The additional accused whose depositions were thus made inadmissible were Mrs Fitzhugh, Mary Astry, Elizabeth Rookes and the maid Bess Walton. They were however now entitled to put in answers on their own behalf, which they did.[29] This stage was accomplished by June, and then the usual delay ensued.

In November, Cranwell and the Fitzhughs put in a Replication to refute points made in the defendants' Answers; and, after the winter was over, more evidence was taken at Little Brickhill. Everything the witnesses said was noted down by a clerk and written up in legal form as their depositions. In all, the commissioners examined fifteen friends and neighbours of the family, nine Wavendon villagers and four servants. The examinations elicited the happenings described in the last chapter and also included such questions as: 'Have you not heard the said Robert Fitzhugh utter words in dislike of the said William Astry?' (Yes, from several witnesses.) 'How often did the said William Astry or his wife watch with him in the night in his last sickness?' (Not at all.) 'Did the said Robert Fitzhugh use kind speeches in expressing his love and affection towards the said Thomas Cranwell, his wife and children?' (Yes.) 'Was the bed wherein the said Robert Fitzhugh died pulled and broken down and the ground under the same digged and broken up ... and what bags of money or silver was there found?' (No, so nothing found.) To a question as to whether the will was read to Robert on the occasion when the women of the family organised the tearing of it, Susan Cranwell said it was not, "for there was none by that could read it." Those present on that occasion were Mrs Fitzhugh, Mary Astry, Anne Cranwell and Elizabeth Rookes as well as the servant Bess Walton and a visitor, Francis Lawson.[30]

That same Francis Lawson, described as a yeoman of Woburn - where the Astrys lived - made a damaging statement to the commissioners, saying that he was with Mr Fitzhugh divers times during his last sickness and heard him call for his will, saying: "If they will not cancel it, bring it to me and I will put it into the privy if they will not." This was presumably the incident described in the Answer of Mrs Fitzhugh and Mary Astry, in which Robert (perhaps exasperated at their nagging) had called for his will to be put into his close-stool for him, as they delicately put it, "to do a homely matter upon it." Since the ladies were keen enough for him to destroy it, perhaps it was only the presence of Lawson that deterred them from taking Robert at his word. Witnesses differed in their opinions as to how far Robert had been in his right mind on various occasions and how much strength had remained in his hands and legs after his recovery from the coma.[31]

In due course the case was heard in the hall in the Palace of Westminster called, from its painted ceiling, the Star Chamber. It was a popular and busy court where decisions were given by the Judge without a jury. All the written depositions were studied, except those excluded because the deponents had later been made defendants. Learned counsel for both parties spoke, the judges conferred, and the verdict they gave was that the defendants had not been guilty of any misdemeanour.[32]

This verdict absolving Astry of criminal conduct did not, however, give, or even imply, any superior validity to his Memorandum over that of Robert's written, but torn, will. So Cranwell and the Fitzhughs took further professional advice as to the possibility of making a second attempt to enforce their rights.

The Star Chamber finds in favour of Robert's original Will

At that time changes were taking place in the family, some of which could affect any further legal action. In 1611 Mary Astry died,[33] and also, in the following year, old Mrs Fitzhugh, Robert's widow.[34] Shortly after that, Henry sold his malting business at Barford and the two brothers left the village of their birth. Henry moved into Bedford[35] near William, but Robert a year later took his family further afield, to a village called Lavendon[36] just over the county boundary in the north-east corner of Buckinghamshire.

The sale of the Barford malting did not mean that Henry was retiring from business. In the county town he acquired, perhaps not all at once, a considerable property in St Paul's parish consisting of houses and tenements, a malthouse, malt loft, pumphouse and mill house, barley shops, barns and stables, an upper and nether yard and an orchard with a dovehouse, also an inn and a brewhouse that were let to a tenant.[37] This property is described as lying on the east side of a street, name not mentioned but almost certainly one of the main ones, so it was probably the one shown on Saxton's plan as Sheps Chipping but now called Harpur Street; but whether the premises stood above or below Silver Street is not known. Henry was prosperous and, though he had been engaged all his life in the making of malt, and trade was looked down on by the upper classes, he had maintained the family's standing in the county, being always designated in official documents as 'gentleman.'[38] His appointment to a collectorship of Lay Subsidy for three Bedfordshire hundreds[39] was to a post reserved to the gentry, but William, who had immersed himself in the commercial life of Bedford, never described himself as anything but 'maltster.'[40]

Shortly before the third brother, Robert, moved from Barford, his wife Anne, in August 1613, presented him with yet another daughter,[41] bringing the number of their surviving children to four: our ancestor William aged fourteen, Elizabeth seven, Anne five, and the baby Amy. Their move to Lavendon was made in mid October,[42] but first Robert sent, or took, his son up to London and apprenticed him to a member of the Merchant Taylors Company.[43] In the record of the apprentice binding the father was described as 'yeoman.' This was a countryman's status next below that of gentleman, and the main difference lay between their ways of life. A yeoman's servants would be farm labourers, male and female, helping him and his wife in working the land and dairy. A gentleman would not till his land himself, and he and his wife would employ domestic servants in the house. The younger sons of the lesser gentry were often described as yeomen until they inherited the wherewithal to refine their mode of living. In the case of some younger sons this might never happen. A yeoman was not necessarily a farmer, so what Robert's occupation at Lavendon was is not known, but malting would seem to be the obvious one.

In January 1614 the three brothers, with Thomas Cranwell and their cousin John, launched their second attack to recover the Wyboston lands and Cranwell's interests in Wavendon. They brought an action against William Astry, this time in the Court of Chancery, to establish the validity of Robert's written will. To save time and costs, they applied for, and were granted, the use of the depositions taken for the Star Chamber suit,[44] but the Court still excluded those made by deponents who had later been made defendants.[45] This time there was little legal delay. The case was heard in May[46] at Westminster Hall in London. That great hall in the Palace of Westminster was, except on rare state occasions given over to several uses of the law. The southern end, furthest from the entrance doors, was occupied by two of the high courts of the realm. In the south-western corner was the equity court of Chancery, and, in the south-eastern, the common-law court of King's Bench. They were raised on rostra and separated from the rest of the area and from each other by partitions and curtains only a few feet high. Round the rest of the hall, the walls were lined with shops and stalls selling

The Fitzhughs attempt to enforce Robert's Will

foolscap paper, pens, red tape and other essentials of the legal profession. The central area was always filled with people, either those, hurrying or waiting, who had business there, the lawyers, ushers and King's Bench witnesses, or passers through, the Abbey clergy, Westminster School boys, people going to and from the Exchequer Court in an adjoining chamber, and members of the House of Commons, the entrance to which lay up a flight of steps near the King's Bench.

Proceedings in the courts tended to advance slowly because they were heard only between the hours of 8 and 11 a.m., but the judges reviewed carefully the whole relationship between Astry and his father-in-law from the time of the marriage to Mary. They studied the Indenture that had been sealed between Robert and Astry to convey to the latter and his wife the reversion of two-thirds of Paslows Manor; and what they saw they did not like. Three parts of the deed had been written by Astry himself, and the remainder by his man, and Robert had had no lawyer to advise him. Worse, it was so worded that if Mary Astry had died before her father, Astry could have turned his father-in-law out of his mansion place, razed his buildings, cut down the timber and committed all manner of waste. Because of this and "some other strange and unusual covenants in the said deed," the Court considered that the Indenture was "not well gotten." In considering Robert's will and the circumstances attending the sealing of the Memorandum, the judges were struck by the facts that the document had been drawn up by Astry without consultation with Robert, that it had been presented to him very late at night after Cranwell, the plaintiff, had gone home, and that although Anne Cranwell had been present in the room, she had not been woken up

In Westminster Hall, to be a witness. They also decided that
the Fitzhughs win Robert had not then been of sound mind,
their case nor had he had the strength in his hands to
seal the deed. The Court therefore decreed that Robert's written will had not been revoked and ordered that if Cranwell would pay the outstanding amount of £100 to Astry in the church porch at Wavendon on or before next Michaelmas Day, then Astry was to hand him a conveyance of the third part of Paslows Manor as from that date. And it was further decreed that the Fitzhughs, their heirs and assigns should from henceforth hold

and quietly enjoy the lands and tenements in Wyboston, Eaton, Roxton and Chawston, and that Astry should pay over to them all the rents and profits he had received from the lands since old Robert's death.[47]

This highly satisfactory judgement was not immediately attended by equally satisfactory results. After a separate legal action that Cranwell had brought against Astry in the Court of Chancery over some sharp practice of Astry's in connection with a bond, Astry had been ordered to pay Cranwell the sum of £80 in Wavendon church porch,[48] but he failed to put in an appearance, so a court order was made for his attachment, which meant putting him under some constraint to compel his attendance in court. The Sheriff however reported that he was nowhere to be found, so a Writ of Rebellion, giving the power of attaching him, was issued to interested private persons including Henry and Robert Fitzhugh and Cranwell's sons Fitzhugh and George.[49] Some one or other of these persons discovered him, and, as he was not able to offer bail, he was taken off to Hertford Gaol. Later he did manage to find sureties and was released *Astry is thrown into Hertford Gaol, and dies soon after.* pending his appearance in court, but again he failed to obey the summons, and his friends lost their bail.[50] So William Astry, the Staple Inn Lawyer, scion of a respected Bedfordshire family, who had hitherto maintained, at least in public, a reputable character, was now in grave trouble. On 23rd June 1615 an order was issued for his committal to the Fleet Prison in London.[51]

On the same day, Fitzhugh Cranwell was granted an order giving him immediate possession of his third part of Paslows Manor; and the tenants of the Wyboston land were ordered to pay their rents to the Fitzhughs instead of to Astry or his agent.[52] All Astry's devious designs had thus ended in failure and disgrace, and in another three months he himself was no more,[53] whether dying in prison or at liberty is not known, but in a will he described himself as "of Staple Inn in the suburbs of London."[54] His passing probably meant little to Cranwell and the Fitzhughs now that they were at last able to feel secure in their possession of the lands of which he had tried to deprive them. In any case, sighs of relief were soon to prove premature.

CHAPTER EIGHT

All this while, old Robert's third son-in-law, Richard Saunders, husband of Frances who had died before her father, had been watching the proceedings from the sidelines, an interested spectator on behalf of his son, who stood to gain from an invalidation of the written will, but seemingly in no position to influence events. Now, however, with judgement passed in favour of the will, he got in touch with a proctor, or canon law attorney, called George Cole.

Back in 1609 the application by Robert's widow for probate of the nuncupative will had been contested by her daughter Anne and Henry Fitzhugh and had been shelved to await the outcome of their legal proceedings. As the widow had since died and the Chancery Court had decided against the nuncupative will, her application seemed a dead letter, but now, when everything appeared to have been satisfactorily settled, the lawyer she had engaged six years before to represent her in the probate court suddenly put in a renewed application in her name. His name was George Cole.

Anne Cranwell and Henry Fitzhugh were probably more annoyed at the inconvenience and expense *But another branch* of maintaining their objection than worried *of the family sues to* about the result, so it must have been to *validate the 'oral'* their amazement and dismay that the *Will, and succeed!* Master Warden of the Prerogative Court gave Sentence in favour of the nuncupative will.[55]

Saunders, though confined to bed at home by illness, swiftly followed up this success by starting a suit at common law to invalidate the original will and in the meantime seized possession of the whole of Paslows Manor and compelled the tenants of the Fitzhughs' lands to pay their rents to him. Cranwell and the brothers appealed to the Court of Chancery, which announced that it would not suffer this attempt "to impeach the judgement of the Lord Chancellor." It ordered a stay of the Prerogative Court's Sentence[56] and of Saunders's action,[57] but he claimed that as he had not been a party to the suit against Astry, he was not bound by the resulting decree. The Court admitted the force of this by giving him leave to apply for its reversal, but in the meantime the Cranwells were to be left in occupation of Paslows, and all the Wyboston rents were still to be paid to the Fitzhughs, who must, however, enter into a bond to repay them if Saunders's appeal went against them.[58]

The pleadings progressed slowly. In May 1617 Saunders requested that the depositions taken for the Star Chamber case but disallowed because the deponents had been made defendants should now be producible. Cranwell and the Fitzhughs objected, but the Court consented.[59] This new evidence was examined by the judges in the following October, and it

The Fitzhughs appeal and win the case...again

seriously affected their opinions. They "did not now think fit to determine whether the said will was revoked or not" and gave Saunders liberty to plead his cause at the common law.[60] This exacerbated the Fitzhughs' worry and caused more delay but at last the whole case was tried afresh in Westminster Hall, this time in the corner occupied by the Court of King's Bench. The result, greatly no doubt to the Fitzhughs' relief, was that their uncle's will was confirmed as unrevoked. They applied to the Chancery Court for an absolute decree in their favour, with costs and possession of the title deeds. The Court agreed, unless Saunders could show good cause to the contrary on the first day of the next law term.[61]

The 1619 Easter Term started on 14th April, and Saunders's counsel appeared. He opposed a decree on the grounds

But Saunders launches yet another action

that the King's Bench jury had decided only that the will had not been revoked. Nothing had been said about handing over title deeds, and he was prepared on behalf of his client to prove that the will was "void in law as to the devise of the lands." The Court gave him leave to present his case; and the Fitzhughs' nerves were once more under strain.[62]

Further delays ensued while Saunders's counsel applied for certain "writings" to be made available by the other side,[63] and these were handed in to the Court for a decision as to how many of them Saunders was entitled to see.[64] As a result of what was revealed to him, Saunders's counsel requested a certain inquest to be inserted into the case, though Cranwell objected that this arose from information "abusively obtained."[65] No details survive, but it had something to do with tenure. The Court found the matter to be of weight, the point in law difficult, and Saunders's desire for a new trial reasonable. So on 29th June it ordered him to renew his suit in the same court, King's Bench, so that a jury could be required to take into account the point raised. If they decided again that the will had not been revoked, then Cranwell and the Fitzhughs were to be granted an absolute decree.[66]

Nearly a year later, on 8th May 1621, a second King's Bench jury confirmed the former verdict in favour of the will. The

The case is tried before a Jury, and the Fitzhughs win

Chancery Court duly ordered that the Fitzhughs should be granted a decree for them to enjoy their lands and be paid costs, but again with the proviso "unless the defendants should show good cause to the contrary," and they were given until the last day of that law term to do so.[67]

On 14th May the Saunders counsel, Mr Serjeant Towse, appeared in court and pointed out that the King's Bench jury had again given only a general verdict without any direction as to possession. He was ordered to confer personally with the King's Bench judges as to whether there had been any matter of law or difficulty in the way of the jury's giving the special verdict required.[68] The judges assured him that they had not overruled the points in law but had put them to the jury to find a special verdict on them if they found

But Saunders finds a technicality, and the whole case goes to trial again

the will to be unrevoked, but they had not done so. Therefore the only thing to do was to try the case all over again.[69] To the Fitzhughs the struggle must have seemed interminable.

Our counsel (if I may so call him) asked that at any new trial the twice vindicated validity of the will should now be taken as admitted and only Saunders's "matter in law" be tried. He also begged that the trial should be speedy.[70] Saunders's counsel objected to any limitation, and on 15th October the Court ordered that a new trial should be heard in King's Bench of the whole case and that its verdict should be final for both parties.[71]

This last order must have been welcome to the Fitzhughs. They had "spent a great part of their estates" on this long drawn out controversy, and now at last an explicit and final verdict in their favour was in sight. In the Easter Term of 1622, the suit was brought to court through Richard Saunders leasing part of the disputed Wavendon land to a tenant and Thomas Cranwell denying his right to do so. Saunders based his case on the

THE ANCIENT INHERITANCE

Memorandum and Cranwell on the written will. When learned
counsel on both sides had made their
After 13 years, the
Jury finds in favour clients' cases and the jury had retired from
of the 'oral' Will the great hall, the Fitzhugh brothers were
hoping that this time the twelve men would
cover all the points in law and so make an absolute decree
possible. One can imagine their utter despair when the jury
returned and gave a verdict that disaffirmed the written will.[72]

After thirteen years of legal struggle and three verdicts in
their favour they were now back where they had started and with
no power to carry the fight further. The Bedfordshire lands,
Paslows Manor and other land in Wavendon were finally to go, in
accordance with Astry's cunning Memorandum, to their uncle's
common law heirs. As both Astrys were now dead, that meant to
Anne Cranwell and Saunders's son Robert. That young man's
inheritance had been increased from a single Wavendon cottage to
half the manor and other land in that parish. The Cranwells had
lost half of Paslows Manor and the rest
of the Wavendon land but retained a *The Fitzhughs lose*
half share of the manor, and gained *'the Ancient Inheritance'*
half the Wyboston lands; and the Fitzhughs had lost the whole of
their "ancient inheritance."

Somebody, on one side or the other, suggested an
arrangement. By common consent of both parties the matter was
referred to their counsel "to be mediated and compromitted."[73]
Those gentlemen conferred together and evolved what they
considered an equitable settlement, and it was accepted by both
sides. On 28th September 1622 a tripartite Indenture was drawn up
between Richard and Robert Saunders of the *A compromise is*
first part, Thomas and Fitzhugh Cranwell of *reached, and the*
the second part and William and Robert *Fitzhughs 'buy'*
Fitzhugh and their cousin John of the third *their inheritance*
part (Henry had dropped out of the case in its
later stages) to the effect that the Saunders and Cranwells would
undertake to convey to the Fitzhughs and their heirs all the farm
lands, tenements and hereditaments in the parishes and hamlets of
Eaton, Wyboston, Roxton and Chawston mentioned in Robert
Fitzhugh's will and that the Fitzhughs would pay therefor to
Richard and Robert Saunders the sum of £225 in two instalments,

the first, of £100, on the next Feast of St Andrew (30th November) and the remaining £125 on next Midsummer Day. At the same time, a conveyance of Paslows Manor and other Wavendon land would be made by Saunders to the two Cranwells.[74] These transactions were duly carried out on the following 20th November;[75] and so, at still further cost, the Fitzhughs at last found themselves the undoubted owners of 'the Wyboston lands.'

Yet, even now, the brothers' litigation troubles were not over. On 28th February 1623, their wonted partner, Thomas Cranwell, entered a Bill of Complaint against them in the Court of Chancery claiming that the £225 they were paying to the two Saunders was only for that family's half share in the Bedfordshire lands, and that they had promised orally to pay the same sum to him and his son for their half share, but were now refusing to do so.[76]

The Fitzhughs made Answer that both the Saunders and the Cranwells had been parties with them to the Indenture of 20th November. The sum of £225 had been the full price of the Bedfordshire lands. It had been made payable to the Saunders alone because the Cranwells' half of it was also due to the Saunders as part payment for Paslows Manor and the other Wavendon land

The costs of the litigations break the Fitzhughs, and they sell 'the Ancient Inheritance'.

conveyed by the same Indenture. Another sum of money, mentioned in that agreement as payable by Cranwell to Saunders, had been only the residue of the amount due from him because of the far greater value of the Wavendon Properties.[77] It does seem surprising that the full price of the Wyboston lands was only 5.6 times its yearly value, but that may have been the compromise amount arrived at by their counsel. Anyhow, their Answer seems to have satisfied the Court, though, some years later, one of the Cranwell sons did try to raise the matter again.[78]

Old Robert Fitzhugh's sentimental intentions for the nearest kinsmen of his name and blood had led to little but bitterness and strife and the expenditure of a great part of the resources of those he had thought to benefit. But the full extent of their frustration was still to appear. The costs of the legal battles in which William, Robert and John Fitzhugh had been so long involved had proved too great for them. In less than a year after paying Saunders the final instalment they sold their hard-won land for an undisclosed sum to three local Wyboston men, one of whom was Richard Stocker.[79] So their uncle's vision of future generations of the Fitzhughs still owning some residue of their ancestral lands had come to nothing, and the last strands of the family's roots in Wyboston were finally severed.

.oOo.

CHAPTER EIGHT

Reference

1   STAC.8/108/1.
2   *Ibid.*
3   *Ibid.*
4   *Ibid.*
5   Wilden Parish Register.
6   Barford Parish Register.
7   *Ibid.*
8   Bedford Archd Wills, 1600-1, 67.
9   Barford Parish Register.
10 PCC PROB.11/110, 90.
11 PCC PROB.11/109, 41.
12 Bedford Archd Wills, 1626-7, 101.
13 Coll of Arms, Ped of Wm. Fitzhugh, 1692.
14 *Ibid.* Bedford Archd Wills.
15 St Paul, Bedford Parish Register.
16 Beds Notes & Queries, C.F. Farrar, *'Old Bedford'*.
17 Bedford Archd Wills, 1632-3, 155.
18 PCC PROB.11/110, 90.
19 *Ibid.*
20 *Ibid.*
21 Ashby-by-Partney B.T.
22 Barford Parish Register.
23 STAC.8/108/1.
24 Beds Foot of Fines.
25 STAC.8/108/1.
26 Sentence PCC 116 Rudd.
27 STAC.8/108/1.
28 *Ibid.*
29 Sentence PCC 116 Rudd.
30 STAC.8/108/1.
31 *Ibid.*
32 C.33/132, f 948.
33 Chan IPM, Ser 2 375/72.
34 Wavendon Parish Register.
35 St Paul, Bedford Parish Register.
36 Lavendon Parish Register.
37 Bedford Archd Wills, 1632-3, 51.
38 E.179/72/215 & 256.
39 E.179/72/256.
40 Bedford Archd Wills, 1632-3, 155.
41 Barford Parish Register.
42 Merch. Tay. Appr Bks; Lavendon Parish Register.
43 Merchant Taylors Appr. Books.
44 Chan D & O C.33/126, f 513.
45 *Ibid.*/132, f 948.
46 *Ibid.*/126, f 1023.
47 *Ibid.*
48 *Ibid.*/129, f 1019.
49 *Ibid.*/128, f 299.
50 *Ibid.*/128, f 1167.
51 *Ibid.*/128, f 1168.
52 *Ibid.*
53 Chan IPM Ser 2, 375/72.
54 PCC PROB.11/126, 96.
55 Sentence PCC 116 Rudd.
56 Chan D & O C.33/130, f 724.
57 *Ibid.*, f 481.
58 *Ibid.*, f 647.
59 *Ibid.*/132, f 948.
60 *Ibid.*/133, f 14.
61 *Ibid.*/136, f 670.
62 *Ibid.*, f 927.
63 *Ibid.*, f 989.
64 *Ibid.*, f 1324.
65 *Ibid.*/138, f 1119.
66 *Ibid.*/ f 1636.
67 *Ibid.*/140, f 1001.
68 *Ibid.*, f 1055.
69 *Ibid.*, f 1100.
70 *Ibid.*, f 1174.
71 *Ibid.*/142, f 45.
72 Chan Proc C.4/15; C.2/C112/50.
73 Chan Proc C.2/C112/50.
74 Chan Proc C.4/15; C.2/C112/50.
75 *Ibid.*
76 Chan Proc C.4/15.
77 Chan Proc C.4/15; C.2/C112/50.
78 *Ibid.*
79 Foot of Fines, Beds.

CHAPTER NINE

THE LONDON APPRENTICE

"When I behold that forest of masts upon your river
for traffic and that more than miraculous bridge ....,
your Royal Exchange for merchants, your halls and
companies, your gates .... and your churches for holy
assemblies, I cannot deny them to be magnificent works
and your city to deserve the name of an augustious and
majestical city."

J. King, Bishop of London, at St Paul's (1620)

W hatever considerations induced Robert, the
youngest surviving Fitzhugh brother, to leave Barford for
Lavendon in the autumn of 1613, they evidently did not seem to
hold out hopeful long-term prospects for his only son. In October,
shortly before his move, Robert took young William, who was
approaching his fourteenth birthday, to be apprenticed in London.
In the capital, the right to become a master tradesman, was limited
to freemen of the livery companies of the city, and hence of the
city itself, a status that could be achieved in *Young William, of*
one of three ways; by apprenticeship to a *the 'English'*
freeman, by patrimony for freemen's sons, *Branch, goes to be a*
and, for an adult, by purchase. Not every boy *London Apprencice*
could become a London apprentice. His
parent had to be possessed of an estate of inheritance or a freehold
worth at least 40s a year and vouched for by justices of the peace
where the property lay. This stipulation helped to ensure that after
the young man became free he would eventually have the means to
set up in business for himself.

CHAPTER NINE

We do not know how Robert, in Bedfordshire, went about finding a Londoner willing to take his son, but as the arrangement was finally made with a resident of the south London parish of St Olave's in the Borough of Southwark, it is possible that he had been an acquaintance of Robert's late brother John. The citizen was Edward Pearce, a freeman of the Merchant Taylors Company, carrying on his trade of drapery in one of the city's most fashionable shopping streets, though admittedly at its less fashionable end.[1] It was a street famous throughout Europe, because its shops and houses stood, firmly founded, right across the flow of the river Thames. In some other countries such structures did exist but nothing in any way approaching the scale of London Bridge.

To reach their destination, father and son had first to find their way through the city's bustling streets - a new experience for the country boy - to where Fish Street Hill led down to the river. They passed under the arched entrance of the bridge, which admitted the roadway into a street-wide arcade formed by the meeting, above their ground floors, of the buildings on either side of the bridge. There, to right and left of them, they passed expensive-looking shops, nearly all of them dealing in the fashions of the day, milliners, drapers, silkmen, haberdashers of hats, haberdashers of small wares, hosiers, shoemakers, glovers and girdlers. Further on, they emerged from under the buildings into an open space, known as the Square, where the thoroughfare stretched the full width of the bridge and there were views up and down the river. To their right they could see upstream the palaces of Whitehall and Westminster and the expanse of the stream dotted with watermen's craft ferrying passengers across and up and down the river. To their left, downstream, lay larger, sea-going ships, crowded together at anchor, and in the distance rose the turrets of the Tower of London.

From the Square, the way led on into the twilight under the next block of buildings, where the shops were of greater variety. In these built-up stretches, the road was only about 12ft wide, and when two loaded pack-horse teams met, there was dangerously little room left for pedestrians. As the Fitzhughs walked out again into the daylight at the next gap, their footsteps made a different sound upon the roadway; they were passing over a great oak drawbridge, one of the ancient defences of the city and formerly a means of enabling masted vessels to pass the bridge. Now they were two-thirds of the way across the river, and all the bridge ahead of them lay in the parish of St Olave's, Southwark.

The Bridge Foot, Southwark, in 1616

The building on the left with its open door is the Bear tavern. The house immediately behind it, with only its roof visible, is the home of Edward Pearce. In the right foreground the market in Long Southwark is in progress. Part of a panoramic engraving by Claesz Jans Visscher, from *The City of London Through Artists' Eyes,* J.L. Howgego, 1969.

There was still a third arcade to go through, and when they emerged again they were faced by a structure that must have been already known to them by repute, the great Stone Gatehouse, straddling the bridge with its portcullised archway. On its battlemented top they saw the grim sight of a number of projecting poles on which were impaled the withered heads of men who had been executed for political crimes. This display had earned for the Gatehouse the same nickname as one of the entrances to the Tower of London, the Traitors' Gate.

Under its deep archway this bastion of the city wore a more prosaic air. It was half a century since it had last been attacked, and though part of it was used as a prison, its downstream side was now leased to a commercial tenant and housed a bookshop. The gateway was strategically placed, not at the end of the bridge but on its second pier. Beyond it the stretch of road over the last two arches was known as Below the Gate. Here the houses on either side did not form an arcade but stood back, partly overhanging their parapets, with their rows of gables facing each other across the roadway. It was here, at the very last house on the upstream side and adjacent to the first on the land that the Fitzhughs found the draper's shop they were seeking.[2]

Each reader must imagine for himself how the travellers were made welcome by young Mr and Mrs Pearce and taken upstairs into their home above the shop and counting-house. Edward Pearce was about thirty years of age[3] and his wife Alice[4] somewhat younger, but there was no sign of any children. They showed William, the first apprentice they had had, the chamber or living space allotted to him. His father must also have stayed a night or two, because there were formalities to be observed before the apprentice-binding could be signed and sealed.

When night fell and the various noises of the traffic, the clatter of horses' hoofs, the patter of cattle droves, the rumble of occasional carts, waggons and coaches and the voices of passers-by, all died down a steady sound, which had continued behind them all, became distinguishable as that of rushing water, a sound which, if listened to in bed - especially by a healthy boy after an exciting day - is irresistibly sleep-inducing. It was the release of the River Thames, its smooth flow impeded and its level raised by the nineteen stout piers of the bridge, successfully forcing its way through the narrow arches. At low tide the difference in levels above and below the bridge was five feet and the sound of the fall was at its loudest. Only near high tide did the downstream water rise to meet and match the freshwater flow, and the rushing sound became quieter and at last silenced.

THE LONDON APPRENTICE

In the Merchant Taylors Company a regulation had just been laid down that before any member could take on a new apprentice, the boy must be brought before the Master and Wardens in Common Hall assembled for them to question him to make sure he was fully suitable, a subject of the King either by birth or naturalisation, of the right family background and under no prior binding. So, as soon as these august personages were available, Pearce took William, perhaps accompanied by his father, into the heart of the city to his interview. Through the narrow streets of half-timbered buildings they made for Threadneedle Street and the group of buildings from which it had acquired its name, the headquarters of the Merchant Taylors Company. They entered the great hall where the public functions of the Company were held. Its broad floor was of red brick strewn with rushes, but its walls were panelled and hung with tapestries on which were worked scenes from the life of the guild's patron saint, St John the Baptist. It must certainly have been the most impressive interior that William had yet seen. There his interview with the five robed chiefs of the Company went off satisfactorily - perhaps his father answered some of the questions. His binding, for nine years, was approved and duly entered in the Company's books.[5]

Having accomplished the purpose of his visit, Robert Fitzhugh returned to Barford to prepare for his move before the month was out to Lavendon with his wife and daughters;[6] and young William, left behind, found himself a full member of the Pearce household, living as one of the family, learning the drapery business in the shop, helping with the household chores upstairs, and running errands for both master and mistress; and he must soon have got to know his way about London's south bank.

Standing outside the shop it was hard to realise that one was on a bridge. The south wall of Pearce's house was the north wall of the first building on the shore, the Bear tavern.[7] That establishment was one of the many houses of refreshment - inns, taverns, alehouses - with which Southwark abounded. Indeed many citizens looked upon provision for eating and drinking as the borough's chief trade. Some of these houses were the termini for the carrier waggons coming in from Kent and Surrey. Others were the resort of Londoners from over the bridge visiting the theatres or Bear Garden, places of public assembly the Corporation of the City was strict in keeping outside the walls. The borough was populous but had a high proportion of mean streets and poor inhabitants, many of them of foreign descent. Its two largest parishes were St Olave's, below the bridge, and St Saviour's upstream. The Bear tavern looked out on a square called the Bridge Foot, from which Tooley Street ran east past St Olave's Church, where the Pearces worshipped. Westwards lay a maze of streets and alleys leading eventually to semi-rural Bankside with its theatres and its ring for bear and bull baiting. Straight ahead from the bridge ran the main thoroughfare, called Long Southwark, where the market was held and where Mrs Pearce will have done most of her household shopping.

The busy life of Southwark's cobbled streets, through which the country lad, used to rough tracks and footpaths, now made his daily way, is reflected in the regulations laid down for the convenience, health and safety of the inhabitants:

"No person shall suffer any cart or dray to stand in the streets longer than they shall unload. No person shall run or trot his cart or dray in the streets or ride upon the same. No person shall suffer their swine to wander or go abroad in the streets. All brewers' servants which carry beer or ale with the tree [yoke] shall go 2ft from the wall and shall in due time speak to passengers [passers-by], that harm may be prevented. No person that useth to buy fish at Billingsgate shall sit down with their fish in the streets to sell, but shall carry the same about the streets. No person shall throw any piss out of their windows, or close-stools, jakes-bowls or other filth or any dead cat or dog out of their doors into the streets to the annoyance or abuse of any of the King's subjects. The Scavenger shall cause the Rakers upon every Tuesday, Thursday and Saturday to take away all such soil as shall be laid upon heaps or brought unto them. Every inhabitant shall sweep the street before their houses every day that the Raker cometh and before he cometh, that the soil, being laid together, may be carried away. And every Saturday, when the Raker is past, no more soil be cast out nor make any dunghill in the streets. The inhabitants (except such as keep their shops open till nine of the clock at night) shall every dark evening hang forth candlelight in lanthorns sound and good from six o'clock in the afternoon till nine. The

Beadles shall warn and charge so many of the inhabitants to watch with the Constables of the nights as that there be a constant number of 30 complete watchmen at the least every night; and every day to give the Constable-in-waiting a note of the names of such persons as he shall warn to watch the night following. The Constables shall every night dispose and place Watchmen as followeth: [among others elsewhere] three at the Bridge Foot."[8] William Shakespeare, walking home after late management meetings at the Globe, had to pass this way, where the raw material for Act 3, Scene 3 of *Much Ado About Nothing* was enacted nightly.

As work went on for long hours and six days a week, it must have been on his errands that William first discovered that, although he was the only one of his generation in the Pearce household, he was not to be altogether without companionship of his own age, and realised that he was a novice member of an unofficial, unincorporated and amorphous brotherhood, the apprentices of London. These youths, though bound by strict rules of behaviour - no cards, dice, wenching or stylish clothes - and obedient to their masters, constituted collectively an urban group to be reckoned with. Brought up in comfortable circumstances literate and wide awake, inhabiting almost every freeman's house in the city, they were aware of everything that was going on, formed their own immature social and political opinions and gave them combined and often violent expression. The leaders were the older apprentices, who might be of any age up to twenty-three, and the younger ones were easily led. Apart from special occasions inciting them to riot, there was one day in the year traditionally devoted to such activity, Shrove Tuesday. On that last day before the rigours of Lent, the City authorities would order a special turn-out of constables and the Trained Bands to keep disorder within bounds. At this period, their choice of targets tended to be directed by the growing influence of puritan austerity in all classes of the community. A favourite one was the row of houses on Bankside called the Stews, the prostitution locality patronised, in that reign, even by royalty. But on Shrove Tuesday 1617, when William was seventeen, the apprentices caused severe damage in several parts of the liberties of London, pulling down houses in Finsbury Fields, St Katherine's, Lincoln's Inn Fields and Wapping and beating those set to guard them. One exploit of that day, at a private theatre in Drury Lane, achieved celebration in verse, of which the following is a shortened version:

> "The 'prentices of London long
> Have famous been in story,
> But now they are exceeding all
> Their chronicles of glory.
> Three score of these brave 'prentices,
> All fit for works of wonder,
> Rushed down the plain of Drury Lane
> Like lightning and like thunder,
> And there each door with hundreds more
> And windows burst asunder,
> And to the tire-house broke they in,
> Which some began to plunder.
> Books old and young in heaps they flung
> And burnt them in the blazes -
> Tom Dekker, Heywood, Middleton
> And other wandering crazes.
> All players and others thrust out of doors,
> Seductive all and gaudy;
> And praise we these bold 'prentices
> Cum voce et cum laude."[9]

Apprentices did have more peaceable relaxations. In Southwark there was the popular holiday period of St Margaret's Fair, held every September; and there were similar occasions elsewhere in London but their regular opportunities for sport came in the afternoons of Sundays and holy days. However, these were under attack from growing puritan opinion within the Church that one compulsory attendance at one's parish church was not enough; the Lord's Day should be given over entirely to devotions. Against this trend, King James himself in 1618 issued a Declaration of Sports in which he condemned the view that "no honest mirth or recreation is lawful or tolerable in our religion" and wished no one to discourage "dancing (either men or women), archery for men, leaping and vaulting, or any such harmless recreation" on Sundays after church, nor from "May-games, Whitsun ales and Morris dances and the setting up of maypoles." For centuries bowmanship had been the sporting skill officially encouraged; and in St Olave's parish there was an Artillery Ground for archers, the word 'artillery' then meaning the shooting of any type of missile.

In 1621, when William was nearing the end of his servitude, a crowd of apprentices took part in a violent political action. Three of their fellows had been arrested for shouting ribald abuse at the Spanish ambassador, the representative of the foreign power that stood for Roman Catholicism and the oppression of Protestants on the continent. They had been arrested and sentenced to be whipped at the cart's tail through the breadth of the City from Temple Bar to Aldgate, but some three hundred apprentices gathered in Fleet Street and attacked the City Marshall who was about to supervise the punishment, and rescued the three demonstrators, at any rate for the time being.[10]

The winter that followed was the occasion of one of the periodic Thames Frost Fairs. The piers of London Bridge were a permanent impediment to the flow of the river and so, in severe weather assisted its freezing on the upstream side. This year the ice was strong enough to support streets of booths, selling all sorts of goods and adding yet another fair to the list of such annual events. As 'numerous diversions' were also practised, the London apprentices must have enjoyed themselves, particularly one who had only to look down from his window to see all that was going on.

In the summer after William's first arrival in London, Mrs Pearce had given birth to her first child, a son whom they called Edward after his father. Two years later came a daughter Mary; then Martha, who lived only a few days; John in 1619, who died at eight months; and Anne in 1620.[11] In March 1622 the house on the bridge took in yet another occupant. William's time was in its ninth and last year, so Pearce engaged a new apprentice, a lad called John Coell from his own county of Sussex,[12] in time to have a six months' overlap under the guidance of his predecessor.

William's indenture finally ran out at Michaelmas, but it was not until the 2nd December that he was formally admitted to the freedom of the Merchant Taylors Company and then of the City and became entitled to style himself 'Citizen and Merchant Taylor of London.'[13]

CHAPTER NINE

Upon the attainment of freedom, the son of a well-to-do father might be set up in business straightaway; but William, like most new freemen, seems to have had to work for a few years as a journeyman, living in lodgings and employed at a wage while he saved enough to be able to put out his own sign. He was given help in this direction by his kind grandmother, Mrs Negus, who sent him a generous present of £20, making it clear that it was to save him from waiting for a legacy when she died.[14]

And there we must leave him, facing the world on his own, while we return to Bedford.

For the young Merchant Taylor's father and uncles, the long-drawn-out legal struggles over the Wyboston land, first against Astry, then Saunders and then Cranwell, were at last at an end. The property they had finally purchased at a favourable price had been sold, so the brothers had probably recouped their onerous legal costs. At any rate, by the mid 1620s, William the maltster and his brother Henry were comfortably off.[15] The latter, after years of successful malting, now derived his income from property. Part of his extensive malting premises were let to Bedford's chief brewer, Simon Beckett, the remainder to an innkeeper, John Wale, and yet other property to another Bedfordian, Robert Fenn.[16]

The brothers had reason to be well off. Malt - William's product and the basis of Henry's rents - was in universal demand. Beer was the staple drink of all classes of the community at all meals. There were two or three brewers in the town and some innkeepers who brewed their own beer, and there was also an extensive trade to private purchasers, mostly the poorer people of the town and nearby villages, who made their own beer at home and bought their malt in small quantities of a peck or half-peck at a time. But demand creates supply; *The Fitzhugh brothers make a success of Malting* the Fitzhughs were far from being the only malt producers in the town, and at some time soon after the brothers' arrivals, one of the Bedford maltsters - it may have been one of the brothers, no one knows - was struck by an idea for attracting more custom to himself.

Malt was sold in the whole grain because it kept best that way, but when about to be used for brewing it had first to be coarsely ground. In Bedford there were three malt-mills that provided this service, two of them operated by horse power and the third by water. The millers kept pack-horses and employed loaders to fetch from the brewers and innkeepers the malt they were about to use, and to return it to them after grinding; but most of the home brewers carried their own small malt bags to and fro on their backs. The enterprising maltster just mentioned took a step that, for these small consumers, cut out the malt-millers altogether. As home brewers normally bought their malt for immediate use, he installed a quern, or handmill, at his malting, and as they paid for their purchases he allowed them to grind the grain on the spot without extra charge. This bonus to the private customer was at first highly successful, but soon every maltster in the town was obliged in self-defence to follow suit.[17] Once the practice became general, the individual maltsters' shares of the market must have remained much as they had been, but the innovation hit the malt-millers badly, and eventually one of the three was forced out of business.[18]

By 1625 William had been presented by the burgess jury to the Common Council of Bedford as a worthy candidate for the College of Burgesses. The Council approved; William paid his fee and was ceremonially sworn in.[19] The Burgesses, some sixty freemen composing the Common Council, were eligible for eventual election to the positions of Mayor, Bailiffs, Chamberlains and Bridgewardens of the borough. Membership also conferred a heritable privilege. The Constitutions of Bedford laid *William becomes a Burgess of Bedford* down "that every burgess inhabiting within the town shall present the name of such man-child as God shall send him at the next Leet here holden after the birth of the same child, and that the Steward, after such presentment made, shall record the same in this Book." By his enrolment the child acquired a patrimonial right to eventual burgessdom. However, the privilege came too late for William. In the fifteen years of marriage to Margaret, the couple had had eight sons, and though, after his election, they did have one more child, this final blessing was a fourth daughter, Sybil.[20]

It was while Sybil was on the way that William, his sister and brothers lost their mother. Mrs Amy Negus must have been eighty years of age or nearly so when she died in 1626. She

CHAPTER NINE

had made her will two years before. Though her latter years had
been passed at Wilden, she remembered the poor both of that
parish and of Bedford, where she had spent her married life with
her second husband; and in her will she mentioned not only her
four children but all her living twenty-four grandchildren by name,
plus a few Negus relations, and left them monetary legacies
totalling £317 and articles from a houseful of chattels. Henry's
daughters received £5 each and his sons £10, but the children of
William and Robert were left double those sums. Henry and
Robert themselves were treated similarly, receiving £5 and £10
respectively. This does not seem to have meant any greater
fondness for the favoured ones, so perhaps Henry and his family
were better off than the others. She appointed William her sole
executor and said that if either of the other sons, or any of their
children, claimed more than their legacies, they were to receive no
more than one shilling. In making William executor she probably
meant him to be also residuary legatee, because he was not
otherwise named, but no residuary legatee was mentioned, so, as
far as the wording went, her trusted son was left nothing.
However, as the other sons were precluded from inheriting more
than their legacies, any residue could only have gone to William
and his sister Elizabeth. She and her husband, John Wilshire, were
left £5 each, and unspecified sums had been handed out in advance
to Elizabeth's three Ward sons.

The legacies of two other grandsons had been given
them in advance. One was to William, the young Merchant Taylor.
Amy's mention of him in her will was a little sharp: "I have
already given him for his part and portion the sum of £20, which
is all that I intend shall come unto him out of my goods and
chattels."[21]   Perhaps William had omitted to thank his
grandmother.

At this period, William's seven surviving sons - the
eldest, John, had just died[22] - were coming, one after the other, to
the age of fifteen where he had to plan careers for them. For the
next son, William (All these Williams!), he was successful in
obtaining a much sought after apprenticeship to a Turkey
merchant,[23] a start that held out prospects of wealth beyond the
hopes of a provincial town tradesman. Turkey merchants were
members of the Worshipful Company of Merchants of England

Trading to the Levant Seas. After serving his apprenticeship in a London counting-house, William would be sent out as a factor, or agent, to one of the cities of the Ottoman Empire, which at that time encircled the eastern Mediterranean. There he could also trade on his own account and amass the capital to return eventually to London as a full member of the chartered company and engage as a principal in its highly profitable import-export monopoly to the middle east.

William apprenticed his second surviving son, Henry,[24] to a woollen-draper in Bedford; and the next two, Francis and Hugh, he sent to London as apprentices to members of the Drapers Company.[25] The remaining three, Thomas, Peter and Robert, were still, in 1632, too young to start

William builds a new house in Bedford High Street. Son Henry is apprenticed to be a Draper

work, but he had his eye on Thomas to succeed him at the malting. With these plans in mind, he set about developing his large and valuable site on Bedford High Street. The northern portion he separated off and built a new house there. It faced the street and had a small irregularly shaped garden at the back and a herb-garden and barn adjoining Duck Lane. Access to the garden from the High Street was through a pair of broad gates shared by both houses and also providing entry to the malting premises behind the Green House.[26]

While William was actively engaged in this scheme, his brother Henry was in failing health, and though he was only in his sixties, which was not old as Fitzhughs went, towards the end of February 1632 he died.[27] His properties he had bequeathed in more or less equal shares to his two sons, William and John; but he and his wife had not been on happy terms with the elder one, and he had felt obliged to dictate an extra clause at the end of his will, saying: "If my son William shall by word or deed in any respect trouble, molest or disquiet my wife, then he shall receive no benefit by this my will."[28] Unhappy family relationships seem to have been a recurring theme among the Fitzhughs at this period.

Two years later, this troublesome son himself married[29] and became a parent of four children,[30] but, as far as is known, he had no further descendants; and his younger brother John never married.

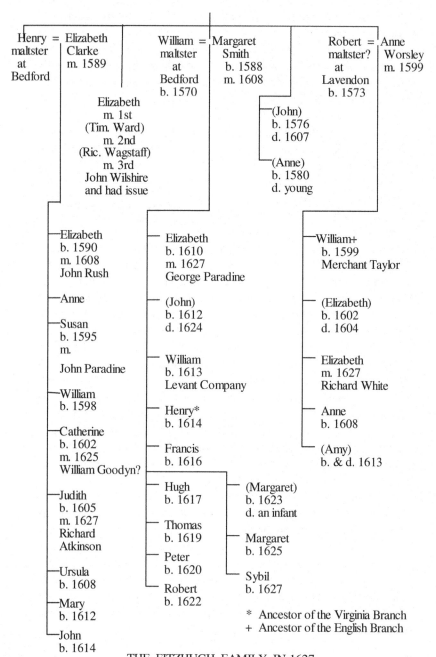

THE FITZHUGH FAMILY IN 1627

At the time of Henry's death, the old malt mill in Mill Street, which had gone out of business and fallen into ruins, with people helping themselves to its doors and other useful parts,[31] was taken over and put into working order again by a new occupant. The property actually belonged to the King, whose 'farmers' the millers had been and as was also the new leaseholder, Robert Bowers. This Londoner entertained a scheme for turning it once more into a busy and profitable enterprise. He contacted the miller operating the other two malt mills and everyone in the town whom he could discover to be grinding malt, including the maltsters who were allowing customers to grind at their querns - among whom William was high on his list - and he informed them that they were breaking the law.[32]

The newcomer maintained that his royal malt mill, called Trinity Mill, was an ancient one to which all the inhabitants of Bedford owed suit of mill. This phrase harked back to feudal times, when each manor had only one mill and that belonged to the lord of the manor. It had been the lord's privilege that all grinding of grain had to be done at his mill; in legal terms the tenants owed it suit of mill. It was a custom existing from time immemorial and so had the force of law. This, Bowers insisted, was the situation for the people of Bedford in regard to Trinity Mill. He demanded that they all abandon their current practices and henceforth have their grain ground by him alone. If they did not, he added, he would take them to court. They listened to what he had to say; they conferred together; and they went on grinding.

Bowers carried out his threat. He entered his Bill of Complaint in the Court of Exchequer because that court was concerned with matters affecting the Crown's revenues, and he hoped to strengthen his case by making the point that, as the defendants would not use his services and pay him for them, he was unable to pay the King his fee farm rent; so the defendants were defrauding King Charles of his rights and dues. He demanded damages so that he could pay his arrears of rent. The rival malt-miller Gascoigne, the brewer Simon Beckett and the maltsters, all named as defendants, met and pledged themselves to raise a fund of £100 to fight the case. At that time the Privy Council was conducting a drive to keep down the price of corn for the relief of the poor, so the maltsters intended to make the point that their free grinding service was a help in that direction. Knowing this, Bowers inserted into his Bill an accusation that the maltsters were making their home-brew customers a concealed charge by raising their prices on small purchases, but this they vigorously denied.[33] However, before the defendants had completed the preparation of their Answer to the Bill, the case lapsed. Robert Bowers had died.[34]

In January 1633 William was feeling "somewhat sickly disposed in body." Doubtless having his brother's recent death in mind, he called in a man called Scott to draw up a will for him. In *Henry is bequeathed* it he left £30 to each son except Henry. To *the new house in the* the eldest, William, he also left a certain *High Street* "provision" which he had made by "a lease in trust" of the Green House to his brother Robert and certain other trustees, which provision the boy was to share with his two unmarried sisters, Margaret and Sybil. It is difficult to know what this 'provision' can have been, since he left the house itself and his malting to his wife Margaret for life and then to his sixth son Thomas, who was also to receive his furnace, brewing vessels and some of his furniture. His new house he bequeathed to his third son Henry, who would be in business in the town. To his eldest daughter Elizabeth and her husband, George Paradine, he left 20s each to buy mourning rings, as was then the custom, and to their son Thomas, 10s to buy himself a lamb. His wife Margaret was to be his executrix and residuary legatee.

Scott composed these intentions into a Last Will and Testament, and William invited his friend William Waller and his son-in-law's father, Thomas Paradine, who was that year's Mayor of Bedford, to come and hear it read and sign as witnesses, which they did.[35]

William did not succumb to his indisposition as soon as he had feared, and by March he was having second thoughts about his will. When his sons William, Henry and Hugh had been apprenticed, he and his wife had had to enter into bonds with their respective masters as security for their truth and honesty. Now he was worried that if, after his death, misbehaviour by any of the three boys caused their bonds to be forfeited, his wife would suffer. So he consulted a local canon law proctor called Whitaker, and on his advice he added a codicil, making his bequests to them payable only after each had completed his servitude, and stipulating, in the cases of William and Hugh, that if any forfeiture was to be paid, the boy's £30 legacy should go towards it. Henry's case was different; he had not been left cash but a house, so for his security his father made some other provision, which is now unknown because, since then, the end of the codicil has been eaten away by mice. This new document was then read over to William by Whitaker in the presence of Thomas Paradine, the Rev. Theodore Crowley, Vicar of St Paul's, and Mr Oliver Cobb, M.A., an ecclesiastical official.[36]

At that time William may have been serving a year as one of the two Bridgewardens of Bedford. The Common Council Minutes for 1651 mention a William Fitzhugh, deceased, as having been Bridgewarden and leaving some unfinished business, and we have no evidence of any other William Fitzhugh with the necessary qualification of burgessdom; but before 1647 there is little documentation, so it is not impossible that his *William serves as Bridgewarden for Bedford Bridge* nephew William, Henry's troublesome son, became a warden later on.[37] The Bridgewardens' duty was the maintenance of the town's bridge over the Ouse, including the lock-up standing on its northern end. In the middle ages it had been the custom for a wealthy bridge builder to include a chapel in the structure, where dry and grateful travellers could offer up a prayer for their benefactor's soul; but, since the Reformation, the chapel on Bedford's bridge had been converted into the town gaol. The larger, county gaol stood in Silver Street. In William's time, the future famous prisoner, who was to inhabit both, was still a small boy at Elstow, and his father, Thomas Bunyan, tramping the roads of Bedfordshire with his cry of "Pots to mend!"

The symptoms of illness that William had suffered in January evidently did prove to be the early signs of some mortal disease. He passed away in April 1633[38] and was buried in St Paul's Church under the wall of the south chancel,[39] leaving his wife Margaret - her elder sons all in apprenticeships and Thomas only fourteen years of age - responsible for the management of the malting as well as, immediately, the settling of affairs arising from his will. Over the latter she was at once in trouble. As soon as her eldest son William heard that he was not to inherit any of his father's real estate, he gave emphatic sign of his dissatisfaction. He would not be of age until the following year, but he contacted a Bedford canon law proctor called Wilbone, who on Sunday, 21st April, while Margaret and her younger children were at morning service at St Paul's, fixed a notice on the outside of the church door – the standard method of making a public announcement – claiming that William, and not his mother, was the rightful administrator of his father's estate.[40]

Margaret at once consulted John Whitaker, the proctor who had drawn up the codicil, and she appointed him her proxy to apply for recognition of her executorship. On 29th April Whitaker attended a session of the Archdeaconry Court of Bedford at Ampthill Church and, in the presence of Wilbone, laid the will and codicil before Archdeacon's Commissary, presiding as judge, who was none other than Mr Oliver Cobb, the friend of the family who had witnessed the codicil. Formally he applied for executorship on Margaret's behalf. The judge then summoned Wilbone's principal, young William, into court, but, though his name was called three times, he failed to appear. As an apprentice he was almost certainly still in London having his impudent nose kept to the grindstone. For his absence the court declared him contumacious and was prepared to grant Margaret's request, but Wilbone demanded proof of the validity of the will and codicil and pleaded for any acceptance to be made provisional. Whitaker was therefore given three sessions in which to produce evidence of their genuineness. Losing no time, he called at Mr Cobb's house on the following Monday accompanied by the three other witnesses, Thomas Paradine, William Waller and Mr Crowley. They were sworn and given notice to attend at the next court to be held at Ampthill, in order to undergo questioning.[41]

The next hearing must have been a bit of a charade, since the judge was personally aware of the validity of at least the codicil. William was summoned again and once more failed to appear. The Mayor, the Vicar and Mr Waller gave their evidence. Nothing effective was adduced to the contrary, so on 25th September Sentence was given in Margaret's favour.[42]

The widow was now the approved executrix and the malting was her inheritance. In the next few years she must have become accustomed to all that was involved in running the business; but in 1636 a former threat once more raised its head. Robert Bowers's lawsuit brought against her husband and others by the late leaseholder of Trinity Mill had lapsed when the plaintiff had died, but now the malt mill had come into the hands of a relative called Leonard Bower, spelt always without a final s, and he renewed the suit in the Court of Exchequer, demanding damages from all the same defendants except that he substituted Margaret's name for William's.[43] Of them all, Robert Gascoigne, the rival malt-miller, was likely to be the one most seriously affected. He owned the water-powered Duck Mill and leased the horse-operated Joel's Mill in Potter Street from the King, as had his father before him. It seemed hardly likely that the King would lease two malt-mills on different sides of the river and in different parishes if one of them could claim exclusive rights over the whole town. He and all the maltsters and inn-keepers involved got busy canvassing townspeople with long memories to give evidence to the Court's commissioners. They mustered ten elderly witnesses of both sexes, including four octogenarians, who all declared that, for as long as they had known Bedford, people had always freely used whichever mill they preferred; that a number of people owned their own querns, the Beckett brewing family even having a horse-mill of their own, all without previous let or hindrance. One witness mentioned that even the county's House of Correction in Bedford had long had a quern at which those confined there - vagrants, unmarried mothers, parents who had abandoned children to the parish - were put to grinding malt.[44] All agreed that one malt-mill could not possibly cope with the trade of the whole of Bedford. But in these efforts the defendants were barking up the wrong tree. When, after the usual delays, the case came to court three years later, the plaintiff let drop a remark, evidently not realising its significance, that Trinity Mill had devolved to the Crown from a religious house at the dissolution. This was an intimation that the Court of Exchequer could easily follow up because the records of the defunct Court of Augmentations, which had administered the dissolution of the monasteries, were now in its keeping. The judges were able to confirm what the plaintiff had said; and that was the end of the case; there was no question of manorial privilege from time immemorial.[45] So Bower lost his claim, and the mills and maltings of Bedford continued their operations without further interference.

Margaret outlived her son Thomas who had been chosen by his father to take over the business. He died just as he came of age.[46] So it was the youngest son, Robert, who for the last twenty-four years of her life was her partner and finally her successor at the Green House and the malting.[47] She lived long enough to welcome the closely spaced arrivals of a remarkable succession of grandchildren. Thirty-two of them were Fitzhughs, but although fourteen were boys, only one was destined to carry our name further than one more generation. Never mind; little William, Henry's ninth child, was eventually to leave Bedfordshire for wider horizons where his family throve and multiplied. In the 20th century his living descendants in the United states of America are numbered in hundreds.

.oOo.

References

1	Merchant Taylors Apprentice Book.	28	Archd Beds Wills 1632-3, 51.
2	Journals of Bridge House Committee.	29	Ravensden, Beds Marr Reg.
		30	St Paul's Baptism Register.
3	Merchant Taylors Freemens List.	31	Excheq Deps E134/12.
		32	Excheq Bills E112/158/27.
4	St Olave's Parish Register.	33	Excheq Bills E112/158/27.
5	Merchant Taylors Apprentice Book.	34	Excheq Bills E112/158/42.
		35	Archd Beds Wills 1632-3, 155.
6	Lavendon Burial Register.	36	*Ibid.*
7	Journals of Bridge House Committee.	37	Bedford Corp Minute Bk, 1647-64.
8	Custmls of Gildable & Gt Liberty Manors, Southwark.	38	St Paul's Burial Register.
9	N.G. Brett-James, *London Anthology.*	39	Coll of Arms, Ped of Wm. Fitzhugh, 1692.
10	L.W. Cowie, *History Today,* June 1972.	40	Archd Beds Wills 1632-3, 155.
11	St Olave's Baptism Register.	41	*Ibid.*
12	Merchant Taylors Apprentice Book.	42	*Ibid.*
13	Merchant Taylors Freemens List.	43	Excheq Bills E112/158/42.
14	Archd Beds Wills 1626-7, 101.	44	Excheq Deps E134/12.
15	Lay Subs Beds E179/72/273.	45	Excheq Decrees E126/5/16.
16	Archd Beds Wills 1632-3, 51.	46	St Paul's Burial Register.
17	Exchq Ct Bills E112/158/27.	47	Archd Beds Wills 1632-3, 155.
18	Exchq Deps E134/12.		
19	Bedford Burgess Roll 1625.		
20	St Pauls Bapt Register.		
21	Archd Beds Wills 1626-7, 101.		
22	St Paul's Bur Reg.		
23	Coll of Arms, Ped of Wm Fitzhugh, 1692.		
24	Archd Beds Wills, 1632-3, 155.		
25	Drapers Company Apprentice List.		
26	Archd Beds Wills, 1632-3, 155.		
27	St Paul's Burial Register.		

APPENDIX ONE

THE ANCIENT MANOR OF BEGGARY

Terrick FitzHugh wrote in Chapters One, Four and Six:

The land [Beggary] ... was part of a Manor that William Fitzhugh held [in 1349] of the Priory of St Neots. In documents from the Middle Ages down to the 16th century it is sometimes called Beggary, sometimes Goodwick and sometimes Goodwick alias Beggary, from two adjacent farms that still exist. ... In Doomsday Book 1087, the property is described as comprising two hides and half a virgate of land with woodland for 100 swine, which means that, apart from the woodland, it contained about 255 acres of arable, meadow and pasture. At the Conquest, King William had rewarded his prominent follower and kinsman, Richard Fitzgilbert with the Honour of Clare and 175 other lordships in various parts of England. Among them were Beggary-cum-Goodwick and other manors in the neighbourhood. ... For its support, he and his wife Rose bestowed lands upon it, including Beggary-cum-Goodwick in 'frank almoign,' free alms. This meant that in perpetuity the only services in respect of that Manor that were due from the black-robed brethren to their feudal overlords the de Clares would be those of prayer for the souls of the founders and their descendants. The monastery was thus able to retain for itself the full service due from the tenants of the Manor, who, by the early 13th century and perhaps earlier, were the Fitzhugh family.

In the hierarchical system of feudalism all the land of England was owned by the King, and his subjects held their estates hereditarily either from him or as sub-tenants; so the de Clares held Beggary-cum-Goodwick of the King as tenants-in-chief; the Priory held it of the de Clares as mesne (middle) tenant; and the Fitzhughs held it of the Priory as terre tenants, the ones actually occupying the land...

Richard Fitzhugh, the great-great-great-great-grandson of William above, changed the name of the Manor from Beggary to Goodwick in about 1527. ... The grandson of this Richard, also name Richard Fitzhugh, sold the Manor in 1572, and thus it went out of the Fitzhugh family.

H.A.F. - 2005

The Manor of Beggary, in modern times Begwary as above. The original land mentioned in the Doomsday Book 1087 is that in the area A-B-C-D, two hides and half a virgate, or 255 acres or 103 hectares. It is about three miles West and one mile South of Eaton Socon. The Manor House was on the same spot as the present White House Farm, Ordnance Survey coordinates TL130578. Map digitally printed March 23, 2005. North is at the top. The featured area of the map is 1700 metres East-West by 1750 metres North-South. Goodwick Farm also shows in the upper right. Reproduced with permission.

The Manor of Beggary – National Monument Record Photograph RAF/541/483, frame 4102, taken aerially on April 7, 1950. North is at the top. A tiny corner of the Manor is out of the frame at the top and a tiny sliver is out of the frame at the right. Goodwick Farm is in the top right corner. Reproduced with permission.

The Manor House of Beggary, now called White House Farm – Selective enlargement of National Monument Record Photograph RAF/82/971, frame 0160, taken aerially on June 24, 1954. North is at the top. The original Manor House is visible very near the centre with its peaked roof running North-South. The outline of the original moat can be seen as an arc to its East running approximately from 'noon' to '5PM' inside the rectangle of garden enclosed from the field. Reproduced with permission.

The Manor House at Beggary, probably early 20th Century. It is believed that this house was built on the plan of the original medieval house.

Another farm building at Beggary.

Part of the original moat around the Manor House.

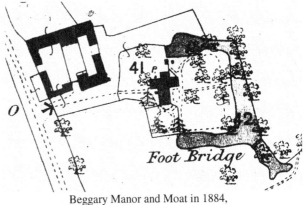

Beggary Manor and Moat in 1884, Ordnance Survey Map 25 inch Sheet VIII 11. Reproduced with permission.

APPENDIX TWO

Horae B.V.M. Secundum Usum Sarum

The British Library Manuscripts Collection contains [Add.43473] a Book of Hours, *Horae B.V.M. Secundum Usum Sarum,* that was once owned by Robert and Elizabeth Fitzhugh. The BL Catalogue states that the Book dates from 1413-1416. [The date of death of Henry IV, March 20, 1413, is written on folio 2.] It may have been owned by the Grene family before the Fitzhughs.

Interleaved within the Book is a cutting from a 19th century auction catalogue, which reads:

XVth Century Manuscript on Vellum from the Bere Court Library
HORÆ BEATÆ VIRGINIS Cum Calendario:
A beautifully executed manuscript of 125 folios by an ENGLISH SCRIBE, written in Red and Black ornamented with 17 INITIAL LETTERS in Gold and Colours with fine Ornamental Borders ROUND THE ENTIRE PAGE OF EACH (The first historiated with a miniature of the Presentation of Christ in the Temple), and many hundreds of Capitals all finely illuminated in Gold and Colours, 4to size, leaves measuring 9in x 6in, bound in Crimson Velvet [but rebound in niger morocco with blind tooling in 1960 by the British Museum].
[...There follows a long description of ecclesiastical content, and the description continues...]
The Illustrations, uniform in character throughout, are singularly well preserved. It has been most carefully collated, the only imperfections being the absence of two leaves quite at the end of the volume. In the calendar (the first leaf of which is soiled) at the end of each month is added what thunder therein betokeneth, and in the month of September is an entry of the obit of Sir Thomas Grene Dominus de Norton in 1462. On the reverse of one of the leaves [97b] is an entry proving that in anno 6 Elizabeth (1563) the MS belonged to Margaret Fitzhugh Cust, daughter of Robert Fitzhugh and Elizabeth his wife born at Wasenden (now Waddendon) in the County of Bucks, near Aylesbury. [This is seriously in error – the auctioneers plainly could not read old Latin. See below. – HAF] At the end of the MS, in a much later hand, is a note saying the MS belonged to Bere Court Library, and a former owner stated that it belonged to Henry VIII, "but whether this be so or not..."

So much for the auction catalogue, which contains inaccuracies. The British Library Manuscripts Online Catalogue entry runs to two full pages, and contains the following:
"A note at folio 97b records the birth on 24 March 1561 (cf. the erased entry for that day) at Wavendon, Co. Bucks., ... of Mary, daughter of Robert and Elizabeth Fitzhugh, afterwards wife of William Astry, cf. *VCH Bucks.*, iii, 346; iv, 492, 495. [This handwritten note is in very tight scribe's Latin, and it seems unlikely that Robert could have written it? However, there are three signs in the margin – perhaps these are the marks of some of the family?] The name of another member of the Fitzhugh family is scribbled in the lower margin of f.106" [This looks very much like the signature of Robert Fitzhugh – HAF].

Rather inconveniently, the interested viewer will need to obtain Reader's Ticket to the British Library before being able to enter the Library. In fact, it is held in such esteem that it is usually necessary to plead a family connection to be able to view the actual Book, and it must be read and handled under the eyes of a librarian.

H.A.F. - 2005

Graffito from Folio 97b
Reproduced with permission.

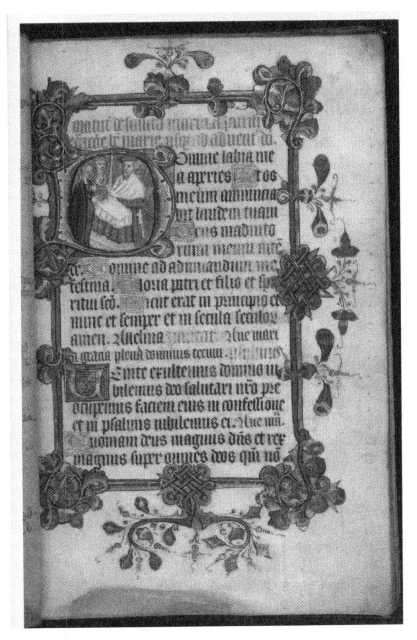

Folio 7f of *Horae B.V.M. Secundum Usum Sarum*   Reproduced with permission.

.oOo.

Volume One
The End…

...Volume Two
The Beginning

THE HISTORY OF

OUR FITZHUGH FAMILY

by
Henry Antonie Fitzhugh
56 Argyle Street, London, WC1H 8ER, England
henryfitzhugh@talktalk.net

TO

ALEXANDER

&

EDWARD

FOREWORD

THIS HISTORY is designed to follow on from a certain point in Terrick V.H. FitzHugh's history *FITZHUGH - The Story of a Family through Six Centuries.* Chapter Nine of that work finishes with these words, referring to the children in William the Immigrant's generation:

> *"Thirty-two of them were Fitzhughs, but although fourteen were boys, only one was destined to carry our name further than one more generation"* (in England, that is). *"Never mind; little William, Henry's ninth child, was eventually to leave Bedfordshire for wider horizons where his family throve and multiplied. In the 20th Century his living descendants in the United States of America are numbered in hundreds."*

The William mentioned above is William the Immigrant, and Henry is his father, both of whom are the subjects of Chapter One of this work. Thus the present volume, taken together with the first nine chapters of Terrick FitzHugh's History referred to above, form an unbroken history of my family down to 1986. A Family Tree covering the entire period of both works is included in this volume, as are some notes on many of the ancestors whose lives are so vividly portrayed by Terrick FitzHugh.

NOTE TO READERS IN
THE BRITISH LIBRARY

This book relates to several other books in The British Library, in that it adds to or corrects information in them. Books which are substantially updated or corrected are:

> *Three Centuries Passed, The Fitzhugh Family*, by Marie Fitzhugh, 1975, Shelf Mark X.809/22316,

and   *William Fitzhugh and His Chesapeake World*, by Richard Beale Davis, 1963, Shelf Mark X.0800/109.(3.).

Other titles to which this book relates are:

> *Cannibals All!, Or Slaves Without Masters*, by George Fitzhugh, 1857, Shelf Mark 8157.bbb.22,

and   *Sociology For The South, Or The Future of a Free Society*, by George Fitzhugh, 1854, Shelf Mark 8156.c.40,

and   *George Fitzhugh, Propagandist of the Old South*, by Harvey Wish, 1962, Shelf Mark X.529/2485.

The author is indebted to Tom French, Head of Modern British Collections at The British Library for suggesting this cross reference.

PREFACE

The ancient Fitzhugh Family of Bedfordshire split into two branches in 1579 when John Fitzhugh, the last common ancestor, died. The next generation contained William (1570-1633) and Robert (1573-1647) who founded the only two branches of the family surviving from the sixteenth century. Two generations after William, another William (1651-1701) was to immigrate to Virginia Colony, thus establishing the family on both sides of the Atlantic. Living members in different branches will generally be ninth, tenth, or eleventh cousins to one another, possibly once or twice removed. Of the two branches, the American is technically the senior, since William was born three years before Robert, and is more numerous as well, both in persons and in sub-branches.

This volume of the History of the Fitzhugh Family begins in the early seventeenth century when the first Fitzhugh of our branch of the family emigrated from England. From then, the History covers William Fitzhugh, the Immigrant and the line of his descent to the author. The Fitzhugh Family is spread far and wide by now, and it would not be possible for anyone to write a history of the whole family and its scores of sub-branches. Some attempt has been made to catalogue as many of family members as possible (see e.g. The Carroll Fitzhugh Roll, and *Some Ancestors Relatives and Descendants of William Fitzhugh of Virginia*, by W. Conway Price, in the Library of Congress). Consequently, this history deals with only the direct ancestors of my own branch, their brothers and sisters, and some other matters of interest.

I am indebted to many people, who have helped with information and constructive criticism. Paramount among these was Terrick V.H. FitzHugh, who brought his lifetime's professional genealogical experience to bear on my behalf. Without this assistance, the early chapters of this volume would have been but a pale reflection of what they now are, and I owe him the utmost gratitude.

Throughout this document the spellings of the Family name Fitzhugh and FitzHugh are used to try to indicate how the person himself would have spelled his name, although sixteenth and seventeenth century spellings such as Fitzhew and Fytzhewgh have been modernised. I would be grateful to any reader who can supply additional information, or any corrections, which will be incorporated into later editions.

All of the research for this history has been carried out from London, a far way from the centre of most of the action in the various States of America. A diligent search of the records in America, notably in Virginia, carried out more thoroughly than has been possible from this distance, would almost certainly produce a clearer picture of the least illuminated part of this history, the eighteenth and early nineteenth centuries.

This edition supersedes earlier editions of 1982, 1983, 1985 and 1988 and contains the results of much more work and a few more interesting facts. Comprehensive indices have been automatically compiled and all of the photographs and drawings have been incorporated digitally. It has been reset in Times New Roman font Microsoft Word97 for Windows. Family Trees were drawn using Microsoft Draw Version 1.0 and imported via Word.

Footnotes and endnotes are treated differently in this 1998 Edition. Footnotes numbered with Arabic numerals at the bottoms of pages provide further information to be read along with the text; endnotes numbered in Roman numerals give sources for reference material only.

H.A.F., London, 1998

PREFACE TO THE SECOND EDITION

A Second Edition of Volume Two finally became absolutely necessary when the Addenda to the First Edition became thirty-seven pages long, with some eighty-five new entries, all accumulated in only two years. The growth of genealogy on the Internet explains much of this, but there have also been some important discoveries, such as the Philip Aylett Fitzhugh Papers in the University of North Carolina.

Following a visit to the family graves in Austin, Texas in December 2000, I have changed the spelling of my great-grandmother's name from Harriet Bullitt to Harriett Bullett, in order to agree with her tombstone, in spite of the fact that many other spellings are found, even in her husband's correspondence. I have also changed my great-grandfather's date of birth by two days for the same reason.

All information known to date has been included in this Second Edition, requiring changes, sometimes very substantial, to eighteen of the separate sections. Three new photographs have been included as well. It is to be fervently hoped that this will not be the last new Edition to appear, as there is still much to learn about the Fitzhugh Family.

H.A.F., London, 2001.

PREFACE TO THE THIRD EDITION

Even though it is only two years since the publication of the Second Edition of this work, there are two good reasons to bring forth a Third Edition. The first of these is the impending Family Reunion in October 2003 in Virginia, but even more important is the hundred or so new pieces of information, some very important and extensive, resulting in a Volume that is a third again larger than the Second Edition, and half again larger than the First Edition. Major new sources include Thaddeus Fitzhugh's Memoirs from the Museum of The Confederacy, an explanation of how our line inherited Marmion, The Dennis Fitzhugh Papers from the Filson Library, a possible explanation for John Henry Fitzhugh's demotion in the Mexican War as well as a definitive explanation for why was befriended by General Sam Houston, and an explanation of how Shooter's Hill came into and out of the family along with much information on its history. The signatures of Henry, Mary, and Robert Fitzhugh of 1657 have been added, as well as the discovery of a Book of Hours of 1413-1416, once owned in the family. Lastly, although clearly not a Fitzhugh, an Appendix regarding Mary Boleyn and King Henry VIII has been added together with the strong suggestion that some of our Fitzhugh ancestors descend from their adultery.

I would like to believe that this Third Edition will be final and definitive. But I rather doubt it, because there is so much we still do not know.

H.A.F., London, 2003

CONTENTS

APPENDICES

PHOTOGRAPHS

ILLUSTRATIONS

HENRY FITZHUGH 1614-1666

CHAPTER ONE

NEW WORLDS FOR OLD

HENRY FITZHUGH

1614-1666

W hen Henry Fitzhugh[1] was born, the Elizabethan Age had only just faded and the Dawn of the Seventeenth Century had scarcely broken. It was both an auspicious and a brave time for the ancient Fitzhugh family, which had inhabited Bedfordshire as landowners under the same surname since the Twelfth Century, to reach upward into the new commercial world of the growing towns. The two present-day surviving branches of the family, which had technically separated in 1579 on the death of their ancestor John, were still linked by two now ageing brothers, William and Robert. William had moved into

John
d. 1579

William
bpt, 1570

Robert
bpt. 1573

The American
Fitzhughs

The English
FitzHughs

---

1   Opposite is a photograph of a painting which, in 1931, was in the possession of Henry Fitzhugh of Washington, D.C. It is a copy painted in 1751 of the original which had written on the back that it was painted when the subject was aged twenty. It is inscribed on the back: "Henry Fitzhugh son of / Willm Fitzhugh of Bedford / Aetatis 20 / 1634 / Cop^d by John Hesselius / 1751." The background has a dark tone, and Henry has dark brown hair and eyes, a white collar and a brown robe. (Private communication from Henry Fitzhugh, the owner, to Rev. V.C.A. FitzHugh, December 2, 1931.) It was owned by Mrs. Robert H. Stevenson of 76 Beacon Street, Boston, Massachusetts, in 1963. It was conserved in 1995 and shown with four other Fitzhugh portraits in an exhibition "The First Fitzhughs of Virginia" by the Virginia Historical Society. See *American Art Review*, Vol. IX, No.2, 1997, pp. 80-85. R.K. Doud states [*The Fitzhugh Portraits by John Hesselius*, The Virginia Magazine of History and Biography, Vol. 75, April, 1967, No.2] "Doubtless the original ... was painted in England and brought to [Virginia] by William the Immigrant..."

and worked in Bedford Town, and had become a member of the Common Council by 1615.[i] In retrospect, we can see that he had succeeded in laying a hard foundation for his family to build on. It was his children's generation which was to reach the family's zenith in the politics and society of Bedford, and the same generation which was to see the first Fitzhughs begin to seek their fortunes across the Seas.

William's fourth child, our ancestor Henry Fitzhugh, came into this world as what even in those days was a large family - he was one of twelve, eight boys and four girls. His younger brother Robert, a Maltster, was the one who made the greatest mark in Bedford, for he was Mayor in 1656 and 1679[ii] and remained an Alderman until 1689. He married Mary Collyer in Turvey, Bedfordshire,[iii] resided at "the Greenhouse in Bedford",[iv] and had eleven children, whose descent we know. Henry's older brother William was baptised on August 1, 1613, went to be a merchant in Turkey, and died unmarried.[v] Perhaps he was in the cloth trade, as England exported 20,000 cloths a year to Turkey at that time.[vi] Hugh was apprenticed to a member of the Drapers Company of London in 1632,[vii] freed in 1642, and went to be a merchant in Amsterdam, dying in 1686.[viii] He married Lydia Potts, and both were *Henry's brothers and sisters* Elders of the English Reformed Church there, and founded a line now known as Fitz or Fitts, the name being changed presumably because the Dutch could not pronounce Fitzhugh accurately.[ix] Probably the reason he went to Amsterdam had to do with religion; Amsterdam would tolerate anything except Catholicism, and all the reformed churches found it easy to exist there. Francis was baptised on March 14, 1615/6,[x] and also apprenticed to become a Draper.[xi] In the Civil War he obtained a Lieutenant's Commission in Lord Wharton's Regiment in the Parliamentary Army. He fought at the Battle of Edgehill, and was captured by the Royalists and imprisoned, first at Ludlow Castle and then in Beaumaris Castle on the Isle of Anglesey.[xii] He survived and returned to Bedford to become a member of the Council in 1648 and 1649 along with his brothers Robert and Henry.[xiii] He married Anne Daniel in about 1646[xiv] and had several children. It was left to Thomas[xv] and Robert[xvi] to follow in their father's footsteps and become Maltsters. Thomas was baptised on January 8, 1618/9, buried June 29, 1639/40,[xvii] dying unmarried at the age of only twenty-one. Another son, Peter, was baptized on September 30, 1620[xviii] and died young and unmarried sometime after 1632/3.[xix] Another son, John, was baptised on March 22, 1611/2, and buried aged twelve on June 4, 1624.[xx] Of the eight sons, it is sad that only five lived into full adulthood.

The girls did somewhat better as far as longevity is concerned. Elizabeth was baptised on May 28 or 30, 1610,[xxi] and married into the prosperous Paradine family, which provided Bedford with several Mayors in the seventeenth century. She married George Paradine on August 19, 1627.[xxii] There was a Margaret baptised on October 8, 1623[xxiii] but she died in less than eighteen months. She was followed by a second Margaret who was baptised on the last day of the year on the Old Calendar, March 24, 1625.[xxiv] She married Henry Zouch in 1649[xxv] and second Matthew Porter of London.[xxvi] Sybil was baptised on February 28, 1626/7,[xxvii] and married Edward Wilson at St. Martin-in-the Fields,[xxviii] which was then surrounded by fields outside London, and not, as today, by Trafalgar Square and the National Gallery.

Into this large family our ancestor Henry Fitzhugh was baptised on December 11, 1614 at St. Paul's, Bedford.[xxix] We know nothing of any education for him, but in a family so large one would not expect the younger sons to aspire to academic heights.

Henry's early life and marriage Instead he was apprenticed[xxx] to become a Woollen Draper of Bedford.[xxxi] He married, in 1638 or before, Mary King, born in 1616, the daughter of Reverend Giles King of Tempsford, Bedfordshire. Their children began to arrive in September 1639,[xxxii] just in time for the Civil War, in which Bedford certainly saw its share of action. The Town was staunchly Parliamentary and almost certainly all of the Fitzhugh family were as well. A Parliamentary garrison of 300 men was at one time stationed in the Town.[xxxiii] Although reports *The Civil War in Bedford* of the time were often a gross exaggeration, it is told[xxxiv] that in October, 1643[xxxv] the Royalists swept through the County with between two and four thousand men, capturing Parliamentary supporters and driving all the cattle to supply the Royalist army at Oxford. The enemy plundered Bedford[xxxvi] and there was fighting on the Bridge[xxxvii] not a quarter of a mile from Henry's and Mary's house. Several of the properties of prominent Parliamentary sympathisers were pulled down.[xxxviii] Levies of horses, men, and arms were demanded of the County,[xxxix] all of which must have been harrowing and alarming, and indeed expensive, for the civilian population who, as ever, were caught in the cross-fire of the opposing armies. Rev. King was expelled from his livings by the Puritans in 1647 as "very disaffected in preaching and ministry."[xl] However, the Fitzhugh family, like the Town of Bedford, was able to bend to the rapidly shifting political winds of the time, and, so far as we know, to emerge at the end of it unscathed.

The end of the decade, which saw the beheading of Charles I, was eventful for Henry and Mary too. A man named William Symonds had been entrusted to carry money to London in 1647 for Henry Fitzhugh but was robbed by highwaymen on the road between Mimms and Barnet, "by which he was utterly undone." Henry had to sue for its return and the case went all the way to the House of Lords.[xli] To make matters worse, in the same year his father-in-law was ejected from his living by the Puritans.[xlii] It must have been in some ways a bad year for the family, but they must have also been prospering, for Henry became Mayor of Bedford in 1649,[xliii] at age *Henry becomes* only thirty-five, one of four Fitzhughs who *Mayor of Bedford* became Mayor, the others being William in 1487, Henry in 1549,[1] and Robert, the present Henry's brother, in 1656 and 1679.[xliv]

The Drapery business must have been good for Henry during his Mayoral year, and he must have been *The Drapery* busy in his civic duties, for he took on an apprentice *business* for eight years, one William Franklin of *prospers* Godmanchester, Huntingdonshire, officially enrolling him on November 20, 1649.[xlv] There may well have been another reason for wanting help. In an Ordinance of four months earlier the residents of the High Street[2] were obliged to put out a candle "of the bigness of at least sixteen in the lb to be kept burning

---

1   This Henry is not identified but would likely have been the same or previous generation as John Fitzhugh (d.1579). He spoke at an important moment in the Court of Common Council in 1566 (*Old Bedford*, C.F. Farrar, M.A., 1926, p.137, quoting from *The Black Book*).

2   See Appendix 8 for a map of Bedford in 1611, plan of the Fitzhugh property in the High Street, and a picture of Bedford Bridge.

and renewed as it is spent" from dusk to 8 AM on alternate nights on the East and West sides of the street.[xlvi] No doubt it was the poor apprentice and not Henry or Mary who watched over the candles every other night.

The job of Mayor was certainly no sinecure. Even beginning the year before he became Mayor, Henry became embroiled in a bitter power struggle involving the *Bedford* Constitution of the Bedford Corporation. The *Politics* Bedford Charter was outmoded by the standards of the times, with most power concentrated in the House of Burgesses. As redress, the Freemen had demanded annual elections to the Council. The dispute was finally submitted to a committee of six - three Burgesses and three Freemen, with Henry being one of the Burgesses. Petitions and counter-petitions were issued[xlvii] and at one stage an adjudication between the six was ratified.[xlviii]

This document[1] is the most personal of all pertaining to our family history, for it contains both the signature and seal in wax of Henry Fitzhugh himself. The Seal is remarkably preserved, showing the Fitzhugh Armorial bearing, Ermine and Chevrons Quartered etc.,[2] and even has the somewhat rough-cut fingerprints of the clerk who moulded the hot wax to take the deep seal impression. It is the earliest surviving example of the use of these Arms by a member of the family, although it is very likely they were in use as early as 1487.[xlix]

---

1   The photograph on the next page shows a detail of Document BorBB6/7 from the Bedfordshire County Records in the Town Hall, Bedford. The signature and seal of Henry Fitzhugh and five others are appended and referred to as such in the document. The Arms are clearly Three Chevrons Quartered, and the impression of the Martlets can still be seen, but the fine detail of the Ermine has apparently not survived. Permission to use this photograph has been given by the North Bedfordshire Borough Council.

2   See Appendix 1 for a complete description, figure etc. Could the fingerprints be those of Henry himself?

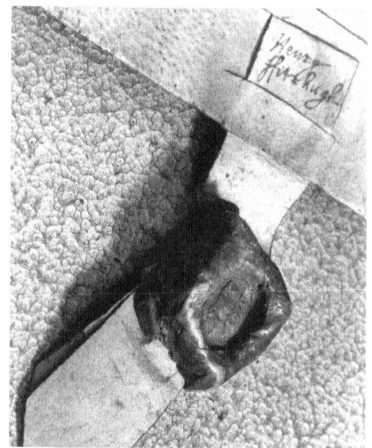

THE SIGNATURE and SEAL OF HENRY FITZHUGH, 1648

One dispute followed another. In 1649 Henry, as Mayor, was commanded[1] to yield the Town Charter to a Parliamentary Committee as evidence in the then current process of rewriting many town charters. *Henry as Magistrate*

On top of all this, Henry had to sit in Court, for it was customary for the Mayor to preside over the Court of Pleas in the Guildhall.[li] The sessions over which he presided were fairly numerous, occurring once or twice a month. They involved the usual plethora of minor crimes and civil actions - granting bail, complaints of nuisance between neighbours, violations of the complex street trading bye-laws, petty theft etc etc. Henry's duties in Court were more or less exactly those of a modern day Magistrate. No doubt this kept Henry pretty busy on top of his drapers business and the general politics of his other Mayoral duties.

Bedford politics in the seventeenth century was apparently not entirely above criticism, even to the point of attracting satire from no less than John Bunyan. It is clear what Bunyan thought of it all[1] when in *The Holy War* he writes that Diabolus (allegorically, the King) made *Bedford* thirteen burgesses and aldermen, the exact number in *Politics is* the Bedford Common Hall, one of the three divisions *mocked* of the Corporation. These were named Mr. Incredulity, *Bunyan* Mr. Haughty, Mr. Swearing, Mr. Whoring, Mr. Hard-Heart, Mr. Pitiless, Mr. Fury, Mr. No-Truth, Mr. Stand-to-Lies, Mr. False-Peace, Mr. Drunkenness, Mr. Cheating, and Mr. Atheism - in other words a normal cross-section of human interest and vice! He further writes "there was also an election of common councilmen and others; as bailiffs, serjeants, constables, and others; but all of the like to those forenamed [the thirteen above] being either fathers, brothers, cousins, or nephews to them...", a fairly accurate description of the composition of the Bedford Council, and of how the Tory party gained power in the local corporations. Incredulity, being the eldest, eventually became Mayor. By such Allegory, the political history of Bedford was presented as a parable of Man's Soul.[2]

---

1   The background to Bedford politics and the reason Bunyan was interested in it is as follows: The King had resolved to make a systematic attack on the Town Charters of the country, because the old Corporations in effect controlled the election of Members of Parliament. He sought to secure control of the Corporations, and through them of Parliament. Bedford at the time furnished a good illustration of the way in which Corporations were manipulated, Charters surrendered, officials displaced, and so forth. [*John Bunyan, His Life, Times and Work*, by John Brown, B.A., D.D., The Tercenteniary Edition, The Hulbert Publishing Company, London, 1928, pp. 316-320.]

2   For further information regarding Bunyan, see Beds. Hist. Rec. Soc., Vol. 59, 1980, *The Internal Politics of Bedford 1660-1680*, by Michael Mullett, *passim*, and therein references 56, 113, & 117. John Bunyan was sent to prison in 1661 for nonconformity. As far as those political upheavals were concerned, our family were certainly Church of England and Parliamentarians, although they were apparently wise enough to

Although they had previously had higher standing as landowners in the County of Bedfordshire, it was this generation which reached the family's peak in Bedford society and politics, producing two Mayors in seven years, *Henry's* as well as being related by marriage to the rich *high water* Paradine family, which produced Mayors of its *mark* own. A picture of Henry exists at age twenty,[1] facing page 1. He is no doubt handsome but his eyes seem to reveal a certain alertness, or even a determination. Perhaps it is this feature of his character that explains his triumphs and failures in later life. His name appears in the Wills of his grandmother Amy Fitzhugh Negus[lii] and his father William[liii] wherein he was left "my newly erected messuage in St. Paul's Parish."[2] This messuage, or house with

---

follow the prevailing political wind after the Restoration. There in no mention of any Fitzhugh in *Recusancy and Nonconformity in Bedfordshire 1622-1842*, Beds. Hist. Rec. Soc., Vol. XX, 1938, ed. W.M. Wigfield, although the names Astry, Negus, and Saunders do appear.

1   See also Richard Beale Davis, *William Fitzhugh and his Chesapeake World*, Virginia Historical Society, University of N. Carolina Press, 1963, facing p. 112; also *Genealogies of Virginia Families*, p. 833.

2   The Will of William Fitzhugh, *Archdeaconry of Bedford Wills*, 1632-3, ABP/W/1633/155, is full of touching phrases showing a concern for his widow and children. The relevant parts dealing with the messuage are lines 32-51, which read as follows: *"I doe give unto my sonne Henrie Fitzhughe all that my newly erected messuage in St. Paul's P(ar)ish in the towne of Bedford neere to my dwelling house and adjoyning east upon the high streete and north upon Mr. Thomas Paradines ground together with my little yard or pigstall adjoyning to the same newly erected messuage on the backside thereof and latelie parcell of and taken out of the great yard of my dwelling house and adjoyning southw(ard)s it is now situated(?) outs(ide) upon the residue of the great yard aforesaid and north upon the said Mr. Paradines ground in the free libertie and passage and all means of carriage at all fitting and convenyent times by and through the broad gates between my said two houses and so by and through the said great yard to and from the said little yard or pigstall. Allso I give unto him my little barne no(r)th (of) the peece of ground now used for an hearbe garden adjoyning thereto and latelie taken out of the backyard next ducke lane adjoyning west upon duck-lane house upon myne orchard and eastw(ard)s it is now hedged out upon the rest of the backyard now late in the holding or occupation of James Bacon to have and to hold the said messuage barne and other (of?) the parcells so bequeathed to him unto my said*

grounds and outbuildings, was a substantial property in the High Street of Bedford. It had four Hearths,[liv] and owning it certainly established Henry as a man of means and position in the Town, which, as we shall see, he was quick to exploit.

But all of this was not enough for Henry. After he finished his term as Mayor, and presumably was riding high on his commercial and political prestige in Bedford, he embarked upon a venture about whose accurate details we can make a good deduction, but which certainly had all the *Henry embarks on a risky speculation* appearances of being highly, or even dangerously, speculative. It was to have consequences for our family which lasted for centuries.

In 1653, Henry obtained loans from Anthony Penniston, a Clerk (i.e. a Cleric) of London and a William Verney[1].

---

sonne Henrie..." It is possible to guess at a plan of how this total estate of two houses, two yards, gates, a barn, a herb garden, an orchard, etc. may have been situated between the High Street and Duck Lane (now Lime Street). Unfortunately there is not enough information in the above to define it other than tentatively, as is shown in Appendix 8. Other extant wills, deeds, or maps may hold some clues from which an accurate reconstruction of William's estate could be drawn. See a later footnote for a description of the house and its contents in 1666. Reference to this estate is also contained on pages 116-117 and 145 of Volume One. The address of its frontage is now approximately 78-88 The High Street.

1 It seems likely that this William Verney was the same as the William Verney who was the Master of the Free Grammar School in Bedford (*Minute Book of the Bedford Corporation 1647-64, op. cit.*, pp. xxvii, 9-10, 94, 98, 138, 180-1). He was a "child" at Winchester College in 1621 (*VCH Bucks.*, ii, p. 164-5), thus making him about the same age as Henry. Verney had been Chaplain of New College, Oxford, and was appointed Headmaster of the Grammar School on October 10, 1636 (Harpur Charity, Letters, H2/15, N. Beds. Bor. Co. Recs.). It was not long before he was in dispute with his Ushers, and asked for their replacement on March 20, 1641 (New Style), (N. Beds. Bor. Co. Recs., H2/16&17). Sometime between 1637 and 1640, a petition to the Harpur Foundation complained that Verney had not only charged fees, which he had no right to do, but had also *"grossly neglected the school by frequent absences from it, by night-walking and mis-spending his time in taverns and ale-houses, and is also very cruel when present to the boys."* [House of Lords MSS, quoted in *John Bunyan, His Life, Times and Work,* by John Brown, B.A., D.D., The Tercenteniary Edition, The Hulbert Publishing Company, London, 1928, p.36]. In 1648, formal

In the case of Penniston, Henry had borrowed £300 with a promise to pay it back a year later or forfeit double the amount,[lv] and presumably a larger amount from Verney, probably £600. Henry must have had some very great short-term profit in sight to make him borrow such a large sum of money (more than his own net worth) over such a short period, with such a large default penalty. Nowadays, no one would borrow, or indeed lend, on such extortionate terms. The details of the Recognizance show that Henry in fact borrowed £300 on May 1, 1653 from Penniston on terms such that if he paid back £318 in Middle Temple Hall by May 5, 1654, the debt was clear. Otherwise, he had to forfeit £600 on the feast of St. John the Baptist, June 24, 1654. The other debt to Verney was almost certainly a similar one for £1200 Bond.

Middle Temple Hall, which had been opened by Queen Elizabeth in person seventy-eight years before, was certainly a suitable venue for such a significant occasion for our family, with its double hammer-beam roof and tables made from oaken planks from Sir Francis Drake's ship, the *Golden Hind*.[lvi] In this case it could hardly have been more important for the Family's destiny, for Henry's resulting bankruptcy is probably the key to everything that

---

complaints were made in the Council that he had *"for a long tyme past neglected ... the dutie of theire said place whereby the same school in in a manner quyte desolate, parents ... of children daily withdrawing them ... and enforced to send theire children to other Schools abroad..."* Verney received £20 salary in 1656, but he was formally ejected sometime later by the Commissioners for Ejecting Scandalous Ministers and Schoolmasters, set up by the previous Parliament. The Council then sought a recommendation from the Master and Fellows of New College, Oxford, to replace him. He did not go easily, for in 1660 the new Headmaster, Mr. Butler, had to request the Council formally to certify that Butler and not Verney was in fact the proper Headmaster, which the Council did, although they did not allow Butler to sue Verney, presumably for damages. Something must have happened to Butler, for on November 9, 1663, the Council had to request New College to recommend a new Headmaster to replace Verney, who was "lately dead". The School was next to the Town Prison. There are several references to boarders, and to fact that the School was a profitable business for the Headmaster. It is also interesting that one of Henry's children, Susan, married a Richard Varney (or Verney?) on September 21, 1659. This was most likely the Richard Varney who signed the Inventory of possessions (PROB4, 9281, Fitzhugh, PRO; also see page 17, footnote 1, Inventory transcription) after his death in 1666.

followed -- his own demise, his widow's penury, his son William's emigration to America, and his son and heir Henry's drinking problem, all of which more anon. Without this disaster, our branch

Middle Temple Hall in 1701, showing the steps, lower left, where Henry defaulted

of the Fitzhugh Family might be Bedford gentry to this day.

But what was Henry borrowing the money *for*? Sketchy in places though it may be, all that has been said up to here of Henry's life is a matter of documented fact. But as we ask the above question and move forward to the greatest, and the most tragic, events in Henry's life, we are forced to rely on deduction in some places and even speculation in others. As the story unfolds all of the factual evidence available will be woven together to support a plausible version of Henry's life, but it will always be made clear exactly where the boundary between fact and deduction lies. As always, if our ancestors had been just a little more diligent in documenting their affairs, then we would be on certain ground in understanding their lives. But then again not all of us would want our own tragedies recorded as well as our triumphs.

Returning to the question of what Henry was going to do with the money, the author strongly suspects that he was trying to revive the River Ouse Navigation Scheme, a plan to enable barges to reach Bedford from the coast. The Navigation had been completed as far as Great Barford by 1640, but had fallen into

Was Henry trying to make the River Ouse navigable? abeyance during the Civil War and Commonwealth.[lvii] A Common Council Meeting was held on February 4, 1653[lviii] whose sole business was to pass a resolution requesting that the Corporation be enabled by an Act of Parliament to make the River Ouse navigable from St. Neots to Bedford. This was three months before Henry borrowed the money, and there were no more meetings until June 27 and 30, from which latter Henry was absent. If this was Henry's plan, it is most likely that he was trying to buy the navigation rights from the heirs of the developer, Arnold Spencer, who had operated the Navigation for many years. It would have been a real master stroke - securing rights to the traffic, and then getting an Act of Parliament to create the traffic.[1]

But alas, Henry must have failed, for no further mention can be found until a Private Bill was presented, but not pursued beyond a First Reading, to the House of Commons in 1662.[lix] Getting an Act passed would have been difficult because the House of Lords, the normal avenue for such Bills, did not sit during the Commonwealth. It may also be that he was unable to overcome opposition. A public Petition[2] of 1660 sets out a strong case for the

---

1   Joyce Godber, *The Story of Bedford*, White Crescent Press, Luton, 1978. The Ouse Navigation was an old cause in Bedford. On April 30, 1628, Henry's father William, as an Alderman on Bedford Council, was party to an attempt to obtain the necessary Act of Parliament (Beds. Hist. Rec. Soc., Vol XXIV, p.33). Spencer and his heir Robert died around 1655 in debt for £1035 16s and the Navigation rights passed to two married daughters. The circumstances could never have been better for Henry to make a bid, and Henry's borrowings are close in value to Spencer's debts, but in the end the Navigation was operated by the creditors for the next 20 years. (Beds. Hist. Rec. Soc. Vol XXIV, *passim* & p. 62.) Certainly the money at Henry's disposal (£1800) was enough to buy the rights. Spencer's creditors were paid off for £1200 in 1674 and a half share changed hands in 1680 for £1250 (*The Great Ouse, The History of a Navigation*, D. Summers, 1973, BL X.529/16238). Failing all this, there is another possibility – the draining of the Fens – which for want of space is discussed in Note 60, following the Family Tree.

2   *A Short Demonstration that Navigation to Bedford is for the Benefit of Bedfordshire*, British Library Shelfmark 816.m.8.(11). The draining of the Bedford Level of the River Ouse, and the Navigation to Bedford were clearly *causes celebres* of the day. There was a true conflict between Navigation and Drainage in the Ouse and Fens – basically the boatmen and millers wanted high water, the farmers wanted low water, and the boatmen and millers could not get along. There is a score of

Navigation, and the tone of it shows that there must have been considerable local resistance. In any event, he failed to get the necessary legislation, and the Navigation had to wait until the latter years of the century for completion.

Had Henry pulled off this coup, he would have made such a fortune that the Fitzhughs would never have needed to leave Bedford. As we shall see, it had the opposite effect of putting the family in considerably reduced circumstances, from which neither he nor his poor widow ever recovered.

While all this was unfolding, Robert Fitzhugh was also having problems of his own. Robert was Mayor in 1656/7 at the time when an attempt was made on the life of Oliver Cromwell by setting fire to Whitehall Palace. It un-nerved Parliament, which responded with a Resolution that Cromwell should become King, thus ensuring a succession, namely of his heirs. Rumours of this got abroad, and in Bedfordshire there was strong opposition. On April 14, 1657 a broadside (i.e. a printed broadsheet) was published entitled *The Humble and Serious Testimony of many hundreds of Godly and Well-Affected People in the County of Bedford and parts adjacent, Constant Adherers to the Cause of God and Nation.*[lx] This strongly put the case for retention of existing constitutional arrangements. It is fairly clear that Cromwell had nothing to do with the original proposal; rather it was being promoted by officials of the government. Secretary of State Thurloe, who had a reputation as a supreme master of spies, as well as being an extremely able administrator,[lxi] thus wrote to Robert Fitzhugh, as Mayor, ordering him to arrest all those who had taken part in *The Humble and Serious Testimony.* There may have been as many as 100 implicated and arrested, for on April 24, 1657 Robert and another Councillor wrote to Thurloe asking for release of their fellow townsmen.[lxii] By reading the entire correspondence[lxiii] it is clear that Robert was, perhaps wisely, prepared to lean over backwards to appear to co-operate with Thurloe even though he must have had great sympathy with *The Humble and Serious Testimony* and its authors. It seems clear that no Fitzhugh was

---

related Petitions, Cases, and Bills published in the mid-seventeenth Century.

among the 100-odd who did sign it, although no signed copy has yet been seen.

Robert had a run of this sort of problem. He and other aldermen were summoned before Major General Boteler in March 1657 to receive strong threats regarding behaviour contrary to Thurloe's wishes.[lxiv] A similar incident occurred in 1680 when a non-conformist was elected to the Common Council.[lxv]

In the midst of all this turmoil, Henry must have spent the years 1654-57 trying to stave off his creditors. In spite of his debts, and the inevitable harrying he must have had, Henry continued to trade as a Draper during this period. This is certain because, quite fortunately, Trade Tokens of his dated 1655 have survived[lxvi] in several museums, as shown and described on the next pages.

Henry was empowered to sign contracts on behalf of the Council in 1650, and this was renewed annually up to 1654. But later he was yet again empowered to sign contracts on March 2, 1657 (New Style). This must mean that he was solvent and at least of good financial reputation just one year before the final Court judgement against him on February 26, 1658

In spite of his debts, Henry carries on.

The Signatures of Henry Fitzhugh, G[en]t, Mary Fitzhugh, and Robert Fitzhugh, Mayor, February 26, 1656/7

(New Style).[lxvii] Also, even though Henry was heavily in debt, or perhaps because of it, the whole family engaged at this time in a good deal of property buying and selling. For this purpose, both Henry and Robert and their wives were involved in a series of actions in the Court of Pleas in the Bedford Guildhall. These transactions appear as Court cases in the seventeenth century as a traditional way of creating an official record of a property conveyance. (Coincidentally, both brothers presided over such cases in their capacities of Mayor.) These cases all took the same pattern. On August 30, 1654, Robert and his wife Mary yielded to Hugh Smith the claim to title of a "tenement" consisting of a messuage, garden, orchard and six acres in the Town, in return for a

TRADE TOKENS of HENRY and ROBERT FITZHUGH

Obv: ROBERT.FITTZHUGH*=R.F.M.
Rev: IN.BEDFORD*=1654

Obv: HENRY:FITTZHUGH:=1655
Rev: IN.BEDFOD.*=1655

Obv: HENRY.FITTZHUGH.=*1655*
Rev. IN:BEDFORD*+*=*1655*

Trade Tokens were a phenomenon which arose about 1648 to fulfil a need created by a shortage of small copper coins of the Realm. They were issued by individual traders, or sometimes by the Mayor of a Town, and more than a hundred species survive from Bedfordshire alone. They were mostly minted in denominations of a farthing but a few were halfpennies, and were obviously meant to be small change. They were eventually suppressed by a Royal Proclamation of August 24, 1672.

These examples of Henry Fitzhugh's tokens, and one of his brother Robert's, are from the British Museum, and are all farthings. Examples are also in a number of local collections (Blundell, *op. cit.*, & *Trade Tokens Issued in the Seventeenth Century*, George C. Williamson, 1889).

The true size of the coins in the photograph the preceding page is 1.5 centimetres in diameter. It is interesting to note that the tokens consistently spell the family name "Fittzhugh" even though Henry signed his name as we would spell it today, as do records of the day such as Hearth Taxes and Lay Subsidies. Photograph reproduced by permission.

payment of £10 only.[lxviii] In the next instance on December 19, 1655,[lxix] Henry, with brother Robert presiding in the Court, "won" a case against Thomas Pare and his wife Elizabeth wherein Henry gained the rights to "one messuage, one dovehouse, one barne, one orchard & one garden with appurtenances in the Towne of Bedford," having to pay only £10 to Thomas. This property was subsequently sold by William, Henry's second son, in 1673.[lxx] Hard on the heels of this acquisition, Henry and Mary together engaged in a case with Robert Lovett on March 25, 1657 (New Style) with brother Robert again presiding in the   Court,   over   three messuages,   one   dovehouse,   an   orchard,   and garden with appurtenances.[lxxi] Henry and Mary granted a Lease to Robert Lovett for ninety-nine years from February 1, 1657 for a rent of "one peppercorne." Henry was paid £10. Henry's signature as well as

Mary's is on the actual indenture[lxxii] and so is Robert's witnessing it in his capacity as Mayor. It is interesting to know that Mary could write, not usual for women at that time. Unless it was subsequently sold, this property should have come back into the family in 1756, even though all of the then living members of our branch were in Virginia. We do not know what happened to this property.

But in the end all of these efforts must have failed, and Henry's creditors must have closed in. In 1658 he *Henry is* suffered what could only have been a major disaster, in *bankrupt* the form of a Court judgement (February 26, 1658 New Style) to pay the £1800 default Bond.[lxxiii] Henry was "attached" for debt to Verney (see a previous footnote regarding this man) and Penniston for £1200 and £600 respectively. Considering that at this time many annual salaries were around a few tens of pounds, and that a substantial property could be bought for ten pounds, this was a staggering sum of money. He was forced to pledge a very long list of business, personal, and household possessions against payment of the debts.[1] This list makes heartbreaking reading,

---

1   The Inventory of Henry's possessions in this Court action [Bedford Court of Pleas, 1657/8] reads (with definitions from the OED and the Librarian of the Textile Institute) as follows: "2 boltes of red cotton, 24 pewter dishes, val(ue) £5, 6 peeces of white cotton, 15 peeces of nap't bayes, 6 peeces of shag'd bayes, 6 peeces of peniston (*a coarse woolen cloth used for garments and linings*), 4 peeces of dornix (*a silk, worsted, or woolen fabric used for hangings, carpets, or vestments*), 20 peeces of broadcloth, 20 peeces of yard-wide woolen cloth, 6 peeces of dyed kersey (*a coarse narrow woolen cloth*), 20 peeces of searge, 18 peeces of yard-wide Norwich stuff (*a worsted dress material*), 12 peeces of English tamcy (*probably tamis, an open plain weave worsted sieve cloth*), 20 peeces of mix't stuff, 15 remnants of taffety & tabbye (*silk taffeta*), 20 peeces of mohayre wrought & playne, 9 peeces of frize (*silk plush*), 4 coates, 8 dozen skinnes, 10 pounds of silk, 12 groose of shalloome (*a closely woven woolen material for linings*), 22 peeces of ribbon, 6 pounds of thred, 12 gros (sic) of great silk buttons, 40 gross of small silk buttons, 12 gross of thred buttons, 20 peeces of silver lace, 8 peeces of coper lace, 10 pounds of worsted fringe, 20 yards of buckeram (*a fine linen or cotton*), 40 yards of dymothy (*dimity, a stout cotton woven with raised stripes or fancy figures, usually for beds or bedroom hangings, occasionally for garments*), 20 els (*an English ell is 45 inches*) of canvis, 30 yards of coloured lynnen, 6 dozen of paddes & collars, 6 peeces of binding and fillating, 4 dozen of rowles (*rolls,*

beginning with his entire stock in the Drapers trade right down to all his silk buttons, and then continuing to his household furniture, kitchen utensils, bed linen, and even fire andirons. Henry was able to satisfy the debt of £600 to Penniston, plus £18 costs, but the entire remainder of his property was valued at only £600 by the Court Serjeant, but Henry got this increased to £800 by two valuers, one of whom was certainly a relation of his. He remained attached for the rest of the £1200 debt to Verney. How or whether he ever cleared this, we do not know. This was total financial disaster, leaving him penniless.

How does a man, once successful and powerful, react to total bankruptcy? It is probable that this disaster holds the key to explaining Henry's migration later on. We know for sure that he died in Cork in Ireland in 1665/6,[1] without making *Undoubtedly* a Will, at only fifty-one years of age. But what *in disgrace,* was he doing there? There is, fortunately, one *Henry goes to* piece of highly suggestive evidence that can be *Ireland* found in the records of Cork. Unluckily, the actual records of the Cork Corporation were destroyed by fire along with the Courthouse in 1891, but there is a reference geographically not

---

probably bands or fillets), chests & drawers belonging to the shop, 4 bedsteads with curtains and vallans, 2 trucklebedsteads (*a low bed designed to be pushed under a higher bed*), fyve fetherbedes, 3 flockbedes (*a bed made of powdered of coarse tufts of wool*), 4 payre of blanketes, 3 ringes, 2 coverletes, 20 pillows, 3 payre of bras & iron andirons, 3 fire-shovelles & tongs, 2 tronkes with 20 paire of sheetes in them, 4 dozen of napkins, 8 board clothes (*table cloths*), 12 towells, 30 chayres, 18 stooles, 4 small silver dishes, one iron --, one hanging presse, 2 chestes, 2 payres of bellows, one jack (*a machine for turning a rotating spit, probably wound up like a clock*) & 3 spites, 4 carpets, 4 window curtains, 4 cushions, 2 bras-kettles, a bras-pot, a preserving pot with a foote, 2 skillettes, 2 pewter candlestickes, 12 pewter porringers, 12 peeces of tyn, 8 sawsers, 10 pewter plates, 2 chests & six tables." All of this was valued at £600 by the Court Serjeant, but at Henry's request was revalued, and sworn, at £800 by Gilbert Negus and Richard Smith, who were probably relations of Henry's. It is obvious that these were not only shop merchandise, but all of Henry's family household possessions. It would appear that they were allowed to keep the clothes on their backs, but not much more.

[1] We are jumping ahead of the evidence here. See following pages for a full explanation.

far away in the Annals of Kinsale to "Mr. FitzHughes, clerk of the [powder] store at Corke...", April 30, 1665.[lxxiv] The date certainly makes it possible that this was Henry, and no other Fitzhugh family can be found in Ireland at the time.[1] The Clerk of the powder store was the manager in modern parlance, and he certainly would have been an Englishman, since one possible use of the gunpowder would have been to control the "Irish Enemy", as they were commonly called.[2] Henry would have been an ideal candidate, (and he might have been appointed by Samuel Pepys), in view of his undoubted political, commercial, and administrative experience.

The powder store would have been located in Elizabeth Fort, Cork, and it is likely that Henry would have been living there.[lxxv] A picture on the next page shows living quarters inside the Fort, and although earlier pictures show a church inside, it is more likely he would have been buried in St Finbarr's Cathedral.

How sure can we be that "Mr. FitzHughes of Corke" and our Henry Fitzhugh are one and the same? A close scrutiny of the *Minute Book of the Bedford Corporation*[lxxvi] for the years 1647-67 gives enough evidence, when properly and intricately interpreted,

---

1   No Fitzhugh is mentioned in any of: *The Surnames of Ireland*, Edward MacLysaght, 1969; *Guide to Irish Surnames*, Edward MacLysaght, 1964; or *Irish Family Names*, Ida Graham, 1973. There is, however, a Fitzhugh in the Dublin Telephone Directory, 1984.

2   However, the reference relates to a raid by the Dutch, and the flavour of the excitement of the times is given by the full quotation: Castlehaven, 30 April, 1665. Rob. Southwell with intelligence from the west. "The enemy are so busy here that the people are running into the hills. They yesterday took a bark from the harbour's mouth of Baltimore... The Gov[r] ... made three shots at them, but could not reach them; they presently set the bark on fire. I am assured there are no less ... than 16 men-of-war, one of 50 pieces of ordnance, one of 42, one of 36, and double manned; their way is, unless it be a prize of value, not to part with any of their men, but to take what the vessel affords, and set them all on fire. This is part of my Lo. Barrymore's letter unto Ensign Browne, unto whom he sent to receive two barrels of powder from Mr. FitzHughes, clerk of the store at Corke. There are four Dutch vessels of great force... They burnt at Baltimore 27 April a small bark..." (Southwell MSS). The munitions could even have been necessary against the Barbary Pirates.

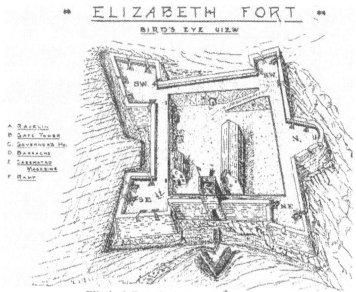

Elizabeth Fort, Cork, latter 17th Century

to make a reasonably safe conclusion. As stated before, Henry was
Mayor in 1649, and, as was the custom, he was appointed an
Alderman after his Mayoral year ended. Henry, like many
Aldermen, had a somewhat poor record of attendance at Council
Meetings after he was out of office. They had to pay a fine of 12d
or 2s as penalty, but perhaps they could all afford it, or perhaps
they were all too busy too attend the eight or ten meetings year.
The fines were automatic and large enough not to be taken
lightly. In 1660, at the end of the Commonwealth, a footsoldier
received 12d a day and a cavalry soldier had 2/6d. The latter was
described as a "gainful profession," good enough to attract
"gentlemen and younger brothers of good family."[lxxvii] Also, the
Mayor's Serjeant in Bedford received only 100s per annum as a
salary in 1657.[lxxviii] Henry was fined sixty-eight times for non-
attendance in the years 1650-59, out of eighty-seven meetings in
that period. However, there were sixty-nine meetings from then
to 1666, of which Henry is recorded as missing only one on
September 5, 1659. According to the Corporation's attendance
rules, he should have been at the meetings, as excuse of fines for
non-attendance was recorded only twice in the entire period to
members who were too infirm to attend. There are also a few

references to excuse for sickness. Thus it seems that either he could no longer afford the fines for non-attendance, or that he had time enough on his hands following the collapse of his Drapers business.[1] Although his attendance seems at first to be exemplary, it is sad to read between the lines of the Corporation Minutes and realise that Henry virtually dropped out of public affairs after 1659. But his supposed attendance record is suspect, as we shall see below. In fact, he was probably not in Bedford at all.

The evidence that Henry was indeed the Clerk of the Powder Store in Cork

Henry and his brother Robert were both listed as Aldermen each year through 1665, and Robert in years thereafter. The Corporation's year began at Michaelmas, The Feast of Saint Michael the Archangel, on September 29, and the last record of Henry's listing was on September 29, 1665. Aldermen were only named at meetings when absent, since a duty to attend was presumed, and we are sure that he knew of the meetings since it was the duty of the Sergeants-at-Mace to "warne each particular

---

[1]   A search of the tax records at the PRO for the mid-seventeenth century in Bedford yields a few suggestions about Henry's financial affairs. He was assessed on three occasions in 1641 and 1642 at a land value of £1 and each time paid 8s tax (Lay Subsidy, 16 Ch. I, E179 72/283 & E179 72/281; 17 Ch. I, E 179 243/3.) This valuation of £1 is very common in the records and is probably the value assigned to any house of moderate proportions. Unfortunately, the tax records of the period are few and far between, because Charles I tried to govern without calling Parliament. The next tax, or "voluntary gift" was levied by Charles II in 1661 (Lay Subsidy, 13 Ch. II, E179 243/6 & E179 243/7.) No Fitzhugh appears in it, suggesting that perhaps it was voluntary after all. (Remember, the Fitzhughs had been Parliamentary supporters.) In the Hearth tax of 1663-4 (Hearth Tax, 15 Ch. II, E 179 243/8) Robert Fitzhugh appears several times, and a John Fitzhugh (whose actual signature as a churchwarden is in the records) appears once, but no Henry. Robert appears in a squabble wherein he was assessed for five hearths, when he claimed he had only four. Four hearths was about right for a reasonably wealthy merchant (*The Story of Bedford*, Godber, *op. cit.*, p. 81). These manuscripts consist of several hundred pages of loose notes written by tax assessors. These were searched reasonably meticulously by the author in 1998, without finding any reference to Henry or his immediate family. Robert appears prominently, which leads to the conclusion that Henry simply dropped out of sight, financially speaking.

Alderman *for the tyme being resydent*[1] within this Towne personallie or by word left at his dwelling howse or other usuall place of abode there, to meet in the Council Chamber...",[lxxix] "such warning to be done by the Mayor's Serjeant..." There were seven Council meetings in the Corporation year 1665-66, the last of which was on September 29, 1666. Robert was fined two shillings for not attending it, but Henry was not mentioned. However, Henry was not listed as an Alderman ten days later at the beginning of the Corporation's new year on September 29, 1666, although Robert was. Thus, if we assume adherence to the Council's attendance rules, then Henry must have died between the nineteenth and twenty-ninth of September, 1666. His widow gained an Administration[lxxx] of his possessions the following November, having filed an Inventory,[2] which is very revealing, probably dated

---

[1] The italics are important. They imply that Henry was only obliged to be at the meetings if he was actually in Bedford. See the argument to follow.

[2] PROB4, 9281, Fitzhugh. This is the original Inventory of Henry's possessions, as filed by Mary to gain Administration of his Estate, and the text is as give below. Much of the ink fell off the parchment as the document was unrolled, and illegible words are each denoted by ( ). "An Inventory of ( ) the goods and chattels of ( ) Henry Fitzhugh late of Bedford Gent. Deceased, valued and appraised by Francis ( ) London Gent., and Richard Varney, London, Girdler the 26? day of October in the Year of Our Lord God 1666. Imprimis: In the Kitchen 25 lb of pewter at 9d per lb. -- 18s 9d. 14 lbs of brass at 5d per lb. -- 5s 10d. five iron spitts, shovells, tongues (i.e. tongs), & jacks at 14s -- 14s. An old looking glass table & other lumber at 3s -- 3s. In the parlour next kitchen 6 old stools a table fire irons shovell & tongs at 10s -- 10s. In the little Room next it a press bed flock bed & bolster coverlid & old table -- 12s. In the Cellar a small Parcell of Coates at 10s -- 10s. In the Chamber over the kitchen an old feather bed bolster blankett rugg curtain vallens six old chairs & stools tongues, fire shovells & tongues & old ( ) hangings with a curtain -- £3 5s. In the Dining Room Six old leather chares T( ) and old carpett and old couch & a par of old broaken har( ) fire irons shovells & Great bellows & old Hangings ( ) -- £2 5s. In the Chamber ( ) ( ) An old feather bed & bolster blankett and Rugg bed ( ) curtins & vallens ( ) & old hangings fire shovells & tongues and old table & carpett & old old hangings to the said room and looking glass -- £3 10s. In the Next Chamber A little old feather bed ( ) and old blankett rugg bed with two chares & a box of ( ) prunelles {*silk or worsted used for uppers of ladies shoes*} fire irons f( ) wood -- £1 4s.

October 26. These dates are at least consistent with the practice that Administrations were granted quickly in those days. However, this line of argument cannot be taken for certain without more evidence. It is also possible that, since we notice that there is no record of any Alderman's death in the Corporation Minutes in the years 1647-67, Aldermen simply may not have been fined for non-attendance if their excuse was that they were dead. If this is the case, we can only narrow Henry's date of death to the period September 29, 1665 to September 29, 1666. In any event, it was not in 1664, as stated in the Pedigree given by William Fitzhugh, the Stationer of London in 1692.[lxxxi]

Probing into the matter further, it is important to point out that before the time of William IV, Aldermen were elected for life, and Henry could have been reappointed automatically even though absent from Bedford. The notes of Aldermen's absences in the Corporation Minutes may in fact be only records of fines collected, and if Henry was in Cork, no fines could have been collected. (See page 22 footnote 1. Henry was not even obliged to be at the meetings if he was not in Bedford.) It seems rather implausible that Henry could have been at a Council meeting in Bedford on September 19, 1666, then travelled over the sea to Cork and died there, and the news to have got back to Bedford all in ten days. Altogether, it seems unlikely that there would have been more than one English Fitzhugh in Cork at the same time, and it is therefore plausible and probable (no more than that) that Henry *was*, in fact, the Clerk of the Powder Store, and that his date of death was between September 29, 1665, the last day his name appears in the Corporation Minutes, and mid-September 1666. The

---

Sum Total £( ). Signed Francis ( ) & Richard Varney 13 November 1666." A Latin statement follows saying that Mary Fitzhugh had sworn this to be a correct Inventory and a further Latin statement saying that it was accepted on the 14th of the Month (probably November). These seven rooms with a cellar and, to judge by the number of fire irons, four to five hearths agrees with the Hearth Tax Assessments (Hearth Tax Return 1671, E179/301, & Hearth Tax 1674, 25 Ch. II, E 179/302.) The sums above add to £13 12s 7d instead of the £17 4s 7d of the Administration. The missing £3 12s could be accounted for by the illegibility of documents or by noting the fact that there is no cash noted in the above. The Richard Varney who signed above may well be Henry's son-in-law.

true date is probably nearer the latter, since, as we have seen, his widow was tidying his affairs in September and October 1666. If this is true, Henry could have gone to Ireland any time after September 5, 1659, the last time he paid a fine for non-attendance at a Council Meeting. The fact that he had no stock-in-trade when he died may give a clue that he went to Cork in other employment not long after his bankruptcy in 1658.

Without doubt, Henry left Mary a poor widow, with young children as well. Some idea of her plight is given by the value of the Inventory submitted by Mary to gain control of Henry's estate, quoted previously. This came to only £17 4s 7d, not a large sum.[1] The Inventory filed with the Administration and its room-by-room description of their house contents shows that they

The Fitzhugh family falls on hard times

had at least replaced some of their furniture lost in the lawsuit of 1657, although they seem to have had a lot of "old" items, a very unusual description for inventories of that time. Their furniture was probably other people's castoffs. Perhaps fortunately, all of the children except William and Henry were grown and out of the house by that time, and perhaps they supported their mother for a while. William emigrated to Virginia seven years later, perhaps partly as a result of his father's troubles. It later fell to him to support his mother in her old age, it being clear that Henry, her son, was not performing this duty. (See the following chapter on William, the Immigrant.)

The fact that Mary went to the trouble and expense of getting the Administration for so small an estate may give a clue to the family situation at the time. There was no compelling reason to obtain the Administration unless she had a need to establish a right to Henry's estate. It may be that the estate was still subject to threat

---

1   *Jacobean Household Inventories*, F.C. Emmison, Beds. Hist. Rec. Soc., Vol. XX, 1938, gives a transcription of a large number of inventories of 1619 and an analysis of their values. From this it seems that £17 4s 7d was certainly not much for the period, being more in keeping with labourers than successful merchants (p.43). The valuation included only movable goods, chattels and credits, and not any fixed item relating to a house or building. In contrast, William Verney, a cleric and schoolmaster, had some £296 15s 6d at his death [PROB 4/2175, December 2, 1663].

from Henry's creditors. After all, so far as we know, the debt of 1657 had never been totally cleared. However, no evidence can be found of an attempt to contest the Administration, as there is no record of any litigation in the diocesan court books of the Consistatory Court of Lincoln,[lxxxii] which was the inferior court of the Prerogative Court of Canterbury. Perhaps Henry's creditors had been satisfied, or given up, or could not be bothered for £17. By law, probably at least one third of the Inventory (not including any land) mentioned in the Administration would have gone to the widow and the rest of the family.

Henry's largest asset was, of course, his messuage.[1] There is no mention of this in any of the Court Actions, and so it seems that Henry's creditors did not get their hands on it. Strong evidence suggests that Mary retained it at least until 1674. The Hearth Tax of that year, as well as for 1671,[lxxxiii] lists "Widow Fitzhugh" living in Mill Lane Ward of St. Paul's parish, as possessing four *Mary at least keeps the family home* Hearths, the same number as his house most likely had, judging by the Inventory description. Robert Fitzhugh is also listed separately in the same Ward in 1671, so there is no confusion with him.[2] The reference is almost certainly to Mary, showing that she still occupied the old Family home. By the Common Law governing inheritance of land of those who died intestate, the messuage should have gone to Henry's oldest son, Henry. On the other hand, there might have been nothing left to inherit. It is possible, although there is no evidence, that Henry could have bought his way out of trouble and settled his debts by selling the reversion of his messuage. That would have meant that he or his widow could occupy it for life and then it would have reverted to the new owner.

---

1   See page 8, footnote 3, Will of William Fitzhugh.

2   Robert Fitzhugh was listed as an Alderman until 1689 in the *Minute Book of the Bedford Corporation, op. cit*. There is a reference in *Boyd's London Burials* to a Robert Fitzhugh who died in 1689 in the Parish of St. Vedast and St Mary Le Querne, the same parish in which Robert's son, William the Stationer, lived. Most likely, they are the same, Robert having died on a visit to his son.

It would have been a clever move on Henry's part, but it would have disinherited son Henry. Another possibility is that Mary could have held onto the messuage by virtue of the terms of her original marriage settlement, as was not unusual in those times. Such requirements were often put into settlements precisely to protect widows from ejection upon their husband's death. However, no such settlement survives in the Bedford County Records. In either case, it could explain why the younger Henry did not live there, and, as will be seen in the next Chapter, possibly why he went to Sea to become a drunken captain. It is very sad that both sons of the Family left Bedford, leaving their mother to fend for herself, probably along with their sister Dorothy. From 1685 onwards, Mary was supported by her son William, who by that time had prospered in Virginia, so it seems likely that she remained in the messuage until her death.

Mary lived long, long after her husband Henry. Later in her life she was in dire hardship, both physical and financial, to judge by the letters[1] from her son William, who had emigrated to Virginia Colony in 1674. Between 1686 and 1698 he went to considerable pains time and again to send her money, and clearly wanted to be sure that she did not lack for continuing support. She could not have lived much beyond 1698, for she would then have been aged eighty-two. William's surviving correspondence ends in 1699, and he himself was to die in 1701. He did, however, make a return trip to England around 1700, but whether he saw his aged mother, or only settled her affairs, we do not know. In any case, Mary knew that her son William had made an illustrious and wealthy position for himself in the New World, something of which his unfortunate father would doubtless have been proud.

Both of the sons leave Bedford forever, but at least Mary is supported by William in Virginia.

---

1   Davis, *op. cit.*, Letters of April 22, 1686, January 30, 1687, June 1, 1688, May 20, 1695, & June 30, 1698. This correspondence is covered in detail in the next chapter.

HENRY FITZHUGH 1614-1666

Had he lived his full entitlement of years, Henry would have known that his downfall had, in an ironic way, profited his family by driving them away from the comfortable confines of Bedford Town to a place where they had a chance to make the fortune that had eluded poor Henry. It is sad that he never knew how successful some of his descendants were to be, far away in the New World.

.oOo.

References

i   North Beds. Borough Co. Recs., *The Black Book*, B1, p.72-3.

ii   *Minute Book of the Bedford Corporation 1647-64*, Beds. Hist. Rec. Soc., Ed. G. Parsloe, Vol.XXVI, 1949, p. 105; Also: Minute Book 1664-88, original manuscript at Bedford Town Hall.

iii   *Bedfordshire Marriage Index*, Bedford Record Office.

iv   *Archdeaconry of Bedford Wills*, 1632-3, ABP/W1633/155.

v   *Pedigree of William Fitzhugh, Citizen & Stationer, 1692*, College of Arms.

vi   David Hume, *History of England*, 1826, Vol. VII, p.300.

vii   *Drapers Company Apprentice List*.

viii   *Pedigree of William Fitzhugh, 1692, op. cit.*

ix   *Ibid.*, and also *The English Reformed Church in Amsterdam in The Seventeenth Century*, Alice Clare Carter, Publication of the Municipal Archives of Amsterdam, No. 3, Schlema & Holkema NV, Amsterdam, 1964.

x   Registers of St Paul's, Bedford.

xi   Drapers Company Apprentice List.

xii   O'Hleiana, in *Collectanea Topographica et Geneal.*, Vol VII; also *The Army Lists of the Roundheads and Cavaliers*; also D.N.B. Philip Wharton.

xiii   *Minute Book of the Bedford Corporation, op. cit.*, p. 17.

xiv   *Pedigree of William Fitzhugh, 1692, op. cit.*

xv   *Archdeaconry of Bedford Wills*, 1640-41, No. 118.

xvi   Haberdashers Company, Binding 1664, p. 68.

xvii   Registers of St. Paul's, Bedford.

xviii   *Ibid.*

xix   *Pedigree of William Fitzhugh, 1692, op. cit.*

xx   Registers of St. Paul's, Bedford.

xxi   *Ibid.*

xxii   *Ibid.*

xxiii   *Ibid.*

xxiv   *Ibid.*

xxv   Registers of St. Peter Martin, Bedford.

xxvi   Registers of St. Paul's, Bedford.

xxvii   *Ibid.*

xxviii   *Pedigree of William Fitzhugh, 1692, op. cit.*

xxix   Registers of St Paul's, Bedford.

xxx   *Archdeaconry of Bedford Wills*, 1632-3, ABP/W1633/155.

xxxi   *Pedigree of William Fitzhugh, 1692, op. cit.*

xxxii   Registers of Tempsford, Bedfordshire.

xxxiii   *The Life & Letters of Sir William Dyve*, H.G. Tibbutt, Beds. Hist. Rec. Soc.

xxxiv   *The Parliamentary Scout*, E71, 25. Public Record Office.

xxxv   *John Bunyan, His Life, Times and Work,* by John Brown, B.A., D.D.,
          The Tercenteniary Edition, The Hulbert Publishing Company, London,
          1928, p.42, quoting reference to *Historical Collections,* VI., 61.
xxxvi   *A Perfect Diurnall,* E252, 3 & E252, 4, Public Record Office.
xxxvii   Joyce Godber, *The Story of Bedford,* White Crescent Press, Luton,
          1978, p. 67.
xxxviii   *The Weekly Account,* E72, 7. Public Record Office.
xxxix   *A Perfect Diurnall, op. cit.*
xl   *Walker Revised, Being a Revision of John Walker's Sufferings of the
          Clergy During the Great Rebellion 1642-1660,* A. G. Matthews, 1948,
          p.65.
xli   Coll. of the House of Lords MSS in Royal Commission of Hist. MSS
          Reports, No. 7, p.3; also *Journal of the House of Lords,* Vol. 9, pp. 491
          & 657.
xlii   *Alumni Cantab.,* p.177, Giles King.
xliii   *Minute Book of the Bedford Corporation, op. cit.* p.17.
xliv   *Ibid.*
xlv   Apprentice Records, C1/1, N. Beds. Bor. Co. Records., Town Hall,
          Bedford.
xlvi   Godber, *op. cit.,* p.69.
xlvii   Godber, *op. cit.,* p.68.
xlviii   *Adjudication in Reference to Certain Persons Named by the Leet and
          other Persons as to the Office of Chamberlain,* August 20, 24 Car. I,
          1648, BorB6/7,Bed. Co. Recs., Town Hall, Bedford.
xlix   Beds. Co. Recs. BorBE2/70, 1487. See Note 16 on the Family Tree.
l   N. Beds. Borough Council Recs., A4/6, Old Town Hall, Bedford.
li   *Sessions of the Peace, Record of the Court Leet & Sessions,* 1649-51,
          F11/4B, N. Beds. Bor. Co. Recs. Bedford Town Hall.
lii   Archdeaconry of Bedford Wills, 1626-7, ABP/W1626-7/101.
liii   *Ibid.,* 1632-3, ABP/W1633/155.
liv   Hearth Tax Return 1671, E179/301; also Hearth Tax Return 1674, 25
          Ch. II, E179/302. Public Record Office.
lv   Chancery Recognizances, C54/3770/41, Fitzhugh and Penniston, PRO.
lvi   *Encyclopedia of London,* Ed. William Kent, London, 1937, p.649.
lvii   Godber, *op. cit.,* p. 63-5, 70.
lviii   *Minute Book of The Bedford Corporation, op. cit.,* p.73.
lix   *Journal of the House of Commons,* Vol. 8, p.447.
lx   British Library 190.g.12.(223).
lxi   Dictionary of National Biography.
lxii   *John Bunyan, His Life, Times and Work,* by John Brown, B.A., D.D.,
          The Tercenteniary Edition, The Hulbert Publishing Company, London,
          1928, pp. 101-103.
lxiii   Bedford Historical Record Society, Vol. 35, pp. 86-89, and *Thurloe's
          State Papers,* Vol. VI, pp. 238-240.
lxiv   *Thurloe's State Papers,* Vol. IV, p. 632.

lxv   Bedford Historical Record Society, Vol. 59, p.17.
lxvi   J.H. Blundell, *Bedfordshire Seventeenth Century Trade Tokens*, New Edition, published privately, 1928; Williamson, *Trade Tokens of the 17th Century,* 1967 issue of 1889, Vol 1, Bedfordshire, BL Shelfmark W43/0582.
lxvii   *Minute Book of the Bedford Corporation, op. cit.*
lxviii   N. Beds. Bor. Co. Recs., B1, *The Black Book*, p. 37.
lxix   *Ibid.*, p. 40.
lxx   *Ibid.*, p. 76.
lxxi   *Ibid.*, p. 42.
lxxii   Court of Pleas Rolls, 1656-7, BorBF9/9, Beds. Co. Recs.
lxxiii   Record Book of the Bedford Court of Pleas, Feb. 26, 1657/8.
lxxiv   *Council Book of the Corporation of Kinsale 1652-1800*, Richard Caulfield, Editor, 1879, p.xlvii. BL Shelfmark 10390.f.22.
lxxv   Private communications from Michael Mulcahy, May 20 & 27, 2002; also: *Elizabeth Fort, Cork*, Michael Mulcahy, *The Irish Sword,* Vol. IV, No. 15, pp.127-134, Winter, 1959; *A Cork City Grant of 1666*, Michael Mulcahy, J. Cork Hist. and Arch. Soc., Vol. LXIX, 1964.
lxxvi   *Minute Book of the Bedford Corporation, op. cit.*
lxxvii   Hume, *History of England, op. cit.*, p. 299.
lxxviii *Minute Book of the Bedford Corporation 1647-64, op. cit.*, p. 100.
lxxix   *Minute Book of the Bedford Corporation, op. cit.*, p. 19, 45-6.
lxxx   PCC Admon Nov. 1666, Henry Fitzhugh, Public Record Office.
lxxxi   *Pedigree of William Fitzhugh, 1692, op. cit.*
lxxxii   Private communication from the Archivist, Lincoln Cathedral, concerning court books Cj 34-5, for years 1665-7, January 13, 1983.
lxxxiii Hearth Tax 1671 & 1674, *op. cit.*

WILLIAM FITZHUGH, THE IMMIGRANT 1651-1701

WILLIAM FITZHUGH,
THE IMMIGRANT

1651-1701

FOREWORD
*So much has been written about William Fitzhugh that it
is difficult to write about him again without merely repeating what
has been said elsewhere. The following draws freely on all the
known texts which refer to William, in order to fill in the theme of
this family history. Some important new discoveries and insights
made by the author are revealed. The reader is referred for more
detail to some of the more lengthy volumes included in the
references in the footnotes and endnotes.*

IN A LAND ONLY PARTIALLY SETTLED some fifty years
earlier, William Fitzhugh[1] chose to make his home far from the
civilised comforts of England. Although he was never to know
what a great country he was to play a part in founding, it is clear, as
will be seen presently, that he had a large hand in shaping the
Colonial society and the political complexion of the Virginia
Colony where he chose to settle. His life story is in many ways
remarkable, one which probably could never have occurred at any
other time in history, and one which required a man of great
character and ability to live out.

---

1   Opposite is a photograph of a copy painted by John Heselius in 1751
of a portrait painted by his father Gustavus Heselius. Inscribed on
back: "Col. William Fitzhugh / son of Henry Fitzhugh Aetatis 46 /
Cop by John Hesselius 1751". [R.K. Doud, *The Fitzhugh Portraits
by John Hesselius,* The Virginia Magazine of History and Biography,
Vol. 75, April, 1967, No.2] The background is a light brown, the
wig black, and the necktie is white. The cloak is a wonderful shade of
blue. (Private communication from Henry Fitzhugh of Washington
D.C. to Rev. V.C.A. FitzHugh, December 2, 1931.) The portrait was
owned by Mrs. Robert H. Stevenson of 76 Beacon Street, Boston,
Massachusetts, in 1963. It was conserved in 1995 and shown with
four other Fitzhugh portraits in an exhibition "The First Fitzhughs of
Virginia" by the Virginia Historical Society. See *American Art
Review,* Vol. IX, No.2, 1997, pp.80-85.

William Fitzhugh was baptised on January 10, 1651,[i] the son[1] of Henry Fitzhugh of Bedford, a Woolen-Draper who was Mayor of Bedford in 1649 and whose vicissitudes were described in the previous pages. William was, as was normal in those times, one of a large family. He was one of three sons, with five older sisters. His brother Henry was a year older, baptised on April 28, 1650 at St. Paul's Church, Bedford.[ii] His other brother Thomas, whose birth date is not known, died as an apprentice in London. It is possible that he was the youngest, and this might explain why he was sent away to an apprenticeship. Henry was said to be a Captain in the Navy[2] and also a "rake and a sot", and married on March 25, 1683 Elizabeth Longe[iii] of Pall Mall, London. Probably, he later married Lettice Hancock on April 25, 1695.[iv] Of the sisters, Anne was baptised on September 8, 1639[v] and died unmarried. Margaret was baptised on November 12, 1640,[vi] emigrated to the New World, married in Maryland and died in Virginia in 1676, having left a daughter.[vii] Susan, baptised on October 27, 1642,[viii] married Richard Varney on June 21, 1659 at St. Albans Abbey.[ix] Elizabeth was born on January 12, 1645 and died on June 12, 1646.[x] Dorothy was baptised on January 24, 1645,[xi] emigrated to Virginia about 1686, married Dr. Ralph Smith, who died in 1688-9, and married again to George Luke, said to be a "neer-do-well."

There is no clear evidence of William's education, although he was probably educated at the Free Grammar School in Bedford, which had been founded in 1561.[xii] If so, he may have had a difficult time of it, for the Headmaster was William Verney, the man who had bankrupted William's father Henry.[3] In any event, it

---

1   Since the first edition of this work, some have expressed doubt that William in Virginia was actually the same person as the William of the Fitzhugh family in Bedford, England. It is clear from the correspondence mentioned later in this chapter between William and various family members in Bedford that they were all of the same family. A summary of the relationships confirmed by that correspondence is given in the Note 70 in the Notes on the Family Tree.

2   This is stated in *William Fitzhugh and His Chesapeake World*, by Richard Beale Davis, University of North Carolina Press, 1963, p. 172 *et seq.*, but there is no record of this in *Commissioned Officers in the Royal Navy 1660-1819*.

3   See footnote 1 on page 9 for an account of Verney and his mismanagement of the School. The School was next to the Town Prison, wherein William may well have seen John Bunyan, who was imprisoned there in 1661.

is clear that he had some scholastic ability, for by the age of twenty-five he was a practising lawyer in Virginia and a member of the Colonial Parliament.[xiii]

The New World was a great lure to the Romantic Heart of the English of that day; their first conquest of the World was just beginning. We do not know William's precise motives for setting out across the Seas, but at a minimum it probably had to do with what he would clearly have seen as far greater opportunity than he could hope for at home. Also, he could never hope to rise far in the social structure of England; as a younger son he could not hope to inherit the family fortunes even if the family had had anything left after his father's bankruptcy. Although his family once had high standing as merchants and gentry, he could not hope to marry into the landed gentry, and even less to acquire wealth to buy himself into that class. William was aged seven when his father was bankrupted and the family impoverished, and he may well have been driven by memories of poverty and disgrace that compelled him to make good, perhaps even to expiate his father's mistakes.

William left Bedford for Virginia sometime between 1670 and 1673. Previous biographers have always believed that he immigrated to Virginia in 1670 or 1671, either with his sister Margaret or at her behest, since she may have already been there.[xiv] We know little of her, but clearly William's luck was better than hers, for, in 1687, two years after her death, in a letter to his Uncle Robert, he said that she *"lived but poorly."* It is also said that William came to Virginia with his friend John Newton, with whom he opened up or "patented" large tracts of land in the Upper Northern Neck. This is possibly the same John Newton who was a member of the Common Council of Bedford in 1648, three years before William was born.[xv] One of Newton's sons came over with him, and Newton himself had been a Master Mariner.[xvi]

It is just possible that William emigrated as late as mid-1673 because he sold on December 10, 1673[1] a property described as *"one messuage, one dovecote, one garden, one orchard, with appurtenances in the Town of Bedford."* This is clearly the same property as previously mentioned that his father had acquired on December 19, 1655,[xvii] and it seems obvious that William had come into it by some transfer from his father, although it was not

---

1   N. Beds. Bor. Co. Recs., *The Black Book*, B1, p. 76. William received £10 for the transaction and the property went to Simon Becket, Gent.

mentioned in the Inventory on Henry's death.[1] However, the most startling feature of this transaction is that William **and his wife Elizabeth** sold it together.[2] Less that six months later, on the other side of the Atlantic William married on May 1, 1674 a second wife, Sarah Tucker. Perhaps Elizabeth died on the crossing; many others did.[3] The existence of William's first wife has never come to light before,

William's first wife, and his second wife

---

[1] It seems that William may well have left for the New World before December (leaving the property sale to be completed after his departure), because he was active as a lawyer in Virginia in early 1674, when his future mother-in-law gave him power of attorney on February 25, 1674. (Davis, *op. cit.*, p.10; The footnote therein is incorrect, referring to the wrong publication.)

[2] It is a pity that this is not the Elizabeth Franklin who married a William Fitzhugh in Ravensden in 1670 (Ravensden Parish Registers, Jan.. 20, 1669/70). That William Fitzhugh was a son or grandson of Nicholas, brother of John who married Amy Negus (Archdeacon of Bedford's Council Book, Vol 5, pp. 133-151, 3 June-6 Nov. 1676).

[3] There is a record in the IGI of a marriage on August 24, 1671 in Gloucester County, Virginia of one Elizabeth Fitzhugh to a William Thornton. She is said to have been born about 1650 in the same County. Her parents are given as John Fitzhugh, born about 1624, and – Fitzhugh, born about 1625, both of Gloucester County. [This record was submitted by an LDS Church Member on November 20, 1957 (film 457242).] According to all that is known of *any* Fitzhugh family, there was no Fitzhugh in Virginia in 1650. Leaving aside a period of two years between 1671 and William's and Elizabeth's property sale in 1673, when the property could have been on the market, allows the author to postulate that this Elizabeth was the estranged or abandoned wife of William the Immigrant. If so, she would have needed marriage for survival, which she could have easily achieved owing to a shortage of women, while concealed her origins. There is a report (private communication from R. M. Coleman, July 26, 2002) that she was married twice, and if so, her marriage to Thornton would probably have been the second, since she had fifteen children by him. The fact that she had so many children in a probable second marriage, and William had eight children in a definitely second marriage may reveal something of their relationship in a childless first marriage. Elizabeth had to vanish somewhere, and it could not have been in England, because the rest of the family would have been surprised when William surfaced twelve years later with a second wife, Sarah. This hypothesis obviously contains speculation and deduction, but if it is not so, then this Elizabeth is yet a further enigma.

and William never made any reference either to his first wife, or his second wife by name, in any surviving correspondence.[1] Perhaps this development in William's life explains why there was a twelve year gap before William contacted any of his family back in England.

John Newton and William proceeded to marry a mother and daughter. Newton married the widow Rose Tucker Gerard, whose daughter, Sarah Tucker, William himself married. Sarah's father John Tucker had been a wealthy planter of Westmorland County, Virginia, although he had originally come by way of Bermuda, according to *Burkes,* and was probably the son of William Tucker of Heronly, Devon. William married Sarah on May 1, 1674[xviii] and received property in recognition of the marriage contract on August 26, 1674.[xix] Sarah, and therefore presumably William, also received 5000 pounds of Tobacco, left to Sarah in her fathers will in 1671,[2] payable on the date of her marriage. This must have been a substantial financial boost to the aspiring lawyer and planter. It was perhaps this property which formed William's initial capital from which his later fortunes grew. Sarah was born on August 2, 1663[xx] and thus was only aged eleven at the time of her marriage. A well established family tradition says that he sent her to England for two years education before the marriage was consummated. But if so, it is hard to understand why she made no contact with any of the many Fitzhugh relations living in England. So, by the age of twenty-three William had been married twice, crossed the Atlantic, and had a substantial property holding in the New World.

In the 17th Century Virginia was a death trap, largely made so by its climate. Robert Beverley, whom William defended for near treason (see p. 45), wrote in 1705 in *The History and Present State of Virginia* of "dampness", and "annoyances" [vermin and thunder]. Newcomers underwent "seasoning", a period of illness, in its mildest form, consisted of "two or three fits of a feaver and ague." Malaria was rife, and often led to dysentery.[xxi]

---

1   There is a firmly embedded family tradition that William sent Sarah to England, and even to stay with his family, to receive an education, but this seems very unlikely in view of her anonymity in all the correspondence.

2   Will of John Tucker, Westmoreland County, Virginia, 1671, *Westmoreland County Deeds and Wills Book,* No. 1, p.386. This part of William's gain on marriage to Sarah was incorrectly stated by Davis, *op. cit.,* p. 11, footnote 10.

It seems clear that William's enterprise was aimed in several directions which included growing tobacco on his property, and at an active legal practice. Perhaps as a sideline, he also traded with ships captains who left goods with him for disposal.[xxii] It is clear that he had a flair for all of it; his estates multiplied, and he had quite an impact in the legal circles of the Colony, defending several famous lawsuits of the time. He apparently took a scholarly approach to his profession, being fluent in both French and Latin. These joint careers saw him into the Virginia House of Burgesses by the age of twenty-five,[1] and eventually he even became a Lieutenant Colonel in the Virginia Militia. By 1681 he was in a secure enough commercial position to land a contract to provision the Potomac Garrison.[xxiii]

William's rise to wealth is well documented in all his letters, now copied in the Library of Congress, and also fully edited and published in R.B. Davis, as footnoted earlier. He built two estates: Eagles Nest, where he lived,[2] and which survives as an

---

1   Although he was not always successful in elections. Wright, *op. cit.*, p.172, relates that " One of the charges made by Scarlet [who won an election against William in about 1688] ... was that there was no law or justice in Stafford County except what Fitzhugh said was so. [William had been presiding Magistrate since 1686.] The truth was that Fitzhugh possessed the greatest store of legal erudition in Virginia, and his technical knowledge had given him a great advantage over planters less well equipped." William was also a known Tory devoted to the Stuart cause, p.171.

2   In a letter to Dr. Ralph Smith, his brother-in-law, of April 26, 1686 (Davis, *op. cit.*),William sought to exchange his estates in Virginia for property in England. He gave the following description of Eagles Nest, which shows what he had amassed in only twelve years: *"As first the plantation where I now live contains a thousand Acres, at least 700 Acres of it being rich thicket, the remainder good hearty plantable land, without any waste either by Marshes or great Swamps the commodiousness, conveniency, & pleasantness your self well knows, upon it there is three Quarters well furnished, with all necessary houses, ground & fencing, together with a choice crew of Negroes at each plantation, most of them in this Country born, the remainder as likely as most in Virginia, there being twenty-nine in all, with stocks of cattle & hogs at each Quarter, upon the same land as my own dwelling house, furnished with all accommodations for a comfortable & gentile (sic) living, as a very good dwelling house, with 13 rooms in it, four of the best of them hung, nine of them plentifully furnished with all things necessary and convenient & all houses for use well furnished with brick Chimneys, four good*

estate today, and Bedford, a short distance along the river.[xxiv] Eagles Nest is now open to visitors, along with its family graveyard.[xxv] (See map in appendix 4.)

It is not to be thought that William was nothing but a workhorse, with his nose always to the grindstone. His social life is tantalisingly glimpsed from many sources. He was lavish in his entertainment of visitors, to the point even of employing jesters, fiddlers, acrobats, tight-rope walkers, etc.[1] on at least one occasion at Christmas, 1686.[xxvi] This hospitality was not forgotten in Virginia, even being remembered in an editorial in the Richmond (Virginia) *Times-Despatch* of Christmas Day, 1946.[xxvii] Perhaps he wanted to show off the various tapestry hangings he had ordered in

---

Cellars, a Dairy, Dovecote, Stable, Barn, Hen house, Kitchen & all other conveniencys, & all in a manner new, a large Orchard of about 2500 Apple trees most grafted, well fenced with a Locust fence, which is as durable as most brick walls, a Garden a hundred foot square, well pailed in, a Yeard wherein is most of the aforesaid necessary houses, pallizado'd in with locust Punchens, which is as good as if it were walled in & more lasting that any of our bricks, together with a good Stock of Cattle hogs horses, Mares, sheep &c, & necessary servants belonging to it, for the supply and support thereof. About a mile & half distant a good water Grist miln, whose tole I find sufficient to find my own family with wheat & Indian corn for our necessitys & occasions. Up the River in this Country three tracts of land more, one of them (Ravensworth) *contains 21996 Acres another 500 acres, & one other 1000 Acres, all good convenient Seats, & wch. in a few years will yield a considerable annual Income. A Stock of Tobo. with all the crops & good debts lying out of about 250000 lb. besides sufficient of almost all sorts of goods, to supply the familys & the Quarter's occasions for two if not three years....the yearly Crops of corn & Tobo. together with the surplusage of meat more than will serve the family's use will amount annually to 60000 lb. Tobo. wch. at 10 shillings per Ct. is 300£ annum, & the Negroes increase being all young, & a considerably parcel of breeders will keep that Stock good forever. the Stock of Tobo. managed with an inland trade, will yearly yield 60000 lb. Tobo. without hazard or risque... The Orchard in a very few years will yield a large supply to plentifull house keeping, or if better husbanded, yield at least 15000 lb. Tobo. annual income."* Clearly William had been industrious and fortunate in his early years in Virginia.

1   For a full account of this carousing, see *The First Gentlemen of Virginia*, Louis B. Wright, *op. cit.*, p.164, and *A Huguenot Exile in Virginia*, Ed. Gilbert Chennard, 1934, p.158-9.

1683, which included a full hanging of a room 20 feet long, 16 feet wide, and 9 feet high.[xxviii] Also, there is a charming story[xxix] about how William wrestled with his conscience and his accounts to convince himself that he could afford £6 or £7 for a calash, a type of light carriage. He hankered after it from 1688 to 1693 when he finally got it, certainly to his great enjoyment for the remaining eight years of his life.

As his prosperity grew, William began to resemble, at least in relative wealth, the manorial class of England. Perhaps he aspired to emulate them, or perhaps it was simply good estate husbandry, but in any case he clearly set out to convert his vast unpopulated estates, now amounting to some 50,000 acres, to tenancies, inhabited by tenants of his choosing. It was only natural that he should aim for this; it was the pattern of land ownership and management in England, and it was a paying proposition. So between 1680 and 1690 he tried to develop a 21,000 acre tract in Stafford County, Virginia with Huguenot tenants, who were at this time fleeing the persecutions of Protestants in France.[xxx] In a single year, 1687, the Huguenot Relief Committee in London sent 600 to Virginia, some of whom settled on William's lands on the Occoquan Creek.[xxxi] William was exceptionally kind to these refugees, by several accounts, but he persuaded fewer than he had hoped, and his dream was largely unrealised. The proposed estate was probably wild in any case, as in 1687 William had to lead a punitive raid against the Seneca Indians.[xxxii]

Nevertheless, by this time William could certainly look back on his achievements with pride and describe himself as "landed gentry" on the English model. Not only did he have a few tenants, but he had some indentured servants (including a cousin, not uncommon at the time), and some slaves. William had probably paid his servants' passage to the Colony in return for their indenture. In 1685, William was able to write with obvious satisfaction to his first cousin William Fitzhugh, a Member of the Stationers Company of Newgate Market, London: *"I have for a long time in a strange land struggled hard with Fortune's adverse hand, but, thank God, in the end, by God Almighty's blessing upon my mean endeavours (having no friend or relative to lend a supporting hand) have overcome, and I praise God, lived very contentedly and well."*[xxxiii] In the same letter, he asked for news of all his friends there, which shows that he had not forgotten the Old Country.

WILLIAM FITZHUGH 1651-1701

This letter to his cousin was the beginning of a long correspondence between William and his family, with whom he had had no contact at all up to then. We do not know why William fell completely out of touch in the years 1671-85. It was certainly true that communications were difficult, sometimes requiring a year for a reply from England. This correspondence began after a chance meeting with a traveller in 1685, who put our William in touch with his cousin William. Through him, contact was made with our William's brother Henry, and then with their mother. The letter between the two Williams of May 18, 1685 was conveyed via a merchant in Virginia Walk, London named John Cooper and shows that they knew each other, but that our William did not know where any of his relations in England were. A letter of April 26, 1686, from William to his brother Henry in London shows that by this time William had heard from his sister Dorothy, Cousin William, and Cooper, but not from Henry. It is a pity that none of these replies survives, but the letter from Dorothy also conveyed news of their mother. William seems to be solicitously begging for a resumption of contact with Henry. One cannot help but wonder if some family rift had kept them apart. Certainly there would have been many strains in the years 1666-73, following their father's death and before William had emigrated. Henry did not even know that William was now married to Sarah and had two children living. Having heard from his sister of his mother's distress, William gave all his money in England (trade account credits, it must be supposed) to Henry for their mother's benefit. In the same letter, he invited his sister Dorothy, who was forty-one and unmarried, to come to Virginia to *"better her Self"* and offered a maid and clothing for the voyage, as well as life-long support. This must mean that Dorothy was not engaged in looking after their mother. In a letter to his mother of the same date, William tells of his marriage (twelve years earlier), but does not name his wife or children!

Contact is finally re-established with William's family

In a letter shortly after dated May 6, 1686 to Henry, William gave £20 to cover his mother's support and Dorothy's voyage, or if she would not come, to support her in England. William would have liked to have given more, but said he could not afford it. In a letter of the same date to Dorothy, he repeated the request that she should come to Virginia.

William's hospitality seemed to be boundless. In the next letter to Henry of January 30, 1686/7, addressed to Pall Mall, London, William invited Henry to come to visit him in Virginia and acknowledges a present from him and his Lady (not named), showing that Henry was married. William refers to Henry's interest and friends being great at Court, and refers to the possibility of Henry becoming a Commander of one of the King's ships. It was in this letter that a disagreement surfaced between William and Henry as to the family's correct Coat of Arms.

A dispute erupts; William has used the wrong Coat of Arms

Henry's wife had sent William a seal stamp, which caused William to reply *"I heartily thank you for ... your Lady's real presents ... & that Steel Seal to myself, had she writ it had been our Coat of Arms, I should have allowed the mistake not esteeming her conversant in Heraldry, or skilfull in Coats of Arms, & for your writing it to be so I must interpret it either to Credulity or mistake ..."* William must have been furious to have been so insulting. Unfortunately, the mistake was certainly William's, for he had been using the wrong Arms - those of the Barons FitzHugh of Ravensworth - (see Davis[xxxiv] and Appendix 1) even though their father Henry had been using the family's correct Arms in 1648 (see previous pages, photograph on page 6, and also Appendix 1). Presumably brother Henry was using the correct Arms; where William got the notion that the family bore the Arms of the Barons FitzHugh is beyond any explanation,[1] and it has certainly has confused a great many family members ever since.

One possible interpretation of the confusion over Arms is that, because William may have been as young as six when his father left for Ireland, there may have been little communication between father and son. William may have known next to nothing about his own family history, and simply picked up the wrong tale later on in Virginia, as many others have done subsequently. Brother Henry, on the other hand, may have had a more accurate picture by having stayed in England. William would have

---

[1] William was, however, not quite the only one in the family using the wrong Arms. His fourth cousin, Thomas Fitzhugh of Walcot, Oxfordshire, descended from Richard Fitzhugh, eldest son of Thomas Fitzhugh and Christine Maidbury, was also carrying the Arms of the Barons FitzHugh (Harley MS 1556, Folio 176, referred to in Harleian Society *Visitation of Oxon. 1574*, Richard Lee, Portcullis Marshall, also per A. Cundy 1634). The Walcot line became extinct in that generation, but it is just conceivable, though unlikely and impossible to understand, that William was following their example. (See *FitzHugh, The Story of a Family Through Six Centuries,* TVH FitzHugh, Supplement Three.)

undoubtedly been annoyed, since he had gone to the trouble and expense of having a large silver sugar bowl and salt cellars engraved with the incorrect Arms, and, in the former, with his marriage date.[xxxv]

William's next family letter to his mother of January 30, 1686/7 is a reply to one brought out by Dorothy, showing that she had come straight away, with an indentured servant, who was sold later on. The news of their mother had been bad, for the letter refers to Mary's afflictions, but again no details. Dorothy was to marry Dr. Ralph Smith, a Bristol and Virginia merchant, on March 5, 1686/7, not long after her arrival. Dorothy must have had some sour words about Henry, because William says *"I am sorry to hear so ill a Character of so dear a Brother & withal to find my expectations so soon disappointed ... in his assisting you in your low & calamitous condition."* So Henry had let their mother down. William sent another £10. William wrote several other family letters to other relations on January 30, 1686/7. William the London Stationer was consoled for the deaths of two of his children. Aunt Margaret Porter got a respectful bread and butter letter, and Uncle Robert, living at the Greenhouse in Bedford, got a friendly letter, which referred to Robert's condition as *"not wealthy, (but) contented."* In a letter to Nicholas Hayward of the same date, William refers to his brother's drinking, saying that if he carries on so, he *"cannot long continue."* The next letter to Henry was two months later on April 5, 1687, and shows that William clearly believed that Henry was now a Commander of one of the King's Ships. William offered Henry the benefit of his experience if he wanted to come to Virginia, and William even suggested, in the strictest of confidence, that the post of Deputy Auditor of the Colony would soon be vacant and might suit Henry. One cannot help but wonder if this was not carrying family loyalty a bit far! On the other hand, it was probably a characteristically generous effort at rehabilitation. At the same time another letter was despatched to mother with a promise of another £10, as soon as Tobacco prices improved.

Correspondence lapsed for about a year until May 10, 1688, when William wrote to the merchant John Cooper with instructions to give his mother £5 is she were still alive. (Perhaps tobacco prices were still low.) The £5 was to be paid to Mary Fitzhugh in person. (Perhaps William did not exactly trust Henry as before?) In letters to his mother and brother of June 1, 1688, he said Cooper was to give her £10, and begged Henry to write. In a letter to Nicholas Hayward of the same date, William acknowledged news of Henry's health, saying that *"large glassing"* (drinking?) did not take up so much of his time now.

A very long gap ensued next. William wrote to his mother on May 20, 1695, saying that he had not had a letter for two years, although Dorothy apparently had, even though she had died on October 1, 1694. William was very ill and near death at the time, but we can only guess that the cause might have been malaria. Mother was in a *"Calamity"* and William wished he were nearer to help. He referred to George Luke, Dorothy's second husband, as a *"Foolish little Knave."* Dorothy seemed to have had bad luck in husbands; her first husband Dr. Ralph Smith had been a Whig and possibly a Dissenter, and in a letter to Hayward of May 30, 1695, William referred to her second husband Luke[1] as so great a fool that Hayward was advised to get his money out of him. Dorothy had also asked Luke on her deathbed to send money to her mother, and all of Dorothy's clothes too, but Luke had not. William promised his mother £6 per annum, forever. Apparently Mary had sent William a box, but its contents were spoiled.

Three more years were to elapse before William's next letter to his mother on June 30, 1698. She had sent him a Bible for which he sent thanks, along with condolences for her sickness and indisposition. William said he was going to double her money. This is the last letter of the family correspondence. What happened to all the rest of the family members, we do not know. Taken as a whole, these letters make sad reading. Out of all the family dealings, the only person to emerge with his judgement, humanity, and condition preserved is William.

It is quite clear from William's actions that he was homesick for England. Perhaps this explains why he named his second estate "Bedford", and probably the reason why Chotank Parish, where William lived, was by 1702 called St. Paul's, after William's home Parish in Bedford, England.[xxxvi] The pull of the civilised Old Country was so strong that he was on the verge of sending his son William, who was then aged only four, to school in England, but relented when he found a Huguenot Minister as a tutor in Virginia. Such was William's longing to return to England that he wrote Ralph Smith, his brother-in-law, that he wanted to trade his estates (then around 23,000 acres) for an estate in England

---

1   George Luke was also the Collector of Customs for the Lower District of the James River in 1702, *Virginia Gleanings in England*, British Library Shelf Mark X.809 66959, p. 485, Will of Nicholas Luke.

worth £300 to £400 per annum.[xxxvii] A year later he was willing to settle for one *"even in Scotland or Ireland."*[xxxviii]

In spite of his longing to return to England, William never flagged in his endeavours to develop his estates and his interests. At one time he thought he had found gold,[xxxix] and all the while he was writing what was apparently the first definitive volume on Virginia Law. He tried to get this published in England as "copy got by accident", (belatedly expressing the Elizabethan Gentleman's reluctance to have his name appear in print).[xl] William's career as a lawyer is well described in his various biographies. Where he trained is completely unknown, although it would seem most plausible that he trained as an attorney's clerk in a law office, rather than having a formal education at an Inn of Court, which his family doubtless could not afford. He apparently made his reputation as a trial lawyer in the case of the defence of Robert Beverley.[xli] Beverley was probably guilty of insurrection bordering on treason, but William got him off with the accused only having to beg forgiveness on bended knee. It was probably his abilities as a lawyer, and even more as a legal scholar, that explain his rapid rise in the House of Burgesses. Also at this time he campaigned heavily for the establishment of the College of William and Mary,[xlii] now the oldest University in North America.

These wishes to move back to England must have subsided eventually, because although William finally did make a trip back in 1700 or 1701,[xliii] there is no evidence that he sought an estate to buy. Clearly by now his roots were firmly in the New World. Like so many immigrants, and indeed their descendants too, William had felt a strong pull back toward the land that had been his and his ancestors. But clearly, after much heart searching, he accepted the exchange of his new worlds for old.

William was, by the end of his life, moving in a society, and at a social level, that closely resembled the upper strata of the hierarchy that prevailed in England. He could never have reached this status had he remained there. His name, through the marriages of his children and grandchildren, became linked to every family of any consequence in the Southern Colonies - Washington, Lee, Aylett, Bullett, McCarthy, Beverley, etc. A portrait of him on page 32 at about this time shows a man who is clearly prosperous, self-confident, and proud of his achievements.

His is the story of the making of a leader, and of the founding of a family, but it is also the story of the development of an economic system. This system, partly based on slavery, and partly on the landed gentry concept of retained tenants on land owned by the Squire, was eventually to come into conflict, two centuries later, with a rather different industrial society and economy being simultaneously developed in the Northern Colonies from Baltimore to Boston. His descendants were to play a large part in the struggle that was to ensue, the American Civil War.

William died of "a bloody flux" on October 21, 1701, contracted from one of the Huguenot refugees that he had befriended, and who he probably had hoped would become a tenant on one of his estates. In his Will, he had asked that his funeral be *"without noise, feasting, drink or Tumult."*[xliv] He is buried, alongside his wife Sarah, at Eagles Nest among a vast number of direct descendants, the last of whom was buried there in 1963.[xlv]

William had accumulated by the time of his death no less than 54,000[1] acres in various estates, but, alas, the original house at Eagles Nest burned down in 1793 during a Poker party held by his great-grandson.[xlvi] An interesting insight is provided into their way of life, for, even with his great wealth, the entire amount of cash bequeathed in William's Will was *"one guinea and one mill shilling".*[xlvii] Obviously they lived entirely by trade and barter. The younger sons, including our ancestor John, were well provided for in land, horses, cattle, household furnishings and silver plate. John, being the youngest son, was last in the pecking order of the Will,

---

[1]   Most historians have written about William Fitzhugh in more or less hagiographic terms, such as those quoted in the following. They saw the accumulation of such vast estates as a triumph of enterprise, initiative, and skill. However, in modern times, a different analysis has been put forward [*Foul Means, The Formation of a Slave Society in Virginia 1660-1740*, Anthony S. Parent, Jr., Omohundro Institute of Early American History and Culture, University of North Carolina Press, Chapel Hill and London, 2003] stating that William Fitzhugh and others of "the great planters" engaged in a "very great cheat" or a "land grab" using office-holding, malfeasance, bribery, and the importation of slaves. The last of these is blamed the laying the foundations of a mass slave society in the American Colonies. In my [HAF] opinion, this book is not only polemic to the point where its objectivity is doubtful, but somewhat Marxist in that it divides the colonists of the era into classes such as "great planters", "small planters", and others, and concentrates on actions as though they were carried out collectively by the classes rather than by individuals. But more importantly, it commits the error of judging the actions of the distant past by our own present standards; everything William Fitzhugh did was entirely within the standards and ethics of his time and place, and was not even questioned by any of his contemporaries.

but he was left a number of small tracts totalling 2175 acres, seven negroes, all named in the Will, five pieces of silver, six spoons, and £50 Sterling.[xlviii]

The Ravensworth Estate,[1] covering 22,000 acres on the Occoquan River, one and a half miles from the Potomac,[xlix] was passed through the Fitzhugh descendants until 1830, when it was sold to Mrs. Robert Lee, General Robert E. Lee's mother, who died there. That Estate, encompassing nearly thirty-five square miles, encompassed what is now most of the western suburbs of Washington D.C., around Arlington, Virginia, and it must be a cause of eternal regret that no part of it remains in the family today. The reader is referred to the maps in the appendices. The Bedford Estate was passed continuously down from William to Henry through eight generations to one A. A. Fitzhugh who died there after 1932 without issue.[1] It remained in the Fitzhugh family until 1953.[li]

In his book,[lii] Wright aptly sums up William's life and accomplishments: *"William Fitzhugh is an excellent illustration of the transition from a Frontier settler to a country gentleman"*; and *"When William died ... he was just fifty ..., but he had accomplished more than most settlers who had come hopefully to Virginia. He had gathered to himself land, riches and honour, and he had risen to a place among the small group of nascent aristocrats who ruled the Colony. If he himself had failed to attain a seat on the Council, his namesake and heir made this final advance to the top of the social hierarchy. The emigrant son of the prosperous woolen-draper of Bedford firmly established his family in a social*

---

1   Ravensworth, a Fitzhugh and Lee family home built about 1796 by William Fitzhugh, great grand son of William The Immigrant. The mansion stood on the largest single land grant in Fairfax County, the 21,966 acres acquired by Fitzhugh's great grandfather in 1685. Ravensworth was untouched by either side during the civil War. After the war Ravensworth came into possession of Robert E. Lee's second son, Major General William Henry Fitzhugh ("Rooney") Lee. Ravensworth, a framed Palladian-style mansion, was one of the most imposing residences in Fairfax County until it burned in 1926. Location - Fairfax Co: Rte. 3090, 0.11 miles south of Rte 620 (Braddock Rd). [Source: *A Guidebook to Virginia's Historical Markers*, compiled by John S. Salmon, University Press of Virginia.] Ravensworth Shopping Center is on Beltway 495, exit 5 west to Braddock Rd on left. The whole area is known as Ravensworth, including an elementary school. For much more detail on Ravensworth, see further notes in the family archives.

position where it might be envied by less fortunate folk for the next two hundred years. " It is not too much of an exaggeration to say that the name of Fitzhugh still commands recognition in Virginia; my mother, Mrs. John H. Fitzhugh, while travelling through, was recognised by strangers by her name and greeted with respect as late as 1966. The author himself has even been referred to by a contemporary genealogist as "a member of the Virginia aristocracy." Indeed, there are still a large number of Fitzhughs living in Virginia.

"Although some of the Fitzhughs distinguished themselves in many ways in later generations, no one of them can compare to the many sided talents of their first American Ancestor."[liii]

.oOo.

WILLIAM FITZHUGH 1651-1701

References

i	Registers of St. Paul's, Bedford.
ii	*Ibid.*
iii	Registers of Rotherhithe 1556-1804.
iv	Registers of Rotherhithe 1556-1804.
v	Registers of Tempsford, Bedfordshire.
vi	Registers of St. Paul's, Bedford.
vii	*William Fitzhugh and His Chesapeake World,* William Beale Davis, University of North Carolina Press, 1963, p. 10 & 200.
viii	Registers of St. Paul's, Bedford.
ix	Registers of St. Albans Abbey, p.92.
x	Registers of St. Paul's, Bedford·
xi	*Ibid.*
xii	Louis B. Wright, *The First Gentlemen of Virginia, Intellectual Qualities of the Early Colonial Ruling Class,* Huntington Library, San Marino, California, 1940, Part Two, p.156.
xiii	*William Fitzhugh and His Chesapeake World,* Richard Beale Davis, University of North Carolina Press, 1963, p.9.
xiv	Davis, *op. cit.,* pp. 10 & 200.
xv	Beds. Co. Recs., BorBB6/7, Town Hall, Bedford.
xvi	Davis, *op. cit.,* p.14; also *Virginia, a Guide to the Old Dominion,* p. 543.
xvii	N. Beds. Bor. Co. Recs., *The Black Book,* B1, p. 37.
xviii	Davis, *op. cit.,* p. 11, footnote 9.
xix	*Ibid.,* p. 10, footnote 7.
xx	*The Vistas of Eagles Nest - A Guide to the Fitzhugh-Grymes Family Home,* King George County, Virginia, by Liza Lawrence.
xxi	*The American Nation – A History of the United States,* 6th Ed., Garrety, John A., & McCaughey, Robert A., Harper & Row, New York, 1987.
xxii	*The First Gentlemen of Virginia,* Louis B. Wright, The Huntingdon Library, 1940.
xxiii	Calendar of State Papers, America and West India Series, 1677-85; also Minutes of the Council of Virginia 244, James City, Oct. 1, 1681.
xxiv	Davis, *op. cit.,* p. 176.
xxv	Liza Lawrence, *The Vistas of Eagles Nest, A Guide to the Fitzhugh-Grymes Family Home,* King George County, Virginia.
xxvi	Davis, *op. cit.,* p. 18.
xxvii	Richmond (Virginia) Times-Despatch Editorial, December 25, 1946, p. 10.
xxviii	*Colonial Virginia, Its People and Customs,* Mary Newton Stannard, Philadelphia, 1917, p.73.
xxix	Wright, *op. cit.*
xxx	*Dictionary of American Biography,* p.438.

xxxi	*The Vestry Book of King William Parish, Virginia,* 1707-1750, Virginia Tax Records, Genealogical Publishing Company, Baltimore, 1983.
xxxii	Davis, *op. cit.*, p. 232.
xxxiii	Davis, *op. cit.*, Letter of May 18, 1685.
xxxiv	Davis, *op. cit.*, p.8-9, 46, 194.
xxxv	*Ibid.* p.241.
xxxvi	Davis, *op. cit.*, p. 147, note 2.
xxxvii	*Ibid.*, Letter of April 26, 1686.
xxxviii	Wright, *op. cit.*, p. 161.
xxxix	*Ibid.*, p. 181.
xl	*Ibid.*, p. 184; This story also appears in *Old Churches and Families of Virginia,* Bishop Meade, 1857, Vol. II, pp. 192-196, British Library Shelfmark 10412.f.11 & 10409.g.15.
xli	Davis, *op. cit.*, p. 115.
xlii	Davis, *op. cit.,* p 35 states that William was a Governor of William & Mary College, but this is misleading. He actually was instrumental in the campaign to establish the College, but was not a Governor [Email of November 12, 2003 from Louise Lambert Kale, Executive Director, The Historic Campus, The College of William & Mary].
xliii	*Ibid.*, preamble to Will of William Fitzhugh.
xliv	Davis, *op. cit.*
xlv	Liza Lawrence, *op. cit.*
xlvi	*Ibid.*
xlvii	Davis, *op. cit.*
xlviii	*Ibid.*, p. 374, 376-7.
xlix	*Ibid.*, p. 171 & 191.
l	Private Communication from A. A. Fitzhugh to Rev. V. C. A. FitzHugh, 1932.
li	Davis, *op. cit.*, p. 177.
lii	Wright, *op. cit.*, p. 154, 185.
liii	Davis, *op. cit.*, p. 55

CHAPTER TWO

BUILDING ON THE FOUNDATIONS

JOHN FITZHUGH

1692-1733

William and Sarah had succeeded in producing a large family of eight children, six of whom survived infancy. In order, they were William (1679-1713), who married Anne Lee, and whose line inhabited Eagles Nest for many generations; Rosamund (b. ca. 1680, d. bet. 1698-1702) who married William Allerton, whose grandfather had come over on the Mayflower; Henry (1687-1758), Thomas (1689-1710), and George (1690-1722). Last of all came John, our ancestor, born about 1692. Much more is known and recorded in our notes about all the older brothers and sister than of John. Perhaps, being the youngest, he got least notice in everything.

With their father's influence and example to build on, it is not surprising that all the brothers became notables in the local society and government. Thomas was the County Clerk, and married Anne Mason around 1710. William became a Governor of the University of William & Mary in 1702, and married in 1699 Anne Lee (ca. 1683-January 12, 1731/2). His line descends to General Robert E. Lee in four generations and to the Fitzhugh-Grymes line who lived at Eagles Nest until this century. Henry was the scholar of the generation; he was sent at age eleven to Bristol to school and to Westminster School at age fourteen, and to Christ Church, Oxford, matriculating on October 30, 1722. He was called to the Bar at the Middle Temple in the same year. Henry later became a Tobacco Agent, Justice of the Peace, and Burgess, and was known as "Blind Henry," because, judging by his portrait, he had one bad eye. John was a Justice of the Court in February, 1720, and a Major in the Militia as well.

William Senior had provided well for all his children, his bequests running to many pages.[i] John was left seven slaves and eight separate pieces of land totalling 2273 acres, all tenanted or leased[1]. All of the children were duly installed in estates modelled on their father's. John's was to be called Marmion, on which he lived, although it fell to his own son to build the house which still survives there. (See maps in Appendix 4.) The name Marmion is interesting in itself in that it is one of the family names of Barons FitzHugh, from whom William the Immigrant incorrectly thought himself to be descended. In fact, Marmion is an ancient landed title, *John inherits Marmion* descended through a female line (Grey) to a wife of one of the Barons FitzHugh. Perhaps William felt so sure of his ancestry as to name his estate after his supposed forbear, or perhaps he was trying to establish a claim to that ancestry.

John married Anne (or Anna) Barbara McCarty, daughter of Daniel McCarty, Speaker of the House of Burgesses, and Elizabeth Pope.[ii] John married Anne before December 15, 1715 (see Note 73.). It appears Anne was only aged 15 at the time of the marriage. We know three more of her ancestors on each side of her family. However, John, his children, and grandchildren are the most shadowy part of our family line. Before them and after them much is known, but information on their three generations is the thinnest part of our family history. John is usually referred to as Major John Fitzhugh, to distinguish him from several other John Fitzhughs of the period.

The McCarty family was both extensive in numbers and in holdings of land, chattels, and slaves everywhere. Anne was mentioned in her father's Will:[iii] "I order to my daughter, Mrs. Anna Barbara Fitzhugh, two female Negroes not exceeding forty pounds sterling value to be purchased by my trustees with said two

---

1   Much later in 1726, John bought a total of 3175 acres in three transactions, Northern Neck Grants A & B, reel 290, pp. 34, 207, 208, Library of Virginia.

Negroes with their increase I give to my said daughter & the heirs of her body lawfully begotten …".

Anne's father Daniel McCarty was married to the widow, Ann Lee Fitzhugh, of John's elder brother William Fitzhugh. So our ancestor John Fitzhugh was both son-in-law and brother-in-law to Daniel McCarty.[iv]   He clearly had high social ideals for his children as shown by another passage from his Will:

"It is my will & desire that my three younger sons have the best education my estate can afford, that one be a lawyer, one a divine, and the other a physician or surgeon or mariner or in the secretary's office or any lawful employment as their mind leads them but rather to the axe & hoe than suffered in idleness & extra vagrancy."

John also got a bit more into the bargain from his father-in-law's Will:

"Mr. John Fitzhugh take my three youngest children to his house & John Warner & his wife to teach & serve them and that they be in all respects supported & maintained out of my estate…"

Probably John Warner was an indentured servant, so John and Barbara must have had a large household by the end of all this. Whether they succeeded in guiding the children to the chosen occupations, we do not know.

In spite of what little we know of John, it is quite clear that he shared his father's business instinct to profit from exploitation of the land of the new Continent. In February 1727, his name appears among many others as a Trustee in the founding of the Town of Falmouth, undoubtedly a commercial venture.[v] There is also a letter[vi] written by one Anne Jones on June 27, 1732, in which she refers to Major John Fitzhugh's copper mine in Virginia. Apparently there was enough "Ore that lay upon the surface of the Earth" to fill "two of the largest ships." The letter gives the impression that hopes were so high that they thought to give up tobacco growing and go into mining, including gold and silver. It is a good thing that they did not, for none of these metals has ever been found in Virginia.

BUILDING ON THE FOUNDATIONS

John died in Stafford County in January,[1] 1733 (New Style), leaving seven children,[vii] one (possibly the oldest) only six. John's will[viii] showed the usual array of property, goods, and chattels befitting a successful colonial planter, especially one who himself had inherited. He left for his wife's use "Negroes ...viz.: mulatto Billy the son of old Sarah, Cesar, Will (Roses' son), black Will old Sarah's son, Jenny, Kate, Betty, Molly (Jenny's daughter), Sabina, Hannibal, Harry, Hannah, Sabina's children Sary, Frank, Sary's children mulatto Sary, Parker's daughter Phyllis", and these passed to his son William, our ancestor, at her death. Also, in a complicated transaction obviously charged with sentimental and emotional considerations, he left a tract of land called "Black Castle", which he had inherited from William the Immigrant, to his step-daughter Winifred. In order to protect this bequest from his sons' possible refusal to agree, he left "The said tract of land whereon I how live [Marmion] containing sixteen hundred acres to my son William" with the proviso that he would make good the bequest to Winifred on pain of losing the entire Marmion Estate. By this means, our ancestor William inherited Marmion instead of his elder brother John. In addition, all else not specifically bequested was left to William. It is amusing to note that the old dream of finding ores upon the land was not quite dead, for John also says "It is my will that if there should be any copper mines found upon my lands, notwithstanding any former bequests, my two sons shall have an equal share of the profits arising from the said copper mines." Sadly, there never were any.

Anne married again, about 1734, Adam Crump, and had issue John Crump, born 17 February 1733/4, and Thomas Crump, born 28 September, 1736, both in St. Paul Parish, Virginia. This line still has living representatives in 1999.

.oOo.

---

1   G.H.S. King, in unpublished notes on the history of "Chatham", 1956, gives a date of January 22, but *Virginia Vital Records*, Gen. Pub. Co., Baltimore, 1984, p. 268, states January 21.

JOHN FITZHUGH   1692-1733

References

i   Will of William Fitzhugh, reprinted in *William Fitzhugh and His Chesapeake World*, Richard Beale Davis, Virginia Historical Society, University of North Carolina Press, 1963.

ii   Liza Lawrence, *Vistas of Eagles Nest, A Guide to the Fitzhugh-Grymes Family Home, King George County, Virginia*, Genealogical Chart; date of marriage from IGI, Virginia, p.3356, 1984.

iii   Will of Daniel McCarty, Westmoreland County, 29 March 1724, *Westmoreland County Deeds & Wills, 1723-1738, pp. 18-20.*

iv   Private communication from Kelly Leighton, May 20, 1998.

v   Unpublished Notes on the History of "Chatham", G.H.S. King, 1956.

vi   Liza Lawrence, *op. cit.*

vii *Virginia Historical Magazine*, Vol. 36; also Liza Lawrence, *op. cit.*

viii Stafford County Wills, Virginia, 1733.

COLONEL WILLIAM FITZHUGH

1725-1791

John Fitzhugh, son of William the Immigrant, had, so far as we know, seven children. It is quite possible there were more, for the records seem incomplete, and families tended to be large in those days. Of the three sons, John, William, and Daniel, John was the eldest, William came second, and Daniel was the third. We know that John lived from 1724 to 1792 and married Elizabeth Harrison, who was born in 1737, on January 31, 1760.[i] We also know that Daniel was born on June 27, 1733,[ii] died in 1786, and married Susannah Potter, producing a son William, and daughters Jane and Sukey. There were also four daughters, Sarah, born on April 30, 1727, Elizabeth, Barbara, and Anna, who possibly died young.

Our ancestor William was born on Tuesday, April 13, 1725,[iii] presumably at Marmion, which was owned by his father. For reasons we can slightly glimpse, this Estate passed to William, even though he was the second son. (See previous pages for the background of this.) We know nothing of his education, although it seems likely that it was in Virginia. But by the age of only seventeen, he was an owner of slaves, at least the seventeen left him by his father John's will (See previous pages.), which is confirmed by the record of the births of slaves made by Rev. Stuart in the St. Paul's Register.[iv] John was able, before 1759, to contract a good marriage to Ursula Beverley, daughter of Colonel William Beverley and Elizabeth Bland of "Blandfield," another Virginia Plantation. Sixty-one of his ancestors, and seven of hers, are known to us. We are fairly certain[v] that our line descends from that marriage, although later he married for a second time to Hannah --. In all there were thirteen children of the two marriages.

William benefited from his grandfather Daniel McCarty's Will:[vi] "I do hereby give to each of my grandchildren two young

THE MARMION ROOM, Metropolitan Museum

Colonel WILLIAM FITZHUGH 1725-1791

THE FRONT PORCH, MARMION

THE HOUSE AT MARMION

.o 60 o.

Negroes & fifteen pounds sterling value each slave to be bought by my trustees to every of them my grandchildren that I now have or at the time of death may have..." This would have benefited William's entire generation.

William must have been prospering on the Estate his father had left him, because in about 1750, he built a new mansion house, known to this day as Marmion.[1] By all accounts it was a fine example of taste of its period, which is the reason that its drawing room was removed to the Metropolitan Museum of Art.[vii] One author said "One cannot be prepared for the sudden transition from the simplicity of the exterior of Marmion to the elaborateness of the richly-decorated drawing room. There cannot be a counterpart to this room anywhere in America."[viii] All of the woodwork, plasters, and panels are elaborately decorated with paintings, said to be the work of a Hessian soldier done after the Revolutionary War, using pigments unearthed on the Estate. This soldier was found starving on the shores of the Potomac by William and nursed back to health. The Marmion Room at the Metropolitan

---

[1]   Two of these photographs were taken this century at Marmion and reproduced on a calendar for 1952 and 1954. The first photograph opposite is of The Marmion Room at the Metropolitan Museum, New York. The 1980 *Guide Book to the American Wing of the Metropolitan Museum* (p.145-6) says: "One of the most interesting of all surviving early American domestic interiors is that from Marmion, the Virginia plantation home of the Fitzhugh family. Here the architectural treatment of the Ionic pilasters and entablature conforms with unusual fidelity to the Renaissance concept of the classical orders. Part of the woodwork is painted to simulate marble; and on the larger panels landscapes suggestive of Dutch paintings, representations of urns with flowers, festoons of leaves, and asymmetrical scrolls are pleasantly composed. The corner fireplace is lined with its original Sienna marble; above it will hang the gilt-gesso rococo looking glass that always has hung in this room." See also *The American Wing at the Metropolitan Museum of Art,* Marshall B. Davidson and Elizabeth Stillinger, Alfred A. Knopf, New York, 1985, p.60-61. The panelling was done between 1735 and 1770 and painted between 1770 and 1780. The Hall and first floor rooms are still panelled and floored in the original wood, no two being the same size or shape. The South chimney is of an unusual design, built to make room for a secret chamber (publicity brochure for visitors to Marmion, early 20th century). See maps in Appendix Four, and more background history in Appendix Seven.

Museum is a memorial to him as well as to our ancestor. The house and outbuildings were laid out by "a man of taste and a lover of beauty."[ix] Marmion was the inspiration for the plantation called Solomon's Garden in *Honor Bright, Parts Unknown,* and *Fieldings Folly,* three of the best known novels by Frances Parkinson Keyes, a popular American novelist of this century whose books were set in the Old South. In *Honor Bright*[1], the major part of the story's action takes place there, and the details of the setting are accurate in every respect. A permanent record of the history and appearance of the house was made and deposited in the Library of Congress.[x] The Marmion Estate was surveyed in 1797, at the request of Philip, William's son, and found to contain 1821 acres with another 792 on the Rapahannock tract adjacent.

Some idea of the life style of William and his wife is given by the diary of Dr. Robert Wellford,[xi] who visited Marmion and knew William and his family well. On February 14, 1814, after William and Hannah were both dead and Marmion had passed into the hands of Major and Mrs George Lewis, he sat alone in the little parlour of Marmion where he "had witnessed much sociality and more merriment than in any other room in the whole course of my life." He reflected on the past and present owners, who "offered in point of management and mode of living almost as wide a chasm of difference as exists between a prince and a peasant. The establishment of [William Fitzhugh] would not have disgraced a nobleman of rank and the establishment of [George Lewis] had with it no evidence that the master of the Mansion had any pretensions to call himself a gentleman. I beheld in various attitudes and a vast variety of situations the former amiable and respectable owners of this Mansion and its large domains. Mr & Mrs Fitzhugh were in their character generous, noble and affectionate. His lady was a pattern of human excellence, no part of her duty was left unfulfilled. She was a most excellent mother [thus showing there were children of William's second marriage], a firm friend, a kind mistress, an affectionate dutiful wife, pious and

---

1   The book contains long and vivid descriptions of the architectural, garden, and historic details of the whole Plantation. Relevant parts of it are reproduced in Appendix 7. Miss Keyes clearly loved Marmion, and registered a strong protest at the removal of the so-called "Pink Parlour" to the Metropolitan Museum.

charitable to all her poor neighbours - in a word she was a sincere Christian and is now in Glory." Later in the diary he wrote "the place of their interment in the Graveyard of the Old Orchard cannot, from the changes that have occurred, be easily visited by their former friends and acquaintances."

William rose to become a member of the Virginia House of Burgesses, like his father and grandfather, and was there privileged to witness one of the most far reaching events to occur in the New World. It was 1765 when Patrick Henry, a fiery orator, revolutionary, (and also a direct ancestor of ours through the marriage of his granddaughter to Philip Fitzhugh, William's grandson), offered his Resolution against the Stamp Act. That Act had imposed a tax upon the Colonies, much resented because it broke the principle of "no taxation without representation," which became the rallying call of the day. The Colonies were not to revolt for another eleven years, but the *William sees the start of the American Revolution, and is visited by Thomas Jefferson* tinder was lit that day when Patrick Henry shouted "Give me Liberty of give me Death!" The following year, 1766, William had the pleasure of a visit at Marmion from Thomas Jefferson,[xii] later to be the leading intellectual behind the Revolution and writer of the American Constitution. The Revolution inevitably came in 1776. Colonel William was once thought to have lost a Commission in the British Army and been imprisoned for refusing to fight against the Colonies, but it is now certain that his first cousin, also Colonel William Fitzhugh of "Chatham"[1] (1721-1798), had that distinction.[xiii] It is likely that our William is the same as listed as a Revolutionary Soldier (no rank given) from Caroline County,[xiv] but we cannot be sure. We do know that a William Fitzhugh signed a

---

1   This William was a fully commissioned Colonel in the British Army and fought in the French and Indian Wars, as well as in the West Indies. He was a good friend of George Washington and used that friendship to get his two sons commissions in the American Army. One of the sons, Peregrine Fitzhugh, was Washington's Aide-de-Camp at Yorktown. The other son, also William, was with the 3rd Virginia Dragoons. (Information from Richard Ledyard, a descendant of the last named William, March 3, 2000)

receipt for arms for Capt. Buchanan's Company of the Caroline Militia in 1775.[xv] It is tantalising to know that George Washington was acquainted with our ancestor,[xvi] but unfortunately we know no more than that.

Whatever his actual part in the War of Independence, all we know is that William lost at least one slave who deserted to the "enemy."[xvii] William lived more than a decade beyond the surrender of Britain, long enough to see the years of debate that preceded the writing of the Constitution, and to see it established as the foundation of the government of new Republic. He died in 1791, (will proved June 2, 1791), leaving Hannah well provided for. In his Will,[1] he described himself as a "planter" and asked that he be "decently buried in my burying ground but without Pomp or other ceremony except such as may be conformable with the Christian Rites; & I request of my family (excepting my wife) that they acquit themselves of that abused custom of wearing mourning and that they wear no mourning for me..." He went on to say "As my wife has ever shewn me the greatest affection and most tender attention towards me in all cases, and also towards my elder children" [probably meaning the children of his first marriage], "I do hereby charge them as they revere my memory that they endeavour in their power to make her life as happy & comfortable as they can..." He also gave her first call on all his estate in case there was not enough for the other bequests. William was, however, worried about his sons, for in his Will, he says: "Whereas some of my sons may be litigious and dispute with one another concerning the bequests herein made them, I do hereby declare that if any of them sues the other concerning this Will, or any of the Bequests herein made, I do hereby revoke every Bequest herein made to the son who shall sue, and do leave the same to the son who shall be sued." He left Marmion to Hannah "during her widowhood" along

---

1   In his Will, William left a total of £3,600 cash (a huge sum), at least eight slaves, ten "working hands" [indentured servants?], a gardener, a cook, all the Negroes [18 or 20?] left to son John (our ancestor), the Marmion Estate mansion and 1,600 acres, gardens, and orchards, the "Carolina Estate", 600 more acres, at least 22 livestock, several horses, coach & harness, many commodities, goods, and other items, King George County Virginia Will Book 2, 1780-1804, Reel 2, p.133-141.

with a very long list of slaves (her choice of eight, together with "my gardener Charles and the choice of a cook"), coaches, furniture, clothes and all manner of things. William also left large sums of money to his six daughters; clearly he had prospered from planting. Upon his death, Hannah moved to the Rapahannock Quarter called "Strawberry Hill," King George County, and died there "in a bad state of health but of sound mind and perfect memory"[xviii] late in 1798. Her Will was made on November 2, 1798 and proved on February 7, 1799. She asked to be buried "beside her dear departed Husband in the Marmion Graveyard...but without Pomp....," the same as he had asked.

Marmion passed to Major George Lewis of previous mention, who was a nephew of General Washington. Lewis' descendant Mrs Lucy Lewis Grymes still presided there in 1956. By then, there was an old Fitzhugh cemetery, but no Fitzhugh stones had survived. However, one of the Grymes descendants in modern times ploughed up a handsome harness buckle with the Fitzhugh coat of arms on it.[xix]

The decade following William's death marks a real turning point in American History. At the beginning of it the Colonies had only just shook themselves free of their colonial overlords and at the end of it the great push West was to begin, in which William's descendants two generations later were to play a full part.

.oOo.

References

i   *Genealogies of Virginia Families,* 1899, p.853; and IGI Virginia, p.3356, April 1984.

ii   IGI, *op. cit.,* p.3555.

iii   Parish Register, Stafford County, Virginia.

iv   G.H.S. King, Private Notes.

v   Private Communication from Howard Steptoe Fitzhugh, 1982, referring to notes (included) from his father and grandfather.

vi   Will of Daniel McCarty, Westmoreland County, 29 March 1724, *Westmoreland County Deeds & Wills, 1723-1738, pp. 18-20.*

vii   The American Wing at the Metropolitan Museum of Art, Alfred A. Knopf, New York, 1985, pp. 60-61.

viii   *Journal of the American Institute of Architects,* March 1916.

ix   *Ibid.*

x   Publicity brochure for visitors to Marmion, early 20th century.

xi   Diaries of Dr. Robert Wellford (1753-1823) of Fredericksburg, Virginia, Microfiche 2548, Southern Historical Collection, University of North Carolina, Chapel Hill.

xii   G.H.S. King, *op. cit.*

xiii   *Some Ancestors, Relatives and Descendants of Colonel William Fitzhugh of Virginia,* W. Conway Price, PhD; also *George Fitzhugh,* by Harvey Wish, University of Louisiana Press, Baton Rouge, 1943, p.6.

xiv   Marshall Wingfield, *A History of Caroline County, Virginia,* Regional Publishing Co., Baltimore, 1975, p.227.

xv   *Historical Register of Virginians in the Revolution 1775-1783,* Gwathmey, John B., 1938, p. 275, British Library Shelfmark 10887.f.6.

xvi   G.H.S. King, *op. cit.*

xvii   *Virginia Gazette,* December 19, 1777.

xviii   King George County Virginia Will Book 2, 1780-1804, Reel 13, p.230-233. Will of Hannah Fitzhugh.

xix   G.H.S. King. *op. cit.*

JOHN FITZHUGH

J ohn Fitzhugh is the most shadowy and least defined of the characters in our family line. We are certain that his mother was his father's first wife, Ursula Beverley, and not his second, Hannah ---. It is certain from the will of his uncle Daniel that there were children of the second marriage, and one source[i] says that at least four sons, William Beverley (born March 27, 1756), Philip (May 6, 1766-1807), Daniel McCarty (born March 15, 1758), and Theodorick (born July 20, 1760) were of the first marriage. Another source[ii] states that there was a fifth son, John, our ancestor, of the first marriage. It is reported that John was born about 1742, in which case he would have been the first born. The other children were Robert, Elizabeth, Anna, Sally, Sinah, Maria, Molly (who married Colonel Brent and had a son Robert Carroll Brent), a daughter who married Finch, and Lucy (who married Campbell and had a daughter Lucy). The same source states that Robert and Lucy were probably of the second marriage. The fact that Hannah, second wife of John's father Colonel William, mentions in her will Philip, Daniel McCarty, Anna, Molly, and Maria could indicate that they were her children, or it could indicate a generosity to her step-children; we cannot say for sure. All of the evidence about the family life of Colonel William and his Hannah indicates that she was a person of extreme generosity of spirit.

Bits and pieces are known of several of the children. Philip was said to be of Fairfax County, Virginia, and married Charlotte Thornton.[iii] Daniel was conveyed 1200 acres in 1780, which had been purchased by his grandfather John in 1725 from John Lisle, a merchant in London. Daniel's actual signature appears in 1782 on the Ancient Record of the Kilwinning-Cross Lodge of Masons, the oldest such charter in the United States,[iv] along with a Thomas and a Francis Fitzhugh, both of whom are unidentified but almost certainly not in our family line. Son Robert came off badly; he was left one shilling, on the condition that he should return to the estate because, as Colonel William said in his Will, "My will is, that if my son Robert should return to this state he shall be paid one shilling out of my estate, my reason for which is that he at the commencement of the late war quit the business which I had allotted for his living, since which I have never heard of him therefore I leave him to the providence of a just and merciful God." The war, the American Revolution, was a good cause, but he finally settled in Logan County, Kentucky, died between 1800 and 1810, and left a line of descendants to this day.[v] Son William Beverley was left two negroes, and John, our ancestor, was left eighteen or twenty negroes already on loan to him. Philip inherited a very large real and personal estate including almost certainly the entire Marmion Estate, but died in 1807 utterly intestate.[vi] William Beverley, Daniel, Philip, and Theodorick were all students of the College of William & Mary between 1771 and 1780.[vii]

John must have had some property to maintain, for his father had left him[viii] "All of the Negroes which I have hither to lent him during his life". William went on to say that these slaves should "...be equally divided between his two eldest sons now living by his present wife...". [Does this imply he had a previous wife, before Lucy?] In any event, John married Lucy Redd[1] of Cedar Vale, Caroline County, Virginia, the daughter of Samuel Redd (born ca. 1720-30) who married Lucy Rodgers before 1749.[2] Cedar Vale is still standing and a portrait of Samuel Redd still exists in Caroline County. Lucy Rodgers was the daughter of John Rodgers and Rachel Eastham, and she died in 1764, at the birth of her son Samuel II, leaving Lucy to a stepmother, Kezia Duke.[ix]

The Redds were a well established and widespread family in Caroline County, with at least six male property owners in the family.[x] Samuel Redd, John's father-in-law, joined the Caroline Militia as an Ensign in 1762, and rose rapidly to Captain

---

1   Lucy was probably born around 1756, and married John around 1774. This can be roughly deduced by a careful reading of the Will of Col. William Fitzhugh, King George County Virginia Will Book 2, 1780-1804, Reel 2, pp. 133-141, which refers to two sons of Lucy's and John's. The Will, whose date is illegible, refers to John's brother McCarty being under age; Daniel McCarty was born on March 15, 1758 (IGI, Virginia), so the Will was written in 1779 at the latest, thus leading, with other obvious considerations, to the above arithmetic.

2   Private communication from Mrs. R. Thomas Baker, June 2, 1986. The above information is correct. References to an ancestry involving a Sir William Lyonel Rufus de Redde are fictitious.

in 1763. Rather than martial activities, business dealings were more his style, and later, when he had established himself at Cedar Vale, he had clearly developed a wide range of business activities, especially for the period and rural setting in which he lived. He joined a partnership in a mercantile business with one Samuel Garlick at Chesterfield, but later forced Garlick out around 1760, gaining total control. He continued at this business throughout the Revolution, although there was strong competition from a rival business run by John Sutton III. Samuel was also one of five owners of a company formed to develop 50,000 acres west of the Ohio River. This was the first attempt at a mass settlement beyond that river, and because of Samuel's interest, many of the original settlers were Caroline men, including his own children, grandchildren, and in-laws.

Land deals figured in Samuel's activities too. There is a tale of an attempt by two executors of an estate to preempt the foreclosure of a mortgage by selling a property to Samuel Redd. This was sailing close to the wind, as far as the executors were concerned, and the Caroline Court set aside the conveyance.

Samuel certainly had some redeeming features, for he at least served some civic duties as a Vestryman. Vestries governed the Parishes, and consisted of twelve men appointed by the Governor. Two wardens, senior and junior, were the executive officers of the vestry. They disbursed alms to the poor and had custody of unfortunates of the parish. The Senior and Junior Wardens for St. Margarets Parish are recorded as John Sutton II and Samuel Redd for 1763-5.

Life in Caroline County was pretty settled by these times. The Reverend Jonathan Boucher wrote[xi] in the 1880s of his travels through the County: "And there is also this peculiarity observable in [Virginia], that the first settlers have usually taken up huge tracts of land, these having since from time to time been divided away and allotted to their descendants in small portions; so that by this means, and by intermarrying, as is common among them, with one another, certain districts have come to be settled by certain families; and different places are there known and spoken of by their being inhabited by the Fitzhughs (and five other family names). ...The family character, both of body and mind, may be traced through

many generations: as for instance, the Fitzhughs have bad eyes[1]; ..."
Luckily this was a mild drawback compared to the characteristics
attributed to the other families.

John was almost certainly young and able-bodied at the
time of the Revolution, and he even qualified as an Officer.[2] He
joined Capt. John Minor's Company as 1st Lieutenant on August
14, 1777. The Roll of Caroline Men shows him as a 1st Lieutenant
in December 11, 1777, in the Captain Samuel Temple's 2nd
Company. He was promoted to Captain on November 9, 1780. This
fleeting glimpse at least confirms that our family were Patriots
during the Revolution, but nothing at all is known of his exploits.
We do know, however, that he supplied the Army during the
Revolution, and was never paid for it.[3] He could well have been in
the Militia for several years.

The only glimpse of the details of John and Lucy's life
comes from the Caroline County Personal Property List of 1783.[xii]
In that year John Fitzhugh is credited with one "white tythe"
(probably a tenant farmer paying a tithe to John), eleven negroes
over sixteen years of age and twelve under, nine horses, twenty
cattle, and two "wheels." This total is above average compared to
many other entries in the List. In the same List are a Samuel Redd,
probably Lucy's father, then aged 54, and a William Redd, each
possessing a similar assortment of property.

---

1   In the latter 20th century, many members of some branches of the family
     were studied by the National Institute of Health and diagnosed with a
     degenerative eye disease *retinitis pigmentosa*, possibly arising as a result
     of many intermarriages between cousins. It is thought that this condition
     may have been inherited from "Blind Henry" Fitzhugh, of "Bedford", a
     son of William the Immigrant. (emails from Katherine L. G. Hope,
     November, 2003).

2   Marshall Wingfield, *op. cit.*, p. 231, and T. E. Campbell, *op. cit.*, p. 370.
     Samuel Temple was Captain, John Thompson was 2nd Lieutenant, and
     George Terrell was Ensign. *Historical Register of Virginians in the
     Revolution 1775-1783*, Gwathmey, John B., 1938, British Library
     Shelfmark 10887.f.6.

3   No less than 110 years later, John's grandson, Thaddeus Fitzhugh, tried
     to gain political support from a Senator for a "claim of Grandfather's
     Estate against the US Government, for supplies furnished during the
     War of the Revolution..." No result seems to have been obtained.
     (Letter of Nov. 25, 1889, MSS Ay 445a 1140-1147, Virginia Historical
     Society Library.)

John's last act of record was to sue, successfully, one George James and Stephen Sutton, and be awarded £10 6s.[xiii] Sadly, from there he drops out of sight, probably living a peaceful life in the early years of the Republic. He died, as far as we know, before 1796.[xiv] Lucy probably died after 1796, in Amherst County, Virginia.

John and Lucy had at least five children, and probably a sixth, William.[1] At least some of them remained settled in Virginia until the generation of John's grandchildren, when they began to desert the East Coast and participate in the great move West.

.oOo.

---

[1] William's name appears in a lawsuit of 1796, wherein their mother Lucy sued on behalf of Dennis and William, both infants, for recovery of certain slaves disposed of by John before his death.

References

i   *Some Ancestors, Relatives and Descendants of Colonel William Fitzhugh of Virginia,* W. Conway Price, PhD; dates, except Philip, IGI, Virginia, pp. 3555-7, April 1984.

ii   Private Communication from Howard Steptoe Fitzhugh, 1982, referring to notes (included) from his father and grandfather.

iii   *Virginia Marriage Records,* Gen. Pub. Co., Baltimore, 1982, p.459.

iv   Marshall Wingfield, *A History of Caroline County, Virginia,* Regional Publishing Co., Baltimore, 1975, pp.94-5.

v   Private communication from E.W. Fitzhugh, a descendent of Robert, Nov. 25, 1995.

vi   W. Conway Price, *op. cit.*

vii   Lists of the Alumni of the College of William & Mary, 1693-1888.

viii   Will of Colonel William Fitzhugh, King George County Virginia Will Book 2, 1780-1804, Reel 2, pp.133-141.

ix   Mrs. R. Thomas Baker, Private Communication, June 2, 1986.

x   T. E. Campbell, *Colonial Caroline, A History of Caroline County, Virginia,* pp. 369, 394, 193, 128-9, 432-3.

xi   Marshall Wingfield, *op. cit.* pp. 17, 21.

xii   Caroline County Personal Property List 1783, *Virginia Tax Returns,* Genealogical Publishing Company, 1983, pp. 30-31.

xiii   Caroline County Court Record, August Court, 1788.

xiv   Mrs. R. Thomas Baker, *op. cit.*; *William & Mary Quarterly,* Vol. XIII, No. 1, Jan. 1933, p. 51.

PHILIP FITZHUGH

1792-1836

Philip Fitzhugh was born in 1792[i] in Caroline County, nearly 120 years after his great-great-grandfather, William, had immigrated to Virginia. Philip was destined to be the last of our line to live out his life in the original Colony, for it was at this time that the great push West was to begin, when new lands west of the Appalachian Mountains were to be opened to descendants of the original colonists and to the hordes of immigrants to come from all over Europe. Of Philip's generation of seven children, Lucy and Alexander both married in Missouri, then an outpost on the Western Frontier, and Dennis, of whom more later, was to make his fortune there. Only Samuel Temple, who moved to Baltimore, and Philip remained in the old Colonies.

On Tuesday, July 13, 1813, Philip married Mary Macon Aylett, who was born in the town of Ayletts[ii] in King William County on December 5, 1793, a daughter of Philip Aylett, and Elizabeth Henry, from one of the older and more illustrious families in Virginia. Mary was educated at the Spotswood Female Institute, Fredericksburg, Virginia, and, much later in life, was chairman of the War History Commission of Virginia, representing Northampton County.[iii] We know her *Our distant connection to the Barons FitzHugh* ancestry back to the early Seventeenth Century in the Aylett line, and, ironically, through a female line directly to the Barons FitzHugh, whose name caused so much delusion to William the Immigrant, and to many Fitzhughs who tried to trace his descent. Consequently, all of the Fitzhughs in our line after Philip have some small amount of the blood of the Barons FitzHugh in their veins. In all, we know 758 ancestors of Mary Macon Aylett.

In a rather bizarre coincidence, Philip Aylett was given by his father in 1809 a negro, two horses, $500, and a gold watch from his grandfather Patrick Henry. Somehow this was related to a quarrel he got into with Colonel Sam Houston, which led to a duel between the two. They fired twice, but neither was injured. Afterwards they became fast friends and Houston presented Philip Aylett with a present of the pistols. The irony of this is that Sam Houston was to be a friend and major influence on Philip's son-in-law John Henry, our direct ancestor, during the Mexican War, as described in the next chapter. Had either been a better shot, our line of Fitzhughs might have become extinct, or Texas might still be a state of Mexico.[iv]

We know very little of our Philip Fitzhugh, but a record has survived of his service in the War of 1812.[v] He served as a Corporal in the Caroline Cavalry, 2nd Virginia Militia, Captain Armistead Hoomes Company, Detachment commanded by Major William Armistead, stationed at Camp Randolph, from March 24 to August 16, 1813. The Militia was frequently called out to meet and expel the British who were landing on the banks of the Rapahannock River, making incursions into the country, destroying private property, and carrying off negroes. They even burned the White House in Washington. These were dark days, with the United States forces crippled by bitter political controversies, which caused the loss of many *The War of 1812* battles. The gloom only began to lift when Andrew Jackson won a splendid victory at New Orleans, which later got him elected President. For all this, Philip was paid $10 per month, plus 40 cents a day for supplying his own horse.[vi] However, it had the belated benefit of providing his son, Thaddeus, with 160 acres of land as late as 1855.[1]

Philip had got married at age twenty-one, but where the family were living then, we do not know. Some references say that Philip lived his entire life at 'Shooter's Hill',[vii] but a sale notice suggests that the family bought that plantation in 1823,[2] - in fact the

---

1   Bounty Land Warrant Application 47336-55-160, War of 1812, U.S. National Archives. This application was lodged on behalf of Thaddeus Fitzhugh, Philip's youngest son, by his older brother and guardian, Patrick Henry Fitzhugh, who was a Justice of the Peace. Thaddeus was still a minor when the application was made in 1855 to take advantage of a new Act of Congress, and he was awarded 160 acres. Possibly the family had decided to let Thaddeus have this benefit since the rest of the sons of Philip were by this time well established.

2   Notice in *The Richmond Enquirer*, Richmond, Virginia, February 20, 1823: "LAND FOR SALE The subscriber will sell a great bargain in his

owner was Philip's father-in-law Philip Aylett - and we know that
Patrick Henry Fitzhugh was born there in 1824. From family
correspondence described in following chapters, we are sure that at
least some of the family members resided in the area until the time
of the Civil War.

As far as the Ayletts are concerned, a small glimpse of the
family and its dealings is revealed by the story of one Benjamin
Hubbard, a businessman in that part of Virginia.[viii] Hubbard
became the head of the Taylor's business enterprises in Lower
Drysdale Parish around 1750 and remained in active command
until he died in the last year of the Revolution. Hubbard was
unscrupulous in his business activities. As a young man, he broke
one Stephen Haynes, seized Haynes' tavern and bound Haynes'
sons out as paupers. Later he wormed his way into Aylett's
warehouse as a minor partner and when the Ayletts and Buckners
engaged in a bitter family quarrel over Philip Aylett's estate seized
control of the business. Although he owned Aylett's, he moved
neither his residence nor his headquarters to King William. Aylett's
warehouse must have been some Aylett family business, and Philip
Aylett is probably the father of Mary Macon Aylett. Sadly, we
have no success stories of any enterprises Philip may have been
involved in, but these depressing tales at least show that the local
economy was mercantile as well as agricultural, and our ancestors
were no longer solely planters. Whatever he was doing, by 1830[ix]
Philip had a total household of sixteen, including eight slaves, two
of whom were children. The census of that year seems to have been
taken before May 9, when Edwin was born, and there is one extra
male child between the ages of five and ten that cannot be

---

tract of land lying in the county of Middlesex immediately on the
Piankatank about eight miles below Urbanna creek, called and known by
the name of Shooter's Hill, containing 519 acres. This land is well
adapted to the culture of corn and wheat; the houses are out of repair,
except the granary, which is new, large, and conveniently
constructed....description of this plantation... by Mr James Stiff,
residing on the premises or George Healy in the town of Urbanna." In
1826, another 615 acres of Shooter's Hill sold for $2406, giving some
idea of the value of this sale. [*Historic Buildings in Middlesex County,
Virginia, 1650-1875*, Ed. Walter C.C. Johnson, 1978.] See Epilogue to
this Chapter.

accounted for, although this is possibly simply an enumeration error.

All we know of Mary is that she died on October 6, 1836, aged only forty-three, leaving eight children, the youngest only eighteen months. Philip died on the following December 21, aged also forty-four.[x] It seems plausible that they may have been carried off in an epidemic, not uncommon in those days. We do not know who cared for the children, although perhaps it was the oldest child, Elizabeth, who was by then aged twenty.[xi]

Philip was clearly content to live the life of a Virginia farmer, but his brother Dennis was more inclined to try his fortune on the Frontier. Dennis' name appears in St. Louis, Missouri, now an industrial town where, among many other things, fighter aircraft are made, but where in 1808, fur trapping and trading were the main activities. Dennis was born in 1777/8[xii,1] and married on May 13, 1805 in Jefferson County, Kentucky, Frances (Fanny) Eleanor Clark (her 3rd marriage). She was from Louisville, Kentucky, the daughter of John Clark and Ann Rogers, and the youngest sister of General George Rogers Clark, known as the Conqueror of the North West Territory in 1778. Dennis was the grandson of Frances' Aunt Lucy Rogers (Note 82) making them 1st cousins, once removed. Their home was in Louisville, Kentucky in the block bounded by Jefferson St., Green St., (Now Liberty St.), Floyd St. and Brook Street. In the 1810 Census of Kentucky, Dennis is listed as living in Jefferson County.[xiii]

Many of the enterprising frontiersmen had banded together to form the Missouri Fur Company including William Clark[2] (of the famous Lewis & Clark Expedition which had first crossed the Continent on foot in 1803-6), and Dennis Fitzhugh. The enterprise was founded to exploit the rich fur trapping of the upper Missouri Valley.[xiv] Dennis Fitzhugh came to Missouri from Louisville, Kentucky, where he eventually returned to become a Judge, although nothing is known of any legal training. Many of

---

1   In the Oath referred to, he is described as: "five feet eleven inches tall, light hair, grey eyes, and [?] complexion."

2   Clark was also from Caroline County, and a first cousin of Dennis, being the son of Ann Rogers and John Clark. Ann Rogers was Lucy Redd Fitzhugh's aunt. (Private communication from Mrs. R. Thomas Baker, June 2, 1986.)

Dennis' personal papers survive[xv] and they give enough clues that he had married into a prosperous and well established family in Louisville. By 1820, he was doing business with, and making purchases on behalf of his step-son John O'Fallon.[xvi] Money was changing hands several thousand dollars at a time and Dennis wrote to John "I have purchased for you a negro girl 15 years of age at the price of $400...", and then justifies having to pay so much. He continues "I will get you a negro boy as soon as I can..." and asks "whether you wish me to get you the sideboard and tables [you] mentioned..." In a letter[xvii] to a Mrs Preston, recently widowed, he gives a great deal of sympathetic legal advice and signs himself as "Judge Fitzhugh". Finally, he gets the sideboard for John for $175, bargained down from $300, paid in Kentucky Notes, making an interesting comparison of the price of slaves and of furniture.

Dennis died in 1822, most likely from a yellow fever epidemic, a sad irony since he was at the time head of a hospital project, begun but unfinished after an earlier smallpox epidemic five years earlier.[xviii] The irony is compounded by the fact that from July 1st of that year Dennis had been appointed to a committee whose purpose was to construct an Episcopal Church in Louisville. This church was surely needed, at least in the view of one Dr Craik, and gives some idea of Dennis' attitudes:

"The effort to establish the Episcopal church in Louisville seems to have proceeded quite as much from the country gentlemen in the neighbourhood as from the residents of the town. Jefferson county, like several other prominent points in Kentucky, was settled at the very earliest period by a class of highly educated gentlemen from Virginia. Of course they were all traditionally Episcopalians, for that had been the established religion of Virginia. But unfortunately, at the period of this emigration, the coarse blasphemies of Tom Paine and the more refined infidelity of the French Encyclopedists had taken a strong hold upon the Virginia mind. The early emigrants brought with them the taint of these principles, and in many cases the books from which they were derived. And alas! there was no church in the wilderness to counteract these evil influences and the new spiritual temptations incident to this breaking off from the ancient stock and from home associations. The consequence was, that this generation lived and their children grew up emphatically without God in the world. But religion of some sort is a necessity for the human soul. The modes of religion prevalent in the country were revolting rather than attractive to educated men, and therefore ... the formation of an Episcopal congregation ... was warmly seconded by the most influential citizens of the country."[xix]

Overall, this picture of Dennis' and Frances' life is much more than one of frontier adventure and trade. He was a well-settled establishment figure in a growing community, and his untimely death at age only forty-four must have robbed it of one of its more dynamic citizens. Frances lived on with her son John O'Fallon in St Louis, Missouri until her death on June 19, 1825.[xx]

By now, the pattern was now well established - our Fitzhugh family was ultimately destined to migrate to the West. The Fitzhughs were not, however, among the first. Indeed, it may be asked why they left it so long. The answer may be that, as the Washington *Herald* put it, the Fitzhughs were universally esteemed (in Virginia) for their "talent, probity, and high morality".[xxi]

Family circumstances, and economic and social forces finally force the Fitzhughs West

A reputation like that might imply much to lose by moving to other parts. However, it is worth pausing to reflect on the social and economic pressures that made some of the new Americans abandon the settled East Coast for the uncharted and often hostile interior. With such large families as were common in those days, the "landed gentry" concept of large estates with a social structure to suit could not maintain itself without vast new areas of land to bring under plantation. This, coupled with the fact that exploration was rapidly opening the frontiers west of the Appalachian Mountains (which had hitherto kept settlers' oxcarts from crossing them until Daniel Boone discovered the Cumberland Gap), meant inevitably that some members of the family would venture West.

The Old Dominion, as Virginia calls itself, and the other Colonies simply could not contain the growing Republic. In fact, Virginia's economy had been in decline since before the Revolution.. Between 1817 and 1829 land values had dropped by sixty percent. Virginians had begun moving away even before these hard times. A third of the white children born in Virginia after 1800 moved elsewhere, followed by a third of the slaves, either moving with their masters or sold on by them. Texas attracted many, even being described as a "Land of Promise".[xxii]

All of this plus the chronic depression in the tobacco market, and the slump in grain sales to Europe with the coming of peace after the Napoleonic Wars, plus the fear that the Virginia soil was exhausted after two hundred years of heavy cultivation, led many with an adventurous spirit to strike out west. A system of inheritance in Virginia Law based on primogeniture and entail[xxiii] meant that the older sons tended very much to remain in Virginia, but the younger sons, not being able to inherit any meaningful part of the main estates, tended to strike out for new lands. Bedford and Eagles Nest had Fitzhugh descendants living on them until 1953 and 1963 respectively, but the younger sons, who are our ancestors, eventually left the relatively civilised Eastern shores to seek their fortunes inland. In any event, our ancestors spent four generations building the foundations so that the Fitzhugh family is still most heavily represented in Virginia, even though other members have by now moved throughout the rest of America. In the case of Philip's son, our ancestor John Henry, these forces were augmented by other events, in the form of two wars, which were to shape his destiny, and ours.

.oOo

Epilogue

Shooter's Hill

Information from
Historic Buildings in Middlesex County Virginia 1650-1875
Edited by Walter C.C. Johnson, 1978

Shooter's Hill was part of a patent granted in April, 1690 to Thomas Dudley and William Elliott, part of which soon came into the hands of one Augustine Smith. He built on the Piankatank River a brick mansion a full three stories high, whose roof held a lead fish tank "where fish could be caught at any time". He must have prospered, for his son John "drove his coach and six [horses] with three postillions in livery". Later, the family requested a "country man" from England be sent over to keep the grounds. By 1751, "planting at Shooter's Hill was poor doings" [possibly owing to over-cultivation and exhaustion of the soil? - HAF].

The mansion at Shooter's Hill burned down in the late 18th century while the owners were in Europe, and in 1797, 1274 acres of the estate were sold to George Brent. In 1810, 515 further acres were sold to Austin Brockenborough, who later sold to George Healy, and Healy sold to Philip Aylett. [Presumably this is the February 20, 1823 sale mentioned in an earlier footnote.] Philip Aylett apparently retained ownership of the tract upon which Philip Fitzhugh and his wife Mary Macon Aylett lived, for according to Aylett's will the tract "on which Philip Fitzhugh formerly resided" was sold to Robert Healy and William T. Fauntleroy. The Fauntleroys reserved a half-acre graveyard, [probably the Fitzhugh graves mentioned below], and in 1888, they sold 320 acres to J.R. Segar, who sold to W.W. Moody in 1893, in whose family it remained until 1941, when it was sold to Harold Barnes. [The further correspondence below is from one of Moody's descendants just before this sale.] In 2002, Mrs Barbara Barnes Robins still owned 240 acres of Shooter's Hill Farm.

**Transcription of Manuscript Mss6:1 F7585:2,
Virginia Historical Society**

"Sylvan Scene"
Machipongo [Va]
October 19, 1940

My Dear Mrs Marchant,[1]

Your very kind letter just received, and I was delighted to hear from you on the subject of "Shooter's Hill". My grandfather was Philip Fitzhugh, who married Mary Macon Aylett, the grand-daughter of Patrick Henry, whose [Philip Fitzhugh's] grave is surely under a tree at "Shooter's Hill". They owned the place, and went there to live, after their marriage – had nine children born there,[2] and my father Dr Philip Aylett Fitzhugh is one of them. Both of their parents died, and of course their children were scattered and [the] place was sold, and their father and mother died a few months apart and their eldest son was executor and settled the estate. My father was 3rd child and married my mother, Miss Tankard, in this, Northampton County (Eastern Share) and died here in 1908, and used to visit his parents' grave [Philip's & Mary's] every year at "Shooter's Hill"; and I have visited the grave also, and I have a tall box plant living from there. – We are all packed up now, to spend the winter in Richmond, and when I unpack after I get there, will send you the list of children from their family Bible, written by my great-grand-mother – my father remembered her and called her Grandma "Henry" [probably Elizabeth Henry] – about a year or two ago Coz Eva Fitzhugh [unidentified] wrote me a similar letter to yours about my great-grand-mother and she gave it to the D.A.R. [Daughters of the American Revolution] who wished to mark her grave. Perhaps they would help your U.D.C. [?] mark the grave. I entered the Dames and D.A.R. also on Patrick Henry. If you look in any first class library you will find all I have written you if you ask for the Fitzhugh pedigree. I married my first cousin W[m] Bullitt Fitzhugh. Thanking you for writing me and I do hope this will help you.

---

1   Cora Lee (Moody) Marchant was apparently resident at Shooters Hill at the time of writing.

2   Eight children are known to us, four of whom were born after the property was, almost certainly, purchased in 1823.

When I visited "Shooter's Hill", the Moodys lived there and seemed very proud of the graves, and they were kept up very nicely. If you know them, they may tell you more. My name and my husband's name are in the Henry Fitzhugh line in the libraries.
Very Sincerely Yrs,
Mary Macon Aylett Fitzhugh[1]
(Mrs Wm Bullitt)
Machipongo, Va.

[This letter was in an envelop dated October 22, 1940, headed "House of Delegates, Richmond, Va., Wm. Bullitt[2] Fitzhugh, Sergeant at Arms, Machipongo, Va.," under the Seal of the State of Virginia "Sic Semper Tyrannis" [referring to the Union side in the Civil War], and addressed to Mrs Cora Lee Marchant, Urbanna, Va.]

In the same papers:
I make this note for further information if ever needed.
The Fitzhugh burying ground is a part of the east end of the yard now at Shooter's Hill. The grave herein mentioned is near or under the guest house built there by Harold Barnes. At that time, when graves were put there, it then was just out side of the yard. There were five or six graves all Fitzhughs. I remember them distinctly, never were any grave stones in my time. About a hundred yards North of this spot, middle of the field another grave yard of the Fauntleroy's.
Cora L. Marchant
1953

Notes on Graves of Fitzhugh's
At Shooter's Hill, Middlesex Co., Va.
At Shooter's Hill Farm, here in Middlesex Co. Va., there is a Fitzhugh grave yard that has passed from time of eternity. And I write these few notes as I am sure I am the last one to remember

---

1   This is the niece "Macon" who visited John Henry Fitzhugh in Austin, Texas in 1891 – see mention in next chapter.
2   Spelled as such, in spite of Harriett Bullett Fitzhugh's name as such on her tombstone.

these graves. My father, the late W. W. Moody acquired the old place in 1893, I think, or about that time. I was then 6 years old and I remember these graves so well and played around them so many times. There never were any tomb stones to mark them, not that I ever saw.

Patrick Henry's granddaughter is buried there, she was daughter of Elizabeth Henry & Philip Aylett, and there are, or were, at least 6 or 7 graves there, maybe more. I am enclosing a letter to me from the late Mrs Bullitt Fitzhugh [letter above], whose husband as you know was Sergeant at Arms at the Capitol Richmond, Va., the Legislature. We were living at Shooter's Hill and were the Moodys she spoke of in her letter. I remember them coming to see these graves.

At one time these graves were right outside the yard fence, but later, years later, father enlarged the yard [and] took the grave yard within the bounds of the yard. They are located in the east end of the yard and there were at [least] 6 or 7 graves. Some of them I dare say are beneath the little guest house there in the yard, built by the late Harold G. Barnes. His widow owns it now, 1964. There was an old rose bush that bloomed for many years and was near these graves, it may still come back, right in the North East corner of the yard.

Then across the lawn from the yard, due North East, probably a hundred & fifty yards there was another grave yard with quite a few graves and this was Fauntleroy burying ground. No stones ever there, my father never had it ploughed or disturbed. There were 2 or 3 large cherry trees growing in it and a tangle of briers and some flowers, but they too are gone. All of these graves long ago, as so the Fitzhughs in time were swallowed up by the earth around them.

I write these notes as I am sure no one else knows anything about them, even now, and certainly in years to come they will not.

Cora Lee Moody-Marchant, Urbanna, Virginia, Box 262

References

i   Bounty Land Warrant Application 47336-55-160, War of 1812, U.S. National Archives.

ii   *Virginia Genealogies* #4, p.465, 1924.

iii   *Virginia Genealogies* #4, p.465, 1924.

iv   *Twelve Virginia Counties Where The Western Migration Began,* Gwathmey, John H., 1937, British Library Shelfmark 010410.1.22.

v   Marshall Wingfield, *A History of Caroline County, Virginia,* Regional Publishing Co., Baltimore, 1975, p.232.

vi   Military Records, War of 1812, Philip Fitzhugh, U.S. National Archives.

vii   *Virginia Genealogies* #4, p.466, 1924.

viii T.E. Campbell, *Colonial Caroline, A History of Caroline County, Virginia.*

ix   1830 Federal Census, Middlesex County, Virginia, Reel M19-196.

x   Bounty Land Warrant Application, *op. cit.*

xi   *Virginia Magazine,* Vol. XL, No. 2, April 1932.

xii   Oath sworn April 16, 1807 in New Orleans, Territory of Orleans, that he was twenty-nine years of age. Dennis Fitzhugh Papers, 1802-1856, Filson Historical Society, Louisville, Kentucky.

xiii FTM Kentucky Genealogy CD #1, 3 volume set of genealogies of Kentucky families; private communication from Susan Hudgens, February 20, 1999; private communication from Charleen Oerding, February 20, 1999.

xiv *The Pageant of America,* Vol. 2, "The Lure of the Frontier," Yale University Press.

xv   Dennis Fitzhugh Papers, 1802-1856. Filson Historical Society, Louisville, Kentucky.

xvi Letters of May 4, 1820, June 15, 1820, July 12, 1821, Dennis Fitzhugh Papers, 1802-1856. Filson Historical Society, Louisville, Kentucky.

xvii Letter of April 9, 1820, Dennis Fitzhugh Papers, 1802-1856. Filson Historical Society, Louisville, Kentucky.

xviii *Two Hundred Years at the Falls of The Ohio,* George H. Yates, p.41.

xix Quoted in *History of Kentucky,* Lewis Collins, 1882, pp. 438-9.

xx   Private communication from Susan Hudgens, February 20, 1999.

xxi Harvey Wish, *George Fitzhugh, Propagandist of the Old South,* Louisiana State University Press, Baton Rouge, 1943, p.6.

xxii Virginia Magazine of History and Biography, Vol. 114, No. 1, pp.18-19.

xxiii Harvey Wish, *op. cit.*, p. 1-2, 101.

CHAPTER THREE

TWO WARS IN TWO DECADES

JOHN HENRY FITZHUGH

1821-1894

IN MANY WAYS the seventy-two years that John Henry Fitzhugh lived were those that saw the creation of America from a small collection of States on the Atlantic Seaboard into a transcontinental nation that we would recognise today. He was born two days before Christmas, 1821 in King & Queen County, Virginia, the original of the Southern Colonies. In that year the continent which was later to become modern America was still shared with Spain and with Russia, which owned what is now Alaska. France had sold all of Louisiana, comprising that State as well as land as far north as the northern Missouri Valley, only some twenty years before, thus enabling Napoleon to finance his various aggressions. It had only been some fifteen years since Louis and Clark had accomplished the first crossing of the continent by land. Their return gave the Congress and the country, which had financed the expedition, some idea of what lay between the East Coast, colonised for two hundred years by the English, and California, held by Spain for even longer. John Henry was to participate in some of the struggles which expanded the Nation to the West and South, as well as the bloody Civil War which almost tore it asunder. By the end of his life in 1894 he was living in a Nation of States stretching between both Coasts whose form and makeup would be instantly familiar to us today, since the forty-eight adjacent States were in the Union only sixteen years later.

In 1821, our branch of the Fitzhugh Family was still firmly settled in Virginia, but the social and economic forces described in the last chapter would soon mean that the family began to spread Westward. John was born in King & Queen County on

December 23, 1821, the fifth of eight children, six boys and two girls. The daughters Lucy Redd (born October 8, 1819) and Elizabeth Henry (born May 12, 1816) married respectively John R. Redd (possibly a distant cousin) and Robert Curtis. Patrick Henry was born on December 2, 1818, and married Mary Steptoe Christian (possibly a cousin), but he was to die, as told below, in the Civil War survived by six children who have descendants to this day. Edwin, born on May 9, 1830, was killed on Walker's Expedition to Nicaragua in 1855, also as told below. Thaddeus was born on March 15, 1835, and married Julia Horsey and two other wives and settled in Kansas City. He left extensive memoirs of his Civil War experiences, told later herein. Lafayette Henry (May 9 1829 - August 1, 1905) served in the Mexican War and was a Colonel in the Confederate Army.[i] He married twice, first to Elizabeth Semple and second to Ann Eliza Bullett and settled in Dallas, Texas. Dr. Phillip Aylett (June 14, 1824-June 7, 1908) married Georgia Tankard, who was a descendant of William Tankard, an original settler of Jamestown, and moved East to Baltimore,[ii] and later to New York, becoming an assistant surgeon at two hospitals.[iii] It is due to a sporadic but close and affectionate correspondence between John and Georgia, also called Georgeanna and Georgie, that much is revealed about John's life at crucial times.

The Fitzhugh children, following the deaths of both parents in 1836, were living in Urbanna, Middlesex County, Virginia. A letter in 1844 from a friend to Philip Aylett Fitzhugh, by then a Cadet at the Virginia Military Academy, refers to Urbanna[1] as *"the poorest place in Creation, a great deal worse than when you left, it is actually whittled down to the little end of nothing...defunct."*[iv]

By now, the financial decline of our branch of the Fitzhugh family becomes all too apparent. As told previously, it was the bankruptcy of Henry Fitzhugh, John Henry's great-great-great-great-grandfather which propelled William the Immigrant to Virginia. William made a huge fortune by any standards, and large tranches of it were passed to William's son John, and then on to John's son Colonel William Fitzhugh of Marmion. On Colonel

---

1   The population of Urbanna in 1990 was 529 (U.S. Census).

William's death, the main Marmion Estate passed out of our line, but he lent and then bequeathed his own son John, John Henry's grandfather, around twenty slaves, which at least implies that John farmed or planted enough of an estate to keep them working and supported. John had twenty-three slaves as well as one indentured servant in 1783, and therefore, although not obviously rich, he was certainly not poor. John's son Philip, John Henry's father, may not have inherited much, since he was one of seven children, but he did at least live on an estate, "Shooters Hill", albeit owned by his father-in-law. Thus, in the space of two, or at most three, generations, our branch of the family had declined from conspicuous and great wealth to, at best, lower to middle income status. The most likely explanation seems to be the effects of increased population together with a declining agricultural economy,[1] as well as the obvious fact that in those three generations there were twenty-eight descendants among which to divide the available inheritance. The family may simply not have been creating enough capital to go around. The death of both of John's parents in 1836 must have been the final straw. In 1830, his father Philip kept a large household of sixteen, but by 1840[v], no trace of his six boys and two girls can be found. The girls were married, and the boys must have dispersed with each going a different way to seek his fortune.

All of the above was bad enough, but as John was approaching adulthood, the country was afflicted by an economic recession that must have seriously affected his prospects. The mid-1830s had been a time of easy credit, good national balance of payments, and heavy speculation in land. In 1836 President Jackson became alarmed by the speculation mania and he passed an Act requiring public land sales to be paid for in gold or silver. This more than slowed the boom. Jackson grossly underestimated the effects of his measures, and this led to the panic of 1837. Cotton prices fell by half and there were demonstrations by the unemployed in New York, who broke into the city warehouses and sacked the supplies. High interest rates followed, and British banks began calling in loans. Crop failures in 1835 and 1837 made matters worse. The effects of all this persisted into 1842-3, by

---

1   See Chapter on Philip Fitzhugh.

which time John was aged twenty-two. This was the economic climate John faced as he sought to make his way in the world.[vi]

John was trying as early as age twenty-one to get into business with a friend, Henry Coghill. Henry would *"like exceedingly to engage with you in the Mercantile Business"* if he *"can raise some funds by next spring."*[vii] John did make it a few years later, but probably not with Coghill.

It is clear from several letters[viii] that older brother Patrick was paying for Philip's fees at VMI, and that he was feeling the expense hard going. Philip, however, was a conscientious and hard working Cadet[ix] who gave a lecture to The Temperance Society of Lexington, Kentucky on New Year's Day, 1845. Life was bleak at VMI, probably not made any more bearable by his friend referring to *"Christmas last winter where he 'frolicked' about with the girls at a rapid rate, didn't kiss any of them though and found that they had not become fond of that during my absence."*[x] Philip, on the other hand, complained that *"the Ladies of this mountainous country"* have *"the largest feet I have ever seen. The Gentlemen have to be very cautious when they walk with them."*[xi]

In the early 1840s, Texas, and its problem with Mexico, were looming ever larger on the American political scene, and ultimately led to the Mexican American War of 1846-48. This War was precipitated when *John enlists in the* Texas, which had been an independent *Mexican War* Republic for nine years since the Texas Revolution and Battle of the Alamo in 1836, decided voluntarily to join the Union in 1845, as the thirty-fifth State. Texas had up to then maintained an independent neutrality between the U.S. and Mexico, and even had an Embassy in London, and so consequently Mexico felt threatened when Texas joined the Union. The US made an offer to Mexico to buy New Mexico for $5 million, and California for $25 million. This was refused and Mexican forces first attacked American troops. War began with Southerners favouring it as likely to extend slave territory, and Northerners opposing it for the same reason.

The first effect of the War on our family appears in a letter from Georgeanna Tankard to her mother of November 28, 1846,[xii] where she refers to the "doctor" going off to the Gulf of Mexico. The doctor is Philip Aylett[xiii], who is obviously favoured by the mother, for Georgeanna says *"you seem to admire that Mr Fitzhugh very much, I should like to know what kind of Genius he is."*

Philip Aylett Fitzhugh

Another letter[xiv] from a distant relation refers to Philip *"going to Texas"* where he will *"have to volunteer"*, as an *"officer or private"*, and *"Patrick ... will find it a difficult matter to furnish you with the means to go to Texas."* Furthermore, *"John is in Gloucester* [County, Virginia] *... he has been expecting for several months to go to Kentucky – probably he will change his mind and accompany you."* So Texas and The Mexican War were proving such an irresistible lure that John was willing postpone his mercantile ambitions in Kentucky.

John enlisted, along with his brother Lafayette, in the First Regiment of Virginia Infantry (Volunteers), Company G, on December 16, 1846,[xv] serving ultimately under General Zachary Taylor (who three years later became the twelfth President of the United States). He enlisted as Private, the lowest rank, but was promoted to Corporal six weeks later, presumably after training, on January 25, 1847. He sailed for the Mouth of the Rio Grande the same month, and the voyage to Point Isabel was, for most volunteers, a wretched experience.[xvi] There were many discomforts, but the greatest was seasickness. Off Cape Henry, the *May Flower* and the *Victory* struck a gale with mountainous waves breaking over the ships, drenching seasick volunteers clinging to the rail. LaFayette was "dreadfully sea-sick from the moment he went aboard until he landed."[xvii] The stifling hot and crowded quarters below offered no comfort, with the putrid odour of the bilge and crawling lice. Even after the storm subsided, high winds prevented the building of fires to cook meals and boil coffee. For five days the men survived on hard crackers and salt pork. The officers fared better as their meals were served from the steward's gallery, where fires were allowed. Some of the men paid several dollars to officers' servants to get a small piece of corn bread or bacon. Members of the company were seen to snatch small bits from plates carried out of the officers' quarters after meals.

But they made it to Point Isabel in Texas and marched inland to Camargo, Monterey, and Buena Vista, which must have been a long, hot, dry walk.[1] Camargo was an advance base up the

---

[1]   Some idea of what it was actually like comes from the letters of a fellow soldier: ... "The weather at this time is unaccountable hot, and were it not for the continual breeze that is stirring, a person could not live here, and a person can see these yellow bellied Mexicans half naked with very broad rimed hats on, some loafing about in the hot sun, and some working, some few are industrious and some are as lazy as anything can be, those that are industrious keep themselves tolerable clean and look tolerable decent but others live like hogs. They build their huts out of cane and mud, and have no chimney, nor anything to sit on old dried cow hide answers for seats and bed and table they have no plates nor forks and are certainly the filthiest of the human race. The women are about the same some clean and decent while others are dirty and filthy as I have seen but five or six Mexican ladies that I considered in any way handsome...Whenever you hear any person say that the Mexicans are handsome, don't believe it and think they are a deceitful set of rascals that will rob, steal, murder every opportunity they have or get. ...because I am tired of this inactive life and would be glad to change it and what is more this miserable hot country. The filthy Mexicans and their ignorance. I do think that if ever I return to the states again I shall thank myself fortunate and will try and stay there. I always was fond of curiosities and I had a desire to come to Mexico and try warfare, to see what virtue there was in soldiering... But my word for it, I found none and shall never forget the twelfth of April 1847, the day I bound myself to Uncle Sam for 'Daring.' I will here add, that I would not advise you to follow my example in that respect, for if you do you will surely rue. But if I should be so fortunate as to return in three or four months from this, I shall never regret my trip to Mexico for it will be worth more to me than I would have made in the States in the same length of time...You have no doubt heard that Gen. Scott is recalled and I think it perfectly right. I never was in favor [sic] of him, and never will be. There is one thing pretty certain, and that is if the administration is of one party and the commanding generals of the other, things will not work well. My opinion is that if Democratic Generals would have had the command in Mexico, they would have managed things in a different way to what they have been managed

Rio Grande, reached by a small fleet of river steamers. From there Taylor marched to Monterrey which he began to attack. The U.S. troops penetrated the town, meeting heavy resistance in the fortified streets and houses. After a four day siege, the Mexicans capitulated. Taylor, disobeying orders, advanced further along the road to Mexico City, encountering the enemy near the hacienda of Buena Vista. The U.S. forces of 4,800, mostly untried volunteer infantry, were entrenched along deep gullies and ravines. General Santa Anna (the same who had massacred the Texans at The Alamo ten

The Battle of Buena Vista

years earlier), whose forces numbered some 15,000, demanded unconditional surrender. Taylor refused. Three days of hard fighting gave him victory, the retirement of Santa Anna's forces, and a termination of the War in Northern Mexico.[xviii] Monterey was captured after a four day engagement that made "Old Rough and Ready" Taylor a national hero.

After some ten months service, John was promoted to Sergeant on November 1, 1847, but for some unrecorded reason he

---

and the war would now be closed." Sgt. John W. Keller, 16th Infantry U.S.A., Letter to his father, Frederick Keller, Lititz, Pennsylvania, 15 June 1847, & 17 Feb. 1848, website pastvoices.com/usa/keller_mexicanwar1.shtml, 2002.

was reduced back to the rank of Private "at his own request" on the following December 8. He remained at this rank for the rest of his service. The most likely explanation for this demotion is that it resulted from some moderately serious disciplinary matter, but the record states nothing.[xix] However, there is a clue elsewhere.[xx] The North Carolina Volunteers had a rather strict Colonel, Robert T. Paine, who used a wooden horse for punishment of minor infractions – the accused had to sit for long periods on its sharp back. The Virginia Volunteers, which included John, were brigaded with the North Carolinians. Fearing that the "horse" might be used on them, the Virginians took pre-emptive action and destroyed it on the night of August 14, 1847. The following night a group of some twenty soldiers shouted insults into Paine's tent, who then followed them to the Virginian camp and attempted to arrest the ringleaders. One escaped, and within an hour the situation became ugly. Paine had not realised the Virginians were near mutiny, and he ordered a detachment of twenty of his own men to disburse them, even though they had begun to walk back to their own camp. Paine changed his mind, and ordered them to halt or he would fire. Apparently not believing he would fire on Americans, oaths were shouted back, and Paine fired, killing one of his own men and wounding a Virginian. Peace was restored after two days, but twenty-five of Paine's officers signed a petition asking him to resign. He refused, and the petitioners were punished. The incident was reported all the way to the White House, and President Polk ordered a Court of Inquiry, which eventually supported Paine.

Morale continued to decline, owing, it is said,[xxi] to the inability to engage the enemy coupled with the boredom of camp routine. Drunkenness featured conspicuously, especially among the Virginia Regiment. Discipline was so lax that men and officers took to leaving the camp after retreat, even though some were murdered in the local town. At least eleven deserted, and Courts Martial were in constant session.

It was in this sort of atmosphere that John must have tried to exercise his new powers as an officer. It is impossible for us to know whether John was involved in any of this ill discipline, but it is clear that at the time morale in the ranks was seriously taxing the ability of the officer corps to maintain order. Perhaps John could not handle the men, perhaps his sympathies were not with the commanders, or perhaps he was implicated in some part of these troubles or their aftermath.

It was probably at this time that he came to know General Sam Houston, former President of the Republic of Texas, who had led the Revolt in 1836. That Revolution saw the bloody fall of The Alamo in San Antonio, and Sam Houston's victory over the Mexican Army at San Jacinto near Houston, and led to, among other things, the annual ten-day Fiesta celebrations in San Antonio to commemorate Texas Independence Day, April 21. It might seem odd that John, a Corporal, should become good friends with a former President who was a generation older, but this is explained by the story in the last chapter where Houston had fought a duel against John's grandfather Philip Aylett, with both surviving to become good friends. As will be seen, this friendship with Sam Houston was to have a crucial effect on John's life.

A peace treaty was signed in 1848 where Mexico ceded all of the future states of California, Nevada and Utah, almost all of New Mexico and Arizona, and parts of Colorado and Wyoming, with a payment from the US of $18,250,000. The War cost in American lives 1,721 killed in action, 4,102 wounded, 11,155 dead of disease, and $97,500,000.[xxii] As far as the Virginia Volunteers were concerned, they lost 88 of 990 for the entire war.[xxiii]

John was honourably discharged at Fortress Monroe, Virginia on August 1, 1848, and given a Land Warrant for 160 acres as his reward for good service.[xxiv] Since there is no record of his occupying any land, it is possible that he sold this to raise capital for his business ambitions.

By 1850, things were looking up. John writes to his brother: *"... I am pleased to inform you that business has been very good since the fall set in..."*[xxv] John was working as a "clerk" and living in a hotel; LaFayette was nearby, working as a "carpenter".[xxvi]

But the next year he had a very narrow escape. Philip writes to Patrick:

"...brother John some three weeks ago informed me, that whilst in Louisville one evening, he was in the back yard of the Hotel & suddenly he heard a shot from a pistol from the hand of an unknown person. The ball entered the fleshy part of his thigh & tho' three physicians were cutting and probing for some time, endeavouring to find it, they finally gave up its pursuit, concluding that it was lodged in the fleshy part of the rump or thigh. It was also

their opinion that he would not receive any serious injury... John I think has returned to Covington." [xxvii]

The year after, May 1852, John writes to his sister-in-law Georgia that he has taken a job:

" I am now at work at the Little Miami Rail Road Depot [Miami, Ohio] *& am kept very busy. I am one of the discharging clerks and am all the time during the day delivering goods ... & can write only during my leisure moments during the day. During the night I am engaged in assorting the freight as the goods are taken out of the cars. ... I was in Louisville ... & did not return for 5 weeks ... do not imagine I went on any courting expedition for that is out of my line, for this is Leap Year and I have too much respect for the 'fair sex' to impose on their time, though I am surely tired waiting for them to propose. ... I got a letter the other day from little Bright that was announcing her marriage, I had a strong notion to send it back to her with respects from Mr & Mrs J. H. Fitzhugh, or send another one ... I will write to her (as we have been corresponding) and put the letter in mourning. I hope she may have a fine time of it, but she is very small for so large a man as she has married. ... I am happy to inform you that my Bullett* [sic] *does not inconvenience me the least and I will try to keep clear of all such random shots but if I could fall in with one of Cupid's Bulletts* [sic] *I will not shun them if I see there is any chance of my sending a return shot, for I do not like this one sided shooting, there should be shot for shot.* {This just *has* to be a reference to Harriett Bullett – HAF} *... Some of the Ladies are marrying off at this time and I hope the may be single next year for then I may be able to find one who would be willing to Emigrate West with me, or that would be willing to take up her abode in the Old Dominion* [Virginia] *with me. ... Who is courting Miss Sally Downing? I should like to see her, she is a Lady I was very much pleased with. ... Miss Yearly, the Misses Fisher, Miss Robins, & I think Miss Winder is a Lady that would or might please those that she thought proper to make herself interesting to, I thought her quite pretty, is your friend Miss Jains married yet? If she is not married ere I go on again I must see her, for from your account of her she must be an interesting Lady."* [xxviii]

John then relates a tale of a man who had 16 or 18 wives, but was arrested on a river boat in New Orleans at the behest of the 19th wife and says:

"I wish I could get in the way of winning the affections of the fair sex that he has, I would not abuse the art as he has but then would

look out for one fair one by the cold weather next winter. You mentioned that you wish something would turn up that would induce me to settle in Northampton [County, Virginia]. *I should like very much to be a citizen of that County if I was married, but to live there and have my lips all the time watering for a kiss from the lips of one that I could call my own, is what I can't stand, for every time I see you & Phil kiss I then wish I had a pair to kiss also, never mind I will try & get a pair one of these days & then I will make up for lost time. Then I will show you all how to Kiss, &c, &c.* [xxix]

But the pursuit of romance must have been difficult, for in July, 1852, John writes:

"I am still much pleased with my situation at the Rail Road Depot, but am kept very busy and closely confined, both day and night."

But he was trying heroically:

"You may want to know how Miss Ellen and myself are getting on with our love (or rather my love) matters, I can only say matters stand as they did last year, I have said nothing more to her, but I do think I will try to see what I can do ere long." [xxx]

Social habits were more constrained in those days, but in some ways they presented more opportunities...

"...got a horse Sleigh & took 4 of our Young Ladies in with me ... the Young Ladies got to snowballing me ... & Miss Ella Watkins was one ... Miss Bush, Miss Broaddus, Miss Riggs, & Miss Ella (last, but not least). ... I am flattered that Miss Rose Windsor enquired after me...Miss Anna Yearly ran off... I like to hear of them getting married even if I am left behind; it is now too cold to think of courting. The weather I am afraid may make their hearts cold, but I intend to make a break in the Spring if I live, for this thing of being alone these cold nights is too bad, just imagine me now of nights seated around a grate of coal burning, with the hearth covered with ashes, with no companion but two or other old chairs, a desk, table, wash stand, & smoking a Cigar & reading a novel, sometimes until 12 or one in the morning too cold to venture to my Cold & Desolate looking Bed, for all the dreary and lonesome looking things in the world, I think an old Bachelor's Bed is the worst, it is time there is a pretty and interesting young lady in the same House, yet she has her Beaux to entertain until ...it is time for her to retire, sometimes I think I will set out & try my luck, but then my Heart fails me ere I could find one that would suit, or rather that I would suit, if I look round and get one that will say

yes, will you & Phil not them come out and see us? For if so that will be another inducement for me to try & get 'doubled'.

"Fayette and A.E. were in Green River in Davis County, he is young to farming. I hope they may be pleased with the life, for then when night comes on you can go to the House & sit by a <u>loving</u> wife & listen to the Sweet Music of her voice, and have her console you after the toils of the day are over, but in the city you have to be in the counting room until a very late hour, ere you can return home, & then your mind is so rapt up in business that you can't rest, or enjoy her company as you can in the country on a farm, but it is still worse with me. I have not any to return to after a long & laborious day's work, but then have nothing but a desolate room, <u>Cold Bed</u> to meet me and console me for the night. I am now more lonely than heretofore as all my old associates have taken off from time to eternity, and now my Room Mate has gone South so I am <u>all</u> alone, but things might take a change one of these days..." But by now John must have left the Railroad, for: *"...our little city is very quiet. The only excitement is from the number of housebreakers that are new in the town, I have sold enough bolts to bolt nearly every house in the city, it has been a fine time for us that are in the Hardware business."* xxxi

Two weeks later, he continues in the same vein:

"Covington has been very dull of late, all the Young Ladies are well. I was to see some of them on Sunday ... I got a large 2 horse Sleigh & got Miss Lucy, then went after Miss Ellen, then Miss Patty & Miss Riggs & off we put for about 3 hours, you may guess I had to sit quite close to them, as there were 4 Ladies – myself and driver in our Sleigh. They got to snowballing one another... I wish I was a medium I would talk to the spirits about Miss M. Price, if she is more beautiful than Miss Sallie. I am only afraid my rough exterior will not suit her. All I can say is that so soon as I can have my business, you may expect me in Davis County, until then keep a good eye on that fair one for me, is she is only like her cousin ... mentally I will be satisfied." Again he refers to local crime: *"It has been a harvest for me as every House had Bolts on the doors, we had to replenish our stock of that article two or three times..."* xxxii

But the hazards to health were never far away. John's letters heretofore contain several references to illness and death among friends and associates, but in March 1853, it hits home:

"...deeply sympathise with you and my Distressed Brother, yet Georgina grieves worst. The poor little Darling has been taken to a

better & happier World, where we all must sooner or later go, we must try to meet him in Heaven, it may not be long ere <u>we</u> be called to follow on after him, the best us see that we are prepared to take a seat with him in Heaven. I know it is hard to part with those we love, and there is nothing I imagine more Heart rendering than to lose a child, Husband, or Wife; yet we must submit to it, it is for our good in the World to Come that we are afflicted in this...There has been much fatality in our city with the Scarlet Fever among children."

But in the same letter there is some good news: *"My business has just begun to open now & will not close until winter,*

JOHN HENRY FITZHUGH (1821-1894)
and HARRIETT BULLETT

and we all look for a larger trade this summer, as there is much building anticipated. Money matters at this time are pretty good, and if it remains so all summer, we will have a good trade." [xxxiii]

Very sadly indeed, there is a gap from now, 1853, to 1865, and we get no further insights into John's wooing and winning of Harriett Bullett, nor any account of the Civil War, until it is over. John's loneliness finally did come to an end when he married, in Gloucester County, Virginia, Harriett Bullett of Ashby, Louisville, Kentucky, on November 30, 1854. She was born on June 11, 1835, a sixth generation descendant of Benjamin Bullett, a Huguenot Refugee, and through her mother Priscilla Christian, was a direct descendant of John of Gaunt through the Beaufort Line and a minor assortment of Scottish Lairds, and also a relation of Fletcher Christian, who mutinied under Captain Bligh on HMS *Bounty.* In all, we know some two hundred and thirteen other ancestors of Harriet Bullett. The photograph on the previous page shows the newlywed couple taken on the day after their wedding.[1] They must have been very avant-garde, because photography had been invented only a few years before. The picture shows her in her "second day dress," with a wedding ring seemingly on her right hand, since the negative was printed in those days by contact and hence the image came out reversed, as though in a mirror.

John was now safely married, but Edwin was about to set out on a military adventure that, had it had lasting results, would have made his fortune beyond the dreams of any of his brothers. Somehow, perhaps he was already in California, he joined Walker's Expedition to Nicaragua.

William Walker was the most active filibuster of the age. He was born in Nashville, Tennessee in 1824. Intellectually gifted, he graduated from the University of Nashville at age fourteen and obtained an MA at sixteen. Further study at the University of

---

1   This photograph is of John and his bride on December 1, 1854. Harriet had come with her mother, aunt, and uncle all the way to Woodville for the wedding. Knowing no one, she had to recruit two local girls as bridesmaids, as the only available niece was too young. As recompense, this niece, later Mrs. M.E. Mitchell, was taken on the one-week honeymoon to visit their Aunt Sarah Fontaine. This story, and many others showing John to be a very kindly man interested in the entire family, come from letters in the Scrapbook of Mary Fitzhugh Thornton, Vol 1, SB 6, Austin Public Library, Texas.

Pennsylvania earned him a degree of Doctor of Medicine. He travelled in Europe and studied in Paris but returned to Nashville in 1848 to study Law. Rootless and dissatisfied, he took to journalism, but his restless spirit found him in California in 1850 to follow the Gold Rush. It seems he became more and more bored by conventional life in the professions, and he then first became involved in filibustering in an attempt to take over Baja California. He was at first successful, but was soon overthrown. His next attempt was upon Nicaragua.

Nicaragua was politically unstable, having thirteen leaders between 1847 and 1855. Two parties, the Legitimists and Democrats, were at civil war. The Legitimists were broadly friendly to the US, UK and conservative landed interests, and the Democrats represented the people and oppressed interests.

Walker recruited fifty-eight soldiers of fortune and set sail from San Francisco. Some were experienced veterans; others included disappointed and luckless miners and prospectors, drifters, wharf bums, and ne'er-do-wells. Those fifty-eight were to be known as "William Walker's Immortals".

Walker's ship, the *Vesta,* had been attached for debt by the San Francisco Sheriff, who had left his Deputy on board to ensure compliance. Walker invited the Deputy into his cabin at midnight for a drink, and the unsuspecting official complied. *Harper's Weekly* reported that Walker, in a slow, quiet, Tennessee drawl, offered the official a choice: "There, Sir, are cigars and champagne, and there are handcuffs and irons. Pray, Sir, take your choice." The Deputy Sheriff took the sensible of the alternatives and the *Vesta* set sail. He was released hours later.

After six weeks at sea, the filibusters landed and made their way in a tropical downpour to the Revolutionary capital of León where they were greeted by a cheering throng. Walker was given the rank of Colonel, and his troops were named *La Falange Americana.* All were immediately naturalised as Nicaraguan citizens.

But Walker had a more extensive agenda. He was secretly glad that things were going badly for the Democrats, since they would need him all the more, and his aim was to dominate and Americanise Nicaragua.

TWO WARS IN TWO DECADES

The Battle of Rivas on July 29, 1855 was the first hot engagement. When the first shots were fired, Walker's native allies

The Battle of Rivas

turned and fled, leaving the Americans to fight alone, outnumbered eight to one. He lost his two most capable officers, plus thirteen other Americans. After several hours of door-to-door fighting, Walker retreated, leaving behind half a dozen wounded who could not be moved. These six prisoners were later chained to a pile of fagots and burned alive.

Additional recruits arrived some weeks later. Walker's strength was now up to 250, all volunteers, and another battle ensued at Rivas, with unspeakable atrocity on the enemy side. In mid-October, Walker attacked Granada, the Legitimist capital, with 100 American and 250 native troops. This time everything worked. Walker captured Granada with no losses on his side. Following a few more skirmishes with no losses, Walker concluded a Peace Treaty on October 23, 1855. A new President and Walker, now a General, were sworn in, but in truth Walker had taken over as virtual dictator of the nation. He had achieved his aim at relatively small cost, but it is horrifying to think that Edwin Fitzhugh may have been one of those burnt alive.

Walker soon had himself elected president of Nicaragua and the US recognised his government. Three months after gaining the presidency he instituted slavery in order to gain favour with the southern states of the US. He aimed to use these slaves to build a Nicaraguan canal to link the Atlantic and Pacific. He declared English the official language, seized Cornelius Vanderbilt's transport company and took out a large loan, putting the territory of Nicaragua up as collateral.

Walker's eventual end came as a result of betrayal by a British Officer. After five more years, and many further adventures, Walker was obliged to surrender, in the face of Honduran opposition, to the British warship *Icarus* under Captain Norvell Salmon at Trujillo in Honduras. Walker gained an assurance from Salmon that he was surrendering to a British Officer and British Authority. Walker's mistake, however, may have been to introduce himself as "William Walker, President of Nicaragua". Salmon then handed him over to the Hondurans, but sixty-eight of Walker's men were treated as Americans and returned to the US. In truth, the British wanted Walker out of the way, as they could meddle more effectively on their own. Without much procedure or ceremony, Walker was executed by firing squad on September 12, 1860, the riflemen needing two volleys and a *coup de grace* to finish the career of the nineteenth century's most notorious filibuster.[xxxiv]

Edwin was dead, but by now John had set himself up as a wholesale hardware merchant in Covington, Kentucky, thus migrating westward from Virginia along with the surge of new immigrants moving to populate the new West. The State of Kentucky had in fact been formed from part of *John settles in Kentucky, but he returns to Texas for his asthma* western Virginia. The western migration began from Caroline, Gloucester, King William, and King & Queen Counties of Virginia, so really John was not moving that far. Business must have been good in Covington for, in 1859,[xxxv] he refers to the town as having *"the finest openings for business I know of anywhere,"* and invites his uncle to join him in business *"to unite the Iron trade with my Hardware."* Unfortunately, John said, he did not have the capital to do it alone. In the same letter, he mentions that he travelled as far as New York to buy goods for his business.

The hardware business was called Fitzhugh & DeGarmo, a partnership between John and David DeGarmo, and was located at "east side Madison 2nd door below Pike", and his (presumed) home address was "south side 3rd between Greenup and Garrard". Street numbers did not get assigned until later.[xxxvi] Later, by 1862, David DeGarmo was in partnership with a certain R. H. Simpcoe for hardware and farm implements at an address in Madison Street.[xxxvii] John had gone to Texas in the first half[1] of 1860[xxxviii], having presumably sold out his interest to Simpcoe.

According to family tradition, John's move to Texas was caused by asthma which he had suffered since 1848,[xxxix] and for relief he went to Texas to visit his friend Sam Houston,[2] by now Governor of the State. John was familiar with the State, of course, having fought there in the Mexican War in 1846-48. Houston apparently recommended the hot, dry climate of Texas as appropriate for asthmatics. How permanent that visit was planned to be, we do not know, but according to the 1860 Census he and the family were living in Cannonville, Texas, a very new settlement between Austin and San Antonio. He was in the occupation of "Stock Breeding" with Real Estate of $800 and Personal Estate of $150.[xl] He had arrived in Texas just in time for the Civil War.

The Civil War touched virtually every family in the South, many with tragic consequences. As already mentioned, John's brothers, Patrick Henry, Lafayette, and Thaddeus all served in the War. Lafayette succeeded in raising the first Confederate regiment from Kentucky. As far as Patrick is concerned, by the outbreak of war in 1861 he must have been someone of considerable local standing although nothing *The Civil War breaks out, and the entire family joins up* is known of any previous military service or training. Having been born in King William County, he had moved to Middlesex County in the 1840's where he established residence at "Woodville," a farm near the present Cash Post Office.[xli] Recruitment for war service in those days was not organised as today into national conscription, but relied largely on volunteers and on certain local

---

1   See Note 100 following the Family Tree.
2   Scrapbook of Mary Fitzhugh Thornton, Vol 1, SB 6, Austin Public Library, Texas, *Austin Daily Statesman*, May 6, 1894, Obituary Notice of J.H. Fitzhugh; also his letter of March 4, 1859, Mary Fitzhugh Thornton Scrapbook, Austin History Center, offers to an uncle a letter of introduction to "my old friend General Houston, who might be of some service to you."

leaders to gather them in. By all the evidence, Patrick was just the sort to whom the community would turn to form a band of patriots.

Patrick began by recruiting a company of volunteers from Upper Gloucester County. Recruiting began in May, 1861, and seventy came forward in one week. Patrick was selected Captain and his own son-in-law, S. B. Shelton, First Lieutenant. Patrick himself had to go to Richmond to buy materials for uniforms and the local ladies made them under the direction of a tailor, the father of the Third Lieutenant. They must have been good seamstresses, for a picture of Patrick[xlii] in the County Shrine of the Gloucester County Courtroom shows him resplendent with full beard, sword, and a uniform with many buttons and braids.

The new Company set off on Sunday, June 2nd, 1861, waved and cheered by their wives and family, in carts supplied by local farmers. At Gloucester Point they were mustered into the Service of Virginia for twelve months, no one believing the War would last very long. They became Company B, the second of ten companies of volunteers to arrive, in the 26th Virginia Infantry. They were issued with arms, which turned out to be flintlocks left over from the War of 1812.

The War, however, turned out to be long and bloody. The South gained the offensive and ascendancy early on, only to slip back to retreat and defeat by 1865. In all, at least 104 men served in Company B, one of whom was Patrick's sixteen year old son, Allen Fitzhugh. Company B's casualties were the highest of the regiment; thirty-one of the 104 did not return, including Patrick himself. He was often mentioned in despatches (Note 101) and was promoted to Major in 1863,[xliii] but he was killed at Petersburg, Virginia on June 17, *Brother Patrick is killed on a revenge raid* 1864. It was Patrick's own bravery that led to his death. Patrick had been informed, erroneously, that his son Allen had been shot while a prisoner on June 16th. On the morning of the 17th, he confided to a brother Officer his desperation for revenge at any cost. The same day, while trying to rally his troops after a collapse of the Confederate lines, he was surrounded by Federal troops and called upon to surrender. Refusing, he was shot down. He was again invited to surrender, but replied that "he would never surrender to such a barbarous and inhuman race." He drew his revolver and shot and killed four of the enemy before he fell. He died while being carried from the field by Federal troops.[xliv] The Rev. William E. Wiatt, Chaplain of the 26th Virginia Regiment wrote of Patrick's bravery in battle, his kindness as a husband, neighbour, and friend: "It was impossible for him to hear or look upon suffering without sharing and endeavouring to relieve it. His home, his heart, and his hand were open to all."[xlv]

Thaddeus had an extremely gallant and indeed swash-buckling war, and he left us a truly graphic account[1] of his exploits. When conflict was inevitable, he was as quick as anyone to enlist. The news came that Virginia had seceded from the Union and in his own words: *"...in a few hours I joined the Cavalry..."* [and the next day] *"was elected second lieutenant."* In a few days, he was *"appointed ... as a surgeon of a battalion of cavalry."* [xlvi] Within two months, the horrors of war became apparent:

> *"I went over the ground* [Cold Harbor, June 27, 1862] *which was literally covered with dead, and at places two or three were laped* [sic] *over each other and the aspect was woefully gay as they were dressed in the most gorgeous Zouave uniforms...many were bayoneted in the act of jumping over the embankments. This was a horrible sight but such is war."* [xlvii]

Shortly after, he observed:

> *"...woe to the man who showed his head above the trenches. Our pickets would frequently place a hat on a bayonet and hold it up, when it would be pierced by one or two balls. This picket firing went off for a couple of days."* [xlviii]

Barely three months into the War, Thaddeus was mentioned in despatches for "conspicuous gallantry".[xlix] However, in the early days at least, both sides were conscious that, in the end, it was Americans firing at fellow Americans. Strange co-operation and even camaraderie broke out:

> *"When on inspection of the line one day, I recognized the officer of the day on the opposite side by the red sash he wore, and in order to attract his attention I raised my white handkerchief on the end of my saber. He immediately recognized my flag by raising his handkerchief... We met on the banks of the river and I asked if that picket firing could not be stopped as it was very*

---

1   Thaddeus Fitzhugh's *Memoirs* are a treasure trove of personal detail and surprising anecdotes, comprising some 35,000 words. They are undated but were clearly written long after the end of the War. These extracts are unjustly brief in order to conform to the style of this History.

annoying to both sides and accomplished no good. He replied by saying he would send back to headquarters for information. I, at the same time, sent a courier to General Hill, informing him of what I had done. Our couriers returned about the same time and both sides ordered the picket firing should be stopped. That afternoon in going along the lines it was amusing to see the number of soldiers of both armies along the banks of the river keeping up constant traffic in tobacco, coffee and sugar. Mr. Yankee would ask Mr. Johnnie if he had any tobacco to exchange for coffee and Johnnie would tie a rock to a plug of tobacco and throw it across the river, and Mr. Yankee would take a piece of pine bark, making a sail out of paper and fix a rudder so that it would sail across the river, bringing over a load of coffee or sugar. This trade went on to such an extent that heavy drafts were made from Richmond for tobacco and the sutler's stores would furnish the coffee, sugar and other stores from the north side, this state of things continued several days and the soldiers would cross over from the opposite sides and intermingle to a certain extent, so much so that it was feared that it might become demoralizing to the army; when an order was issued that no soldier should appear nearer than one hundred yards of the stream.

"In my first interview of the federal officer of the day (a major) we met on the trunk of a tree that had been thrown across the stream when we had a lengthy and interesting visit, and found that major an intelligent and accomplished gentleman. In our interview he remarked he had friends in the confederate lines, from whom he had not been able to hear or communicate with for a long time and I offered to take any letters he wished to send through and see that they were properly mailed. He asked if it would be convenient to meet him at the same place that afternoon. We met there again at about 3 o'clock in the afternoon when he gave me several letters all unsealed, with the request that I would read them to be sure there was nothing countermand in them. On our parting he presented me with a fine pipe..." [1]

For a time at least, the same spirit prevailed during an organised exchange of prisoners:

"...an orderly reported to me the arrival of some prisoners and among them was General Reynolds and several members of his staff. On my reporting it to General Hill, he directed that General Reynolds be conducted to him. The most affecting scene occurred, not a word was spoken, they shook hands most cordially and each

placed his left hand on the other's shoulder. When General Hill turned to those present and requested them to retire, these two general remained in the room for about half an hour when breakfast was announced, after which General Hill sent General Reynolds and his staff in his headquarter ambulance with an escort to Richmond, with a request that General Reynolds be sent down the James with the first batch of prisoners for an exchange. General Hill stated that he had never loved one so dearly as General Reynolds. They were class mates at West Point, graduated in the same class and assigned to the same regiment and messed together until the war called them to different fields." [li]

Soon came the first of narrow escapes: *"...on their [federal troops'] arrival at Mathews Court House and finding that we had escaped they entered the room I had formerly occupied at the hotel and destroyed everything they could find of mine, my books, diploma and other things I valued they burned. My clothing they gave to negroes."* [lii] But Thaddeus was clearly in fear of his own life, for few soldiers would forego a good pair of shoes: *"strapped to the haversack of one of the confederate dead was a fine pair of shoes which he had evidently taken from a sutler's store at Mechanicsville, as they had never been worn. I took up the shoes and finding they were exactly my size, jumped on my horse, but thinking that I might meet with the same fate as the poor soldier I threw the shoes on the ground..."* [liii]

In spite of the well documented slaughter, chivalry still had a place in this war:

"I was ordered to take a train of ambulances and wagons and move all sick and wounded [NB enemy sick and wounded] *... In each of these field hospitals were federal surgeons left in charge, and in consequence of my humane action Dr. Ellis of the* [federal] *Maryland Brigade of Lancers presented me with a handsome present in behalf of the surgeons. ...a cartel* [was formed] *for the exchange of prisoners ... [and to escort] a lady who was the wife of one of the officers of the War Department, who wished to go through the lines and to her old home in St. Louis, Missouri..."* [liv]

And later, during another exchange of prisoners, a fine banquet was fixed for the officers of the opposing sides, much wine flowed and Thaddeus wrote *"In all my life, I don't think I ever spent two more pleasant days..."* [lv]

But beneath all of this decorous behaviour there was clearly a daring and bold man:

JOHN HENRY FITZHUGH 1821-1894

"I suggested to Colonel Jones that we go ashore and capture these men as they were there in a strange country and knew nothing of the surroundings, to which he refused and I replied that if they would not go with me I would go alone, so I took off my boots, rolled up my pants and as soon as we founded the point from the island started for the shore. The water being about knee deep as it was low tide, they could not see me until I rounded the point and was about one hundred yards distant. I had shoved my pistol around to my back and started up the beach as carelessly as possible. When reaching thirty or forty yards and in full sight of the men, one of whom was standing on the beach with a gun evidently on guard, the others were around the fire drying themselves, as they were wet as rats, the bank was four or five feet high, and the arms were stacked along the beach. On approaching them I suddenly drew my pistol and ordered the man to drop his gun, and the first man to approach the beach would be a dead man, and as my camp was just across the woods, the first fire would bring a whole regiment down on them. I ordered them to fall in line and as I was barefooted and knowing we would have to go at least a mile and a half through some pine timber, I ordered one of the men to give me his shoes, when he said there was a pair in one of the valises. I directed him to get them and to throw them to me, thinking there might be a trick to get my pistol by throwing me off my guard. He soon threw me a fine pair of gaiters. We marched down the beach in full view of the gun boat ... when we were about one mile they wanted to know where my camp was, to which I replied, not to be uneasy, we would approach it in due time. We soon reached Mrs. Edward's farm, where I knew two of my men were, and as we approached the house, my men and several young ladies from the neighborhood and some from the mainland were eating watermelons. I remarked to my prisoners that there was my camp. I had thirteen men and one woman, who had been a laundress, of one of the regiments of the brigade. She turned to the men and in all my life I never heard such abuse as she heaped upon them, calling them miserable cowards and other names – thirteen men to surrender to one man." [lvi] This was good for war propaganda too: *"...The next morning after the arrival of these prisoners in Richmond, the* Richmond Dispatch *came out with an article saying that thirteen men and a woman were surrounded and captured by one man."*

But then another narrow escape: *"Soon after ... I was some distance in advance when I heard the whiz of a minnie ball close to my*

*head, and as I turned saw two federals, one who was in the act of firing. I
dodged just in time to miss the ball."* [lvii] In this incident, he captured *"a
number of prisoners"* including a lieutenant. Thaddeus placed the enlisted
men in the King & Queen Court House jail, but, out of respect for a
fellow officer:

> *"The lieutenant I took with me in the Hotel, and that night both of
> us retired in the same bed. I hung my arms on the bed posts and
> had a good night's rest, but on waking the next morning asked the
> Lieutenant how he had rested and he informed me he had hardly
> slept a wink, as he had been deliberating all night over making me
> his prisoner and taking me across the York River into the Federal
> lines, but as I had treated him so kindly and been so white, after
> he had deliberately shot at me, he could not betray my confidence
> to the extent of making me a prisoner, or escaping over to his
> lines. I saw at a flash the position I had placed myself in, as I had
> not even a picket out and my feelings can be well imagined. I had
> the cold chills to think how easily I could have been made a
> prisoner, and the Lieutenant could have freed himself. I thanked
> the Lieutenant for the confidence he had imposed in me and
> promised that he should be rewarded as soon as we reached
> Richmond. I went to Libby prison and stated the circumstances to
> the Commandant as I knew him well, and asked that the
> Lieutenant should be sent down the James with the first prisoners
> for exchange..."* [lviii]

Thaddeus obviously had a positive outlook on life and a
capacity to remember the good parts:

> *"While we were in Mathews we had a most delightful time when
> not engaged in war, as the county was celebrated for its beautiful
> ladies and the hospitality of its citizens. It is with pleasure at this
> late date we refer to the happy times we had, attending to the
> gaiety of the dance and partaking of the splendid dinners during
> the day, and the delightful sailings on broad waters bordering the
> bay, when the gun boats were not too close to be neighborly..."* [lix]

and make light of the hardships: *"The winter was unusually
severe and as we had no tents, we prepared a shed to sleep under
by putting two forked posts, and a cross pole with fence rails
placed obliquely, with blankets and oil cloths spread to shed off
the rain and snow, but for beds we procured straw and spread our
blankets overlapping each other under which six of us slept. A big
log fire was in our front and when one wanted to turn the order
was given 'all turn'."* [lx]

JOHN HENRY FITZHUGH 1821-1894

The War continued in this mixed vein of gallantry, pleasure, and horror. After a battle in which Thaddeus had two horses shot from underneath him, and had *"to retire to the rear with my saddle and accoutrements on my back,"* [lxi] there followed not only a Grand Military Ball, but a Society Wedding in which Thaddeus was a groomsman:

"...Colonel T. L. Rosser of my regiment was married to a Miss Winston of Hanover Court House. It was one of the grandest weddings I had ever had the pleasure of attending. General Lee furnished the Colonel and his party with a special train. Generals Fitzhugh Lee, Dearing, Young of Georgia, Quarles of North Carolina and another General ... Major Von Bach, a Prussian officer... and Major Taylor of Fitzhugh Lee's staff and myself were the groomsmen. Mrs. Winston's mansion was about a mile from the courthouse and a beautiful place it was that night, with a large lawn, brilliantly lighted up. In the hall were two large tubs, well filled with toddy, one of apple brandy and the other of peach brandy. After the ceremony came a dance and then the supper and a most sumptuous one it was, as every delicacy was supplied. The bride was a charming lady, and as beautiful as she was charming. Well do I remember how brilliant she looked that night. The dance was kept up to a late hour at night, and at an early hour the next morning we started on our return to the army. A few days after the severest cavalry battle of the war ensued." [lxii] War in those days was clearly different from what we know now, but the horror was never very far away: *"When we reached Carlysle* [Pennsylvania], *General Stuart sent in a flag of truce to demand its immediate surrender, or else we would shell that city. His demand was refused and he was told he must capture it first. Stuart opened a heavy artillery fire and as my regiment was at the head of the column and I commanded the first squadron, we could easily hear the screaming of the people and witness the burning of the houses from the exploded shells. ...Before leaving Carlysle Stuart ordered fire set to the barracks and as we marched out, they were in full blaze. We made a rapid march* [to the Battle of Gettysburg]...*All day we could hear a continuous heavy boom of the cannons. That night was the first night's rest we had had in seventeen days, all of which time I had not taken off my boots nor the saddle from my horse...or a square meal except what we could pick up along the line of march."* [lxiii]

TWO WARS IN TWO DECADES

Many now believe, half-mistakenly, that the Civil War was about freeing slaves, and today we think of slavery as totally iniquitous and intolerable, but an interesting insight into the relationship between master and slave comes from Thaddeus' own words:

> "My servant Peter was as faithful a negro as ever saddled a horse or polished his master's boots, and he remained with me until the close of the war. He was captured twice, but always got away and returned. On one occasion I sent two of my horses back home to recruit and get a fresh mount and as Peter was passing through Gloucester County, he met a regiment of cavalry. The Colonel of the regiment questioned him closely as to where he was from and as to where had got such fine horses. He told them he had stolen them from the rebel camp, back in the valley, and was then on his way to Gloucesters Point to dispose of them. The Colonel ordered him to turn back and go with the regiment, which was out on a scout, when Peter asked him if he might go on to the point as he had been located there before the evacuation, and he would remain until the return of the regiment. The Colonel gave him a note to the Commandant at Gloucester Point, who would give him feed for his horses and rations for himself. As the regiment moved on and was soon out of sight, Peter started through the woods in the direction of the adjoining county, and going to Mrs. Christian's house, my brother's [Patrick Henry Fitzhugh's] mother-in-law, where he left my horses and procuring a fresh horse returned to the army bringing the note with him to me, and on another occasion... a lot of our horses were captured, and Peter was captured along with the horses and taken back to General Wright's headquarters where he took in washing for the staff officers and at the battle of Fisher's Hill, ... Peter secreted himself in a cellar and as soon as our command came up he came out, and was most delighted to get back to my camp. I thought a great deal of Peter." [lxiv] By this time, President Lincoln had signed the Emancipation Act, and Peter could much more easily have simply asked the federal soldiers for passage to the North and gained his freedom.

By now, Thaddeus had moved from being the Regiment's Surgeon to become a front line commander, and a rather buccaneering one at that. His *Memoirs* contain a long account of how he captured the federal ship *Titan*,[lxv] but the text of his official report[lxvi] must suffice:

JOHN HENRY FITZHUGH 1821-1894

Report of Captain Thaddeus Fitzhugh, Fifth Virginia Cavalry
Steamer Titan,
Piankatank River, March 5, 1864

SIR: I have the honor to report that I have just returned from an expedition across the Chesapeake Bay to Cherrystone, Northampton County, Va., where I captured the entire guard (cavalry) with their horses, arms &c., and a large supply of subsistence stores, consisting of a large supply of army bread, 600 barrels of pork and bacon, and as many barrels of flour, rice, molasses, beans, sugar, coffee, &c.; also 9 army coats and several army cooking stoves, all of which I had to destroy by burning, not having the force or time sufficient to put on board the following vessels, which I afterwards captured, viz: The steamers *Iolas* and *Titan* and a large schooner, with their entire crews. I sunk the schooner, bonded the *Iolas*, and brought the *Titan* safely across the bay into this river. I cut the submarine telegraph cable and destroyed machinery and captured the operator,[1] whom, together with the crew of the *Iolas*, I paroled, not having the force sufficient to guard the prisoners and work the boat across the bay. All this I accomplished with 13 men of my company, assisted by Messrs. Maxwell and Burley, acting masters, C. S. Navy, who acted gallantly and were of great value to the success of the expedition. All my men acted nobly, particularly Sergeant Marchant.

T. FITZHUGH
Capt. Co. F, Fifth Va. Cav., Lomax's Brig. [2]

---

1   In fact, Thaddeus is being both modest and economical with the truth here. The telegraph operator's wife had *"rushed up to me making the most pathetic appeal that her husband might be released, and I could not resist an appeal from a lady in her condition."* [*Memoirs,* p.30]. Much later, Thaddeus was to learn that the child she carried was called Fitzhugh out of gratitude, and the operator became *"a most valuable friend"*, [*Memoirs, p.63*].

2   By a strange coincidence, the federal report on the same incident contained the statement: *"The Captain of the party happened to be the brother of an old friend of mine in the Pacific, named Fitzhugh."* This old friend almost certainly must be Edwin Fitzhugh, killed in Nicaragua in 1855, as told above; Union report of 5 March, 1864 by Wm. Webster, Fortress Monroe, on the capture of the steamer *Titan,* United States War Department, Record and Pension Office, and War Records Office, 1897, *The War of the Rebellion: A Compilation of the Official Records of the Union and Confederate Armies, Series 1,*

TWO WARS IN TWO DECADES

This report was endorsed by Major-General Fitzhugh Lee, at the Headquarters of Lee's Cavalry Division, then by Major-General J. E. B. Stuart, at Headquarters Cavalry Corps, and by General R. E. Lee, at Headquarters, April 1, 1864. Word of it got around, for Thaddeus further relates:

"*Gen. Stuart ... informed me that there was to be given him and his staff a grand entertainment that night at the house of one of the most prominent citizens of* [Fredericksburg] *and he wished me to attend... On reaching the house and being admitted to the hall, I met the General in the hall awaiting me. The parlors were large and were brilliantly lighted, and well filled with Virginia's beauties, and the gallant officers arrayed in their most splendid uniforms. When the general conducted me to the front, remarking 'Ladies, I have the honor of presenting you to the hero of Cherrystone', after which I spent a most delightful evening.*

"*It was pleasant even now after so many years to look back to the hard marches, and skirmishing with the rear, or advance guard of the enemy, and on going in camp after a hard day's work, he* [General Stuart] *would send an orderly around the camps and direct such officers as he wished to join him in a ride of five to ten miles to have a dance where he had made a previous arrangement, where there would always be collected a houseful of ladies, for to be known that General Stuart and his officers would be there, would invariably demand a large attendance. The dance would be kept up until a late hour at night, the next day there would be marching, and fighting as before. There seemed never to be any tire to General Stuart and after being up all night, the next day he would be as gay and as fresh as ever.*" [lxvii]

Thaddeus was getting quite a reputation. It is interesting to note from Federal correspondence[lxviii] that they feared a repeat raid by Thaddeus himself in the months that followed, but he did not go back to naval exploits, at least for a while. On the field, his lucky escapes continued:

"*In a cavalry charge near the Rapahanock I was wounded, a flesh wound in the right thigh, as it was a spent ball and lodged in the region of the Femeral* [sic] *nerve, caused me the most excruciating pain, but after being assisted from my horse, and the ball was removed, the pain was greatly relieved.*" And later "*had

---

Volume 51 (Part 1), page 1150, Government Printing Office, Washington DC.

a ball to pass through my coat sleeve, cutting my undershirt sleeve, then through my coat and undershirt, next to my body, and I thought I could feel the blood passing down my side...I unbuttoned my coat about that time and passed [my] *hand along my side and on its removal expected to find blood, but found none, much to my relief...”* [lxix]

It is well appreciated that Civil War loyalties divided families, and the Fitzhugh family was no exception:

“There was a Mrs. Wise living not far from the place where I was wounded and on calling and informing her who I was, she told me that Major Fitzhugh, a quarter-master in the federal army left there that morning and before the retreat he filled their cellar with enough groceries to last her for a year... I had the pleasure of meeting with the Major after the war, when the above circumstance was referred to. He remembered Mrs. Wise well. He was from Buffalo and connected with a New York regiment and I in conversation found that he was a distant relative.” [lxx]

Sadly for Thaddeus and the Confederate cause, not all actions were a success:

“I cautiously moved back to the road on which I had retreated, and found the valley strewn with the dead and wounded from my regiment. I had been in a great many engagements but never heard ball fly so thick, ... My Company had been recruited up but a short time before and I went into this fight with 49 men and officers. We had twenty-three captured,... and nineteen killed or wounded. It was a distressing sight to see so many of those I loved so dearly killed and wounded. Of the five captains with the regiment, Captain Boston and myself were left.” [lxxi] And later, after having yet another horse shot from under him, Thaddeus writes: *“The field was thickly strewn with dead and wounded, among them my attention was drawn to that of a captain who had received a mortal wound, from which he had lost a great deal of blood, and seemed to be in much pain. Seeing his suffering condition I dismounted and raising his head placed my canteen to his mouth, from which he drank most heartily, after which he expressed great gratitude and when about to leave I told him to keep the canteen as he would need more water for which he thanked me and took from his pocket a fine pearl handled knife, remarking that he would not live to meet me again, but asked that I would keep the knife as a remembrance of my kindness. I kept that knife for years and when it was lost, much to my regret.”* [lxxii]

TWO WARS IN TWO DECADES

The Confederacy had done well in the early War, but by now, November 1864, its Army had been reduced to a pitiable state:

"[General] *Early's army was in a most distressing condition, for want of food for his men and horses, and at times the infantry in their marches along the pike could be tracked by the blood from the feet of the soldiers. It was sad to see them in this pitiable condition and their bodies but little better clothed than their feet. The horses were so much reduced in flesh that they hardly could bear their riders. Early's army was truly in a sad plight... Lee's army was in very little better condition ... and at times entire regiments, deserted for want of food, it was evident that the Confederacy was on its last legs.*" [lxxiii]

However, this did not stop Thaddeus' gallantry. In a letter [lxxiv] to the Secretary of War General R.E. Lee writes: "*Captain Fitzhugh ...led the assault on Fort Kelley and was the first to enter the works and pull down the flag.*"

But even after three years hard fighting, and by now realising that defeat must come, Thaddeus' evident humanity and compassion held up:

"*I made my men relieve* [the prisoners] *by letting* [them] *ride their horses until they were somewhat rested, by riding and tieing* [sic], *and at times when I would see a prisoner about to give out, I would take him up behind me. Some years since an old soldier I met in Kansas, on his learning my name, asked if I was the officer that conveyed some prisoners up the valley that had been captured at New Creek. When I told him I was, he remarked he was most glad to meet me and to thank me for the kindness I had extended to himself and other prisoners, on that occasion. It made me feel proud to hear such an expression and I was glad to meet him after so many years.*" [lxxv]

By some nine months after Thaddeus' spectacular capture of the *Iolas* and the *Titan*, supplies were getting desperately short for the Confederate Army. General Lee asked Thaddeus in person and in confidence if he thought it possible to repeat the exploit on further federal supply ships. Thaddeus agreed readily, and gives a long account in his Memoirs, [lxxvi] but a heavily edited version of his official report [lxxvii] must suffice:

JOHN HENRY FITZHUGH 1821-1894

APRIL 4, 1865 – Capture of the steamer Harriet De Ford, near Fair Haven, Chesapeake Bay, Maryland

Report of Capt. Thaddeus Fitzhugh, Fifth Virginia Cavalry

Fredericksburg, Va., April 16, 1865

GENERAL: In February 1896, in obedience to orders from you, I reported to General R.E. Lee, ... to submit to him the expediency of an expedition to Cherrystone... for the purpose of capturing the steamers *Iolas* and *Titan*. In the interview the general inquired whether a transport laden with supplies for [the federal] army could not likewise be seized... Thinking such a thing possible I so informed him and offered to undertake it. I was directed ... to capture the steamers *Highland Light* or *Harriet De Ford*... ... we reached Cedar Point, I with one man went to a small village and reported ourselves as deserters from [the federal] army ... learning that [the *Harriet De Ford*] would make a landing at Fair Haven, I decided on that place. ... Equipping nineteen of my best men in the clothes of the boat crew we went on shore... I secured a wagon and team, stating that we were wood choppers... but we reached the wharf just in time to see the [*Highland Light*] majestically moving out into the bay... We awaited the arrival of the *De Ford*. As soon as [she] landed we went on board and procured passage under the guise of wood choppers. I immediately proceeded to place my men in positions to command all the points of the boat, from the engine room to the pilot house, and when about five miles from shore, finding all in readiness, I went to the pilot house, where the captain was, exposing my uniform and arms, and demanded the surrender of the boat in the name of the Confederate States. Seeing resistance useless, he ordered the surrender of the boat, and at a signal of the whistle my men quickly drew the pistols, to which was yielded the most perfect obedience. ... At the wharf we landed all the non-combatants and a part of the boat's crew, demanding of them their parole of honor to give us such time as to get down the bay in safety. During the day before we could hear the heavy guns at both Annapolis and Washington City, and from the capture of the *De Ford* we learned [of the defeat of Lee's army] rendering the object of the expedition futile... We started in three open boats, going nearly 100 miles by water in three nights. Our captures, 2 vessels, 1 steamer, 1 cannon, 62 stands of small arms, and many other valuable stores, and 205 prisoners, including about 60 negroes. Our loss none.

Respectfully submitted.

T. FITZHUGH

Capt., Comdg, Company F, Fifth Va. Cav., Payne's Brigade

Brig. Gen. W.H. Payne, C.S.A.,   *Commanding Brigade.*

Thaddeus was of course never to know, but the success of his mission was all the more remarkable considering that the Federal forces had intelligence of his orders and plans.[lxxviii] But on return, the fruits of that success turned sour, and he must have been heartbroken to learn that the War was over, and hear of the assassination of President Lincoln.

> *"I had gone but a few miles when I met some of Lee's men, when they informed me that General Lee had surrendered and that the war was over. Though I had suspected as much, it was a sad blow to me. I felt that in the impoverished condition of the south, from the ravages of war, that we were all ruined ... I learned of the death of President Lincoln. I felt before that our condition was pitiable, but we had learned to look upon President Lincoln as our only preserves, as he had proved himself to be a friend to the south as well as the north, hence we looked on him as our only salvation, having no confidence in Mr. Johnson and considering him a traitor and the assassination of President Lincoln would exasperate the northern people and that they would avenge his death by increasing the punishment of the south. Truly our last hope was gone."* [lxxix]

As if all that was not bad enough, he was horrified to learn of a federal reward of $10,000 for his arrest, on a charge of piracy in the rivers. The *Memoirs* do not say, but these charges must have been dropped after a few months of house arrest.

But what does an old soldier do?: *"I became restless and determined to leave the country and go to Australia, as some of my friends were about to leave for that country. I wrote to General R. E. Lee, informing him of my intentions and received a reply 'that he hoped the young men of Virginia who had comprised the flower of his army, would not leave their native land, but remain at home and assist in building up what had been pulled down and prove as true to the Stars and Stripes as they had in the past to the Stars and Bars, and he hoped the Stars and Stripes would float over an again reunited country.'"* [lxxx]

.o 116 o.

JOHN HENRY FITZHUGH 1821-1894

Thaddeus did not go to Australia.[1] We know that he was paroled at Richmond, Virginia, May 18th, 1865. Much later, he went to Fort Worth, Texas in the fall of 1878, on to Runnels County in April, 1886 to the prospective town of Ballinger, and practised as a physician. His first wife was Maria Savage, who may have died. He then married Julia Horsey, by whom he had two sons, John Golden and Edgar Horsey Fitzhugh. Thaddeus and Julia were divorced sometime after 1880. Later he married Laura Sharpe and had four daughters.[lxxxi] He was living in Kansas City, Kansas, in 1890/91.[2] Ever the Old War Horse, Thaddeus, aged sixty-three at the outbreak of the Spanish-American War in 1898, "…in a letter full of patriotism preferred his services to President McKinley expressing his willingness, if need be, to sacrifice his life in support of 'the principles of a firmly united country'."[lxxxii]

Luckily for the survival of our Branch of the Family, John was already in Texas when the War began in earnest. He did not join the Confederate Army until July 15, 1863, when he was enrolled as a Private in the 4th Battalion Cavalry, Texas State Troops.[lxxxiii] He officially enlisted on August 10, and was mustered on August 15. The record shows that he was discharged after serving one month and sixteen days at $12 per month plus $19.40 "for use of horse, arms, etc. total $37.80." Presumably his short term was due to his ill health. However, he was mustered again on March 16, 1864 at Camp Terry, when he was detailed to establish a tanning yard to produce leather for the Army boots. The only record of his exploits is that he served as a Scout from Liberty to Smithfield on November 3-14, 1863, and as a Scout of twelve men under Corporal Goforth from Camp Terry to Walnut Creek, Llano, after Indians. The dates given for this venture[lxxxiv] do not reconcile with those given above, even though they are on the same record, which may reflect something of the chaotic nature of warfare or bureaucracy.

John next surfaces soon after the Confederate surrender. He writes[lxxxv] to "Sister" Georgia on September 22, 1865:

---

1   Although he did try to join the Army in Egypt in 1870, asking Robert E. Lee for a recommendation.

2   See Notes, Note 105.

"I have booked up last night since the first of September $209. That is doing pretty well, don't you think, for a beginner?" He was back in business, but at what?

In February, 1866, he pours out his misfortunes:[lxxxvi]

"This War has not been the cause of my losing less than $6,000⁰⁰ in Money, 3 years ago when I went in the Army I had 111 head of Horses & 20 colts, and the most I have seen since is 98 head... and when I went to the front I had in my Tannery (for I had turned a Tanner) over $3,000⁰⁰ worth of [ ] all nearly tanned, and when I returned I did not realise more than $150⁰⁰ from all I left, not enough to pay for the skin of our hand. I had invested in the yard $1,100⁰⁰ in Money, my own time for 12 months & the labour of two men all the time & our Tanner for some months. The Horses I have on hand at my Ranch are not worth anything in the Market, I owed $2,000⁰⁰ on my entire stock ... I compromised by giving my entire interest in our bunch of Horses ... should be some 80 head ... I refused 4 years next spring $500⁰⁰ for one of them... I have got an old Governor Tanner to run my Yard and am in hopes to make 'Finish Calf Skin & Uppers' in Texas... all that is in the way now is hiring Garfield for the want of Means to begin, having lost all the available Means at my command."

He was not the only one to be affected, however:

"I was much pained to hear of Sister Mary's misfortunes, not only in losing a devoted husband [Patrick Henry], but all this World's goods, ...they lost all they had and that the negroes stole nearly every vestige of clothing the Girls had, she had not the means to replace them with, wish it was in my power to give you some aid. You may not believe you when I tell you, but I have made every pair of shoes my family has used for 3 years, so you see I have turned a Tanner & Shoemaker."

But at least he has some good news:

"With all my misfortune I am happy to say Texas has sustained the health of Myself, Wife and little Daughter, though at this time all of us down with the measles, 3 of my children have it & 2 of the negroes. I have 4 children, one daughter and 3 sons, and a finer looking suit of children cannot be found anywhere..."

He must have been really pressed for cash, as he tried to collect an old loan from his younger brother:

"Learned that Thaddeus is living in Acomack [County, Virginia] & doing well. I loaned him some money in 1854 & some when he was at College, & wrote to him asking for some back, but no reply. Please jog his memory... The last 2 years have been living 1¼ miles

from Austin" [because of the smell of the Tannery?]. *"When I was in the Service the Bush Whackers ran my family from my Ranch & I have not been able to get my wife to return to the Mountains, we are much more pleasantly situated here on account of security, yet the Mountains were healthy, I became attached to it, I may in another year move to Austin an account of sending my children to school."*

John did return to Austin, Texas and went into the hardware business there. Two Wars in two decades, the first of which brought our ancestor to Texas, and the second of which drove him out of his home and back to Texas, had the result that our Family was finally forced to desert the East and follow the Nation as it filled up the new West.

From 1865, John and Harriett settled down to family life in Austin with their children. It was at least stable, but by no means prosperous. In 1869, John had paid Poll Tax only, having no land, personal property, or animals and an income of $300 per year. The Tax Record[lxxxvii] lists him as "salesman with Sampson & Henricks, Merchants." We have a photograph of where he worked then. In 1874, he had land valued at $2,900 and Personal Property of $450, and by 1877 he was a clerk with George H. Drury & Co. By 1876, the land was worth $2,500, and there was no personal property. 1879 was worse still, with no land, a carriage ($80), 4 horses ($80), 20 cows ($120), and $18 miscellaneous. By 1881, he was employed as a clerk at Walter Tips & Co., where he stayed until around 1891. Walter Tips & Co. were hardware merchants in a building restored and (in 2001) standing in Austin, of which we have pictures. JHF's gold headed walking cane was given to him by Walter Tips, with his date of death on it; perhaps it was given posthumously to P H Fitzhugh whose name is also on it? In 1888, he paid Poll Tax only, listing no property at all, and in 1890 he did not even pay Poll Tax. However, he clearly tried to start a new venture around then, for in the *City Directory* of 1891/2 there is listed "Fitzhugh & Sons (John H., Henry A., & John G.) Fire Insurance Agents, Office 111 W. 7th St." His sons were still listed as employees elsewhere in the city, so maybe the insurance business had yet to prosper. This continued until 1893/4, the last year of his life.

Further insight into John's circumstances is shown by his successive addresses in Austin. In 1872, the family lived at the corner of Bois D'Arc and Colorado Streets, near the centre of town. In 1877, it was the corner of College Avenue and San Antonio Street, further out. 1881 saw the family at the corner of Rio Grande and Magnolia, yet further out. All of this is clearly rented accommodation. But by 1891, after Harriett's death, the father and two sons (H.A. and J.G.) are all boarding with Joseph Harrell, Sr. His last address was 205 W. 7th St, the address of his fire insurance business, but he was alone; his sons were boarding with their married sister Mary Thornton. The business did not continue, for in 1895, the year after John's death, John G. is listed as a land dealer, and the *City Directory* makes no mention of Fitzhugh & Sons. But at least he had a close and social family around him. He attended the First Baptist Church,[lxxxviii] even though his family in Virginia had probably been Episcopalians (Anglican).[lxxxix] He was Treasurer and always took collections there, but he was never a preacher.[xc] A picture of him and four of his five sons on page 121, probably taken in the early 1890's, shows a father sitting straight and erect, with his four sons doing him credit on both sides. Our ancestor, Henry Alexander, is seated on the right.

John wrote[xci] to his sister-in-law Georgina at this time:

"Oh! Georgia, how often I do wish it was so I could spend one more Summer in your county & renew those pleasant associations formed the Summer I spent at your House... Things have got better now. Harriett's main problem is her flowers and frost, & they have peaches & plums. Two of my boys, Henry & John, have a farm with about 5 or 600 acres in cultivation but all of it rented out, and one of them nearly 100 acres of corn up, and all cut down... Harriett has had pneumonia for a week, and was in danger, but she is now on the mend (I hope). She caught it from nursing the son of a friend." [Harriett died of this three days later.] *"...and I not having got over my spell of Asthma... Henry & John nurse their mother all day & ½ the night each. I have a very good old V^d Negro Woman who is a* professional *nurse to attend to her. This old Woman at one time was owned by the family of Thomas Cheesman who at one time I knew very well... I don't cough as much as I did... but I suffer from the want of breath. I can inhale, but not exhale".*

"Now with reference to my Boys,... I have no cause to be other than pleased with them, except their apparent indifference to their final end they are good moral young men, ... and can live in hope they may yet be brought their Error ere it is too late, I feel I

have great cause to be thankful they are as they are. One of them, Henry, is said by the Monied Men of Austin to be one of the best business young men in Austin, and the finest Trader in the City... Georgia... I can't write as easily as I could some years back, it is a task for me now..."

Harriett had died in 1890, but John lived four more years in rather sad circumstances, while putting a brave face

JOHN HENRY FITZHUGH 1821-1894 and HIS FOUR SONS

John is pictured with four of his sons, Phillip Aylett, Henry Alexander, John Glasscock, and Patrick Henry. Henry Alexander, our ancestor, is seated on the right. This photograph was probably taken in the early 1890's. Their sister Mary Ann is not shown, although photographs of her at this period do exist.

on it. He writes[xcii] and refers to a Lady "Macon", the daughter of Patrick Henry,[xciii] who came on a visit to Austin and was presented to the Governor, but John could not get out that night owing to his Asthma, but *"my general health is good"*. *"We have two very comfortable rooms opening in to each other"...* *"my little Land Lady, you would be loath to part with her... Myself and the boys are all pleasantly located as we could ever expect to be." ... "The weather will not permit my going out at night."*

Left to Right: LaFayette, John Henry, Philip Aylett, and Thaddeus

John had been granted a pension of $8 per month in 1887 for his Mexican War service.[xciv] For some reason, Congress had authorised the increase of pensions to $12 per month to any pensioner who was wholly incapacitated for manual labour and for whom $8 per month would not provide the necessities of life. John applied,[xcv] stating that that he had had asthma since 1848 and now had a rupture and included sworn statements substantiating this. Sadly, two of these statements were from tax assessors who verified that John had no property at all known to them, and John stated that he was "dependant on relatives for subsistence." He was granted the pension of $12 per month on September 13, 1893. Perhaps mercifully, he only endured until May 5th, 1894, when he died in Austin, at two o'clock on a Saturday afternoon, of heart trouble.[xcvi]

John and Harriett are buried in Oakwood Cemetery in Austin. John: May 6, 1894, Section 2 Block 740 Lot 14; Harriett: March 16, 1890, Lot 13. Also buried there are Patrick Henry, Mollie, and Mary Fitzhugh Thornton.

The many twists and turns of John's life characterise, in a way, everything that was happening in the country. It was his generation that saw the most change in America, and it was men like him who, beginning in a colonial civilisation, paved the way for businessmen and entrepreneurs, like his sons, to come later and to capitalise, quite literally, on the exploits of their forefathers.

.oOo.

References

i   *Genealogies of Virginia Families*, 1899, p.866.

ii   Most of these dates are confirmed in *Virginia Historical Magazine*. Vol XL, No. 2, April 1932, p.175ff.

iii   Scrapbook of Mary Fitzhugh Thornton, Vol 1, SB 6, Austin Public Library, Texas, *Austin Daily Statesman*, May 6, 1894, Obituary Notice of J.H. Fitzhugh.

iv   Philip Aylett Fitzhugh Papers, Southern Historical Collection, University of North Carolina Library, Chapel Hill, Manuscripts #4872-z, Letter of September 28, 1844.

v   U.S. Federal Census, 1840.

vi   *Encyclopaedia of American History*, 7th Edition, Ed. Morris, RB & Morris JB, Harper Collins 1996, pp. 200 & 708.; *The American Nation – A History of the United States*, 6th Edition, Garraty, JA & McCaughey, RA, Harper & Row, 1987.

vii   Philip Aylett Fitzhugh Papers, *op. cit.*, letter Henry Coghill to John Fitzhugh, October 1843.

viii   Philip Aylett Fitzhugh Papers, *op. cit.*, letter of January 9, 1845, VMI Account of April 1, 1845, letter April 5, 1845.

ix   Philip Aylett Fitzhugh Papers, *op. cit.*, VMI Report of January 9, 1845.

x   Philip Aylett Fitzhugh Papers, *op. cit.*, Letter of September 8, 1844.

xi   Philip Aylett Fitzhugh Papers, *op. cit.*, Letter of April 5, 1845.

xii   Philip Aylett Fitzhugh Papers, *op. cit.*, Letter of November 28, 1846.

xiii   The author has seen the Philip Aylett Fitzhugh Papers in the Duke University Rare Books, Manuscripts, and Special Collections Library, Durham, North Carolina.

xiv   Philip Aylett Fitzhugh Papers, *op. cit.*, Letter of May 29, 2846.

xv   Mexican War Service and Pension Records, U.S. National Archives: Honourable Discharge of John Henry Fitzhugh, August 1, 1848; Land Warrant 28862, Vol. 17, p.158, October 5, 1848; Declaration of Survivor for Pension, March 25, 1887; Affidavit of Witness A.J. Dorn, March 25, 1887; Affidavit of Witness Lafayette Fitzhugh, March 25, 1887; Declaration of Pensioner for Increase of Pension, March 27, 1893; General Affidavit of Witnesses, June 26, 1893; Record and Pension Office - Return to Commissioner of Pensions, June 19, 1893.

xvi   *The First Regiment of Virginia Volunteers 1846-1848*, Lee A. Wallace, Jr, Virginia Magazine of History and Biography, Vol. 77, pp.46-77, British Library Shelfmark Ac.8545/6.

xvii   Letter of E. C. Carrington to the *Martinsburg Gazette*, from Point Isabel, Feb. 21, 1847,

xviii   *Encyclopaedia of American History*, 7th Edition, Ed. Morris, RB & Morris JB, Harper Collins 1996, pp. 226-228.

xix   Mexican War Military Records, U.S. National Archives.

xx	McCaffrey, James M., *Army of Manifest Destiny*, New York University Press, 1992, British Library Shelfmark YC.1994.b.947.
xxi	Wallace, *op. cit.*
xxii	Carruth, Gorton, *The Encyclopedia of American Facts and Dates*, 10th Edition, New York, Harper Collins Publishers, 1997)
xxiii	Wallace, *op. cit.*
xxiv	Mexican War Service and Pension Records, *op. cit.*
xxv	Philip Aylett Fitzhugh Papers, *op. cit.*, Letter October 14, 1850, Covington, Kentucky, from John to his brother.
xxvi	1850 U.S. Census of Covington, Kenton County, Kentucky.
xxvii	Philip Aylett Fitzhugh Papers, *op. cit.*, Letter February 29, 1851 from Philip A. Fitzhugh to Patrick H. Fitzhugh.
xxviii	Philip Aylett Fitzhugh Papers, *op. cit.*, Letter from John Fitzhugh to sister-in-law Georgina Tankard Fitzhugh, Cincinnati, May 6, 1852.
xxix	Philip Aylett Fitzhugh Papers, *op. cit.*, Letter from John Fitzhugh to sister-in-law Georgina Tankard Fitzhugh, Cincinnati, May 6, 1852.
xxx	Philip Aylett Fitzhugh Papers, *op. cit.*, Letter from John Fitzhugh to Georgina Tankard Fitzhugh, Cincinnati, July 3, 1852.
xxxi	Philip Aylett Fitzhugh Papers, *op. cit.*, Letter from John Fitzhugh to Georgina Tankard Fitzhugh, Cincinnati, February 9, 1853.
xxxii	Philip Aylett Fitzhugh Papers, *op. cit.*, Letter from John Fitzhugh to Georgina Tankard Fitzhugh, Cincinnati, February 22, 1853.
xxxiii	Philip Aylett Fitzhugh Papers, *op. cit.*, Letter from John Fitzhugh to Georgina Tankard Fitzhugh, Cincinnati, March 31, 1853.
xxxiv	*Freebooters Must Die!*, Frederic Rosengarten Jr, Haverford House, 1976, British Library Shelfmark X.800.27094. Other useful books on Walker are shelfmarked 10880.W.25, 010880.i.36, X.709.52200, WP/6458/1.
xxxv	Letter from John H. Fitzhugh, Covington, Ky., March 4, 1859, to his uncle Spottiswood Fontaine, Scrapbook of M.F. Thornton, *op. cit.*
xxxvi	*Covington City Directory*, 1860, p.399; communication from Charles King, Kenton County Library, June 7, 1999.
xxxvii	*Covington City Directory*, *op. cit.*, 1862.
xxxviii	Census Return for Cannonville Post Office, Hays County, Texas, July 11, 1860.
xxxix	Mexican War Pensions Records, Declaration of Pensioner for Increase of Pension, March 27, 1893.
xl	1860 Census, *op. cit.*
xli	Ludwell Lee Montague, Gloucester (County) in the Civil War, *Gloucester-Mathews Gazette Journal*, Thursday, April 19, 1962.
xlii	*Ibid.*; *Twelve Virginia Counties Where The Western Migration Began*, Gwathmey, John H., 1937, British Library Shelfmark 010410.l.22.
xliii	*Twelve Virginia Counties Where The Western Migration Began*, Gwathmey, John H., 1937, British Library Shelfmark 010410.l.22.
xliv	Anonymous letter in Mary Fitzhugh Thornton Scrapbook, *op. cit.*

xlv	Ludwell Lee Montague, *op. cit.*
xlvi	*Memoirs of Thaddeus Fitzhugh*, Eleanor S. Brockenborough Library, The Museum of The Confederacy, Richmond, Virginia, p.1.
xlvii	*Ibid.*, p.5.
xlviii	*Ibid.*, p.6.
xlix	Confederate report of 28 February, 1863 by Maj. Gen. A.P. Hill on the June/July 1862 battles of Mechanicsville, Gaine's Mill, Frazier's Farm, and Malvern Hill. United States, War Department. 1880-1901. *The War of the Rebellion: a Compilation of the Official Records of the Union and Confederate Armies*, Series I, Volume 11, (Part II), pp.837-840. Government Printing Office, Washington, DC
l	*Memoirs of Thaddeus Fitzhugh*, *op. cit.*, pp.6-7.
li	*Ibid.*, pp.7-8.
lii	*Ibid.*, p.7.
liii	*Ibid.*, p.7.
liv	*Ibid.*, p.10.
lv	*Ibid.*, p.12.
lvi	*Ibid.*, pp.14-15.
lvii	*Ibid.*, p.15.
lviii	*Ibid.*, p.16.
lix	*Ibid.*, p.17.
lx	*Ibid.*, p.18.
lxi	*Ibid.*, p.20.
lxii	*Ibid.*, p.21.
lxiii	*Ibid.*, p.23.
lxiv	*Ibid.*, pp.26-27.
lxv	*Ibid.*, pp.27-32.
lxvi	United States, War Department. 1880-1901. *The War of the Rebellion: a Compilation of the Official Records of the Union and Confederate Armies*, [Series I (53 Volumes), Series II (8 Volumes), Series III (5 Volumes), Series IV (4 Volumes)], Series 1, Volume 33 (1891), p.232. Government Printing Office, Washington, DC. The Federal report of the same incident is on p.231.
lxvii	*Memoirs of Thaddeus Fitzhugh, op. cit.*, pp.32-33.
lxviii	Union letters of 28 April, 2 May, and 5 May, 1864 regarding intelligence on the movements of Thaddeus Fitzhugh, United States War Records Office, Office of Naval Records and Library, 1897, *Official Records, of the Union and Confederate Navies in the War of the Rebellion, Series 1, Volume 5, Operations on the Potomac and Rapahanock Rivers, (December 7, 1861 – July 31, 1865)*, Government Printing Office, Washington, DC, pp. 414-416.
lxix	*Memoirs of Thaddeus Fitzhugh, op.cit.*, pp.35&45.
lxx	*Ibid.*, p.35.
lxxi	*Ibid.*, pp.39-40.
lxxii	*Ibid.*, pp.45-46.
lxxiii	*Ibid.*, p.48.

lxxiv   Letter of 8 December, 1864, *The War of the Rebellion, op. cit.,* Series 1, Volume 43, (part I), pp. 667-668.

lxxv   *Memoirs of Thaddeus Fitzhugh, op. cit.,* p.54.

lxxvi   *Ibid.,* p.55-60.

lxxvii   *The War of the Rebellion, op. cit.,* Series 1, Volume 46, Part 1 (1894) pp.1305-1307; also reported in *The Washington Times,* Saturday, May 24, 1997, p. B3.

lxxviii   *Official Records, of the Union and Confederate Navies in the War of the Rebellion, op. cit.,* Series 1, Volume 11, pp. 599-600.

lxxix   *Memoirs of Thaddeus Fitzhugh, op. cit.,* pp.60-61.

lxxx   *Ibid.,* p.64.

lxxxi   Email from Kirk Fitzhugh, January 16, 2004, quoting information from Michelle Dukler, great-granddaughter of one of them.

lxxxii   *The Atlanta Constitution,* April 4, 1898.

lxxxiii   Confederate Army Muster Roll, Texas State Archives.

lxxxiv   *Ibid.*

lxxxv   Philip Aylett Fitzhugh Papers, *op. cit.,* Letter of September 22, 1865.

lxxxvi   Philip Aylett Fitzhugh Papers, *op. cit.,* Letter from John Fitzhugh to Philip Fitzhugh, Austin Texas, February 27, 1866.

lxxxvii   Travis County, Texas Tax Records, 1869, 1874, 1876, 1879, 1888, 1890]. In 1872 the *City Directory* [Austin *City Directories* 1872/3, 1877/8, 1881/2, 1883/4, 1885/6, 1889/90, 1891/2, 1893/4, 1895/6.

lxxxviii   *Austin Daily Statesman,* Sunday, May 6, 1894, Funeral Announcement.

lxxxix   *A History of Caroline County, Virginia,* Marshall Wingfield, Regional Publishing Company, Baltimore, 1975, p. 297.

xc   This sketch of his life is taken from a letter from "Aunt Dot" Thornton, daughter of Mary Ann Fitzhugh Thornton, 1939.

xci   Philip Aylett Fitzhugh Papers, *op. cit.,* Letter from John Fitzhugh to Georgia Tankard Fitzhugh, Austin, Texas, March 13, 1890.

xcii   Philip Aylett Fitzhugh Papers, *op. cit.,* Letter from John Fitzhugh to Georgia Tankard Fitzhugh, Austin, Texas, December 30, 1891.

xciii   1880 US Census, Eastville, Northampton, Virginia, FHL Film 1255379, National Archives Film T9-1379.

xciv   Mexican War Pension Certificate 3047, June 10, 1887. U.S. National Archives.

xcv   Mexican War Service and Pension Records, *op. cit.*

xcvi   Newspaper clippings, Scrapbook of Mary Fitzhugh Thornton, *op. cit.*

GEORGE FITZHUGH

1806-1881

George Fitzhugh, though not in our family's direct line of descent, deserves a mention because of his place in American history. He was a fourth cousin of our ancestor John Henry Fitzhugh, being descended from William the Immigrant's son Henry. George was an intellectual, given to analysis of the developing economic system of America, and particularly the South. Like many others, he observed a failure of mid-nineteenth century capitalism and its seeming exploitation of workers. Unlike the socialists who were also motivated by this observation, he preached the doctrine that the patriarchal society and economy of the slave-owning South provided the only lasting solution, because, once a worker had become the chattel of his employer, the latter had a direct interest in the health and well-being of the former. George Fitzhugh was an articulate and convivial man, who preached this doctrine to the North, and debated it in the highest fora, for example with Wendell Phillips in 1855.[1] According to *The New York Times* in 1856, George was "A genuine Virginian, conservative, talented, refined – one of the old school heroes of the South whose presence and counsel in this age of turmoil should be regarded as a benefaction. Mr Fitzhugh, probably more than any other writer in the South, has given the world correct ideas of our institutions and our resources."

George's books *Sociology for the South* (1854) and *Cannibals All!* (1857), among others, aroused the ire of Abraham Lincoln more than most pro-slavery books. Lincoln took great note of George's views as expressed in pamphlets and editorials and went to considerable pains to refute them in his speeches. However, George's was not a doctrine which had much chance of success, and he lived to see the total collapse of the Society he hoped would lead the way to his social revolution. The Civil War finished the slave-owning South, and it is no exaggeration to say that George

---

1   The photograph opposite was taken just before the Fitzhugh-Wendell Phillips Debate at New Haven.

did a great deal to sow the seeds of that conflict. Indeed, George Fitzhugh had come to represent "The South" in many Northern minds. Despite his peaceful intentions, he had done his full share to make the Civil War inevitable. He lived to 1881, in time to see America thoroughly industrialised, having left any thought of his ideas far behind. It is sad that in some Fitzhugh family circles, he is referred to as "Crazy Cousin George."

For a complete description of George Fitzhugh's life and times, the reader is referred to the *Dictionary of American Biography*, and to a biography of him.[1] The latter is a fascinating account of the ante-bellum political and social background of Virginia and the South, provided the reader has a strong constitution for ideas totally alien to any modern liberal viewpoint.

.oOo.

---

[1]   *George Fitzhugh, Propagandist of the Old South*, Harvey Wish, Louisiana State University Press, Baton Rouge, Louisiana, 1943.

GEORGE FITZHUGH 1806-1881

HENRY ALEXANDER FITZHUGH 1862-1932

CHAPTER FOUR

BUSINESSMAN AND DEVELOPER

HENRY ALEXANDER FITZHUGH

1862-1932

It was after John Henry Fitzhugh had been compelled to settle in Texas that Henry Alexander Fitzhugh was born on April 1, 1862 during the second year of the Civil War. It is said that he was born in Huntsville, Texas in the home of General Sam Houston, at whose suggestion John Henry had come to Texas in the first place. Henry Alexander was the fourth child of six in all. The first three, William Bullett (1855, died 1856), Mary Ann (1858), and Philip Aylett (1859) were born in Covington, Kentucky, and the last two, John Glasscock (1863), and Patrick Henry (1867), were born in Austin, Texas.

Such are the hardships of war that it must have been a difficult time to have five young children, two born during the Civil War and one more afterwards, but at least Texas was far removed from the fighting front. The fact that the family was in financial difficulties brought on by the Civil War is told in the last chapter and also shown by the story of the naming of John Glasscock. Harriett could not find material for her baby's clothes, so she traded the family's silver water pitcher for a bolt of cloth from a neighbour named Glasscock with the understanding that when times were better the pitcher would be retrieved. The infant was named Glasscock to remember the bargain. The two families sadly lost touch and the pitcher was never recovered. John Glasscock was later to become a businessman, probably a wheat broker, but a quarrel alienated him from the rest of the family and contact was lost.

BUSINESSMAN AND DEVELOPER

In early adult life, all of the sons stuck close to home opting for employment rather than adventure, as the previous generation had done. In 1880, Henry Alexander was a "Druggist Clerk",[i] but by 1881/2, he was a clerk with JJ & WH Tobin in Austin and living at home with his family. John Glasscock was a clerk with Walker Brothers at the same time, also living at home. Philip Aylett was still living at home (no occupation mentioned).[ii] By 1883, John G. was a clerk with McKean & Co., and he and Philip A. were still living at home. In 1885, Henry Alexander was still with JJ Tobin and John G. had been elevated to city salesman with Crow, McKean & Co. By 1889, Henry Alexander was still a bookkeeper at JJ Tobin, John G. was now with Nelson Davis Co., and Philip A. worked as a travelling salesman, but had moved up to being a buyer for Brenham Oil Mills and boarding at Joseph Harrell's in 1891-2.[iii] In 1890, Henry and John had a 600 acre farm between them, and Henry was said to be "one of the best business young men in Austin".[iv] This situation held through 1891, except that father John Henry and two sons Henry A. and John G. were also boarding with Joseph Harrell Sr.

Philip Aylett invented a new "seed handler" capable of emptying railroad cars of seed much faster than by manual means. He must have done this around age fifty, and patents were applied for, but nothing more is known of this invention.[v] John G. Fitzhugh later went into business as "McDonald & Fitzhugh – Miller's Agents - Flour, Meal & Grain" in Jackson, Mississippi in the early 1900s.[vi]

Although his father had settled into a conventional hardware business, Henry Alexander seemed to have a bit more flair for enterprise, if not to say business adventure. Nothing is known of his education, which is perhaps why he seemed to lead a life of business ventures or adventures. At one time he managed a ranch in Meridian, Texas for the English owners, Rogers Brothers. Luckily for Henry, this period was a little late for the range wars which had recently afflicted the area. Texas had been a battleground for the conflicting interests of the cattlemen on the one hand and the farmers and sheep owners on the other. Neither form of agriculture was compatible with the other because the farms and fences limited the open range, and the sheep cropped the grass so short that it was useless for cattle. Many bloody conflicts had arisen and the State had finally decided to set a dividing line, the 100th West Meridian, as a boundary. East of it was farmland, and West was cattle country. Needless to say, the truce did not always hold, and the Town of Meridian was directly in the middle of the conflict for many years. It seems as though Henry tried to keep a foot in both camps. It was at this time that he registered the cattle brand **HA**, shown on page 137 and now registered in the name of Henry Antonie Fitzhugh. At the same time he tried to grow wheat while managing the ranch, but he was unsuccessful. Around 1904, he and four others bought the machinery and landleases of the Cincinnati Beaumont Oil Company, but they lost it later through a shareholders battle, which required a Supreme Court action before final settlement. After this, he moved to New Roads, Louisiana, where he lived until 1917. Apparently he abandoned Louisiana because of the bad water and fever conditions which even at that date had not yet been conquered. He moved to Memphis, Tennessee and worked in the Cotton Seed business with mills through Arkansas, Louisiana, and Mississippi. Some of our early genealogical notes are written on his company letterhead, which simply says "H. A. FITZHUGH COTTON SEED." After World War I, there was a big drop in cotton seed prices owing to the cancellation of many orders for war supplies, and he lost all the mills. By all accounts, he was never one to take things too hard, and he simply started up again.

Henry Alexander was a seasoned businessman of forty when he married Mary Scott, twenty, the daughter of an Austin lawyer, John Lyle Scott, and Emma Cable. We know sixteen ancestors of John Lyle Scott. Mary was born in Meridian, Texas on February 17, 1881. She had been to Stanford University in California, probably at the time less well known that the famous University it is today. It must have been quite an adventure for a young Texas girl to live near San Francisco in those early post-frontier days. The Scott ancestry is known for several generations, but it is not quite clear why they were married, on July 9, 1902, in Blairfield, Iowa, rather than in Texas.

Henry Alexander died in Memphis, Tennessee on March 22, 1932, never having seen a grandchild of his. Mary died in St. Louis, Missouri, where she was living with her daughter Irene, on April 19, 1943.

BUSINESSMAN AND DEVELOPER

By this route our branch of the Fitzhugh Family thus moved back to Texas, but of course by this time there were many other Fitzhugh relations in various parts of the State. For whom the town of Fitzhugh, Fitzhugh Road, and the Fitzhugh Baptist Church, all in central Texas, were named, we do not know. But what is certain is that the first Fitzhugh who came to a western frontier during the Mexican War played his part in paving the way for the next generation, such as his son Henry Alexander who followed him to become a businessman and developer. By the time the latter had died, the country they both inhabited had been transformed from a frontier to modern America in only two generations.[1]

.oOo.

---

[1] Much of the information in this chapter from a letter from Henry A. Fitzhugh (b. 1916), grandson of the first Henry A. Fitzhugh, May 29, 1981.

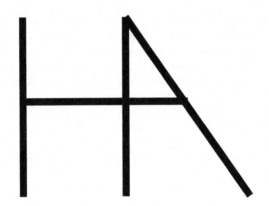

The cattle Brand of Henry Alexander Fitzhugh and Henry Antonie Fitzhugh, see page 135.

References

i	1880 US Census, 3rd Ward Austin, Travis County, Texas, National Archives Film T9-1329 Page 194B.
ii	Austin *City Directory* 1881/2 and following years.
iii	Austin, Texas, City Directories, 1889-92.
iv	Philip Aylett Fitzhugh Papers, Southern Historical Collection, University of North Carolina Library, Chapel Hill, Manuscripts #4872-z. Letter from John Fitzhugh to Georgia Tankard Fitzhugh, Austin, Texas, March 13, 1890.
v	Undated newspaper clipping from *The Daily Democrat-Times,* possibly Greenville, S.C., from Mary F. Thornton Scrapbook, Austin, (Texas) History Center.
vi	Compliment Slip in Mary F. Thornton Scrapbook, Austin, (Texas) History Center.

JOHN HENRY FITZHUGH 1904-1965

.o 140 o.

CHAPTER FIVE

MODERN AMERICA

JOHN HENRY FITZHUGH

1904-1965

J OHN HENRY FITZHUGH, the eldest child of Henry Alexander and Mary Scott Fitzhugh, was born on September 26, 1905. Such were conditions in New Roads, Louisiana, where the family were living, that Mary had to flee a yellow fever epidemic, and hence John was born in Jackson, Mississippi. Yellow fever, so called because doctors hung out a yellow flag outside of infected premises, was a terribly virulent infection, capable of wiping out whole streets and even villages. It was rife throughout the South, so much so that the U.S. Post Office would fumigate with sulphur all mail going from the South to the North during the summer months, even puncturing envelops with nails to ensure the contents were gassed as well. This was quite ineffective, as it was proved in 1900 that mosquitoes were the carrier. Fumigation projects in cities worked extremely well, and this epidemic was the last in the U.S.[i] Mercifully, our family survived it.

It seems inconceivable to look back from our twentieth century viewpoint and realise that not only were the swamps of Louisiana then still pits of contagion, but John and all his brothers and sisters to follow were reared with the help of an ex-slave. He may have been an old family retainer, and he loved children, saying they "had diamonds in their eyes." There were five other children: George, Harriett Irene, Lyle Scott, Henry Alexander, and Mary Aylett. Irene, Lyle, and Henry married and left descendants whose details are on the tree following Chapter Six. Mary remained unmarried and George adopted Natalie, his wife's daughter by a previous marriage.

John spent his early childhood in New Roads, Louisiana, where his father had a cotton seed oil mill. A few years later the epidemics became so bad that the family moved North to Memphis, Tennessee, and Henry Alexander managed his cotton seed business from there. For the first recorded time since William the Immigrant, the education of all the sons was taken seriously and they were sent to Webb School in Bell Buckle, Tennessee. This was a boarding establishment, rather unusual in America, especially as far "West" as Tennessee.

Some time after he finished School, John set about the first really serious genealogical work undertaken by anyone in our branch of the family. All his manuscript notes and a good deal of his correspondence survive, along with the family tree of total ancestry that he prepared. However, he never made any contact with any FitzHughs in England, and so was never to know any of his own Fitzhugh ancestry beyond Henry, the father of William the Immigrant. The work that he did was of high accuracy, as far as I have checked it, but he never learned of the mistake William the Immigrant made regarding the Family Arms. Consequently, John is buried under a tombstone with the Arms *Azure, three Chevrons interlaced in Base Or, a Chief Or* carved on it, and he left us two signet rings with the same Arms carved on them. Nevertheless, his work in genealogy provided the foundation without which no further work would have borne much fruit.

It was about this period, around 1926, that John had an illness, possibly a serious nervous breakdown, that hospitalised him for some time. The niece of the hospital Superintendent was Eleanor Jeanes, whom he was to marry. Their only child, Mary Eleanor, was born on September 9, 1935. They were divorced some time later around 1939.

John moved to San Antonio, Texas and there he met Mrs. Marie van O. Halverson, also divorced, with three young children. Marie[1] had been born in Belgium, where her father had been

---

[1]   This story of Marie's life is a greatly condensed version of a long history written by her brother, Derek van Osenbruggen and the present author. The full manuscripts of both of these are in the family

working as a consulting engineer. He travelled all over the world at that time and it was for this reason that Marie was born and travelled abroad, even though she spent all of her childhood in London, at 78 Alexandra Road, Wimbledon SW19. She went to the Greycoat Hospital in Westminster, becoming Captain of the School and of athletics and winning a number of school prizes in the form of books which we still have.

Marie developed a strong and independent character and will from an early age, possible due to a personality clash between her and her mother. Relations were not good between the two, although what is cause and effect is now hard to know. The positive effect of this is that she developed a determined will, and unbreakable constitution, and a sense of purpose that was to be needed to see her through a difficult life.

Both she and her brother did well academically, each finishing the London University BA and BSc certificates, and Marie went on to study at the Sorbonne. Their farther, who evidently wanted to see his children move away from home for the broadening of their education, arranged for Derek to go to America to the University of Michigan. This was arranged through business contacts of their father's. Derek found Michigan entirely to his liking, so much so that it was decided to send Marie as well. She went, and took a Degree in Journalism. One year before graduating, during a summer vacation, Marie and some friends got jobs as waitresses in Yellowstone National Park in the far West. It was there that she met Arnold Halverson, somewhat older and of Scandinavian descent. They became closely attached, and at the end of the summer she decided to go to Los Angeles to be near him, rather than to return for her final year at Michigan. However, she was dissuaded from this by Derek, who had to make a special trip to Yellowstone at their parents' behest, which was a cause of some rancour between Marie and her parents. Arnold then moved to Chicago, within visiting distance of Michigan, and got a job in a power station. After graduation, Marie got a job in Chicago working on the newspaper *The American*. She worked there for a

---

notes. Marie was the daughter of Antonie van Osenbruggen and Clare Elizabeth Groom. We know twenty-eight more her ancestors.

year before she and Arnold were married in Bowling Green, Ohio in 1927 before a Justice of the Peace.

Arnold wanted a ranch of his own, rather than power station work, and so they gave up their jobs and headed West. They ended up in Spokane, Washington where Arnold got another job in a power station. Their first child Dagny (which in Norwegian means Dawn, the time she was born) arrived in 1928, but unfortunately Arnold lost his job and they had to move to Alaska, of all places, where Arnold could find another power station job. Clemence and Michael were born there.

Dagny, Marie, and Arnold Halverson in Alaska, 1930

Possibly because of the Depression, Arnold lost his job again in 1931, and the family decided to move to Carmel, California, where some friends of Marie's lived. When money ran out in the middle of the Depression, there was no other choice but to go back to Arnold's family in Minnesota. His family were Scandinavian immigrants, who treated Marie as little more than a servant. Marie put up with it for about a year until she could take it no longer. They got an old car, somehow, packed the children into it, and headed South, as did many a Depression stricken family in those days. They arrived in San Antonio, where they were literally destitute. In the depths of the Depression, such families were looked after by charities and State authorities, and there was nowhere else to turn. By contrast, Marie's parents were on a Caribbean cruise, one of three round-the-world cruises they made, and they called in to Texas and San Antonio. Horrified at the situation, her father found them a house and plot of land on the edge of town, bought them some food, and gave them some money. They kept goats and chickens and grew vegetables, but Arnold never had steady work. This episode was the cause of a total break in relations between Marie and her parents, which was not healed until after her mother died in 1952, and her father visited us all in Texas on his own.

Marie eventually got a job with one of the agencies that looked after them, while Arnold took care of the children, goats, chickens, and garden. Marie's job was secure enough to enable her to study and take exams to enter the U.S. Civil Service. But the strain of this life was too much for their relationship, especially when Arnold wanted to move on again. Marie and Arnold were divorced around 1939. Marie always said that at the time she would have moved back to England, but was prevented from taking her children, who were American nationals, with her, so she stayed in San Antonio.

In the meantime, John had moved to San Antonio, where he had met Marie. In her words, they "got along extremely well together." They were married on November 30, 1940, and she continued to work in the Civil Service, even until she retired. Because of this, the family managed to become more secure and set up house at 215 West Myrtle Street.

By this time World War II had begun in Europe, and America was pulled into that conflict at the end of the next year. John volunteered for the Army even though he was exempt from the Draft owing to his age. He was trained in chemical warfare, which mercifully was never used anywhere. He was demobilised before the end of the War, probably because of his age, then approaching forty. He went to work in the Post Office in San Antonio, and their only child, Henry Antonie, the author of this work, was born on September 9, 1944. As soon as the War was over, the family, including the Halverson children, Dagny, Michael (Mickey), and Clemence built a new house at 174 Sherwood Drive. This was soon outgrown and, in 1948, a much bigger house was built next door on five and a quarter acres of vacant land at 168 Sherwood Drive.

By 1949 or so, Marie was firmly into a career with the U.S. Air Force at Lackland Air Base, where the training of all recruits was done. She was working her way up eventually to become the Head of Budget. She started work at 7 AM, finished at 4 PM, shopped every day on the way home, and did her housework between 4 and 6 in the morning every day. One of the habits that helped her relax and keep calm under all this work was her knitting - she knitted every moment she was not doing something else with her hands. She even won First Prize at the Texas State Fair for some of her Fair Isle sweaters.

Taking advantage of a more stable situation, John wanted to engage in the import business of silverware, china and fine arts, possibly because use could be made of the van O. family connections then still active in Holland. For this purpose, a company called *van Osenbruggen & FitzHugh* was formed. Much silver and china was imported from Europe, many exhibitions were held, and most of it eventually sold. However the fatal flaw in the whole scheme was that John loved the best pieces too much to sell them, and he was probably aiming at too high a place in the market. In any event, the business pottered on while the family collected and retained an enormous amount of silver, delft, pictures, and even some furniture that was all considered too good to sell. In the end, John was too much a lover of beautiful things, and too little a businessman, and the import business eventually petered out. He turned his thoughts to custom made jewelry, designed by himself. He obtained commissions for some beautiful pieces, all of which were hallmarked VOF. We still have three rings so marked. As a young boy, I can remember visiting Joe Bettancourt, his silversmith, and Levitt, the diamond merchant. Visits to Levitt's office were a real treat - to touch diamonds spread all over table tops is more than many are privileged to do. My father was allowed to bring home dozens of stones "on approval" to show to potential clients. The business was fascinating, never made any real money, and only had the positive result of supplying the next generation of Fitzhughs and Halversons with splendid engagement rings and the like.

JOHN HENRY FITZHUGH 1904-1965

On top of all the activity of trying to operate an import business part-time, John also set about conversion of the Sherwood Drive property into something of a landscaped park. It was a daunting prospect in view of the hostile climate, which meant that all of the new plants had to be watered constantly throughout the hot summers, and also because of the Martinez Creek which flowed through the property. The Creek was normally dry, but it would flood to be six feet deep and 100 feet across in a matter of minutes whenever there was a heavy rain, on occasion even cutting off the house from outside access. Ours was the largest residential property in San Antonio, and clearing it of trees, brush, and stones was backbreaking work, all done by John's own labours. The land became known within the family as *The Plantation*, and nothing befitted it more than to have a plantation bell to summon home the plantation worker. This bell was duly mounted on top of the garage, and as a small boy it was my duty to ring it to call my father in to lunch. In the end the plantation took on the aspect of a dry mediterranean semi-desert garden, but it was soon to be altered irrevocably as a result of neglect during John's forthcoming illness, and by a motorway which was built over part of it.

At about this time, John and Marie achieved something which meant a great deal to them - a reconciliation with the Church. Since both were divorced, they felt that the Anglican, or Episcopal Church is it is called in America, would not welcome them, and they had not participated in any significant Church activities since they were married. However, they made contact with a father Joseph, the vicar of a local High Episcopal Church, who took the view that Church attitudes had become more liberal. They were welcome, he said, and from then on they were both heavily involved in Church activities for the rest of their lives. John became a Lay Reader; he had the voice for it, loud and booming, just right for putting across the Word to a large congregation.

John had always been a dedicated Anglophile, solely because of his appreciation of his family and ancestors and his own romantic sense of history. In spite of being married to an English lady, who had been home several times, it was not until 1960 that a family trip, including me, was organised. It was the trip of a lifetime for him, made all the more poignant by the fact that less than five year later, he was to be buried at one of the beautiful spots he had visited, St. Martha-on-the-Hill, near Guildford. It was within a month of the return from that trip that John felt the first signs of the illness that was eventually to take him away. The illness was progressive, and in spite of the fact that he visited several of the best clinics in America, it remained undiagnosed. Even after an autopsy, to this day we do not know of what he died. He retired on disability from the Post Office in 1963 and passed away on May 20, 1965. It shows how fast progress has been in modern America in the twentieth century, and how near in time the past really is to us, that a man could be reared by an ex-slave, live to see men in Space, and die before he was sixty.

John's death, and the fact that I had left home by that time, left Marie more or less free. She worked on to retirement from the Air Force in 1967, and then took a round the world trip in 1968, which involved a coach trip from London to Calcutta, lasting 12 weeks. In 1969, I persuaded her to move back to England, about which she had hesitated, having got used to living in the States for so long. Even though she claimed to have regretted living in the USA all her life, she paid one last tribute to San Antonio by writing a historical novel, *Irish Flats*, set there in the 1890s.[ii] She also wrote another book, *Three Centuries Passed*[iii], a short history of the Fitzhugh family, which, though touching and valuable in many parts, unfortunately repeats many of the ancient historical errors that this Volume has corrected.

She lived long enough to see her last two grandchildren, Alexander and Edward. These last years were peaceful, but very active. Unknown to anyone, she was developing an internal cancer, which went unnoticed owing to her strong constitution and Spartan way of life. Even though she was planning a trip to Siberia in September 1977, she was suddenly stricken down at Sunday midday and passed away at 8 AM on Monday, September 5. It was a shock to everyone, and many of her friends were simply disbelieving. Nevertheless, it was a merciful end to what at times had been a hard life. At least she had seven good years of retirement, living in Hope Cottage in her beloved Sussex, so happy that she used to say to her friends that she could not wait to wake up in the morning.

JOHN HENRY FITZHUGH 1904-1965

Mrs. MARIE Van O. FITZHUGH, 1906-1977
From the dust jacket of her novel, *Irish Flats*

Marie had during her lifetime been over most of the World, and she had a lot of experience to show for it. The most extraordinary thing, however, is how her outlook and personality changed through her life. In her early years, she was self-determined and strong-willed, even difficult at times. In later life she was completely different - always working to the benefit of others, usually her family or many friends in need. For example, she financially supported Mary Eleanor, her stepdaughter with whom she had never lived, for some years after John's death, even though the two hardly knew each other. She showed almost no concern for herself, either material or emotional, but spent most of her fortunes and effort making it possible for others to do what they themselves wanted in life. It was a life of almost total self-denial. I am sure that it was a reaction - a very positive one - to the resentment she had to her relationship with her own mother. I remember she once told me that she wanted to be sure that her own children had enough pocket money, because she had, she felt, been deliberately deprived as a child, and wanted to see no child of hers suffer like that. To my mind, this exactly sums her life up. She suffered very grievously in the first half and spent the second half making sure no one she loved suffered in like manner. Many lesser people would have become twisted by such a life as hers, but we the beneficiaries have much for which to be grateful. For her, these experiences, not all told in this story, served only to make her into a true Christian, who then devoted her life to others, and to us. Her example will shine like a Beacon to me always, but will probably prove impossible to emulate.

.oOo.

References

i   *New Scientist,* 14 October, 2000, pp. 48-49.

ii   *Irish Flats, A Ghost of San Antonio's Past,* Marie Fitzhugh, The Naylor Company, San Antonio, 1972.

iii   *Three Centuries Passed,* Marie Fitzhugh, The Naylor Company, San Antonio, 1975.

HENRY ANTONIE FITZHUGH
at a London Underground Board Meeting

CHAPTER SIX

FULL CIRCLE

HENRY ANTONIE FITZHUGH

1944 -

I WAS BORN[1] at the old Physicians' & Surgeons' Hospital in San Antonio, Texas at 7.45 AM on Saturday September 9, 1944. By my mother's account, my first act in this world was to urinate in the face of Dr. Pinson who had delivered me seconds before, and this may explain why he never filled in the year on my birth certificate. This has caused me a minor problem here and there, but at the time I simply let it pass.

I was named, according to a loose family tradition, for my two grandfathers, Henry Alexander Fitzhugh, and Antonie van Osenbruggen. The former I was never to meet since he died in 1932, but of the latter I have fond memories, from when he visited Texas for several months in 1953.

I was the baby in a large and older family. My mother's three children were living at the family home at 215 W. Myrtle Street. Mickey (Michael), Clemence and Dagny's father Arnold was around from time to time, and I got on well with him until he died about 1957. My father's daughter, Mary Eleanor, nine years to the day older than myself, never lived in our family. She was raised by her mother, Eleanor, in Memphis, Tennessee.

After an episode where the Landlord tried to evict our family, and mother faced down the Sheriff on our own doorstep, the

---

1   This Chapter is a condensed version of a much longer and more detailed account contained in the family history archives, telling many stories not touched upon here.

family decided to build a house on what was then the extreme northern outskirts of town, at 174 Sherwood Drive. Later we built a much larger house next door at 168.[1] The land was so wild that at one time about 1946 my mother had to climb a tree to kill a mountain lion (about the size of a medium dog) for fear that it would jump on my father when he came home from work.

My mother went back to work when I was an infant, about 1946, purely to aid the family finances. Fortunately she found a very kind lady, Mrs. Stark, to look after me. Mrs. Stark usually had six or eight children, some her own grandchildren, in her house at once. It was like having two homes and families, and what I can remember of it was extremely good fun.

My first education began in kindergarten, where I went to Zion Lutheran Church along with Alice Chadwell. However my first real educational experience was at my next school, the Redeemer Lutheran, where I began in the first grade. All went well until near the end of my second year. I had been a keen fossil collector because that part of Texas is so rich in them, and I brought in my collection for a show-and-tell. I can remember the teacher looking very unhappy at the back of the class as I drew a picture of a fossilised Octopus (which I had never seen, of course) and expanded of the Theory of Evolution and Age of the Earth. Unfortunately, the Lutherans do not support the Theories of Darwin. I cannot remember what I said exactly, but it must have had some impact, because the teacher spoke to the Headmaster, who spoke to the School Board, who suggested to my parents that it might be better if I did not come back the next year. I had been expelled for Heresy! I did not learn of this until many years later. In fact, it was the best thing that could have happened to me, because it had the result that I went to Keystone School the next year. This was a far better school, which made me into everything I am, academically and intellectually. This was the first big stroke of luck in my life. I was to stay at Keystone until I graduated from High School. After having been there in the third grade for a half year, they decided to promote me into the fourth grade, so that I advanced one year overnight. It was my first taste of hard work.

---

1   This was a very strange house and property. A full description of it and its intermittent river is in the longer version of this account.

HENRY ANTONIE FITZHUGH 1944-

My early memories of this time are ones of pure delight. My older brother and sisters were very good to me, and Mickey even used to take me along with his teenage friends for their days out. Later, when he moved away from the house, he used to come home weekends and take me to drive-in movies. These were sublime occasions that I always cherish. Once, even, one of his girlfriends took me out to a film and a snack later on, no doubt trying to win Mickey's heart.

Something that I look back on with the fondest of memories is the Boy Scouts, which I started at age eleven. My Scoutmaster, E.K. Melton, was a wealthy owner of a meatpacking factory who had a ranch north of town on several thousand acres. Over the years the Scout Troop had developed a permanent campsite beside a river on hilly ground covered with cedar trees. It was a fabulous place - the Troop had the run of the whole ranch. It had two high hills on it, about a mile apart, and we used to play capture the flag, at night, between them. "Junior", as we called our Scoutmaster, also had a forty-two foot cabin cruiser on the Coast. Once he took me and two other Scouts down there for the weekend. Mine was the best Scouting career I know of.

At this point in my life, an event was to happen which affected my future so much that, in a sense, it has probably put me where I am today. It is hard to believe that when I was young in the mid-1950s, such things as computers, hand calculators, video recorders, and earth satellites had yet to be invented. One of these things came along in 1957, and it was to have a great effect on my life. Russia put up the first satellite, Sputnik I, on October 4, 1957. It is impossible to describe the shock to the American public that this was. There was much national heart searching, Congressional Investigations, and a general sense of National failure. Luckily for me, good was to come of it. Mr. Greet, Keystone's Headmaster, had always wanted to start an accelerated curriculum with a very heavy bias toward Science. He wanted to take in students who had high ability and interest in science and give them what amounted to an extra year of work, thus covering the first year of University as well. Competitive examinations were held all over San Antonio, and, even though I was already in the School, I had to sit in competition with all the rest. Twenty places were awarded, and I got number eighteen. (I was eventually to work my way up to number three, and then number two, when the existing number two left the School.) Without doubt, the superb start that this curriculum gave me was what got me into the Massachusetts Institute of Technology (MIT), and opened the door to much that followed. I can genuinely say that Sputnik set me on my course, and this was yet another of the lucky events in my life.

In 1960, another event happened which was to have a profound effect on my life. My parents and I came to Europe on a trip. We spent a week in Holland, with Aunt Louise, and a week in London, staying in Wimbledon. We travelled around a lot, did all the sights, including Richmond and its Riverside - little did I know I would one day live there. The trip was an eye opener for me. Up to then, Texas had been the centre of the world, and it broadened my outlook considerably. It was the start of my romance with England.

I had been a practical sort of boy from very early on, by which I mean that I was always interested in making things, and how things worked. It was natural that I eventually turned to science and technology, although at various times I must record that I wanted to be an archaeologist, and even a lawyer. Keystone had given me a superb preparation in science and mathematics, so I aimed very high, and wanted to go to MIT. I took the nationwide examinations and scored 705, 712, and 736 out of 800 in Physics, Mathematics, and English. This was good enough to get me in, somewhat to my surprise, and to the delight of everyone, because MIT has the very highest reputation in the world.

I enrolled in Chemistry, rapidly grew tired of that, flirted with Metallurgy, and then went into Aeronautics & Astronautics. I was very much a product of my time; it was then that the Space Race was really on and Defence was really an issue, and America was committed to putting a man on the Moon by the end of 1969.

MIT was dedicated to the Fraternity system of living - in fact there were 28 Fraternities over and above the big halls of residence. In a Fraternity House, the Brothers organise their own living entirely. It was traditional for the freshmen to come to Rush Week, a week ahead of the start of the first year. This was a week of non-stop parties and social occasions designed so that the Brothers could look at the freshmen and vice-versa, with the aim of each House getting the new entrants, or Pledges, they wanted. It was terrific fun for the freshmen, although I was to learn that it was hard work for the Brothers. We had to be on duty and sociable from 7.30 AM until long after the freshmen had gone to bed - say 2 AM. After that, we cleaned the House, decided which of the freshmen we wanted to see the next day, and then slept of the floor, because the guests had all the beds. All of this followed what we called Work Week, where we assembled beforehand to renovate the House and do other big repairs. Work generally went on 24 hours a day, in shifts. All in all, it was a hard two weeks of the year, but well worth it for the fun and comradeship of Fraternity life the year round.

I pledged to Kappa Sigma, KΣ, one of the largest fraternities with about 150 Chapters at Universities all over America. The first year Pledges had to clean the House, serve meals, tend the Bar, etc, which was not actually all that bad. After that, in the following three years it was really great fun being waited on hand and foot. We had our own cook, who would even make breakfasts to special order.

After my first year at MIT, I came home for the summer. I had managed to get a vacation job with the Texas Highway Department, working on one of their Survey Crews, doing land survey for new motorways. It was terrible work in hot sun, over 100 degrees F every day, and being the junior man of the gang, it was my job to do all the hard work like chopping out brush and trees that obstructed sight lines, carrying all the equipment etc. The rest of the gang were not educated at all, and looked on me as some sort of freak. Now that I look back on it, it was a valuable experience which certainly taught me the value of an education.

Life at MIT was hard work. Students in Britain do not know what really hard work is in the American style. We had so much homework to do, and exams generally every week, that we worked every evening and most of the weekends. In my second year, my folks got me a Volkswagen Beetle, toward which I contributed my entire earnings from my vacation job, and this improved my social life quite a bit. All in all, it was a great experience, one that every MIT man is proud that he survived.

In the year 1963/4, my Junior year, I had yet another great stroke of luck, which was to have a decisive effect on my future. By a long series of very unlikely coincidences, too tedious to go into, I met Professor Ham in the Aeronautics Department at MIT. He was Canadian who had been educated in England, partly at the College of Aeronautics at Cranfield, Beds, now called the Cranfield Institute of Technology. He revealed to me that MIT had an unofficial exchange programme with Cranfield, whereby they exchanged a few students each summer, and, to cut a long story short, I ended up going to Cranfield for three months in the summer of 1964.

The decisive influence of this trip was that it changed my education plans dramatically. I had seriously thought of continuing on to do a PhD Degree, largely for the reason that I wanted to go as far as I could. I had toyed with the idea of applying to Cambridge, because it was well-known, as well as a few Universities in America. When I mentioned this at Cranfield, they immediately told me that Imperial College, London University had the best facilities and suggested I go down there to see the Professor. I did so, and a year later I was a postgraduate at I.C. It would not have happened if I had not met Prof. Ham a year and a half before.

I returned from Cranfield to MIT to finish my final year. Because I had taken extra courses in the summer one year and extra courses most terms, I was able to finish in three and a half years instead of the normal four. This let me graduate in February 1965 instead of June. I had nine months spare before I was able to enter I.C., so I started looking for a job. I was extremely lucky to find one working on a contract to determine whether a short-haul air transport system would be appropriate for the Boston-Washington Megalopolis. I was working for MIT, which meant I did not have to move, and it earned me some money and taught me to program a computer.

I came to I.C. in September 1965, and moved into Beit Hall, Prince Consort Road, next to the Albert Hall Steps. I began to get my research organised, and had the extreme good luck to become a student of J.L. Stollery, who was Reader in the Aeronautics Department. He was superb at guiding his students, and my efforts prospered under him. As a result, I had three really good years of pure enjoyment pursuing my research into hypersonic boundary layer theory and heat transfer. It was the happiest time of my life.[1]

I finished writing my thesis in June 1968, and my supervisor took over six weeks to read it. After finding a job in the States, I had a week to spare, so I looked for a short holiday. In the Personal Column of *The Times* I spotted an advertisement for a House Party in Devon, with water skiing, etc. On the spur of the moment, I went. This was to be another decisive event in my life, because one of the girls there at the same time was Hilary Smith. My Lotus Elan apparently made quite an impression, I was to learn later.[2]

I had planned to go back to America to work, solely for the reason that there was more scope for my profession and salaries tended to be about five times higher that in Britain. McDonnell-Douglas Research Division offered me the best salary, and there I went to work on Transonic aircraft. The job itself was very good, but St. Louis was a dump, and an unattractive place to live, especially after London. The aerospace industry was in a period of contraction and there was little chance of finding a job elsewhere, and, what is most important, my outlook had been thoroughly changed by three years of living in England. By this time I was willing to sacrifice a high salary to live in civilised surroundings, so I decided to look for a job in London. My mother tried for a while to talk me out of it, saying that it would lessen my career chances, but I still decided it was what I wanted to do. I have never had a second thought about it.[3]

It was here that another great piece of luck came my way. Two political events in England were to combine in my favour. First, the British Government had been shamed into setting up a research unit for Hovercraft, largely because of public outcry at yet another British invention going abroad. Second, the Government was also embarrassed that so many British scientists were leaving

---

1 For a long and intriguing yarn involving Russian spies, the CIA, and me, see the longer version of this Chapter in the family archives.

2 For the tale of how we were rescued from the tidal rocks by helicopter, see the source in the footnote above.

3 This was the time of the Vietnam War. I had a very narrow escape from being conscripted into it, the lucky tale of which is contained in the longer version of this chapter in the family notes.

the country, the so-called Brain Drain. To combat this, the Government set up a recruitment scheme in North America. At just the right moment, an advertisement appeared in the *New Scientist* for a job at the National Physical Laboratory (NPL) doing research in Hovercraft. I applied direct to NPL, and they put me onto the recruitment scheme. They paid for me to fly to the British High Commission in Ottawa for an interview. I was offered the job at NPL, and they even paid all my travel expenses, right down to overweight baggage on the plane. So I immigrated back to England at the British taxpayer's expense!

The job at NPL was very exciting and worthwhile. I did some of my clearest and most original thinking there, getting two patents in a few months as well. I went on a month long trip to Iran, driving around in a Land Rover, in August 1971. On that trip, I realised I was in England to stay, so I came back determined to buy a house to live in. With the benefit of a loan from my mother, I bought 44 Ham Street in Ham, Richmond, and moved in December 1971.

All this while, since coming back to England, I had been going out with Hilary. She had been a Lecturer in Leeds in 1970, but she moved to Chelmsford in September of that year, and since she was nearer, we saw more of each other. We used to meet at Liverpool Street, because it was halfway for both of us. I proposed to her on a bar stool in Dirty Dick's, just up the road, in January 1972. We were married on September 9, 1972, my twenty-eighth birthday.

In the meantime, the Government had changed in Britain. Wilson was out, and Heath was in. Reductions on the Civil Service were the order of the day, as well as a cutback in Hovercraft research. Not being a British citizen, I was on a three year contract at NPL, and I was one of the most expendable. The Director did his best to keep me on, but it was obvious that it was not going to be easy to stay. Then, still another great piece of luck came my way.

Stan Smith, who had been Research Director at British Rail, and before that at Rolls Royce, came to London Transport, and decided to set up a Dynamics Section. An advertisement appeared in the *New Scientist,* and Hilary talked me into applying, even though I had eight months to go on my NPL contract. I went to LT on November 1, 1972, and it was to turn out to be one of the best things I have ever done.

Ham Street was a sweet cottage, but very small, and Hilary and I began, at first idly, to look for a bigger house. There were many reasons, one of which was that we wanted children, and Ham Street was too small by far. We hunted for many months, were let down a few times, and eventually saw 18 Denton Road come on the market. We rushed very quickly to beat the developers, and then had to wait several nerve wracking months while the tenants were found other accommodation. I had paid £7,250 for Ham Street, and we sold it for £15,950 nineteen months later. We bought Denton Road for £17,750.

Denton Road was a real dump when we moved in. It had had a lot of old men in bedsits. Edward's room was a kitchen, and so was the present washroom, and dressing room. I did most of the work myself, nearly exhausting myself in a year, but finally the house was modernised. I worked every evening from 5 to about 11, and all day and night over the weekends, but it was worth it in the end. It took two more years to finish the last two bedrooms, but I built the Grandfather Clock in the meantime, partly as a diversion.

Another event was to happen now that had a major effect on my career. In my new job at LT, I was the deputy head of the Dynamics Section, under Chris White. Although I did not realise it, he had a very unstable personality, and in early 1974, he collapsed with a nervous breakdown. I was suddenly in charge, on a few hours notice. We never saw him again, and this was the start of my administrative career. Shortly after, Alexander was born on September 5, 1974.

Now that I was a Section Head, I came more into contact with S.F. Smith (SFS), the Chief. This was to be yet another decisive piece of luck for me. In effect, I became his protégé. He sent me on a three month management course at the British Transport Staff College, Woking, for all rising managers in the transport world. Because I did well on that course, and because A.G. Collings, the Scientific Adviser and Head of the Research Laboratory decided to retire early, SFS decided to put me into the job. I knew nothing of this, and applied in competition with five other candidates. I was to learn some years later that SFS had rigged it all in my favour. I owe it all, really, to him and the trust he put in me. It was a busy time; the Woking course was May to July, 1976, Edward was born on August 25, and I was in the new job at the Laboratory in October.

It was at this time that I had to do, and did, the thing that, in retrospect, I consider the finest I have done in my life. It was to force London Transport to get rid of the polyurethane foam seats which had lately been introduced into Underground trains. Polyurethane foam is an extreme lethal hazard in a fire, and my staff realised that the seats could be set alight by a smouldering cigarette, extremely worrying since smoking was then still legal in the Underground. The man who could take such a decision was my own boss, Stan Smith, the Chief Mechanical Engineer, and he understandably resisted on cost grounds, especially as the hazard was still unproven. My staff and I staged a series of tests which proved beyond doubt that the danger was real, and in the end I had no choice but to expose the evidence at a high level meeting of the Chief Mechanical Engineer and the Chief Operating Director. After my presentation, the latter turned to Stan Smith and said "Stan, How the Hell did you get me into this?!" That forced the correct decision. Stan was a big-hearted man, and held nothing against me for it.

At it happened, about eighteen months after the last seats were gone, there was an electrical fire on a train near Wood Green Station. Three hundred people were evacuated, with only one case of mild smoke inhalation, but if the seats had been there, 300 people would have been cremated beyond any remains, and the train would have burned down to its motors and wheels.

As I look back, that is the action of which I am most proud. The work led to the development of the Underground *Code of Practice for the Fire Safety of Materials,* all of whose main principles were mine. After another disastrous fire at Kings Cross in 1987 in which 31 died, the ensuing Public Enquiry, the longest in British legal history at over 100 days, gave its only praise to that *Code of Practice.*

I was substantively in the job at the Laboratory until 1983, but actually I did several other jobs at the same time in the last three years, such as selling telecommunications facilities, project managing a computer network, and management auditing. In October 1983, I came under the wing of a powerful and dynamic woman named Rosemary Day, who was reorganising the computer side of the whole of LT. She persuaded me to take over the Telecommunications network, which meant that I finally severed all connections with the Laboratory. All went smoothly for the first year when, to my surprise, Bob Dorey, the Development Director, retired for medical reasons. Quite by chance, I soon after had a conversation with Dr. Tony Ridley (TMR), the Managing Director of the Underground. I asked him what he would be doing about filling the post, and he said he was unsure, but added that he was under a lot of pressure to have a Marketing Director. I indicated that I was interested, and that was that for another year. In September 1985, a very strangely disguised advertisement appeared in the papers for a "Marketing and Development Director." I recognised it as being for the Underground, but did not apply thinking that the disguise meant that only an outside candidate was wanted. Quite out of the blue, some six weeks later, the telephone rang, and it was TMR asking if I was still interested in the vacant Director's job. After a remark about the advertisement, I said yes, and immediately put my entire heart and soul into the ensuing process of interviews. I got Ian Round to help, and worked as hard on that as I have worked on anything. Finally I was called up to an interview before a collection of Board members, including Basil Hooper, who comes into this tale later.

The interview was one of the more beastly experiences of my life. It became apparent very soon that I was a pawn between two factions, one of which wanted an outside candidate, and TMR who wanted someone he knew. I stuck to my script, and did the best I could. Afterwards, I waited for some time, until TMR rang me to say that the job had gone to an outside candidate, one of 53 who applied.

Needless to say, I was feeling considerably less than gruntled, when two weeks later Basil Hooper contacted me through Rosemary Day. He came straight out and said that the only reason I had not got the job was lack of experience, but if I was really interested in Marketing, he would take me onto his staff and train me up. He proposed to send me to an advertising agency for six months, and then onto another company, because he was looking for a successor. All of this was said on the telephone, and after a little thought, all of my instincts told me this was a big opportunity.

FULL CIRCLE

I accepted soon after. It was a total break with all of my previous career experience. I knew nothing of the future, had several mouths to feed and school fees to pay, but somehow it felt right.

Basil was true to his word, and in February 1986, I started at Foote Cone & Belding in Baker Street. They treated me very well, and I found it riveting as an Account Director for Typhoo Biscuits.

Suddenly, as everything seems to happen in this phase, I came home one evening in March 1986 to find that TMR had tried to ring me at home. Eventually I went to see him that night at his home in Richmond. He got straight to the point: the man he had hired as the new Director had decided to leave, partly as a result of a bad case of culture shock, and partly because he had had a better offer. TMR was willing to let him go in three weeks, and inside four days, I was the new Director. I finished my commitment to FCB, and became a full Director on June 29, 1986.

This brings events up to the present. The reader can see that there were a lot of lucky coincidences involved in this story. As I look back on it, I can see that at every major juncture, luck has played a big part in the good life that I have had so far. I have often asked myself why things worked out so well. Perhaps it is all Destiny, but I believe the answer is that I have manufactured most of the luck that I have had. I did this mostly by taking advantage of the opportunities as they came, and by being able to recognise them for what they were. Luck is preparation meeting opportunity. Most opportunities are not too obvious at first sight, and have to be correctly interpreted. More than that, one must be prepared to take a radical change of direction on short notice. This is my parting observation to anyone who reads this. I only hope that some of the extraordinary luck I have had can be visited on my children, and that they can have as much luck as I have had.

To those same children, I bequeath this history of my life up to the time they can take over writing the rest of it. It is very difficult to write about oneself, and this chapter is too long as it is. I only hope it will provide the inspiration, example, and source for someone to carry on writing the History of our Fitzhugh Family.

.oOo.

EPILOGUE

"What's it all about anyway?" - everyone asks themselves at some point in life. I certainly was forced to ask this question when writing this History. I could not help but feel insignificant compared to the events and long timescales of this story, and I felt even less significant after a trip to Bedfordshire to see all of the Family sites. I visited all of the ones mentioned in this and Terrick FitzHugh's History. None of them bore any trace of our Family, although it was possible to find the exact spots where they lived and died. The question may seem difficult, but the answer is obvious: significance can only be seen in terms of continuity - we are each but a link in a chain. I hope that in this History I have succeeded in putting together the links firmly enough so that future generations can appreciate its continuity and their place in it. Without that, it is only a collection of stories.

I have also realised that words are the only things that are real, because only words are capable of lasting forever. All of us in this piece will fade away, but I hope what is written here will have meaning and value to someone in the far future, just as the old words and documents from the past have meaning for me.

In the hope that someone who reads this will be interested, I make a point and pose a challenge. An expedition into ones family history is a voyage that should never be finished; truly it is better to travel happily than to arrive. The pleasure of a new discovery is always a real possibility since new records are always being catalogued and published. Here are some of the unanswered questions concerning our ancestry that may some day be answered, and which would help fill in the complicated mosaic of centuries of family endeavour.

Absolute proof is needed that Henry Fitzhugh of Bedford was the same as the Mr. Fitzhughes of Cork. The Ordnance Records (WO Series) at the Public Record Office, Kew may have a clue, although expeditions in 1986, 1993, and 1998 only proved how difficult it is to search unindexed records. Extensive speculative searches of the British Library have as yet turned up nothing.

What did Henry really want to do with all the money he borrowed? Was it really the River Ouse Navigation Scheme?

Who was William the Immigrant's first wife, Elizabeth? And who is the Elizabeth Fitzhugh said to have been born in Virginia about 1650? As of 2004, all references to her seem to be bogus.

Can any more details of the lives of John Fitzhugh (who married Lucy Redd) and Philip Fitzhugh be found?

The local records of all kinds in Austin, Texas may still have more to say about the life of John Henry Fitzhugh (1821-94), even though I have had them searched three times.

There may still be missing Parish Record Entries to be found.

There are Fitzhughs in Bedford in the 15th and 16th centuries that may have unidentified descendants, and the other Fitzhugh families mentioned in Appendix Three could be descended from them. It should be possible to determine whether any of those families are actually related to our family. DNA Y-chromosome analysis could, in principle and probably in practice, determine whether there is a common ancestor to living male line representatives of each family and give an estimate of how far back in time the common ancestor lived. This would be of benefit mainly to the other families rather than our own, but in my opinion it is worth doing. However, a proposal put out on the Fitzhugh web newsgroup in 2002 failed to excite any support.

A trip to the Library of Congress in Washington and to the Virginia State Library may well offer references not possible to find from London, although I visited both libraries in 2003 during the Fitzhugh Family Reunion in Fredericksburg, Virginia.

H.A.F., London, 2004.

THE FITZHUGH FAMILY TREE

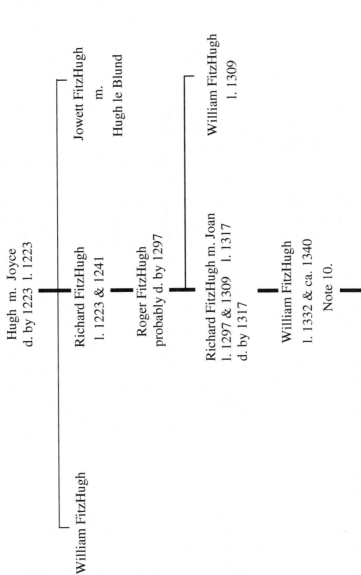

Hugh m. Joyce
d. by 1223 l. 1223

William FitzHugh

Richard FitzHugh
l. 1223 & 1241

Jowett FitzHugh
m.

Hugh le Blund

Roger FitzHugh
probably d. by 1297

Richard FitzHugh m. Joan
l. 1297 & 1309   l. 1317
d. by 1317

William FitzHugh
l. 1309

William FitzHugh
l. 1332 & ca. 1340

Note 10.

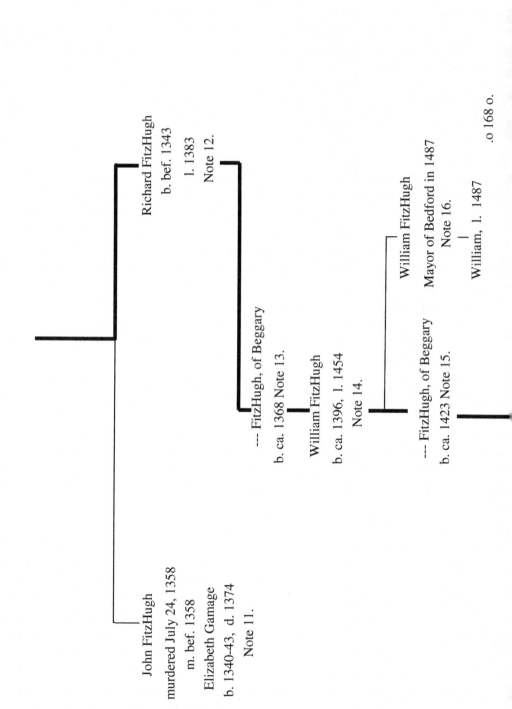

John FitzHugh
murdered July 24, 1358
m. bef. 1358
Elizabeth Gamage
b. 1340-43, d. 1374
Note 11.

Richard FitzHugh
b. bef. 1343
l. 1383
Note 12.

--- FitzHugh, of Beggary
b. ca. 1368 Note 13.

William FitzHugh
b. ca. 1396, l. 1454
Note 14.

--- FitzHugh, of Beggary
b. ca. 1423 Note 15.

William FitzHugh
Mayor of Bedford in 1487
Note 16.

William, l. 1487

.o 168 o.

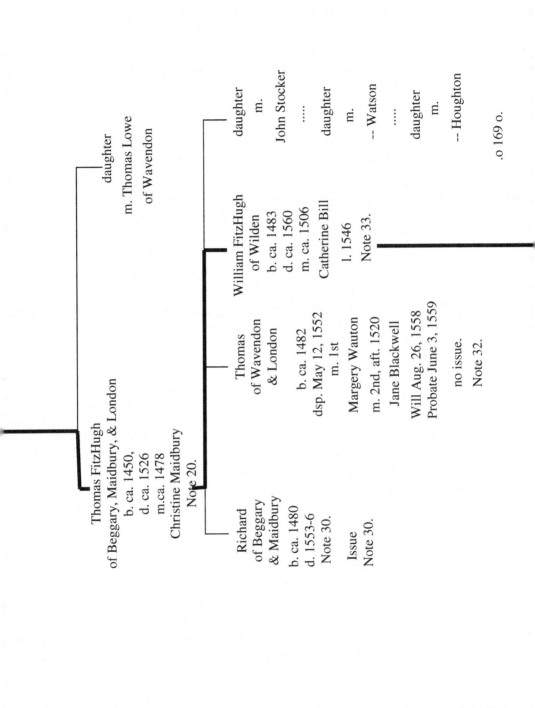

Thomas FitzHugh
of Beggary, Maidbury, & London
b. ca. 1450,
d. ca. 1526
m.ca. 1478
Christine Maidbury
Note 20.

daughter
m. Thomas Lowe
of Wavendon

Richard
of Beggary
& Maidbury
b. ca. 1480
d. 1553-6
Note 30.

Issue
Note 30.

Thomas
of Wavendon
& London

b. ca. 1482
dsp. May 12, 1552
m. 1st
Margery Wauton
m. 2nd, aft. 1520
Jane Blackwell

Will Aug. 26, 1558
Probate June 3, 1559

no issue.
Note 32.

William FitzHugh
of Wilden
b. ca. 1483
d. ca. 1560
m. ca. 1506
Catherine Bill

l. 1546
Note 33.

daughter
m.
John Stocker
.....

daughter
m.
-- Watson
.....

daughter
m.
-- Houghton

.o 169 o.

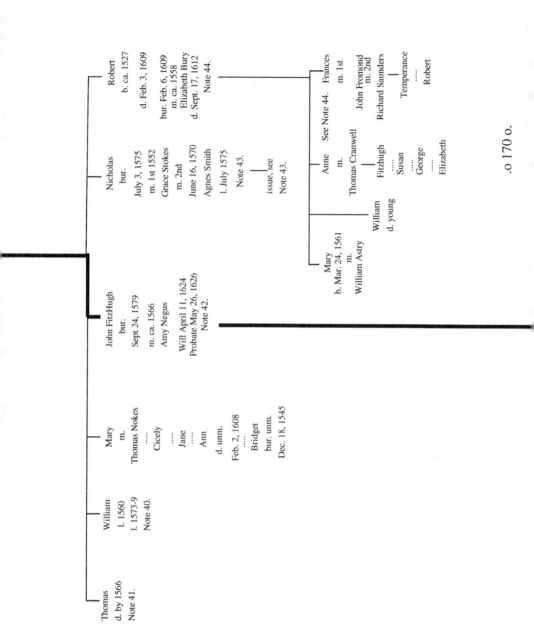

Henry
bur.
Feb. 28, 1632
m. 1589
Elizabeth Clarke
Note 50.

Issue died
out in 2nd
generation

John
bpt. Jan. 6, 1576
bur. Nov. 16, 1607
d. unm.
Note 51.

William FitzHugh
bpt. June 21, 1570
bur. Apr. 5, 1633
m. Sept. 6, 1608
Margaret Smith
b. Aug. 26, 1588
d. Feb. 13, 1665
Note 52.

Elizabeth
m. 1st
Timothy Ward
(Issue)
m. 2nd
Richard Wagstaffe
Note 54.
.....
Anne
b. posthumously
bpt. Feb. 15, 1580

Robert
bpt. July 23, 1573
bur. Aug 7, 1647
m. Sept 25, 1599
Ann Worsley
bur. Nov. 23, 1658
Note 53.

Line to the English
Branch of the Family
Including Terrick V.H.
FitzHugh Note 53.

Elizabeth
bpt. May 28
or 30, 1610
m. Dec. 29, 1627
George Paradine
.....
John
bpt. Mar. 22, 1611/12
bur. June 4, 1624
.....
William
bpt. Aug. 1, 1613
d. unm.
Note 63.

Francis
bpt. Mar. 14, 1615/6
m. ca. 1646
Anne Daniel
(Issue)
.....
Hugh
bpt. July 16, 1617
d. 1686
m. Lydia Potts
(Issue 9 children)
Note 63.

Henry FitzHugh
bpt. Dec. 11, 1614
d. 1666
m. Mary King
b. 1616
d. aft. 1698
Note 60.

Thomas
bpt. Jan. 8, 1618/9
bur. Jan. 29, 1639/40
w. pro. June 18, 1640
d. unm.
.....
Peter
bpt. Sept. 30, 1620
d. unm. after 1632/3
.....
Sybil
bpt. Feb. 28, 16267
m. Edward Wilson
Note 64.

Margaret
bpt. Oct. 8, 1623
d. soon after
.....

Margaret
bpt. Mar. 24, 1625
m. 1st July 6, 1649
Henry Zouch
m. 2nd
Matthew Porter
Note 64.

Robert
m. 1647
Mary Collyer
Note 61.

William
Note 62.

Anne
bpt. Sept. 8, 1639
.....
Margaret
bpt. Nov. 12, 1640
d. 1676
.....
Susan
bpt. Oct. 27, 1642
m. June 21, 1659
Richard Varney
.....
Mary
b. Dec. 22, 1643
.....
Elizabeth
b. Jan. 12, 1645
d. June 12, 1646
Note 72.

Thomas
d. young
Note 72.

William Fitzhugh
"The Immigrant"
b. Jan. 8, 1651
bpt. Jan. 10, 1651
d. Oct. 21, 1701
m. 1st
Elizabeth ---
m. 2nd May 1, 1674
Sarah Tucker
b. Aug. 2, 1663
d. after 1703
Note 70.

Henry
bpt. Apr. 28, 1650
m. bef. 1687
Elizabeth Long
m. 2nd?
Lettice Hancock
Note 71.

Dorothy
bpt. Jan. 29, 1645
m. 1st Mar. 1, 1687
Dr. Ralph Smith
d. 1688/9
m. 2nd
George Luke
Note 72.

Thomas
b. ca. 1689
d. ca. 1719
dspm
m. ca. 1710
Anne Fowke
Mason
Note 76.

Henry
b. Jan. 15, 1686/7
d. Dec. 12, 1758
m. Feb. 24, 1718
Susannah Cooke
b. Dec. 7, 1693
d. Nov. 21, 1749
Note 74.

Line to
George Fitzhugh
See original Tree
and notes.
Note 74.

John Fitzhugh
b. ca. 1692
d. Jan. 21 or 22, 1732/3
m. Dec. 15, 1715
Anne Barbara McCarty
Note 73.

William
b. ca. 1679
d. Dec. 1713
m. 1699
Ann Lee
b. ca. 1683
d. Jan. 12, 1731/2
Line to Gen.
Robt. E. Lee
in 4 Gens.
Line to
Fitzhugh-Grymes.
Surname Fitzhugh
extinct in 3
generations
Note 75.

George
b. 1690
d. 1722
m. ca. 1712
Mary Mason
issue 2 sons

Rosamund
b. ca. 1680
d. ca. 1700
m.
William Allerton
d. ca. 1724
Note 77.

a girl
b. 1677
d. infancy

....

a boy
b. 1682

John
1724-1792
m. Jan 31, 1760
Elizabeth Harrison
b. 1737
Note 84.
Issue-
Note 84.

Daniel
b. June 27, 1733
d. 1786
m. Oct. 24, 1772
Susannah Porter
Issue: William,
Jane, Sukey
Note 81.

Philip
b. May 4, 1766, at
Marmion, d. 1807
m. March 9, 1788
Charlotte Thornton
d. 1813
Northumberland
Co., Virginia

Sarah
b. April 30, 1727
m. April 2, 1747
Francis Thornton
Note 87.
....
Rosamond b. bef.
1733

Col. William Fitzhugh
b. April 13, 1725
Will pro. June 2, 1791
m. 1st Ursula Beverley
m. 2nd bef. 1759
Hannah –
Will pro. Feb. 7, 1799
Note 80.

Mary
m. Col.
George Brent
Issue: Robert
Carroll Brent

Lucy
m. Dec. 3,
1788
--Campbell
Issue:
Lucy

John Fitzhugh
b. ca. 1742
d. ca. 1796
m. Lucy Redd
Note 82.

Philip Fitzhugh
b. 1792
d. Dec. 21, 1836
m. July 13, 1813
Mary Macon Aylett
b. Dec. 5, 1793
d. Oct. 6, 1836
Note 90.

Frances
b. 1781

Lucy
m.
Dr. Hall
Note 93.

Alexander
m.
Cason
Note 94.

Barbara
m. Feb. 6, 1739
Rev. Wm McKay
Note 86.
....
Elizabeth Note 88.
.....
Anna Note 85.

Theodoric
b. July 20, 1760
d. October, 1800
Caroline Co. Va.
......
William Beverley
b. at Marmion
Mar. 27, 1756

Elizabeth,
Anna,
Sally,
Maria,
dau. m.
Finch

Samuel Temple
m. Miss
Fitzhugh
(cousin)
Note 92.

Daniel McCarty
b. Mar. 15, 1758
m. Ann ---
.....
Robert
Note 83.

Dennis
b. 1777/8
d. 1822
m.
Miss
Clark
(cousin)
Note 91.

William
l. 1796
Note 95.

Patrick Henry
b. Dec. 2, 1818
d. June 17, 1864
m. Mary Steptoe Christian
Line to Steptoe Fitzhughs of Baltimore
Note 101.

Elizabeth Henry
b. May 12, 1816
m. Nov. 22, 1833
Robert Curtis

Dr. Philip Aylett
b. June 14, 1824
d. June 7, 1908
m. April 7, 1849
Georgia Tankard
Note 104.

John Henry Fitzhugh
b. Dec. 23, 1821
d. May 5, 1894
m. Nov. 30, 1854
Harriett Bullett
b. June 11, 1835
d. March 17, 1890
Note 100.

Edwin
b. May 9, 1830
d. 1855
Note 102.

Thaddeus
b. Mar. 10, 1835
d. Nov. 21, 1918
m. Maria Savage, Julia Horsey, Laura Sharpe, Issue
Note 105.

Lucy Redd
b. Oct. 8, 1819
d. 1894
m. April 23, 1838
John R. Redd
issue: daughter

LaFayette Henry
b. May 9, 1829
d. Aug. 1, 1905
m. 1st
Elizabeth Semple
m. 2nd
Ann Eliza Bullett
issue 2nd marriage
Note 103.

Philip Aylett
b. Dec. 4, 1859
d. Mar. 23, 1932
m.
Mrs. Mary Fornais

Mary Ann
b. Feb. 4, 1858
m. Nov. 20, 1877
Edwin Thornton

William Bullett
b. Aug. 13, 1855
d. June 21, 1856
Note 112.

Henry Alexander Fitzhugh
b. April 1, 1862
d. March 22, 1932
m. July 9, 1902
Mary Scott
b. Feb. 17, 1881
d. April 19, 1943
Note 110.

John Glasscock
b. Dec. 15, 1863
d. Nov. 25, 1934
m. June 3, 1900
Mrs. Ida Tatom Daughtry

Dr. Patrick Henry
b. Aug. 29, 1867
d. Nov. 5, 1914
Note 111.

Mary F. Thornton
"Aunt Dot"
Note 115.

John G. Fitzhugh
b. June 23, 1904

Paul Tatom Fitzhugh
b. Sept. 29, 1904
m. April 13, 1935
Kathleen Willis
Note 113.

.o 175 o.

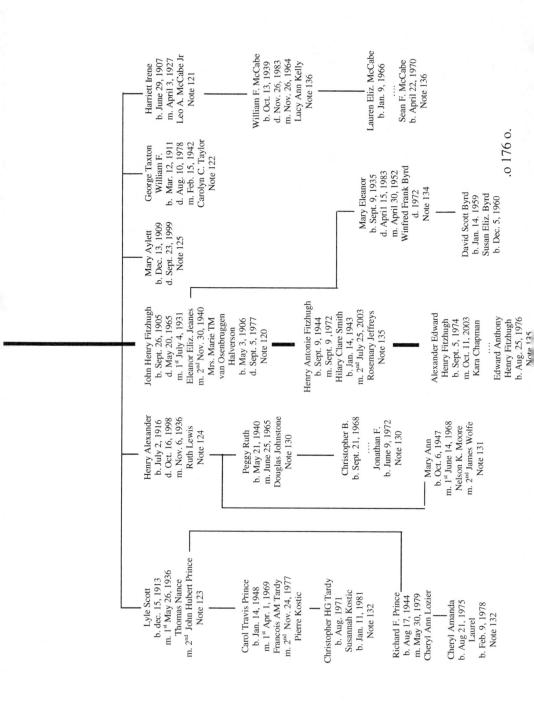

A CONDENSED LINEAGE

1. HUGH d. by 1223 m. Joyce l. 1223
2. RICHARD l. 1223 & 1241
3. ROGER d. by 1297
4. RICHARD l. 1297 & 1309 m. Joan l. 1317
5. WILLIAM l. 1332 & 1340
6. RICHARD b. bef. 1343, l. 1383
7. ----- b. ca. 1368
8. WILLIAM b. ca. 1396, l. 1454
9. ----- b. ca. 1423
10. THOMAS 1450-1526 m. 1478 Christine Maidbury l. 1546
11. WILLIAM 1483-1560 m. 1506 Catherine Bill l. 1546
12. JOHN d. 1579 m. 1566 Amy Negus d. 1626
13. WILLIAM 1570-1633 m. 1608 Margaret Smith 1588-1665
14. HENRY 1614-1666 m. ca. 1638 Mary King 1616-ca.1698
15. WILLIAM 1651-1701 m. 1st Elizabeth ---- d. ca. 1673-4
       m. 1674 Sarah Tucker 1663-aft.1703
16. JOHN 1690-1733 m. 1715/9 Anne McCarthy d. bef. 1733
17. Col. WILLIAM 1725-1791 m. 1st Ursula Beverley d. bef. 1759
       m. bef. 1759 Hannah ---- d. 1798/9
18. JOHN d. by 1796 m. Lucy Redd
19. PHILIP 1792-1836 m. 1813 Mary Macon Aylett 1793-1836
20. JOHN HENRY 1821-1894 m. 1854 Harriet Bullitt 1835-1890
21. HENRY ALEXANDER 1862-1932
       m. 1902 Mary Scott 1881-1943
22. JOHN HENRY 1905-1965 m. 1st 1931 Eleanor Jeanes d. 1984
       m. 2nd 1940 Marie van O.
       Halverson 1906-1977
23. HENRY ANTONIE 1944- m. 1st 1972 Hilary Clare Smith 1943-
       m. 2nd 2003 Rosemary Jeffreys 1955-
24. ALEXANDER 1974- m. 2003 Kara Chapman 1975-
    EDWARD 1976-

NOTES ON THE FAMILY TREE

The numbering system of these notes deliberately leaves gaps, possibly to be added to later. Basic information on names and dates is given on the Tree; additional information wherever it is known is given below. All references to archives, trees, etc. refer to information held by Henry A. Fitzhugh, the author. Dates between January and March are in New Style, unless indicated otherwise.

Abbreviations are: b.-born; bpt.-baptised; d.-died; bur.-buried; w. pro.-will proved; m.-married; liv.-living; bef.-before; ca.-circa; unm.-unmarried; dsp.-died without issue.

10. William Fitzhugh of Beggary Manor, or Goodwick Manor, Eaton Socon, Bedfordshire.

11. Elizabeth Gamage was the daughter of Nicholas Gamage of Wizebury, Netherlye, Gloucestershire who died in 1349, and who was the son of William Gamage. Nicholas Gamage married second Elizabeth's mother Eleanor de Stokes, widow of Thomas de Waughton of Basmead (l. 1346). She died in 1349 and was the daughter of John de Stokes of Boughton who died in 1349 and who married Margaret --. John Fitzhugh, the first son, was murdered by his wife and Richard Stocker on July 24, 1358.

12. Richard Fitzhugh, the second son, obtained livery of the Manor of Beggary (or Goodwick) in 1374.

13. The name of this generation is unknown, but he was born circa 1368, of Beggary Manor.

14. William Fitzhugh was seized of the Manor of Beggary.

15. The name of this generation is unknown. He was born circa 1423, of Beggary Manor. He may have been the brother of William Fitzhugh who was Mayor of Bedford in 1487.

16. There is a conveyance (BorBE2/70, Beds. Co. Recs.) of William Fitzhugh acting as executor of a Will of Richard Lenton in 1487. William is referred to as "Mayor" as well as by name, but there is no signature and only vestiges of sealing wax remain.

20. Thomas Fitzhugh was of Beggary, Maidbury, and Wavendon. Christine Maidbury was of Maidbury Manor (which still exists as Medbury Farm), Elstow, Bedfordshire, and Paslows Manor, Wavendon, Buckinghamshire. She was the daughter of William Maidbury, who was dead by 1488, and who was the son of Thomas and Joan Maidbury, both of whom were dead by 1488. See the various Maidbury trees in the notes.

30. Richard Fitzhugh, the first son, was of Beggary (or Goodwick) and Maidbury Manors. According to *V.C.H. Beds.*, iii, p.282, he died in 1557. His wife's name is unknown but he had issue: Richard, who married Frances Wyatt, who later married Edward Bridges and died on November 3, 1557; Nicholas, who died circa 1581; Christine, who married -- Townsend; and Alice, who married George Bowles. This line became the Fitzhughs of Walcot, Oxfordshire. See Terrick FitzHugh *FitzHugh – The Story of A Family Through Six Centuries*, and also Appendix One. Richard's grandson, also Richard, married Elizabeth Giffard, daughter of John Giffard of Itchell, Hants. The latter Richard was born ca. 1544 and sold the Manor at Beggary cum Goodwick in 1572, acquiring instead an estate at Walcot, on the outskirts of Charlbury, Oxford, which was formerly owned by the Catesby family. His father, yet another Richard, had died in 1557, leaving his widow, Frances, with a family of six children: The grandson Richard, the eldest, who would have been about 13 then, and three other boys, Nicholas (who sought his fortune in London, became a member of the Haberdashers and died in 1576), George and Thomas, and two daughters, Elizabeth and Alice (who married Robert Claydon of Ashdon, Essex). Richard's male descendants died out in the third generation.

32.   Thomas Fitzhugh, the second son, was of Paslows Manor, Wavendon, Buckinghamshire, and Charterhouse Lane, London. He was admitted to Middle Temple on July 1, 1505, Justice of the Assizes 1512, and accused of fraud in the Court of Chancery on a trumped-up charge, but acquitted. He also obtained a pardon for Treason in the Reign of Edward III, probably only as a precaution in uncertain times. His first wife Margery Waughton was the daughter of Sir Thomas Waughton of Basmead, Eaton Socon, Bedfordshire. His second wife Jane was widow of Robert Blackwell who died in 1520. See. *V.C.H. Beds.,* iii, p.193 for reference to Thomas and moiety of Basmead. See also *V.C.H. Beds.,* iii, p.329-30 for a legal action regarding the Manor of Blundells in 1547, resulting in Thomas receiving one sixth share of the Manor.

33.   William Fitzhugh, the third son, was of Wilden, Bedfordshire. He succeeded to Paslows Manor on the death of his brother Thomas. Catherine Bill, of Ashwell, Hertfordshire was daughter of John Bill, a Draper, who died in 1503, and Agnes Bill, living in 1503. John Bill was the son of Thomas Bill of Ashwell, Hertfordshire. See various Bill trees in the notes. See Terrick FitzHugh *FitzHugh – The Story of A Family Through Six Centuries,* Tree for Fitzhugh of Walcot, for relations of Katherine Bill and line to the Spencers of Althorp.

40.   William Fitzhugh, the first son, was of Paslows Manor. He sold Wavendon to his brother Robert in 1560.

41.   Thomas Fitzhugh was the second son.

42.   John Fitzhugh was of Great Barford, Bedfordshire. He was the fourth son and a Maltster, and was buried at Great Barford. His wife Amy Negus was the daughter of Henry Negus of Shelton. She married second her cousin, William Negus.

43.   Nicholas Fitzhugh, of Wilden, Bedfordshire was the third son. His first wife, Grace Stokes, was of White Notley, Essex, and died circa 1569. His issue had descendants surviving to the end of the seventeenth century. At the Visitation of Bedfordshire 1566 he obtained confirmation of the Arms: *Ermine, on a Chief Gules, three Martlets Or; Quartering, Argent, three Chevrons Sable, each charged with a Bezant.* His second wife Agnes married second Robert Carter on November 26, 1576. See *V.C.H. Beds.,* iii, p.195 for

reference to a lease on Honydon, or Camoys, Manor. Nicholas had been ill in Warwickshire for a long period circa 1570.

44. Robert Fitzhugh, fifth son, bought Paslows Manor from his brother William in 1560. His wife Elizabeth Bury was the daughter of Richard Bury of Toddington, Bedfordshire. See *Harleian Visitation of Bedfordshire XIX, 1566, 1582, & 1634* p.8 for four generations of ancestry of Elizabeth Bury, and also our notes copied from Terrick FitzHugh. Their issue were: William, who died young; Mary, who married William Astry of Wavendon; Anne, who married Thomas Cranwell, of Simpson, Buckinghamshire; and Frances, who married first John Fromond and second Richard Saunders. See Terrick FitzHugh's notes, Vol. 1, p.97. Anne had issue: Fitzhugh, Susan, George, and Elizabeth. Frances had issue, by her second husband, Temperance and Robert. See *V.C.H. Beds.* iii, p.193 for a reference to Robert being seized of a messuage called Farm House, by descent from Thomas, note 32.
The British Library Manuscripts Collection contains [Add.43473] a Book of Hours, *Horae B.V.M. Secundum Usum Sarum,* that was once owned by Robert and Elizabeth Fitzhugh. It is 130 pages of some of the most beautiful illuminated text, handwritten mostly in Latin on fine vellum, and the BL Catalogue states that the Book dates from 1413-1416. [The date of death of Henry IV, March 20, 1413, is written on folio 2.] It may have been owned by the Grene family before the Fitzhughs. A handwritten note at folio 97b records the birth at Wavendon of Mary, daughter of Robert and Elizabeth who married William Astrey. [The Catalogue quotes *VCH Bucks.*, iii, 346; iv, 492, 495.] This handwritten note is in very tight scribe's Latin, and it seems unlikely that Robert could have written it? However, there are three signs in the margin; perhaps these are the marks of some of the family? The name of another Fitzhugh is illegibly scribbled at folio 106, but it could be Robt Fitzhugh. Later the Book belonged to Mary, daughter of Robert and Elizabeth. See Appendix Two to Volume One for a full description of this Book.

50. Henry Fitzhugh, of Barford in 1609 and then of Bedford, was a Maltster. They had issue: Elizabeth, bpt. 1590; Anne; Susan, bpt. 1595; and William, bpt. February 26, 1598/9 and died in 1644/5. Henry died February 25, 1631/2, and was buried on February 28, 1631/2. His Will was made February

3, 1631/2, proved October 8, 1632, and a transcription is given in CRT 190/205 in the County Record Office, Bedford. See Terrick FitzHugh's History for six other children.

51. John Fitzhugh, Embroiderer and Hosier of Southwark, died unmarried and was buried on November 16, 1607, at St. Olaves, Southwark.

52. William Fitzhugh was a Maltster of Barford in 1607 and then of Bedford in 1609. He died in April 1633, and was buried in St. Paul's Church, Bedford in the South Chancel, West end, under the South wall. During excavations in 1981, some unmarked lead coffins were found at that location, and left in place. Margaret Smith was the daughter of Lawrence and Elizabeth Smith. She was born on August 26, 1588 at Milton, Buckinghamshire, and died on February 13, 1665. She was buried at St. Michael le Querne, London. See Smith trees in the notes. The Church of St. Michael le Querne, between St. Paul's Churchyard and Cheapside, was destroyed in the Great Fire and not rebuilt (Kent, *Encyclopedia of London*, 1937, p.110). William was a Bridgewarden for the High Bridge in Bedford. See *Minute Book of the Bedford Corporation 1647-64*, p.55 & xvi. Although these records pertain to the 1650's, we can guess what William's duties and emoluments were for his post of Bridgewarden. The *Minute Book* (*op. cit.*, 11-12, 108) indicates that an annual inspection was required at a payment of 12d "for his dinner", and that he was responsible for having the Bridge cleaned on certain days of the week in a precisely specified manner, and charges were borne by the Corporation. In slightly earlier times, around 1578-83, the Bridgewarden was responsible for prisoners kept in the town lock-up on the Bridge. He collected various fines from them as well, although they do not seem to have amounted to much (*The Black Book*, B1, N. Beds. Bor. Co. Recs.). In 1343, The Great Bridge was endowed with two messuages, 17 shops, three acres of land, and 7/- rent in Bedford. It is likely that the Bridgewarden had to look after these properties as well. (*Old Bedford*, C.F. Farrar, M.A., 1926) Bridgewardens Accounts still exist (D6/1) but it is difficult to say whether they were made out by William. William's name appears in *The Black Book* in a list of Councillors' names substantiating a collection of forty-one bye laws, the earliest of which is August 14, 1615. This shows that he was a member of the Common Council of Bedford before 1615. William is a signatory on a document of April 30, 1628, whereby the Town of Bedford promised to pay the cost of an Act of

Parliament opening the Navigation of the River Ouse (BHRS, Vol. 20, p.33). In 1649 and 1656, long after William's death, the Bridge tolls were leased for £12 per annum. It appears in any case that tolls and revenue were payable to the Corporation, so it seems likely that the Bridgewarden was simply paid a salary. Almost certainly this could only have been a subsidiary activity to William's Malting business.

53. Robert Fitzhugh was of Barford, Bedfordshire, and of Whitehills Manor, Olney, Buckinghamshire, formerly of Lavendon, Buckinghamshire in 1613. He and his wife Anne Worsley were both buried at Lavendon. The English Branch of the Fitzhugh Family descends from Robert and Anne. See *Burkes Landed Gentry, 18th Edition,* Vol. 2, 1969, p.203ff for a complete Genealogy of this Branch, as well as Terrick FitzHugh's History of the FitzHugh Family. Terrick V.H. FitzHugh, the author of the family history in England, is a direct descendant of Robert.

54. Elizabeth Fitzhugh had by her first husband Timothy Ward: John; Amy, died in 1588; Timothy baptised in 1589; Thomas baptised in 1592; Henry died in 1598; and William baptised in 1596. By her second husband, she had Agnes, and a son who died as an infant. Later she married John Wilshire.

60. The text and footnotes on Henry Fitzhugh suggests that he borrowed money to buy the Navigation Rights to the River Ouse. But there is another possibility: he may have been trying to invest in the biggest local scheme of the day – the draining of the Fens known as the Bedford Level. This project, which eventually cost $500,000 by the time it was finished, had beginnings in 1593, but by 1653 a group of 14 "Adventurers" had succeeded in draining the Fens, and their own finances too. It is just possible that Henry was seeking to get into the action, but the copious records of the period do not give any further clues. See British Library shelfmarks 725.c.44, 291.a.42, 523.a.35, 725.c.42, 725.c.43, 725.c.40, 725.c.41, 725.c.39.1, 725.c.39.2, 1651/125, 725.h.20, 725.e.1, 08777.aaaa.16, & 8776.cc.35.

61. Robert Fitzhugh, of "the Greenhouse in Bedford," was Mayor of Bedford in 1656 & 1679, and an Alderman until 1689. Mary Collyer was the daughter of Phillip Collyer. Almost certainly Robert died in 1689 in the Parish of St. Vedast & St. Mary le Querne in London, where his son William the Stationer was living, (*Boyd's London Burials.*)

62. William Fitzhugh, Stationer, was one of eleven children of Robert and Mary. For the five sons and six daughters, see Terrick FitzHugh's notes, Vol.I, p.80.

63. John was baptised at St. Paul's, Bedford, and became a merchant in Turkey. Francis fought at the battle of Edgehill; his wife Anne Daniel was daughter of Richard Daniel, and they had issue. Hugh was apprenticed as a Draper in 1632, freed in 1642, and became a merchant in Amsterdam. See notes for the descendants of Hugh.

64. Thomas Fitzhugh became a Maltster. Sybil Fitzhugh married Edward Wilson in St. Martins-in-the-Fields, London.

70. William Fitzhugh, the Immigrant, was baptised January 10, 1651 at St. Paul's, Bedford. He immigrated to Virginia Colony in 1674. Sarah Tucker was the daughter of Rose Tucker Gerard Newton, who died in 1712, and John Tucker, of Bermuda, whose will was proved on May 31, 1671.

John Tucker, was born about 1639 in England; and died about May 31, 1671 in Bermuda. He was the son of Capt. William Tucker and Mary Thompson. He married Rosanna Sturman, born about 1629 in England; died 1712.

The will of John Tucker was proved in Westmoreland County May 31,1671. His legatees were his daughters Sarah and Rose Tucker (who married, subsequently, Mr. Blackistone, of Maryland), 5,000 pounds of tobacco each; and unborn child, 5,000 pounds tobacco; eldest son (whom he does not name) and wife Rose. Appoints Captain (Thomas) Phillpot and Mr. Richard Kenner, of Westmoreland, overseers. Mrs. Rose Tucker married (II) Thomas Gerrard, of Westmoreland (formerly of Maryland, she was his second wife); and he, on January 28, 1672, made a deed of gift to the children of Mr. John Tucker, deceased, and of "my now wife, Mrs. Rose Gerrard," vizt; John, Gerrard, Sarah and Rose Tucker. On April 24, 1674, Mrs. Rose Gerrard, widow, made a deed in consideration of a marriage contracted between her eldest daughter, Sarah, and William Fitzhugh. Mrs. Gerrard married (III) John Newton, of Westmoreland prior to May 16, 1677. (*Virginia Historical Magazine*)

Notes for Rosanna Sturman: The maiden name Sturman is not positively proved but Norma Tucker gives evidence that leads one to believe that this is most likely correct. (footnote from *The Fitzhugh Family of King George Co., Virginia* by Elizabeth N. Lee, referring to Norma Tucker, *Virginia Colonials and Their Maryland Relatives*, Baltimore, 1994, p. 35).

NOTES ON THE FAMILY TREE

The will of Rose Newton, widow, was proved in Westmoreland, January 28, 1712. She gave her son Thomas Newton her lands in Virginia and Maryland and all rents and arrearages for lands left her by her former husband Thomas Gerrard, &c, &c. Thus it appears that Thomas was omitted in his father's will, and the only child named in his mother's. (*Virginia Historical Magazine*)

Rosamund "Rose" Fitzhugh was mentioned in the Will of James Ashton, proved September 8, 1686, and September 14, 1687 in the P.C.C.: "Rose Fitzhugh, daughter of Col. William Fitzhugh, two heifers and two calves..." From the context, Ashton was probably her godfather. William Fitzhugh and others were Executors. *Virginia Gleanings in England*, Lothrop Willington, Genealogical Publishing Company, 1980, British Library Shelfmark X809.66959.

Since the publication of the first edition of this work, some have queried whether William in Virginia was really the same person as the William of the Fitzhugh family in Bedford, England. The clinching evidence comes from his correspondence with five members of the family in the years 1685-1698. These letters are all in Davis' book *William Fitzhugh and his Chesapeake World,* and page numbers here refer to that book.

William the Immigrant knew and was on good terms with William Fitzhugh, the Stationer of London, and exchanged news of <u>family</u> and friends, [Davis, p.169, letter of May 18, 1685]. It is clear they thought they were related to each other, as cousins, and there is simply no dispute that William the Stationer was of the Bedford family.

The letter of April 22, 1686 to "Brother Henry" [p.170] makes it clear that the two Williams were cousins.

The same letter refers to "Sister Dorothy" (who was definitely in the Bedford family) shows that William was related to her.

A separate letter of April 22, 1686 (p.172) to "Miss Dorothy Fitzhugh", addresses her as "Dear Sister".

A separate letter of April 22, 1686 (p.173) to "Mrs Mary Fitzhugh" addresses her as "Dear Mother".

A letter of January 30, 1686/7 (p.200) <u>at the Greenhouse in Bedford</u> addresses him as "Most Worthy Uncle".

The conclusion from this is that the Bedford family, Mary, Dorothy, Robert, Henry, William the Stationer, clearly accepted William the Immigrant as respectively their son, brother, nephew, brother, and cousin. William the Immigrant clearly believed he bore the same relationships to them, and, what is more, was willing to subsidise, give money to, and support in other ways his sister, brother, and mother. There can be no better evidence than that.

The entire correspondence between family members is tabulated below.

Letter of Date	Page	To Whom	Mode of Address
May 18, 1685	169	William the Stationer, Asks for information on Mother, brother and sister, Uncles and cousins	Dear Cousin
April 22, 1686	170	Henry Fitzhugh, also refers to "Sister Dorothy"	Dear Brother
April 22, 1686	172	Miss Dorothy Fitzhugh	Dear Sister
April 22, 1686	173	Mrs Mary Fitzhugh	Dear Mother
May 6, 1686	186	Henry Fitzhugh, Gave money to Mother and Sister	Dearest Brother
May 6, 1686	187	Miss Dorothy Fitzhugh	Dear Sister
January 30, 1686/7	192	Captain Henry Fitzhugh	Dear Brother
	197	Mrs Mary Fitzhugh	Dear Mother
January 30, 1686/7	198	William Fitzhugh (the Stationer)	Most Kind Cousin
January 30, 1686/7	200	Robert Fitzhugh, **at the Greenhouse in Bedford**	Most Worthy Uncle
April 5, 1687	215	Captain Henry Fitzhugh	Dearest Brother
April 1687	219	Mrs Mary Fitzhugh, sends money	Dear Mother
July 18, 1687	229	Henry Fitzhugh	Dear Brother
June 1, 1688	242	Mary Fitzhugh	Dearest Mother
June 1, 1688	243	Captain Henry Fitzhugh, expecting Henry to come to Virginia	Dearest Brother
May 20, 1695	333	Mrs Mary Fitzhugh	Dear Mother
June 30, 1698	358	Mrs Mary Fitzhugh	Dear Mother

71. Henry Fitzhugh was baptised on April 28, 1650 at St. Paul's, Bedford. Elizabeth Longe was of Pall Mall, London. He may have married second to Lettice Hancock. The *Registers of Rotherhithe* 1556-1804 list the following: 1683 March 25, Henry Fitzhugh married Eliz. Longe; 1695 April 25, Henry Fitzhugh married Lettice Hancock. Terrick FitzHugh's notes show clearly that he strongly suspected this was "the brother of the Colonist".

72. Anne Fitzhugh was baptised on September 8, 1639 at Tempsford, Bedfordshire. Margaret Fitzhugh married in Maryland and died in Virginia. Susan Fitzhugh married Richard Varney in St. Albans Abbey. Dorothy Fitzhugh was Baptised at St. Paul's, Bedford, and immigrated to Virginia circa 1686. Her second husband George Luke was said to be "a neer-do-well." Thomas died as an apprentice in London.

73. John Fitzhugh owned the Marmion Estate, but the present house there was built by his son William. Ann Barbara McCarty was the daughter of Dennis McCarty and only aged 15 at the time of marriage. Ann's father Dennis was married to the widow Ann Lee Fitzhugh of John's eldest brother William Fitzhugh. So John was both brother-in-law and son-in-law to Dennis McCarty. See notes for the McCarty ancestry. John was born in Stafford County and married in Westmoreland County, Virginia. Anne Barbara McCarty was born in 1700 in Westmoreland County, Virginia and died December 12, 1737 in Stafford County, Virginia.
Excerpt from Bill McCarty's unfinished book ms., *The McCartys of the Northern Neck*:
Anne Barbara McCarty (1700-?) was the eldest (proven by the inscription that was on the McCarty tomb in Old Yeomocico church listing the children). She was born ca. 1700 (Capt. Daniel was m. 19 Oct 1699) and married Major John Fitzhugh of Marmion in Stafford County by 5 Dec 1715 (MRC:246), (VMHB, VII:317-19). It appears that Anne Barbara was only 15 at the time of her marriage. We know that Capt. Daniel McCarty was pleased by this marriage because on 5 Dec 1715, he made a deed of trust of 9 negro slaves (six females with "one large girl" and three males) for the newlywed couple (Wco DB 5:510-13). Another reason for his pleasure might have been that he was married to the widow Ann Lee Fitzhugh of John's eldest brother (William Fitzhugh). Thus John Fitzhugh was both son-in-law and brother-in-law to Capt. D. McCarty. Even more indicative of his regard for John Fitzhugh, Capt. D. McCarty made him executor of his will and John Fitzhugh was to "take the three youngest children" to raise. Perhaps Capt. D. McCarty

remembered his own childhood when he had non-related guardians. By Maj. John Fitzhugh, Anne Barbara had seven children.

74. Henry Fitzhugh, born at Eagles Nest, built the Bedford Estate in Virginia, and married and died there. Susannah Cooke was the daughter of Mordecai Cooke of Gloucester County, Virginia. Henry was sent to school in Bristol, England at age eleven, was High Sheriff of Stafford County, Virginia in 1715, and a JP and Burgess in 1714. He was known as "Blind Henry." He and Susannah had nine children, and this line goes to George Fitzhugh (Chapter Three) in four generations. See the original family tree for details. George Fitzhugh (November 4, 1806-July 29, 1881) died in Huntsville, Texas. He married in 1829 Mary Metcalf Brockenborough (March 4, 1806-October 14, 1877). See original tree for seven children. George was the son of Dr. George Fitzhugh (1776-1824) who married in 1804 Lucy Stuart (1786-1862). Dr. George was the son of John Thornton Fitzhugh (1749-1809) who married Mrs. Margaret (Helm) Foote. He was the son of John Fitzhugh (June 30, 1727- May 14, 1804) who married on October 30, 1746 Alice Thornton (August 21, 1729-March 5, 1790). John was one of nine children of Henry Fitzhugh, son of William the Immigrant. Another of these nine children was Thomas (1725-1768) who built "Boscobel." Henry Fitzhugh was a Member of the Assembly Resolution of 1720, Virginia Assembly. (Hist. Soc. of Fairfax Co., Virginia Vol 3 1954 p.19) He inherited Bedford plantation and married Susannah Cooke, the daughter of Mordecai Cooke of Gloucester County. He was born in 1686 and died in 1758. His half of the Ravensworth patent remained in the family intact until his grandson Henry Fitzhugh who also lived at Bedford partitioned it in 1783 among his five younger sons, Nicholas, Richard, Mordecai, Battaile, and Giles. By the end of this generation the northern half of the tract had been sold out of the family. (Hist. Soc. of Fairfax Co. vol 3 1954 p. 28) Boscobel was inherited by Henry Fitzhugh (1686-1759) of Bedford in 1701. From *Colonial Families, Southern States*, p.226: Hon. Henry Fitzhugh owned 17,598 acres of land in Stafford Co., and he served as High Sheriff, 1715; as Burgess, 1736; liberal supporter of the Established Church, and a Vestryman.

75. William Fitzhugh, of Eagles Nest, was a Captain in the Militia, in the House of Burgesses in 1700, and a Governor of the College of William & Mary in 1702. Anne Lee was the daughter of Richard Henry Lee. They had two sons, four daughters, leading to the Fitzhugh-Grymes line, as given in

our archives. The Fitzhugh surname became extinct in this line in four generations, and led to General Robert E. Lee, Commander of the Confederate Army, in four generations. See original 1927 family tree, 1927 notes, loose notes etc.

William inherited 1800 acres of land in Stafford and Westmoreland Counties. He was the Justice of Stafford Co., and High Sheriff in 1707; member of the House of Burgesses in 1700, and a Governor of the College of William and Mary in 1702. He inherited under his father's will 18,723 acres of land in Stafford and Westmoreland; was residuary legatee of all lands not bequeathed, and rights to lands in Virginia, Maryland and England; eight negroes; 18 pieces of silver plate; £200 Sterling out of his father's money in England; half the household furniture; "my own and my wife's pictures, the other six pictures of my relations, and the large map in the study", half of his father's "study of books", &c. He was appointed clerk of Stafford County, July 18, 1701, and was a member of the House of Burgesses for that county, 1700, 1701 and 1702 (Stafford Records). Possibly he was a member in other years. On Dec. 13, 1711, the Lords of Trade and Plantations presented a representation to the Queen, recommending William Fitzhugh, Esq., as a person fully qualified to fill a vacancy in the Council, being a good estate, and being well affected towards Her Majesty's Government (Sainsbury Abstracts). The appointment made on Dec. 19 and he took the oaths in Virginia, October 15, 1712 (Council Journal). His tenure of office was short, for his last appearance in Council was in Nov. 8, 1713, and Jan. 27, 1713-14, there is an entry in the Council Journal that he was dead. Besides the offices named, He was a justice of Stafford, and high sheriff in 1707. If he made a will it was doubtless recorded in Stafford, but the books of that date have been lost. He married Ann, daughter of Richard Lee, Esq., of Westmoreland County (member of the Council.)

Anne Lee [Charleen had Ann McCarty, but it has to be Ann Lee – HAF] Will dated November 7, 1728; Proved May 31, 1732. To each of my own brothers and their wives a ring; a ring to Col. John Tayloe; son Henry Fitzhugh all my lands, my 1st wedding ring and my grandfather Corbin's mourning ring; to Elizabeth dau. of Major J. Fitzhugh a gold ring; to daughter Lettice 2 negroes; dau. Sarah Fitzhugh 2 negroes; Billington McCarty my last wedding ring; to Thaddeus McCarty a stone ring; to Sarah Beale my hoop ring. I discharge my brothers   [-in-law] H. Fitzhugh and Thomas and Henry Lee from the bills of exchange to my late husband McCarty. Negroes in the hands of the husband of my daughter Lettice to be hers." Anne Lee had grown up at Mt. Pleasant with her five brothers in a most erudite atmosphere. Her father, "who neither improved nor diminished his estate" could write in Latin, Greek, Hebrew, French, but he paid little attention to his business affairs, he left Anne 4000 acres in Stafford county that he no longer owned. Her tombstone in the family cemetery (at Eagle's Nest) reads: Here Lies The Body of Anne the Daughter of The Honorable Richard Lee Esq. She was first married to The Honourable William Fitzhugh esq. Whom she surviv'd By whom she had Issue, Henry, Lettice & Sarah who are still living. She was afterward married to Daniel M'Carty, Esq. Whom she also Surviv'd, By him, she had Issue, Anne Who d'yed (an inf.) Her surviving Children erect this Monument To Her Precious Memory Wou'd They like Her obtain In this Life the Love & Praise of all And in the next Eternal Happiness Let Them Imitate The Good & Pious Pattern. she departed this Life Jan'Y. 12th 1731. In the 49th year of her Age. (from *The Vistas of "Eagle's Nest"* by Liza Lawrence).

76.   Thomas "Bell Aire" Fitzhugh was County Clerk in 1714. His wife Anne Fowke Mason was the daughter of George Mason. They had one daughter. He was born in 1689 in "Bedford", King George County, Virginia; and died in 1719 in Richmond, Virginia. He married Ann Fowke Mason, daughter of George Mason, about 1716. She was born before 1695. Thomas was County Clerk in 1714. Thomas received by the will of his father nearly 5,000 acres of land. A tract of 1,100 acres lay near Fredericksburg. At the time this property was in Richmond County and his last will and Testament is recorded there. He served as clerk of Stafford County a few years, dying in office. Anne Fowke (Mason) Darrell, daughter of Col. George and Mary (Fowke) Mason, was widow of William Darrell (16??-1715) by whom she had a son Sampson Darrell (1712-1777) who died testate in Fairfax County, Thomas and Anne Fowke (Mason) Fitzhugh had an only child, Mary Fitzhugh, who died in infancy. Anne Fowke (Mason) Darrell Fitzhugh married thirdly Thomas Smith (d. 1764) who died testate in Fairfax County; his will mentions three children, viz: (1) Susanna Smith; (2) Mary Smith (married Mr. Hancock); and (3) William Smith (172?-1802) who died testate in Mason Co. Kentucky. As Thomas died without male issue and his father had entailed his estate, his property came into possession of William Fitzhugh, Esq. (1741-1809) and in 1769 he built the handsome brick mansion called Chatham upon the land overlooking

Fredericksburg. (*The Register of Overwharton Parish* compiled by King, p. 226)

77. Rosamund Fitzhugh married William Allerton, grandson of Isaac Allerton, who immigrated in the Mayflower. Willoughby (William) Allerton married Sarah Taverner about 1702 in Westmoreland County, so Rosamund Fitzhugh must have died between 1698 (probable marriage date) and 1702 (remarriage date estimated from birth date of Sarah's and Willoughby's first child). [Private communication from Kathleen Much, February 20, 1999.]
Westmoreland County Wills: ALLERTON, WILLOUGHBY, gent., January 17, 1723; April 8, 1724 Land, stock and 3 slaves to wife Hannah; son Isaac land whereon I live and 300 acres or land and two-thirds of estate; dau. Elizabeth Allerton 200 acres and one-third estate; son exr; my wife's daus. Hannah and Sarah Bushrod personal property of the father and mother. Land on Machotick; land formerly Capt. Joh[n?] Bushrod's and person estate of his to my wife and her daughters.; to wife the school master Joshua Nelson and 3 more white servants. From *English Duplicates of Lost Virginia Records* compiled by Louis des Cognets, Jr., Genealogical Publishing Co., Inc., 1958 (current printing 1990): on p. 3 in List of Sheriffs Appointed April 25, 1707 Willoughby Allerton is listed for Westmoreland Co.

80. Colonel William Fitzhugh was baptised May 14, 1725, godfathers Col. John Tayloe and Daniel McCarty, godmothers Sarah McCarty and Winwood McCarty. He built the present mansion at the Marmion Estate. The living room of this house is now in the Metropolitan Museum in New York. (See Chapter Two and Appendix 7.) The name "Marmion" is a very early family name of the Barons FitzHugh of Ravensworth (see Appendix 1), descended through the Grey family, and has no real connection with our family. He married first Ursula Beverley, daughter of Colonel William Beverley of "Blandfield." He married second, before 1759, Hannah --, whose will was proved on Feb. 7, 1799. It is fairly certain that there was issue of both marriages, and we are fairly certain that John (Note 82) was a son of the first marriage. See notes for the Beverley ancestry. The marriage to Ursula Beverley was about 1741. She was born about 1729 in 'Blandfield', Essex County, Virginia, and died after 1766. Hannah was born between 1727-37 in 'Strawberry Hill', King George County, Virginia, and died in 1799.
There is recorded in King George County of a deed dated May 31, 1786, from William Fitzhugh, of Marmion, and Hannah his wife. Also a deed dated March 6, 1780, from

William Fitzhugh, of King George County, conveying to his son Daniel Fitzhugh, 1,200 acres "where Rappahannock Quarter now stands," purchase by John Fitzhugh, father of said William from John Lisle, merchant, of London, by deed dated October 26, 1725, and recorded in Lancaster Co., July 13, 1726. He was probably the William Fitzhugh, Jr., who was major in the Stafford militia in 1752 (*Cal. Virginia State Papers*). It is possible that he, instead of William Fitzhugh, afterwards of Maryland (who, as appears from a deed, lived in Cople parish, Westmoreland, in 1744), was burgess for Stafford 1748 and 1751. His will was dated March 13, 1789, and proved in King George June 2, 1791. Legatees: to wife her clothes, all her jewels, her gold watch, such furniture, plate and books as she should choose, the coach and horses, eight slaves, and, during her widowhood, the Marmion plantation mansion, with houses, gardens, orchards, a supply of groceries, &c., and also 60 pounds per annum. He states that he had provided for his sons, Daniel (McCarty) and Theoderick. Gives son John the negroes he had lent him. To son Philip the remainder of the estate not otherwise bequeathed. If son Robert should return to the State he is to have one shilling, "because at the commencement of the late war he quitted the business I had allotted for his living, since which I have heard nothing from him.' Son William Beverley Fitzhugh, two negroes. Daughter Lucy Campbell 600 pounds, Daughter Elizabeth 500 pounds if she marries, if not 25 pounds per year. Same provision for daughter Anna. Bequests to daughters Sally, Molly and Maria, and daughter Finch. William Hooe, of "Pine Hill," and "my son-in-law" Alexander Campbell, executors. (*Virginia Historical Magazine*) William Fitzhugh, son of John and Anne Barbara Fitzhugh, was baptised on May 14, 1725. God Fathers: Colonel John Tayloe and Daniel McCarty. God Mothers: Madam Sarah McCarty and Winwood (sic) McCarty. Westmoreland Co., Virginia. Book V. p. 510 show that "John Fitzhugh of Stafford Country, Gent." married Anne Barbara, the eldest daughter of Daniel McCarty, Gent., of Westmoreland county before or about Dec. 5, 1715. (*St. Paul's Parish Register 1715-1798*, compiled by John Bailey Calvert Nicklin, p. 75,note 18) In 1797 Marmion was purchased by Major George Lewis (1757-1821), nephew of George Washington, and is now in possession of his descendant Mrs. Robert Carter Nicholas Grymes (née Lucy Lewis), as of 1961.

Doctor Robert Wellford (1753-1823), physician of Fredericksburg, was several days at Marmion attending

Catherine (Daingerfield) Lewis (1764-1820), wife of Major George Lewis, in her last illness. As Doctor Wellford sat by the fire in the little parlour at Marmion on a cold day in February 1820 he wrote in his diary, reflecting upon former days:

"At the particular desire of Mrs. Lewis I remained the whole day in the house and slept on the subsequent night once more and for the last time in the little parlour in which room in time past I have witnessed such sociality and more merriment that in any other room in the whole course of my life. ...Mr. William Fitzhugh, the hospitable owner of the mansion (Marmion) and the estate surrounding same, his sons, his brother Daniel, and his son William; the Rev. Thomas Thornton; that truly respectable Gentleman, the late William Fitzhugh (of Chatham); Mr. Grymes of the Wilderness and his namesake of Eagle's Nest; Mr. Robert Allison; Mr. John McCoy (with the musicians, Victor, Olliver, &c. in the subordinate range of assembly) formed a group not often collected together in the Northern Neck of Virginia. But they are all gone and 'the place that hath known them shall know them no more.' The worthy proprietors of this most hospitable mansion are also removed from the cares of this world and are (I sincerely hope) at rest in Heaven although the place of their interment in the Graveyard of the Old Orchard cannot (from the changes that have occurred) be easily found by their former friends and acquaintances." (*The Register of Overwharton Parish* compiled by King, p. 227.)

81. Daniel Fitzhugh was of King George County, Virginia, and is buried in Colonel William's graveyard. Daniel McCarty Fitzhugh was born in 'Bedford', Stafford County, Virginia. He married first Catherine – before 1770, and second Alice Riden in 1771 in Stafford County, Virginia, and third Susannah Porter on October 24, 1772 in Stafford County, Virginia.

William A. Crozier, ed., *Westmoreland County Wills* (Virginia County Record Publications, n.s. 1, 1913), p. 80, citing Will Book 16: "Fitzhugh, Daniel September 17, 1777; March 28, 1786 To be buried in brother William's burying yard; son William negroes which I had by his mother Catherine; daughter Jane negroes which I had with her mother Elcey; daughter Sukey negroes I had with her mother Susanna, also sum due from estate of Philip Grymes which was due my wife Susanna; brother William's children by his wife Hannah; niece Lucy Fitzhugh 1 negro; nieces Ann and Sally daughters of brother William; nephew McCarty Fitzhugh; friend William Fitzhugh of Chatham. *From The*

Register of Overwharton Parish Stafford County Virginia 1723-1758 compiled and edited by George Harrison Sanford King, 1961 Daniel Fitzhugh (1733-1786) married three times and left issue a child by each wife, viz: (1) Catherine, probably née Hore, who is mentioned as a granddaughter of John Triplett of King George County in a deed there in 1766 - she was the mother of his only son, William Fitzhugh, mentioned by Doctor Wellford; (2) in 1771 to Alice Riden (Riding) and (3) in 1772 to Susanna Potter. By his last will and Testament of record in Westmoreland County, William Fitzhugh (I think the author must mean Daniel) requested that he be buried "in my brother William's burial ground." Daniel Fitzhugh's will was dated September 17, 1777 and recorded March 28, 1786; it indicates his three wives predeceased him. Jane, his daughter by his second wife, married on June 17, 1790 Henry Dade Hooe, and Susanna, his daughter by his third wife, married on May 13, 1790 Rice Wingfield Hooe.

82. Lucy Redd married in Hanover County, Virginia and was the daughter of Samuel Redd (b. 1729) who married before 1749 Lucy Rogers. Samuel was the son of Thomas Reed (or Redd) of Cedar Grove, Caroline County, Virginia, who married a Sarah Ferguson. Lucy Rogers was the daughter of John Rogers and Rachel Eastham. See notes for more ancestry of many of these names. From *The Virginia Historical Magazine*: From a record in King George it appears that in 1797, "Marmion" was surveyed at the request of Philip Fitzhugh. It contained 1,821 acres, and the "Rappahannock Tract," adjoining, contained 792 acres. Both had belonged to William Fitzhugh, father of Philip. About 1800, is a deed in King George from Philip Fitzhugh and Charlotte, his wife, and Daniel McCarty Fitzhugh, and Ann, his wife, conveying the "Rappahannock Tract" to Hooe and Wallace. There is also in King George a deed dated June 9, 1804, from Philip Fitzhugh of Fairfax County, conveying land in King George to Daniel McCarty Fitzhugh, of Fairfax. Daniel Fitzhugh (no doubt the same) and Susanna Potter were married in King George, October 24, 1772. In a case in one of the Virginia reports, it is stated that Philip Fitzhugh, son of William Fitzhugh, of Marmion, inherited a very large real and personal estate; but died in 1807, utterly insolvent.

An interesting family story that occurred in this generation is told, two generations later by John Henry Fitzhugh. In an undated letter in Mary Ann Fitzhugh Thornton's Scrapbook in the Austin History Center, John writes in a beautiful old hand harking back to Secretary Style the following. Informing his correspondent of Uncle Spotswood Henry's death, he says "...the Henry papers have been returned to Pa. [Pennsylvania?] as Uncle Spotswood kept them during the latter part of his life. ... Among them is Grand Pa's resolutions against the Stamp Act with letters of the most interesting nature from General [George] Washington and LaFayette. He intents to present them to Congress..." This must refer to John Henry Fitzhugh's mother's father, who was the son of Patrick Henry, the fiery orator who shouted in the Virginia House of Burgesses "Give me Liberty or give me Death!" The Stamp Act was an attempt in 1765 by George Grenville, Prime Minister of Great Britain, to raise revenue by taxing the American Colonies, who rightly objected by quoting William Pitt "No Taxation without Representation". Such was the colonial agitation that George III conspired to replace Grenville with Lord Rockingham, who repealed the Act in 1766 in order to pacify the Colonies, [Oman, *History of England*, 1907, pp. 539-41]. The bitterness left behind led to the tax on tea, to the Boston Tea Party, the Boston Massacre, and then to the Declaration of Independence.

83. Robert Fitzhugh ran away to the War of Independence, leaving the estate his father had provided for him. He settled in Logan County, Kentucky and left a line of descendants to this day. See notes. Daniel McCarty Fitzhugh, born March 15, 1758 in Marmion, Stafford, Virginia; died December 1, 1796 in Spring Hill, Wicomico Co., Maryland; Robert Fitzhugh was born in 1743 in Virginia, and died between 1800 and 1810 in Logan Co., Kentucky. He married Margaret Bell about 1757; she was born about 1740; died in Logan Co., Kentucky. Robert Fitzhugh sold 155 acres to John Bales for 160 pounds Virginia currency on 26 Sep 1797 in Bedford, Virginia.

The following is from a 1955 letter from Mary Trowbridge Elkins (a descendant of Solomon Fitzhugh):

"The first records we have of Robert was when he went to Bedford County, Virginia on a small farm and his son Peter was born in Bedford Co., Virginia in 1760. They paid taxes there from 1782-1797 and the record of Peter's, Robert Jr's, and Hannah's marriages are there in Bedford County all before 1797. The record shows also that they sold all this land they owned in Bedford County on Sept. 26, 1797 about 155 acres. Some of the family were in the revolution, but so far no one has taken the trouble to prove it. Until now the family had not been traced. One relative got in to the D.A.R. on the strength of Robert Jr., but she traced the family wrong and we are able to prove that now.

In the tax lists of 1799 the first Robert, Peter and Robert Jr. are given as living in Logan Co. Kentucky. After that only the names of Peter and Robert Jr. show on the tax lists. Robert Sr. must have died or gone back to Virginia. We know nothing more of him."

1787 Bedford Co. p. 194, Per. Prop. Tax List A: Robert, Sr. (1 horse, mare, colt, or mule and 3 cattle) not tithable. (Reasons for being exempt included: being a woman; being old and infirm, in which case one should be able to find in the county Order Books a law making him exempt; and an occupation of clergyman or professor. Certain political jobs, from constable, at county level, to governor, at the state level, made one exempt. White males between sixteen and twenty-one were subject to a county parish tithe, but not to the state poll tax. Indians were exempt. Persons living out of the county may be listed because they owned property in the county, but they themselves were exempt except in the county in which they resided. Sometimes the tax commissioner notes the county or state in which out-of-county taxpayers lived.) p. 211 Taxpayers By Date Commissioner Received Their Lists. (The commissioner was required to note the day he visited each taxpayer. This makes it possible to rearrange the lists and determine probable neighbours.) Robert, Sr., also Peter, Robert, Jr., and George Potter who married Robert, Sr.'s daughter, Hannah. Jan Wolford of Texas visited Logan Co., Kentucky cemeteries in Sept. 1996 to locate Robert's grave; they did not find it but found that of Robert's son, Robert in Terry Burying Ground.

According to Walter Guy Lane, first mention of Robert Fitzhugh is in the Bedford Country, Virginia, Deed Book, No.2 on page 198, dated May 24, 1763, when Richard Stith of Bedford on behalf of the executors of Richard Randolph deeded to Robert Fitzhugh of the same county 105 acres in Bedford County on the south side of Jones Fort of Otter River adjoining Yoatem, being part of the land conveyed by the executors of Richard Randolph, deceased, to the said Richard Stith by power of attorney, Nov. 7, 1761 and recorded in the General Court. Recorded, Bedford, May 23, 1763.

In the Library of Congress there are eight "Early Virginia Petitions" dated between June 3, 1782 and October 27, 1785. Robert's signature is on page 5 of the last.

84.   Elizabeth Harrison was the daughter of Nathaniel Harrison of Prince George County, Virginia. They had issue five girls and two boys, named in *Genealogy of Virginia Families*, 1899, p. 853, which lists John's death on October 10, 1772. According to Kelly Leighton (see files), John married first Alice

Thornton and had at least 10 children. "Major" John Fitzhugh is said to have been born January 4, 1729/30 in Stafford County, Virginia and died October 10, 1792. He first married Alice Catlett Thornton about 1745, who was born August 21, 1729 in Crowes, King George Co., Virginia; died March 5, 1790 in 'Belle Air,' Stafford Co., Virginia. Their daughter Anne married George May in 1783. The record of his marriage to Elizabeth Harrison is in Lunenberg County. He married (2) Elizabeth Harrison January 31, 1760 in St Paul's Parish, King George Co., Virginia; born 1737.

85. Anne Fitzhugh was born about 1718 in Virginia and married William Allison on November 21, 1740 in King George County, Virginia.

86. Barbara Fitzhugh was born about 1720 in 'Bedford', Stafford County, Virginia. Rev. William McKay was born in Hanover Parish, Prince George County, Virginia, and they were married in Stafford County.

87. Sarah died August 3, 1784 in 'Society Hill', King George County. She married in Stafford County, Virginia. Francis Thornton on April 2, 1747 who was born July 20, 1725 in Stafford County. Sarah Fitzhugh, born May 30, 1727 in Bedford, Stafford Co., Virginia; died 1784 in 'Society Hill', King George Co., Virginia; Francis was of 'Society Hill', King George Co., Virginia, and was referred to as Col. Francis Thornton. He was Justice of Peace and Col. of Militia in that County.

88. Elizabeth Fitzhugh, sister of Colonel William Fitzhugh, was born in 1728 in 'Bedford', Stafford County, Virginia. She married Nathaniel Gray.

90. Philip Fitzhugh was of Caroline County, Virginia, and Mary Macon Aylett was of King George County, Virginia. The Aylett Family ancestry is known for a considerable period, and it is through that family that we are linked to the Barons FitzHugh of Ravensworth. See the separate family tree, volume of notes on the Barons FitzHugh, and the notes regarding the founding of Emanuel School.

91. Dennis Fitzhugh and his wife Frances had issue Clark Fitzhugh, and Ann Clark Lee Fitzhugh who married Allen Polk and had issue. Dennis Fitzhugh is listed in the 1810 Census of Kentucky as living in Jefferson County.

92. Samuel Temple Fitzhugh was born about 1784 and married a cousin, the daughter of William Fitzhugh of Baltimore. Later they moved to Kentucky.

93. Lucy Rose Fitzhugh, born about 1790, married Dr. Benjamin Harrison Hall October 28, 1824 in Jefferson County, Kentucky; he was born in 1781 in Fredericksburg, Virginia.

Lucy Redd Fitzhugh married Benjamin Harrison Hall on October 28, 1824 in Jefferson County, Kentucky, and lived in St. Louis, Missouri.

94. Alexander Campbell Fitzhugh was born in 1794 in Hanover County, Virginia, and died January 2, 1895 in Calloway County, Missouri. He married Nancy Cason on April 14, 1812, in Harrison County, Kentucky; she was born in 1792 in Spotsylvania County, Virginia. They settled in Pike County, Missouri in 1823. Alexander Fitzhugh moved to Harrison Co., KY about 1810 with his older brother, William. Alexander and Nancy lived on Gray's Run, a creek near Cynthiana, Harrison Co., Kentucky where they had a farm. In 1820 they moved to Louisiana, Pike Co., Missouri, where they had a town load and also a farm. Around 1835, the family moved to Callaway County, Missouri, and lived on a 160 acre farm near the town of New Bloomfield. (Information from Charlie Abernathy). This line descends in two generations from Alexander Campbell Fitzhugh to Lucas D. "Luke" Fitzhugh (1866-1944), a Deputy Sheriff to Wyatt Earp.

95. William Fitzhugh is first known from a lawsuit of 1796, when he was an infant. See also Note 94 above. Of this generation, Dennis and William are stated to be the oldest sons, 2 H & M 290, 1808, referred to in *William & Mary Quarterly*, 2nd Series, Volume XIII, No. 1, January 1933, p.51. William Fitzhugh is listed in the 1810 Census of Kentucky in Henry County, and was born about 1775.

100. John Henry Fitzhugh's life is covered in Chapter Three. Harriett Bullett's ancestry is known back to medieval times; see notes and other family trees. John Henry Fitzhugh styled himself as "Major" Fitzhugh in later life, and indeed there is a reference to a Major John H. Fitzhugh in the records of the Aztec Club, an association of Officers of the Mexican War, but after extensive research, I am convinces that this is inaccurate and unreliable. See archive notes.

The Census Return dated July 11, 1860 for Cannonville Post Office, Hays County, Texas lists John, Harriett, Mary, and a male child "Abyth", aged 8 months, all of them living with a JPT Fitzhugh and a Frank Fitzhugh, who have been identified by Charleen Oerding as 4th and 5th cousins to John. This child Abyth is most likely (Philip) Aylett, the name "Aylett" having been corrupted on the Return to become "Abyth". This seems obvious because Philip Aylett was 7 months and 7 days old on July 11, 1860, which accords with Abyth's Census age of "8/12". Abyth, or Philip Aylett, was listed as having been born in Kentucky, which means that the family moved from there to Texas sometime between late December 1859 and early July 1860.

101. Patrick Henry Fitzhugh may have had 10 children: Mary Elizabeth, Page, Shelly, George, Allen, Philip, Helen, William, Martha, Lena. He first married Hannah Maria Coalton of Richmond, Virginia, licence dated October 25, 1837. He married Mary Steptoe Christian of Middlesex County, Virginia on November 10, 1840. This line goes to the Steptoe Fitzhughs of Baltimore. See the Scroll Tree. During the Civil War, Patrick was mentioned in despatches several times: "Captain P.H. Fitzhugh, in command of the infantry at Long Bridge, is throwing up redoubts at that point, for its more successful defence." [United States War Department, Record and Pension Office, and War Records Office. 1889. *The War of the Rebellion: a Compilation of the Official Records of the Union and Confederate Armies*. Series 1-Volume 27 (PartIII), p.975. Government Printing Office, Washington DC.] Later, "Major Fitzhugh deserves special praise and thanks for his signal gallantry throughout this action. [He] volunteered to rescue the bridge while exposed to the fire of the enemy's guns." ... "Maj. P.H. Fitzhugh, commanding the two companies of the Twenty-Sixth Virginia, gallantly volunteered to take 20 men and extinguish it [a fire on the bridge]." [*Ibid.* Part II, pp.264, 363]

The Virginia Regimental Histories Series. (VARosterC) Published in 1987:Enlisted as a Captain on 23 April 1861; Commission in Company B, 26th Infantry Regiment Virginia on 23 April 1861, Transferred on 31 October 1863 from company B to company S. Promoted to Full Major on 31 October 1863. Killed on 18 June 1864 in Jordan's Farm, VA

Robert Edward Fitzhugh Gentry has in his possession the regimental battle flag of Major Patrick Henry Fitzhugh, C.S.A. - at least it is claimed to be. His mother had it preserved and framed prior to her death.

Residence: 1850, Gloucester
Notes for HANNAH MARIE COALTON:
Their marriage is listed in: Annals of Henrico Parish, Diocese of Virginia, 1611-1884. Name: Patrick Henry Fitzhugh, Spouse: Hannah Maria Coalton, At Richmond, of Gloucester, of Richmond; license dated October 25, 1837.
Notes for MARY STEPTOE CHRISTIAN: In the 1860 US Census she was listed as living in Gloucester Co., VA. 1880

US Census, Census Place:Petsworth, Gloucester, Virginia, Source: FHL Film 1255367 National Archives Film T9-1367 Page 152.

102. Edwin Fitzhugh, thought to have been a soldier of fortune, was killed on Walker's Expedition to Nicaragua in 1855.

103. LaFayette Henry Fitzhugh was born on May 9, 1829 in "Shooter's Hill", Middlesex County, Virginia, and died on August 1, 1905 in Dallas, Texas. He married first Elizabeth Garlick Semple, on December 15, 1849 at Covington, Kentucky, [*Richmond Whig & Public Advertiser*, Tuesday, December 25, 1849] born, June 4, 1827, died June 4, 1851. He married five weeks later on July 13, 1851, Ann Elizabeth Bullett, born March 9, 1831 Louisville, Kentucky, died February 8, 1908, Dallas Texas, daughter of Cuthburt Bullett, and sister of Harriett Bullett (note 100) (wife of John Henry Fitzhugh). They settled in Dallas, Texas, and had issue two sons, one daughter, and three others, Bullett, Fayette, and Lillie. He served in the Mexican War; and was a Colonel in the C.S.A. He took a Bachelor of Arts degree at the University of Virginia. At the age of sixteen, while visiting Kentucky, he enlisted with a Kentucky regiment for service in the Mexican War, and was on duty throughout that period of hostilities. After the war he returned to Middlesex Co., Virginia. In the 1850 Census of Covington, Kentucky, he is listed as a "carpenter". In the 1860 Census of Kentucky, he is listed in Hartford, Ohio. At the outbreak of War Between the States he raised and brought to Virginia the first Confederate regiment from Kentucky. During the war he served as sergeant at arms of the Confederate Senate. He was chosen the first Democratic doorkeeper of the House of Representatives at Washington during Grant's administration. In 1867, he was a "Commission Merchant" and Partner in Fitzhugh, Wilmer, & Co., Commission Merchants, 40 & 42 Broadway and 53 New Street, New York In the 1870 Census for Kentucky, he was listed as a "hotel keeper" with real and personal estates of $8000 & $3500. In 1880 he moved to Dallas, Texas where he became a railroad official and oil operator, although he is listed in the Austin, Texas *City Directory* for 1887-1892 as a Clerk for Downs, DeCordova, & Raymond at 605 W. 10th St. However, he is also listed in Dallas, Texas in 1889/90 in the firm of Fitzhugh & Wozencraft and Alfred P. Wozencraft, Fitzhugh & Wozencraft, Attorneys, at 503 Elm St. This continues for 1891-1894 with LaFayette described as a "real estate agent". He had charge of the building of the Chicago, Texas and Mexican Central Railroad and died at Dallas, August 10,

1905. He was a Democrat, and a very zealous member of the Baptist Church and the Masonic fraternity. [*Virginia Genealogies* #4, p.466, 1924] "Mr. L. H. Fitzhugh had, for a while, the management of Crab Orchard Springs in this State" (Kentucky). [*The Ticket,* December 9, 1875, Covington, Kentucky, p.3, col. 2.]

104. Dr. Phillip Aylett Fitzhugh married on April 7, 1849 [*Richmond Whig & Public Advertiser*, Friday April 24, 1849] Georgina Tankard of Baltimore, a descendant of William Tankard of Yorkshire, an original settler of Jamestown. They had two daughters, one of whom, Mary Macon, married William Bullett Fitzhugh, her first cousin. P A Fitzhugh was practising medicine in Johnsontown, Northampton County, Virginia. Georgina Tankard was from that County, married in 1849. She was a graduate of the Wesleyan Female Institute of Wilmington, Delaware, and the author of *The Life of Dr. John Tankard,* (1907).

Philip A. Fitzhugh, born 1824, Mddlesex Co., VA; graduate, Virginia Military Institute Class of 1846, physician; CSA veteran/ d. 1908 Northampton Co., VA. Descriptive note: Misc. paper, most dating from cadetship. Include 6 letters from Fitzhugh to his brother, containing many references to cadet life (graduation; hazing "plebes"; death of Henry C. Reid, Class of 1846, Washington College student, called "minks"; handwritten issue of a cadet newspaper called "The Royal Caroline," dated March 21, 1846; VMI letter of appointment and 2 grade reports; invitation to Society of Cadets meeting, medical school speech; letter to Fitzhugh from Henry T. Lee regarding Daniel Lee Powell, VMI Class of 1844.

Genealogies of VA Families p.866 says that Dr. Philip Aylett Fitzhugh died 2 October 1878.

Manuscripts Department, Library of the University of North Carolina at Chapel Hill, SOUTHERN HISTORICAL COLLECTION, #4872-z Inventory

Abstract: Correspondence by and relating to Philip Aylett Fitzhugh (1824-1908), physician of Northampton County, Va.; his wife, author Georgiana Tankard Fitzhugh (1827-1899); and his siblings. Included are six letters, 1844-1845, pertaining to his education and training as a doctor at the Virginia Military Institute and society in Lexington, Va.; and letters, 1850-1853, 1866, 1890-1891, from his brother, John

H. Fitzhugh, who emigrated to Kentucky and Austin, Tex. Two letters, 1845 and 1866, discuss the emancipation of slaves. Also included are two letters on legal issues: one, 1876, from Judge John Critchen (1820-1901) and one, 1879, from University of Virginia law professor John B. Minor (1813-1895). Provenance: Purchased from Terry Alford, Annandale, Va., March 1997 (Acc. 97048). Correspondence pertaining to Fitzhugh's V.M.I. years includes: Six letters, 1844-1845, by Fitzhugh on cadet life at V.M.I., including a description of Christmas Day celebrations, Whig politics, a speech by Fitzhugh to the Temperance Society of Lexington, the decline of Washington (later Washington and Lee) College, Lexington society, and other events;A letter, 22 November 1845, which mentions the freedom of a slave named Betsy and a servant named Andy, "but owing to his peculiar dark complexion which characterizes the true African race, we gave him the appropriate appellation of Snowball"; Two printed forms, signed and completed in manuscript, showing the academic, moral, and financial standing of Fitzhugh, by F. H. Smith, Superintendent of V.M.I. Family and related correspondence includes: Letter, 29 May 1846, to Fitzhugh from William Spotswood Fontaine of Fontainbleau, King William County, Va., discussing their friend, Henry Aylett (1825-1870), great-grandson of Patrick Henry; Letter, 18 May 1849, from Fitzhugh and his wife to his mother-in-law, Anna K. Tankard, while the couple were on their bridal tour; Letter, 29 February 1851; from Fitzhugh to his brother informing him that their brother John had been shot and wounded by an unknown assailant in Louisville, Ky.; Six letters, 1850-1853, from the Covington, Ky., area from Philip's brother, John H. Fitzhugh, who emigrated west, describing his loneliness, railroad and freighting work, wounding by an unknown assailant, and the collapse of a church floor while a bishop was giving a sermon; Three letters, 1866, 1890, 1891, from John Fitzhugh in Austin, Tex. The 27 July 1866 letter describes the financial ruin which ensued from his enlistment in the Confederate Army, the loss of his horses, and how "bushwhackers" had driven them from their home. He mentioned that their sister-in-law Mary in

Virginia had also suffered with Negroes stealing nearly all of her clothing. The 1891 letter states he was pleased with the new minister at the Austin Baptist Church, W. B. Garrett, at whose Virginia home John Wilkes Booth died. The collection also includes three additional letters: 10 November 1867, from John A. Fitzhugh of New York, nephew of Philip Fitzhugh; 27 March 1876, from Judge John Critchen (1820-1901), sending legal opinions; 24 March 1879, from John B. Minor (1813-1895), sending legal opinions to Mr. Williams of Baltimore (connection to Fitzhughs unclear). http://www.lib.unc.edu/mss/inv/f/Fitzhugh,Philip_Aylett.html In the 1860 US Census he was living in Northampton Co, VA. In the 1870 US Census he was living with his wife in Eastville, Northampton Co., VA. 1880 US Census Census Place: Eastville, Northampton, Virginia Source: FHL Film 1255379 National Archives Film T9-1379 Page 462B

Notes for **GEORGIANNA TANKARD**: Georgia Tankard of Baltimore, a descendant of William Tankard of Yorkshire, an original settler of Jamestown. They had 2 daughter, one of whom married William Bullitt Fitzhugh, next generation. In the 1860 US Census she was living in Northampton Co., VA. In the 1870 US Census she was living in Eastville, Northampton Co., VA born 2: 1827, Northampton Co., VA.

105. Major Thaddeus Fitzhugh's own biographical statement, July 26th, 1887: "Born March 10, 1835, in Middlesex County, Virginia, enlisted in the Confederate service April 1861, Company F, 5th Virginia Cavalry, Pane's Brigade, served in General Lee's army and participated in most of the battles fought by Lee's army, remained in service until the last and was paroled at Richmond, Virginia, May 18th, 1865. Came to Texas in the fall of 1878, Tarrant County, post office, Fort Worth, and to Runnels County April, 1886 and located at prospective sight [*sic*] of Ballinger. By occupation, a practising physician, a thorough Confederate." Source: Mary Love Berryman, on website: *126 Biographical Sketches of Confederate Soldiers.* He published two articles on medical journals in 1884: *A Monstrosity – A Second Rita-Christina,* The Texas Courier of Medicine 1(5): 6-8, and *A Case in Practice - Placenta Praevia Centralis,* The Texas Courier of Medicine 1(8): 39-41. He was living in Kansas City, Kansas, in 1890/91. His 1st wife: Maria Savage (b. 1834

Northampton Co. Va., daughter of Thomas Lyttleton Savage and Louisa Mayo, m. 27 Feb. 1868, d. 7 Jan. 1869, Accomack Co. Va.; son Henry Aylett, b. 31 Dec. 1868, d. 19 Jun., 1869, Accomack Co., Va.). Thaddeus Fitzhugh married 2nd Julia Horsey on January 27, 1870 as St. Peter's Protestant Episcopal Church, Baltimore, and had issue by her: Julia, John Golden (7 June 1879 – 9 April 1962), and Edgar Horsey Fitzhugh. Thaddeus and Julia were divorced sometime after 1880 [source: Harold Dean Davis via Kirk Fitzhugh, email of 1/1/03]. John Golden Fitzhugh married Mary Ella Meredith and had issue: Mary Ella, and William Neale Fitzhugh (18 February 1915 – 31 August 1981) who was General Doolittle's co-pilot in the Second Tokyo Raid in 1942. John Golden Fitzhugh married Dorothea Louise Pursley and had issue: John Patterson Fitzhugh (22 August 1945 -) Michael Dean Fitzhugh (25 January 1949 -) and Mark Lee Fitzhugh (25 April 1961 -). Mark Lee Fitzhugh married Cheri Smith and had issue Emma Smith Fitzhugh (29 May 1998 -). His 3rd wife: Laura Sharpe, (1858-1938) by whom issue Virginia 1892, Georgia 1892, Gordenia 1894, Hilda 1897.

Note from Kirk Fitzhugh, November 13, 2003: Driver, Jr., Robert J. 1997, *5th Virginia Cavalry*, The Virginia Regimental Histories Series. H.E. Howard, Inc., Lynchburg, Virginia. The book chronicles the activities of this unit during the Civil War, of which Thaddeus was in Company F. The author cites extensively Thaddeus' memoirs. There is an appendix listing the roster of the 5th, with information on individuals derived from a variety of sources. The following is provided for Thaddeus (p. 207): Fitzhugh, Thaddeus: Captain, Co. F(3rd). b. Middlesex Co. 3/10/35. M.D. Enl. Mathews CH 7/23/61 as 2nd Lt. Reenl. 3/8/62. Elected Captain 7/23/62. Presence or absence not stated 5-10/62, however, ab. on furlough from Richmond hosp. 10/21/62. Pres. 11-12/62. Paid 1/8/63. Signed for forage for 40 horses 7/31/63 and for 35 horses 9/30/63. WIA (right thigh) 11/63. Pres. 11/63-4/64. Signed for forage for 32 horses Orange CH 1/31/64, for 40 horses 2/28/64. Captured the Chesapeake and took 20 prisoners in report to President Davis. "A gallant officer of great dash and skill." Signed for 12 pair of shoes, 2 jackets, 5 pair of pants and 4 pair of socks 4/17/64. Reported 62 men pres. 5/64. Signed for 18 jackets, 13 pair of pants, 7 pair of shoes, 16 pair of drawers, 7 shirts, 4 pair of socks and 2 caps 5/25/64. Signed for forage for 16 horses 6/30/64, for 32 horses 8/31/64 and for 19 horses 9/30/64. Paid 10/28/64. Pres. 11/28/64. Assigned as Captain, Co. D, consolidated regiment. Ab. detailed on Secret Service 1/29-2/28/65, and had been recommended for retirement. Pres. 4/4/65. Paroled Richmond 5/17/65. Moved to Texas 1878. M.D., Runnels Co., Texas 1887. Received Cross of Honor, Richmond 1909. [Certification for Dau. of The Confederacy, 2003]. Died November 21, 1918.

110. Henry Alexander Fitzhugh was born in Hayes County, Texas, (said to have been in the home of General Sam Houston), and died in Memphis, Tenn. He married Mary Scott in Blairfield, Iowa. She was born in Meridian, Texas and died in St. Louis, Missouri. For the Scott ancestry, see the archives.

111. Dr. Patrick Henry Fitzhugh was born in Austin, Texas. In the 1887/8 *City Directory* for Austin, Texas, Patrick Henry is listed as a Medical Student, working for T.D. Wooten (as an intern?).

112. William Bullett Fitzhugh was born in Covington or Hopkinson, Ky. There is a Notice in the *Covington Journal* of June 28, 1856, p.2, as follows: "DIED In Covington on the 21st inst. WILLIAM BULLITT (*sic*), son of John H. and Harriett Fitzhugh, at the age of 10 Months and 8 days." This accords exactly with his birth date of August 13, 1855. Previous editions of this History have stated that this William Bullett was the same as the William Bullett who was the son of LaFayette Henry Fitzhugh, i.e. this William Bullett's first cousin. Now it seems that the two brothers, John Henry and LaFayette Henry, who both married sisters surnamed Bullett, had sons named William Bullett. The son of John Henry died young in 1856, whereas the son of LaFayette Henry died in 1944.

113. John Glasscock Fitzhugh was born in Travis County, Texas. He married Mrs. Ida Tatom Daughtry, a widow, in Terry, Mississippi. Their son John G. was born in Jackson, Mississippi. In the *City Directory* for Austin, Texas of 1887/8, John Glasscock is listed as a "city salesman" for McKean, Eilers & Co., living at home with J.H. Fitzhugh, and in 1889-92, the same occupation but with Nelson, Davis & Co., later boarding with J.H. Harrell, Sr. In the last two years, he is also listed with J.H. Fitzhugh, Fire Insurance Agents.

114. Phillip Aylett Fitzhugh was born in Covington, Kentucky.

115. Mary F. Thornton was born on April 11, 1882, in Kansas City, Missouri and died in Austin, Texas on July 25, 1971. An interesting family story surfaces from Mary F. Thornton's Scrapbook in the Austin History Center [note typed in the 1890s by Dr. P.H. Fitzhugh entitled *History of the Old*

Table]. She was in possession of a marble table whose history is as follows. It was brought to Virginia in 1656 by the Aylett family and stood for two centuries in the Aylett homestead in King William County, Virginia. Guests who gathered around it include George Washington, Marquis de LaFayette, Richard Henry Lee (Light Horse Harry), James Madison (later President), Patrick Henry, President Tyler, and others. It was badly damaged by Federal Troops in the Civil War, but later repaired, then seeing the decision by the Confederacy to surrender. It came to Texas in 1872, and descended to Aunt Dot (Mary F. Thornton). As a boy, I must have seen it, but was unaware of its history. Dot died childless and unmarried, and the table's whereabouts are unknown.

120. John Henry Fitzhugh was born in Jackson, Mississippi and died at San Antonio, Texas and was buried at St. Martha-on-the-Hill near Guildford, Surrey, England. See van Osenbruggen family tree for other children and van Osenbruggen ancestry. See also the History of the van Osenbruggen Family, by Derek van Osenbruggen, for the life of Marie. T. van O. Fitzhugh.

121. Harriett Irene Fitzhugh was born in New Roads, Louisiana and died at St. Louis Missouri, on June 29, 1970, and married Leo A. McCabe, Jr in Marion, Arkansas.

122. George Taxton William Fitzhugh was born in New Roads, Louisiana, and died in Pinehurst, North Carolina. He married in St. Louis, Missouri and adopted the daughter of his wife Carolyn Cress Taylor. That daughter Natalie married Walter Strange, U.S. Army, and had issue Gee and Shelly.

123. Lyle Scott Fitzhugh was born in New Roads, Louisiana.

124. Henry Alexander married in Marion, Arkansas Ruth Lewis, daughter of Volney Carlisle Lewis and Nancy Edith Drake.

125. Mary Aylett Fitzhugh was born in New Road, Louisiana.

130. Peggy Ruth Fitzhugh Johnstone was born in Memphis, Tennessee and married in Vail, Colorado. Christopher Blake Johnstone was born in Portland, Oregon and Jonathan Fitzhugh Johnstone was born in Eugene, Oregon.

131. Mary Ann Fitzhugh was born in Chatanooga, Tennessee, and married first in Memphis, Tennessee and second in Montgomery, Alabama. Issue: Jesse Alexander Wolfe, b. March 10, 1981; Heather Elizabeth Wolfe, b. February 7, 1983.

132. Carol Travis Prince was born and married first in Washington D.C., and second in Paris. Christopher Hubert George Tardy was born in Chicoutimi, Quebec, Canada and Susanna Kostic was born in Paris.

133. Richard Fitzhugh Prince was born in St. Louis, Missouri, married in Arlington, Virginia. Christine Amanda was born in Eureka, California, and Laurel was born in San Diego, California.
134. Mary Eleanor Fitzhugh was born in Memphis, Tennessee. Both children, David Scott and Susan Elizabeth were born in Memphis, Tennessee.
135. Henry Antonie Fitzhugh was born in San Antonio, Texas and married in Loughton, Essex, England. Hilary Clare Smith was born in Theydon Bois, Essex. See Smith family tree for her ancestry. Both children, Alexander Edward Henry and Edward Anthony Henry were born in London. Rosemary Anne Jeffreys was born in Essex on June 4, 1955, and was married to Henry Antonie Fitzhugh on July 25, 2003 in Richmond Registry Office, Surrey, and on July 26, 2003 in Gray's Inn Chapel, Gray's Inn, London.
136. William Fitzhugh McCabe was born in Toledo, Ohio and married in St. Louis, Missouri. Lauren Elizabeth was born in Washington D.C., and Sean Fitzhugh was born in San Francisco, California. William and Lucy were divorced in the late 1970s and William died in San Francisco on November 26, 1983.

.oOo.

APPENDIX ONE

THE RELATIONSHIP OF OUR FITZHUGH
FAMILY
TO THE BARONS FITZHUGH
AND THE ARMS OF EACH FAMILY

For the last thirty years or more it has been known that there were in fourteenth and fifteenth century England at least two FitzHugh families. Prior to the 20th century it was believed by the American Fitzhughs, our family, that there was only one Fitzhugh family, and that we must be descended from the Barons FitzHugh who bore the Arms emblazoned as: *Azure, three Chevrons interlaced in Base Or, a Chief Or.* The Barons FitzHugh became extinct in 1512, but the American Fitzhughs have always used those same Arms ever since William Fitzhugh immigrated to Virginia Colony in 1673.

What was not realised until the 1930's, and did not become well known until the biography of William Fitzhugh was written by Richard Beale Davis, was that this belief was in fact an error on the part of William himself. My father, John Henry Fitzhugh, even though he was interested in genealogy, did not know it, and at his request the family had the Arms of the Barons FitzHugh cut onto his tombstone.

The misunderstanding goes back to a dispute between William Fitzhugh and his brother. William believed the family Arms to be those of the Barons FitzHugh, and his brother believed them (correctly) to be those of the Fitzhughs of Wilden and

THE RELATIONSHIP TO THE BARONS FITZHUGH

Wavendon, as given in the *Harleian Visitation of Bedfordshire 1566*, (Harleian Society, 1884, p.26). These Arms are emblazoned as: *Quarterly, 1 & 4 Ermine, on a Chief Gules, three Martlets Or; 2 & 3 Argent, three Chevrons Sable, each Charged with a Bezant.*[1]

It is remarkable that such a dispute could have arisen, because Henry Fitzhugh, the father of William the Immigrant, was using the correct Arms in 1648, when he pressed them into a wax seal on a document (B6/7) still in the North Bedfordshire Borough Council Records Office. (This extant seal was discovered by the present author in 1984.) See a photograph of this seal on page 6, where there is also a complete version of the dispute between William and his brother.[2] The correct Arms were confirmed to the Rev. V.C.A. FitzHugh on January 17, 1930.

The Barons FitzHugh were an ancient titled family dating back to the Conquest. The Fitzhughs of Bedfordshire would be classed as gentry, without anything like the landholding (in Yorkshire) that the aristocratic Barons FitzHugh had. The Barons FitzHugh founded Jervaulx Abbey, fought on the Crusades and in the War of the Roses, and were in the company of Kings for many generations, unlike the Fitzhughs of Bedfordshire who were minor landholders at the time.

It was largely out of curiosity, and based upon a hunch, that I began the genealogical work that led to a connection between our family and the Barons FitzHugh. I reasoned that since at least

---

1 Around 1770, the English FitzHughs adopted a motto "In Moderation Placing All My Glory". This is derived from Horace and Pope and is explained in Terrick FitzHugh's *FitzHugh, The Story of a Family Through Six Centuries*, pp. 518-520, British Library Shelfmark YA.2002.b.526.

2 See also *William Fitzhugh and his Chesapeake World*, William Beale Davis, pp.8-9, 46, & 194, for an account of this dispute.

some records went back far enough to where our ancestors were equal in number to the population of the country, that there was a good chance that one of our ancestors might include a member of the Barons FitzHugh family.

Without going into great detail, the link was found just as I was about to give up. I found several links by marriage, of varying degrees of closeness, when I suddenly spotted the missing link in the More family. See the separate family tree that outlines this link between the Barons FitzHugh and ourselves. The link goes from Joan, daughter of William, 4th Lord FitzHugh, who married into the Scrope family, through three generations of Scropes, into the More family for five generations, then in eight generations of Ayletts to our family Fitzhugh, and then in six generations to Alexander and Edward. Thus it is only the last six generations of our branch of the Fitzhugh family that are descended by that particular line from the Barons FitzHugh, although Terrick FitzHugh, the genealogist and author of Volume One as well as the complete history of his English branch of the family *FitzHugh The Story of a Family Through Six Centuries*, has descent from four other lines to the Barons FitzHugh.

The Title of Baron FitzHugh was claimed by two descended families, namely Parre and Feinnes, as described in *Burke's Dormant and Extinct Peerages,* 1883.

H.A.F., 1983, 2001

Following a debate that erupted over the internet in 2002, I have now decided to expand upon and lay out the evidence and arguments that apply to the question of any relationship between the Barons FitzHugh of Ravensworth and our Fitzhugh family of Bedfordshire. This debate ranged over all aspects of the question of whether, and how, our family could be descended from the Barons, and how such a mistake could have been made by William the Immigrant. Most of the debate is fueled by the fact that the American Fitzhughs have been using the Arms of the Ravensworth FitzHughs, and not the Arms of the Bedfordshire Fitzhughs, ever since William's time. An account of this error on William's part is given on pages 42-43 of this Volume.

The first point to note clearly is that the Bedfordshire family adopted the surname Fitzhugh at least some fifty years before the Barons of Ravensworth did the same. This is seen by comparing dates described on pages 12-14 of Volume I, which shows that our family began using the Fitzhugh surname no later than 1241, and *The Complete Peerage*,[1] which shows that the first of the Barons to use the surname FitzHugh must have been born around 1290. Thus, our family was called Fitzhugh some fifty or so years before the Barons were so named. This point was noted in 1932 by The Rev. V.C.A. FitzHugh in the first modern published article to address the correct ancestry of the Fitzhughs of Bedford and America.[2] We also know our own Bedfordshire ancestry back to 1223, when Hugh was living. The Barony of FitzHugh was not established until 1321 (by writ). It would thus seem impossible for a younger son of the Barons line to found our family as a related line of Fitzhughs because our family was already in existence. This argument so far should obviate any possibility of our family being directly descended from any of the Barons, but there are several other points to consider as well.

Another line of debate tries to suggest that Hugh, our patronymic ancestor in Bedfordshire, was in fact part of the Barons FitzHugh family, namely the same person as Sir Hugh Fitz Henry, the second son of Sir Henry Fitz Randolph, who was the 6th Lord of Ravensworth.[3] Unfortunately the dates do not support this; Sir Hugh died on March 12, 1304/5, and so he could not have been born much before 1250, which is not contemporaneous with Hugh, the founder of our family. In any event, "Hugh" was a very common name in England at that time. It has also been suggested

---

1   *The Complete Peerage of England, Scotland, Ireland, Great Britain, and The United Kingdom, Extant, Extinct, or Dormant*, by G.E.C., Volume V, 1926, re-issued by Alan Sutton 1982, p.417. Sir Henry FitzHugh was old enough to be pardoned for crimes on October 16, 1313; he died in 1356.

2   *The Fitzhugh Family*, by Victor C. A. FitzHugh, The Virginia Magazine, Vol. XL, No. 2, April 1932, pp. 187-204 (with Tree).

3   *The Complete Peerage, op.cit.,* p.416; Burke's *A Genealogical History of the Dormant, Abeyant, Forfeited, and Extinct Peerages of the British Empire*, Sir Bernard Burke, 1883, p.207.

that Sir Hugh was despatched to Bedfordshire to look after family lands, but the lands our family occupied were firmly owned by the Priory of St Neots, which was subordinate to the Abbey of Bec in Normandy, and had been made so by Richard FitzGilbert following the Norman Conquest. (See pp. 3 & 7 of Volume I.) This leaves no room for any form or ownership or control by the Barons FitzHugh.

This line of argument has also been carried further - there is a reference to a "Hugh" in Harrison,[1] given as *temps* King John (1199-1216). It is odd that this Hugh is not mentioned in any of the other references to the Barons FitzHugh, and no descendants of Hugh are given. Harrison does not give his sources. Nevertheless, even though this Hugh [fitz Hervey], a younger son of the Lord of Ravensworth, would have been roughly contemporary with our Hugh of Bedfordshire, there is still no evidence at all to connect them, and even less to suggest they are the same person. If they had been the same, Hugh fitz Hervey would have carried his Arms with him to Bedfordshire, differenced in cadency as a second or third son. His father Hervey died in 1182, so the cadency differencing would have vanished from that year. So, without doubt, at the time of our Hugh (ca. 1223), Hugh fitz Hervey would have carried the Barons' Arms - *Az, Three Chevrons interlaced in Base Or, A Chief Or.* Turning to our Fitzhugh Arms, it is highly likely that they were in use before or during the reign of Henry V (1413-1422), since this was the time that the College of Arms began to function. (It was not Incorporated until 1484.) We can be sure that our Arms were in use this early because the College has no record of such a Grant of Arms (vast numbers of ancient Arms predate the College) and because no claim of such a Grant was made at the Harleian Visitation of 1566. If, somehow and against all the Rules of Heraldry, the Barons' Arms were had been transmuted into the Arms of Fitzhugh of Bedfordshire, there would have been only a maximum of 175 years for the process to take place. In addition, there is a huge question as to why would a descendant of the Barons want to have Arms so differenced from his ancestors as to be unrecognisable as a descendant of a Peer of the Realm? Such

---

1 *The History of Yorkshire*, Harrison, George Henry de Strabolgie Neville Plantagenet, Vol 1, 1879 (BL 1854.c.5; The BL Catalogue states that there were no further volumes published.)

hypothetical descendants of the Barons had no need to difference their Arms and would have had every reason not to have wanted to. They could have reverted to the original Barons' Arms any time they chose. It would be very difficult to explain why they would have allowed such a differencing process to take place, especially since there was no College of Arms to control them. It is simply beyond belief and comprehension – Ermine would have to appear; Three Martlets would have to appear; the Chevrons would have to become Simple and not Interlaced, and the Bezants would have to appear, and all the while the bearers of these new Arms would be losing their identity as descendants of the Barons. Thus, there is no evidence at all to connect Hugh fitz Hervey and Hugh, our ancestor of Bedfordshire, but there is considerable and compelling circumstantial evidence to conclude that there can be no connection.

Confusion has also arisen over the names of some of the lands owned by the Barons FitzHugh, namely Barforth (-on-Tees) and Barwick (-on-Tees), where the Barons FitzHugh had property.[1] These are actually called Barford in some references,[2] and thus they have been confused with Great Barford in Bedfordshire, where of course our family did have property. But the river Tees is 160 miles north of Bedfordshire, and these places are irrelevant to our family history.

Another line of argument starts from the fact that one of the distant relations of the Bedfordshire Fitzhughs, Richard Fitzhugh (1544-1602), of Walcot, Oxfordshire, quartered our Fitzhugh Arms with those of the Barons FitzHugh.[3] The arms in the

---

[1]   *The Complete Peerage, op.cit.*: Barforth-on-Tees (p.418, footnote f); Barwick-on-Tees (p.430, footnote b, & page 432, footnote c).

[2]   Harrison, *op. cit.*, p. 136.

[3]   The Visitation Pedigree for "Fitzhugh of Walcot" appears under Harley MS 1556, Folio 176 [British Library reference: Harley 1556, 36a, F.18, Manuscript Room] referred to in the *Visitation of Oxford 1574* by Richard Lee, Portcullis Marshall and Deputy. 'The rest are descents of the same county, not extant in any visitation' per A. Cundy 1634. It is odd that this reference appears only in Cundy's manuscript notes of the Visitation of 1634, by which date this line of FitzHughs was extinct, and does not appear in the earlier Visitations of 1566 or 1574. It gives the impression, to me [HAF] at least, that the Barons FitzHugh Arms were not seriously used or claimed by the

Walcot pedigree are emblazoned *Quarterly, Azure 3 Chevrons Interlaced in Base Or, a Chief of the Last...* i.e. the Arms of the Barons FitzHugh of Ravensworth. Richard Fitzhugh of Walcot would appear to have distanced himself so far from his Bedfordshire cousins that he was not aware of his true Arms and imagined himself descended from a junior line of the FitzHughs, Barons of Ravensworth. The fact that Elizabeth Fitzhugh, née Giffard, was the great-granddaughter of Elizabeth FitzHugh, co-heiress of the Barony of FitzHugh of Ravensworth, may have led to this wishful thinking. (See Pedigree "Connections of Elizabeth Fitzhugh née Giffard" below). The marriage of Richard's son Thomas Fitzhugh into the baronial Cromwell family may also have encouraged this process. This, in turn, may have led William the Immigrant to adopt the same Arms in error. In fact, Richard was entitled, although very loosely, to use the Barons FitzHugh quartering, since his wife's great-grandfather was married to Elizabeth FitzHugh, daughter of Henry 5th Lord FitzHugh. Another way of expressing this complicated relationship is that William the Immigrant had a second cousin twice removed (Richard) whose wife (Elizabeth Giffard Fitzhugh) had a great-grandfather who was married to one of the 5th Baron's daughters. This is such a tenuous relationship as to be totally irrelevant. It is really nothing more than an example of the degree of intermarriage between families in England, something that genealogists are used to. See the two trees on the next two pages for clarity.

 Another way of looking at this is as follows: The Harleian Visitation of 1634 actually recorded the Barons FitzHugh quartering in the Walcot branch, even though Thomas FitzHugh, the last of that line, was by then dead since 1613. It is therefore contemporaneous and within the realms of possibility that our family (William who died in 1633 and Henry who died in 1666) may have known of that quartering well enough to where William the Immigrant also knew it. He would have been only a young boy, but that just might be the reason for his misunderstanding. His father Henry was using the correct Arms in 1648 (see Chapter One of this work), so nothing can excuse William using the wrong

---

Walcot FitzHughs, but got picked up as an afterthought or as a later addition.

Arms, but it simply might be explained by this relatively close juxtaposition of the two FitzHugh Arms within our widely extended family. The ancient names "Marmion" and "Ravensworth", old estates of the Barons FitzHughs, may well have been family lore in the Walcot branch, and William the Immigrant as a young boy might have heard of them. It is also interesting that the title Lord FitzHugh Marmion was in public use in the 1640s and 1650s as a minor title of the Earl of Pembroke,[1] who had inherited the Barony through the Parr family after the Barons became extinct. By 1686, when the dispute over the Arms broke out (see pp. 42-43), William the Immigrant had been out of touch with his family for twelve years, and he may have been only aged six when his father left for Ireland. He may simply not have known, understood, or remembered what his Arms were.

It is easily possible that William the Immigrant could have acquired a reference book giving the Arms of the Barons FitzHugh in a manner that confused him. There are many such bogus books being pedalled today, and many descendants have made that same mistake in the following three centuries. Could William have made the same error? First of all, the *English Short Title Catalog* lists 79 books on English Heraldry published before 1686, the year by which we know William had adopted the wrong Arms. These are scattered all over the world, but four of them are now in the British Library, and one of them is a very likely candidate. It is: *A Display of Herauldry, A more Easie access to the knowledge thereof than hath hitherto been published by any, through the benefit of Method;...* by John Guillim, late Pursuivant of Arms.[2] On page 94 (of the first part) it gives the Barons FitzHugh Arms (*Az, 3 Chevrons*, etc) with a picture and refers to estates in the North of England. Page 7 (of the second part) refers to Henry, Lord FitzHugh (*Az, 3 Chevrons Interlaced, Or*). This was a very widely published book. The copy in the British Library is the 6th edition of 1666, which was published by three separate printers, and was intended as the definitive reference book. This is the point: our family is <u>not</u> represented in the book, but the Barons' Arms are, and William could easily have read that. Indexes and abridgements

---

1   References *passim* in the English Short Title Catalog.
2   British Library Shelfmark 9917.h.19.

were published after the author's death, and in all it was in print from 1610 until its last edition in 1755. William could easily have seen it and even purchased a copy before he left England, and also it probably would have been available in Virginia since several original copies are now in American libraries. It does not actually mention Marmion or Ravensworth, but many other books of the period would have done so. This may well be an answer as to how William discovered by the wrong Arms. It is also possible that William was simply trying to impress some of his more anciently aristocratic associates of his own supposed illustrious family forbears. After all, he must have been conscious that he never quite made it to the levels of social status of the older "Virginia Aristocracy".

Attempts have been made to link the two FitzHugh Arms, the Baron's and our family's, by showing a way that the former could have evolved to become the latter by the Heraldic rules of quartering and cadency. This is impossible within the rules, even if they are stretched beyond the limits, as they sometimes were. For example, even though both Arms have *three Chevrons Or*, there is no valid way to get from *interlaced in Base* to *three Chevrons* (simple). Although Martlets are the cadency device for fourth sons, this is relevant only when they are applied in the proper cadency manner over (impaled upon) an existing coat of Arms, and is not relevant when they are an integral part of the Arms, as they are for our FitzHugh Arms. The two Arms are quite distinct, and always have been.

Lastly, but not insignificantly, the English FitzHughs have never used the Arms of the Barons, and have always used the correct Arms of the Fitzhughs of Bedfordshire. In modern times, they are aware of the use of the Barons' Arms in America, but regard this as an error.

So, somehow, by one means or another, and from far away in the New World, as his wealth and position grew to need to display family Arms, William got the wrong ones, and it has taken over three centuries to unravel the error.

H.A.F., 2002

.oOo.

Fitzhugh of Walcot

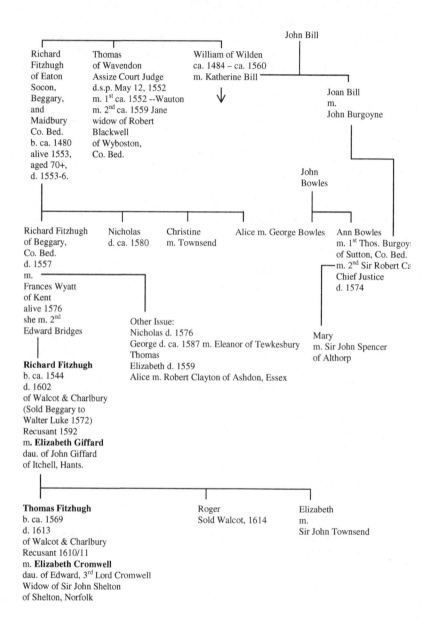

John Bill

Richard
Fitzhugh
of Eaton
Socon,
Beggary,
and
Maidbury
Co. Bed.
b. ca. 1480
alive 1553,
aged 70+,
d. 1553-6.

Thomas
of Wavendon
Assize Court Judge
d.s.p. May 12, 1552
m. 1st ca. 1552 --Wauton
m. 2nd ca. 1559 Jane
widow of Robert
Blackwell
of Wyboston,
Co. Bed.

William of Wilden
ca. 1484 – ca. 1560
m. Katherine Bill

↓

Joan Bill
m.
John Burgoyne

John
Bowles

Richard Fitzhugh
of Beggary,
Co. Bed.
d. 1557
m.
Frances Wyatt
of Kent
alive 1576
she m. 2nd
Edward Bridges

Richard Fitzhugh
b. ca. 1544
d. 1602
of Walcot & Charlbury
(Sold Beggary to
Walter Luke 1572)
Recusant 1592
m. **Elizabeth Giffard**
dau. of John Giffard
of Itchell, Hants.

Nicholas
d. ca. 1580

Christine
m. Townsend

Alice m. George Bowles

Ann Bowles
m. 1st Thos. Burgoy
of Sutton, Co. Bed.
m. 2nd Sir Robert Ca
Chief Justice
d. 1574

Other Issue:
Nicholas d. 1576
George d. ca. 1587 m. Eleanor of Tewkesbury
Thomas
Elizabeth d. 1559
Alice m. Robert Clayton of Ashdon, Essex

Mary
m. Sir John Spencer
of Althorp

Thomas Fitzhugh
b. ca. 1569
d. 1613
of Walcot & Charlbury
Recusant 1610/11
m. **Elizabeth Cromwell**
dau. of Edward, 3rd Lord Cromwell
Widow of Sir John Shelton
of Shelton, Norfolk

Roger
Sold Walcot, 1614

Elizabeth
m.
Sir John Townsend

THE RELATIONSHIP TO THE BARONS FITZHUGH

Connections of Elizabeth Fitzhugh, née Giffard

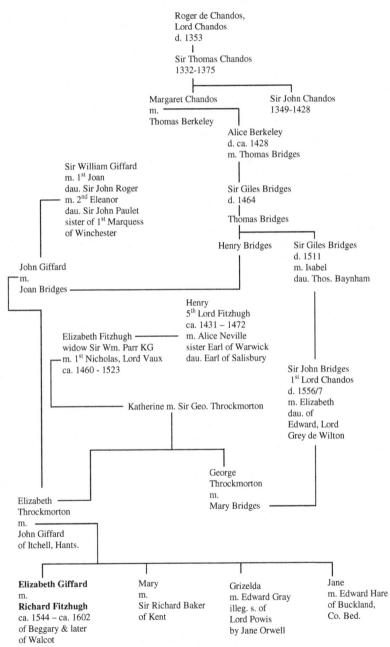

Roger de Chandos,
Lord Chandos
d. 1353

Sir Thomas Chandos
1332-1375

Margaret Chandos
m.
Thomas Berkeley

Sir John Chandos
1349-1428

Alice Berkeley
d. ca. 1428
m. Thomas Bridges

Sir William Giffard
m. 1st Joan
dau. Sir John Roger
m. 2nd Eleanor
dau. Sir John Paulet
sister of 1st Marquess
of Winchester

Sir Giles Bridges
d. 1464

Thomas Bridges

Henry Bridges

Sir Giles Bridges
d. 1511
m. Isabel
dau. Thos. Baynham

John Giffard
m.
Joan Bridges

Henry
5th Lord Fitzhugh
ca. 1431 – 1472

Elizabeth Fitzhugh
widow Sir Wm. Parr KG
m. 1st Nicholas, Lord Vaux
ca. 1460 - 1523

m. Alice Neville
sister Earl of Warwick
dau. Earl of Salisbury

Sir John Bridges
1st Lord Chandos
d. 1556/7
m. Elizabeth
dau. of
Edward, Lord
Grey de Wilton

Katherine m. Sir Geo. Throckmorton

George
Throckmorton
m.
Mary Bridges

Elizabeth
Throckmorton
m.
John Giffard
of Itchell, Hants.

Elizabeth Giffard
m.
Richard Fitzhugh
ca. 1544 – ca. 1602
of Beggary & later
of Walcot

Mary
m.
Sir Richard Baker
of Kent

Grizelda
m. Edward Gray
illeg. s. of
Lord Powis
by Jane Orwell

Jane
m. Edward Hare
of Buckland,
Co. Bed.

APPENDIX TWO

THE FITZHUGHS AND
THE MAGNA CARTA

In the Magna Carta there is a John FitzHugh who is listed as one of the advisers of the King, and there is a copy of the Magna Carta (bought by John Henry Fitzhugh in 1945 through the British Information Service in New York) showing the Arms of the Barons FitzHugh (*Azure, Three Chevrons*, etc.). These facts have caused much confusion among American Fitzhughs regarding their ancestry.

To deal with the first point, the name John FitzHugh is purely coincidental, since families did not keep the same surname in each generation until more than a century later. (Thus, for example, any son of that John FitzHugh would have been known by the surname FitzJohn.) There was a John FitzHugh, a Judge, who was of a Yorkshire family, a firm adherent of King John and high in the King's employ, but there is no evidence to link him to the family later known as Baron FitzHugh, although much is known about him.

The copy of the Magna Carta which shows the Arms of the Barons FitzHugh is simply a fake. According to the Assistant Keeper of Manuscripts at the British Museum (in 1981), it is a copy of the Lincoln Cathedral Magna Carta and the seal at the bottom is possibly that of King John on the City of London Charter of 1202 A.D., or possibly the one attached to the Articles of the Barons. The Coats of Arms shown are probably Victorian pastiches. The reason that J.H. Fitzhugh was able to buy it in 1945 was that it had been in the USA for the duration of World War II and it was sent on tour of the USA in that year to raise money for Lincoln Cathedral restorations. It was a worthwhile cause, so far as our family is concerned, because an ancestress of ours, Katherine Swynford, third wife of John of Gaunt and mother of the (illegitimate but later legitimised) Beaufort Line, is buried beside the Altar at Lincoln Cathedral.

THE FITZHUGHS AND THE MAGNA CARTA

In any event, there is certainly no evidence to link our family to the Magna Carta, or the Barons FitzHugh to the Magna Carta either.

.oOo.

APPENDIX THREE

OTHER FITZHUGH FAMILIES

Terrick FitzHugh has written the following:

THE YORKSHIRE FITZHUGHS: In the Middle Ages there was a well-known Baronial family, the Lords FitzHugh of Ravensworth. They have no connection with my (Terrick's) family... They died out in 1512. (See Appendix One and Chapter One of this Volume. - H.A.F.)

THE FITZHUGHS OF KINGSTHORPE: This, the most numerous family of Fitzhughs, lived at Kingsthorpe, now a suburb of Northampton, from 1688 onwards. They are now spread all over England, with probable migrants in the U.S.A.

OTHER NORTHAMPTONSHIRE FITZHUGHS: Fitzhugh families lived at various places in the South of the County from as far back as 1562. They and the Kingsthorpe family may all have a common origin, but it has yet to be traced.

OTHER MEDIAEVAL FITZHUGHS: The practice of adopting a common hereditary surname for all members of a family only became the custom very gradually during the period 1200-1400. Until the later date, many people's second name was purely personal, usually derived either from their place of abode, occupation, or father's name. FitzHugh means 'son of Hugh,' 'fitz' being the Anglo-Norman for 'son,' a corruption of the French 'fils du.' Most Mediaeval persons called FitzHugh did not belong to a family of that name but just had a father called Hugh, and their male-line descendants have other surnames. (See Appendix Two.)

There were two more Fitzhugh families that existed for at least a century each, one in Buckinghamshire in the fourteenth and fifteenth centuries, and one in Essex in the seventeenth and eighteenth centuries, but these have probably died out. (Other Fitzhugh families have been identified in Morayshire and Cheshire between 1110 and 1214, and Durham and Lancashire in 1412-1428. – HAF)

There are many black Fitzhughs in the USA. All of us welcome them as family members, but of course they could be members of one of the other Fitzhugh families, and we have over the years done what we could to determine which.

In 1996, I became aware of another Fitzhugh family active in Colonial Maryland, by way of a book[1] which traces their lineage. It is stated that they are not related to William Fitzhugh The Immigrant but descended from one Thomas Fitzhugh (d. 1723) and his wife Susanna. There are many thousands of descendants of that family now in America.

The Fitzhugh Family of Dorchester County Maryland 1684 - 1992, (Three Volumes), Harold Dean Davis. Copy kept in Clayton Library, Houston, Texas.

OTHER FITZHUGH FAMILIES

DNA analysis[1] carried out in 2005-6 by the University of Arizona confirms that the Dorchester Maryland Fitzhughs are not related to the Fitzhughs of Virginia and Bedford, England. This result depends upon three DNA samples from their family, and seems conclusive.

There is also some circumstantial evidence that the Kingsthorpe Fitzhughs are not related to either our family or the Maryland Fitzhughs. The evidence is tenuous, relying on one DNA sample from a Fitzhugh unrelated to either family who can trace his family back to Kingsthorpe, where the tree goes cold in 1801. Interested readers can follow progress at the website below, and more DNA samples are always welcome.

There are also descendants of Thomas Fitzhugh and Priscilla Drew of Southampton Co. Virginia in 1769. No DNA tests have been done on this family, and we have no idea where they fit in.

In addition to our own Arms and those of the Barons FitzHugh, *Edmondson's Heraldry*[2] lists three other Fitzhugh Arms:

- *Azure, Fretty Or, A Chief of the Second*
- *Argent, A Fesse between Three Buckets Sable, Hooped Or*
- *Argent Three Buckets Sable Hooped Or, Two and One.*

The localities and genealogies of these families are unstated. Edmondson also gives our Arms as follows: Fitz-Hugh, or Fitz-Hewe [Wanenden (*sic*) in Buckinghamshire] *Ermine, on a Chief Gules, Three Martlets Or.* Crest: - *A Cornish Chough Proper.* The Colville Quartering is not mentioned.

In summary, there appears to be four Fitzhugh families that have living members today:

- The Fitzhughs of Virginia, descendants of William Fitzhugh The Immigrant, who are co-descendants of Hugh and cousins of:
- The FitzHughs of England, the family to whom Terrick FitzHugh belongs.
- The Fitzhughs of Dorchester County, Maryland, who, according to them and to DNA analysis, have no relation to either of the above.
- A second Fitzhugh family in England, presumed to be the Fitzhughs of Kingsthorpe and/or of Northamptonshire, with no known relation to the other English FitzHughs, but who almost certainly have numerous descendants in the USA.

It is presumed, but not at all proved, that any living Fitzhugh or FitzHugh will be a member of one of these families.

.oOo.

Fitzhugh DNA Project: http://www.familytreedata.com/public/Fitzhugh/.

Joseph Edmondson, FSA, Mowbray Herald Extraordinary, *A Complete Body of Heraldry:* [&c., title contains 310 more words], 2 Vols., Vol. II, London, 1780, British Library Shelfmark HLL929.82, (also 138.i.3., L.40/1., C.44.k.6.) All of these Arms are also mentioned in Burke, *General Armory,* 1884 (HLR929.82), and *The British Herald,* Thomas Robson, Vol. I, 1830, (HLR929.82), and Berry, *Encyclopaedia Heraldica,* 1828, (HLL929.603).

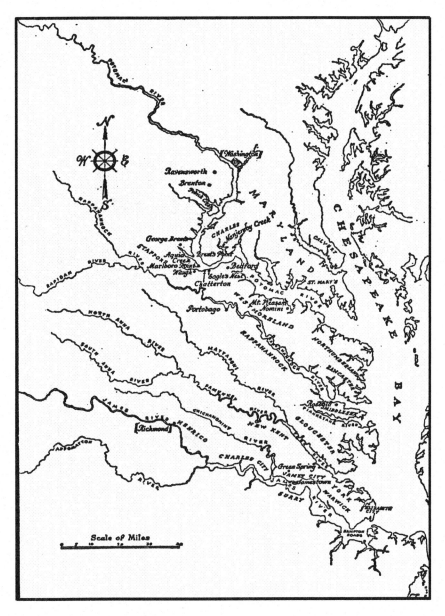

The Northern Neck of Virginia, showing Eagles Nest and
Ravensworth. Reproduced with permission.

APPENDIX FOUR

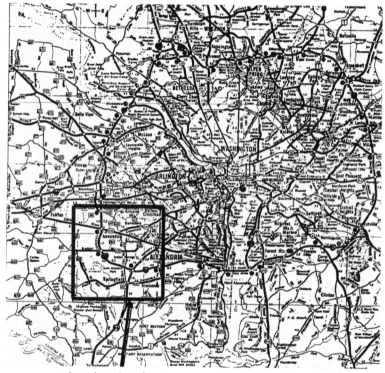

Approximate Area of
Ravensworth Estate

Metropolitan Washington
Reproduced with permission

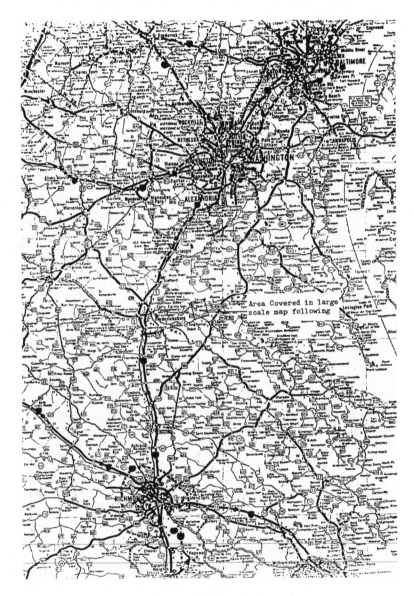

Area of Marmion
Reproduced with permission

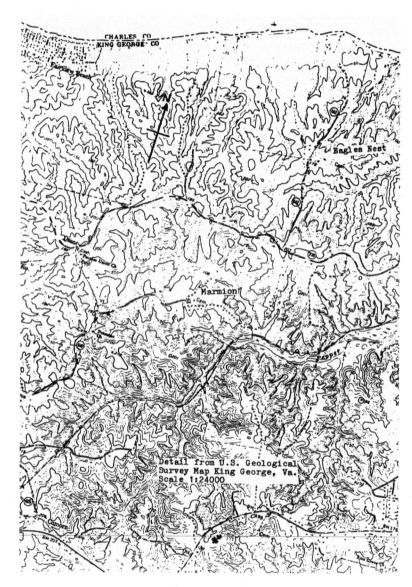

Detailed Map of Marmion
Reproduced with permission

APPENDIX FIVE

THE ANTIQUITY OF THE FITZHUGH SURNAME AND THE PROPER SPELLING THEREOF

The Fitzhugh surname derives directly from an ancestor named Hugh. His descendants either wished to be known as his sons, or wanted a constant surname as was becoming customary in the thirteenth and fourteenth centuries, and hence used the prefix "fitz", which means "son of" derived from "fiz" or "fils du" in Norman French. The "t" was added to give effect to the common pronunciation in French at the time. It is commonly believed that the prefix Fitz denotes illegitimacy of some ancestor, but this is incorrect; that meaning only applies to certain offspring of Royalty, mainly in later Stuart times, e.g. Charles, George, and Henry, the sons of Charles II and Barbara Villiers, all named Fitzroy and all created Dukes, and earlier, Henry Fitzroy, Duke of Richmond, son of Henry VIII and Elizabeth Blount. It is also commonly thought that Fitz indicates an Irish surname, but this is only true for certain names descended from some Anglo-Norman knights who settled in Waterford in 1170.

The earliest traceable use of our Fitzhugh surname yet found occurs in 1309 in the Calendar of Patent Rolls, Vol. xi, and Subsidy of Edw. II, 1309-10 (Beds. Hist. Rec. Soc.), although the Hugh in question lived a full century earlier. A full account of this evidence is given in Volume One, Chapter Two, pp. 13-18 by T.V.H. FitzHugh's History. Previous to that evidence becoming known, it was thought that the earliest reference was in 1339, as quoted in the Rev. V.C.A. FitzHugh's article in 1932 in the *Virginia Magazine of History and Biography*, Vol. XL, No. 2, April 1932, pp. 187-201. Between the fifteenth and seventeenth centuries the spelling is usually Fitzhugh (sometimes looking as though it were ffitzhugh, because of the way the capital letter F was written in Secretary Hand) or Fittzhugh as on the Trade Tokens shown in Chapter One of Volume Two. However, instances of Fitzhew, Fytzhewgh, and the like do crop up. It is characteristic of the non-standardisation of spellings that Henry Fitzhugh signed his name Fitzhugh in 1648, but had Fittzhugh on his Trade Tokens in 1655. The English Fitzhugh family changed its name to FitzHugh in 1835 during the Gothic Revival of the 1820s to 1830s. A statement by the Rev. V.C.A. FitzHugh in the article quoted above that the change happened around 1715 is not correct, as shown by Terrick V.H. FitzHugh in his *Dictionary of Genealogy* (1985), p.276 under the heading "Spelling" and reinforced by private correspondence of August 30, 1989 between him and the author. The American Branch was firmly established by that time, so this means that its members are more likely to be correctly addressed as Fitzhugh, rather than FitzHugh, unless someone took the latter spelling upon himself. However, my father, John Henry, spelled his name FitzHugh, and so, I suspect, do quite a few others.

H.A.F., 1985.

.oOo.

APPENDIX SIX

THE ORIGIN OF THE
FITZHUGH CHINA PATTERN

The Fitzhugh pattern of China has been in existence for two centuries, although it has only been comparatively recently identified with the Fitzhugh family. Indeed, when I was a boy, we believed that the name of the china arose from a corruption of the name of the Chinese city of Foochow. However, we now know that that city was a closed port until the 1840s, long after the Fitzhugh pattern had become well established.

It is now certain that the generations of eighteenth century sea Captains in the English Branch were responsible for the initial imports of the pattern, at least to England. Senior Officers in British East India Company ships were permitted to deal up to a certain value in goods for their own private account, and they all naturally took advantage of it. Captain William Fitzhugh (1674-1730), whose life is so well portrayed in T.V.H. FitzHugh's *FitzHugh The Story of a Family Through Six Centuries* (Chapter 15 onwards) first sailed to China in 1704, but there is no proof that he imported any of the china pattern. However, his son Thomas (1728-1800) also went to sea and first sailed to Canton in 1746. He resided there for many years as President of the Company's factory, and documentary evidence exists of his private trade in "Boxes [of] Chinaware." Thomas Senior rounded out his career as a Director of the East India Company, and his son Thomas and nephew William also went to sea and were in Canton in the 1780s and 1790s. Thomas Junior did not apparently ship any more china, but his cousin William certainly did. All in all, it seem most likely that we owe the naming of the Fitzhugh China Pattern to Thomas Senior.

The pattern is better known in America than in England, ever since its earliest appearance in the late eighteenth century. This may have arisen because American sea captains first arrived in Canton in 1784, and may have found it easy to purchase china already in the pattern already developed to supply to Thomas Fitzhugh.

    The pattern is described (J.A. LLoyd Hyde, *Oriental Lowestoft,* 1964, p.72) as: "A trellis-work border with four split pomegranates showing the fruit inside, and butterflies with wings spread. In the centre of the pieces appear four separate groups of flowers as emblems, martial or otherwise, surrounding a medallion or an oval monogram. Fitzhugh Pattern china is most frequently in blue, but it also occurs in sepia, gold, pink, brown, black, and bright green..." The pattern is most often found with a "post and spear," or Nanking, border, although this is not regarded as an integral part of the design. The modern pattern (in 1985) is made by Spode, and available in blue or red. Much of the information above comes from an article by J.B.S. Holmes in the American magazine *Antiques*, January 1966, pp.130-131, which also contains much biographical detail.

Thomas Fitzhugh Senior (1728-1800), was a fifth generation descendant of John Fitzhugh (d. 1579), which makes him a direct fourth cousin and contemporary of our ancestor Colonel William Fitzhugh (1725-1791) of Marmion. It is interesting to realise how far the habitats, and indeed the destinies, of the two Branches of the family had diverged over the century since they each had deserted their ancestral home in Bedfordshire.

H.A.F., April 1985

.oOo.

APPENDIX SEVEN

A DESCRIPTION OF MARMION, AS SEEN BY FRANCES PARKINSON KEYES IN THE NOVEL *HONOR BRIGHT*

Frances Parkinson Keyes wrote a great many historical novels based in the Old South in the early part of this century. *Honor Bright* is one of her better known books, first published in 1936, and still in print in 1973. As with most authors of fiction, her settings and characters are based on fact, and we know, as explained on page 66 of this History, that Marmion was the inspiration for Solomon's Garden, where much of the action in *Honor Bright* takes place. Honor Bright is the strong-willed and calculating heroine of the piece. The following are extracts from the novel, describing the lives and adventures of the family associated with Solomon's Garden, together with a few added explanatory notes, all designed to give the reader of this history an impression of Marmion as it is today.

The Foreword of *Honor Bright* begins...

The old plantation of Solomon's Garden, described in *Honor Bright*, has its prototype in reality. It is presented in fiction form with the knowledge and approval of its present owner, the nearest living "kin" to George Washington. The name, of course, has been changed; one which formerly belonged to a nearby plantation but which has now become obsolete having been used instead...

Referring in Chapter 4 to the "Lower Garden" of the plantation called "Solomon's Garden"...

A DESCRIPTION OF MARMION

A fringe of Judas trees, delicately pink, surrounded it; then came a slope, bright with the first lush green of spring, piercing deep gashed of rich red soil, and an orchard fluffy with a profusion of blossoms. Beyond, a white-clapboarded, green-shuttered house, with a wide brick walk leading up to it, and wide brick chimneys towering above either end of it, rose on a little knoll before them. It was surrounded by four outbuildings, also white-clapboarded, which combined to make a symmetrical square, and which gave it an air of solidity and strength. Though it was partially concealed by the branches of the beautiful trees which shaded it and the glossy ivy which climbed over it, John was immediately conscious of the atmosphere of permanence and peace that enfolded it.

This is an exact description of the layout and construction of Marmion. A few pages later in Chapter 5, Honor takes her guests into the Painted Parlour...

The quaintly hinged doorway leading from the stoop already stood hospitably ajar; and as they passed through it into a low-studded hallway, suffused with soft light from another wide door at the other end, John saw that this house was not overwhelming, like the one at the Upper Garden, but that it was mellow with age and redolent with charm. Mrs. Brockenborough led the way past two small wainscoted sittingrooms which opened out on either side of the entrance, their chimney-piece and corner-cupboards visible from the hallway. Then she paused smilingly at a threshold beyond a spreading staircase.

"This is the Painted Parlour in which we feel so much pride at the Lower Garden," she said. "It was decorated for us by a Hessian soldier - a refugee - whom my great-grandfather rescued. He was found on the riverbank in a critical condition, and was brought tenderly up to the house. He was so grateful for the care which he received that after he recovered, he begged to be allowed to show his appreciation. Being an artist by profession, he was familiar with the fashions of the day in Europe; and though he made his own paints from the clay here on the plantation, and had only our garden and grounds for inspiration, we feel that the effect he achieved is very pleasing."

This is an exact repetition of the story of the creation of the Sitting Room at Marmion, now the Marmion Room at the Metropolitan Museum in New York. The story continues...

She threw open the door. Through the many-paned windows, the sun streamed in across the satinwood with which the room was sheathed, ringed with warmth and radiance the festoons of flowers, the overflowing cornucopias, the sylvan glades and rustic landscapes with which the panels were alternately painted. A mirror, hung above the fireplace which slanted diagonally across the corner shone like a sheet of silver. The delicate arches surmounting the panels, the sculptured wreaths entwining them, the perfect proportions of the room as a whole, and the restraint and elegance of all its appointments, combined to give it an effect of complete harmony and grace.

"Don't you think it is beautiful?" Honor asked anxiously, as Reeves Stone did not speak at once.

"Yes, Honor. So beautiful that I hardly know how to put my feeling about it in words. I may have to ask you to help me do that."

Reeves had place his arm around her shoulder, drawing her closely to him. Now as he stood beside her, his fine eyes rested in deep appreciation on every detail of the Painted Parlour, and John knew instinctively that nothing Senator Bright had shown him had made such an impression on him as this.

A DESCRIPTION OF MARMION

"I am more eager than ever now to learn something about the story of Solomon's Garden," he said at last. "Was it customary in Virginia to build two houses on the same estate?"

"It was not at all unusual. The earlier house was generally much the simpler of the two, as it is here. Then as a settler's family expanded, numerically and financially, a landowner built more pretentious houses for his sons and grandsons than he lived in himself... It was partially finished before 1678. That was when James Fitzhubert brought Sally Hunter here as a bride. He had been formally betrothed to her for several years before that. But she was so young that he sent her to England to complete her education."

This is exactly the Fitzhugh Family tradition surrounding William Fitzhugh's marriage in 1674. Clearly James Fitzhubert is William Fitzhugh and Sally Hunter is Sarah Tucker, who was aged eleven when she married William. Marmion was not actually built, however, until the best part of a century later, and we now know, as they did not know then, that William could not have been betrothed to Sarah "several years" earlier. The story continues a page later...

Honor unlocked one of the deep cupboards flanking the characteristic corner fireplace.

This is accurate in detail. The conversation turns to other parts of the plantation...

"Well, why don't we just walk through the garden and down to the graveyard?"

"The graveyard!"

"Yes, our own little burying-ground. It's lovely - not a bit like a regular cemetery."

Honor was already doubling back the screen-shaped sections of the side door at the rear of the hallway. A broad brick walk, similar to the one at the front of the house, and bordered with yellow primroses led across a lawn scattered over with ailanthus and catalpa trees; then by a succession of low steps through an open garden where the flowers and shrubs merged gradually into the general landscape. Jonquils were springing up from the ground everywhere; beyond them, big beds of blue periwinkles stretched out in-definitely; lilac bushes laden with scented bloom formed a natural hedge. John was amazed when Honor, turning a little to the right, opened a small gate, so completely concealed in a thicket where Easter roses were just beginning to bud, and so thickly overhung with glossy vines, that he had not even seen it until it had actually swung against him. Now he perceived that it led into a small enclosure, sheltered by the tall trees which rose caressingly around it, but still overspread with sunshine and fragrant with flowers.

This is most likely a description of the Graveyard at Marmion in the early twentieth century, although it has without doubt changed since Colonel William Fitzhugh's day. The text continues after a page...

"Did you notice that all the trees around the graveyard are maples?", she asked. "That is because they are the first to bud in the spring and the last to shed their leaves in the fall, and in our family we have always liked to feel that there was pleasant shade in our burying-ground. But it is peaceful here in the winter, too, when there are no leaves at all, and lovely when there is snow. Of course, that does not come often, but when it does, all the marble seems to try to outsparkle it. I like this little stone, don't you, John? - with the scroll unfurled from the carved wreath of pansies - of course, those are for loving thoughts. And I like the inscription too: 'I go to him but he will not return to me.' My great-Aunt Estelle's husband, who is buried here, was killed in the war between the States, and she was simply disconsolate. I think she really died of grief. Anyway, that is what she wanted written on his grave."

A DESCRIPTION OF MARMION

These are probably not Fitzhughs, but after a search through more tombstones, we are treated to the following...

> "'In here were blended all the virtues that adorn the woman and grace the matron,'" John read aloud. "'She lived in the exemplary perfection of all the duties that her domestic and social relations imposed... And died exulting in the swift faith of a Redeemer and in the blessed hope of a happy Resurrection... Let her husband and children mark, remember and follow her bright example.'"

It is just possible that this describes Hannah, second wife of Colonel William Fitzhugh, both of whom are buried at Marmion.

At Marmion, one bedroom known as the "Safe Room" can only be entered by passing through the Master Bedroom. This is explained in Chapter Seven...

> "Honor," he enquired, "how does it happen your room has no door into the hall? It seems funny to build a house like that!"
>
> "Well, it wasn't so funny as it was necessary, at the time the house was built," Honor answered unconcernedly.
>
> "What do you mean, necessary?"
>
> "That has always been the room of the daughters of the house. It was safer for them if no one could get in there except by passing through their parent's room."
>
> "Safer?"
>
> "Yes, safer" Honor reiterated a little impatiently, as if she were tired at the necessity of explaining an obvious situation, though she remained unembarrassed by it. "You see, life was very lonely on the plantations in the early days, and when the settlers and their families went to stay with each other they naturally tried to make up for the dull periods between visits.

A DESCRIPTION OF MARMION

There was a great deal of drinking and love-making. So
girls were protected - that is, as much as they could be."

Some pages later, the genteel poverty of the family is mentioned.
They live off the produce of the plantation entirely, but raise such
cash as is necessary by selling off heirlooms...

"And it is only by exercising the strictest self-denial
that they have managed to cling to the panelling in the
Painted Parlour."

"You mean - they might have to sell it?"

"Several museums have urged them to do so. It is
unique."

"But it would be terrible to take it away from here.
Almost as bad as desecrating a church."

"Yes, it would. I hope with all my heart that such a
tragedy may be averted. But I fear that it will only be
postponed."

The menace of poverty had never before been
brought home to John. He sat, bewildered and
dismayed, picturing the beautiful Painted Parlour
stripped of its shining satinwood and bright festoons,
and visualising the incongruous effect which would be
produced by installing these in some bleak New
England museum.

This is exactly what happened. The Painted Parlour is now the
Marmion Room in The American Wing of the Metropolitan
Museum in New York. The author is obviously registering a
protest. The story proceeds to Chapter Nine when, some years
later, Honor is married to a Professor at what must be the
University of Virginia at Charlottesville, and is feeling rather
cloistered in a desolate University Campus house. She says...

"...Sometimes the high brick wall around the
campus seem to contract and contract until it constricts
my heart! It's Solomon's Garden that I love! Think

what it must be like there tonight! The woodlands and the meadows all so free and open, and the river winding along in the distance, cool and grey and broad! The big beds of mertensia and the periwinkle in the garden, and the feverfew springing up around the milkhouse, and the Easter roses climbing over the graveyard gate! All the little forest creatures quiet for the night, and not a sound from the kennels and stables either; but the feeling that the friendly dogs and horses are there just the same, and the little ducks and chickens safe under the old hen's wings! 'Liza shuffling over the flagstone floor in the kitchen, putting away the hotwater plates and the hominy mortar with the cedar pestle, and the big waffle iron with the pattern of clubs and hearts and diamonds and spades; the looking up, as she steps outside, to make sure the hornet's nest is still hanging over the door for good luck, before she starts across the knoll to her cabin with Gratty beside her, chanting 'Swing low, Sweet Chariot!' as she trudges along! Grandfather standing beside the sideboard mixing juleps in James Fitzhubert's silver goblets, and Grannie sitting in the Painted Parlour, waiting for him to come back to her, and with that far-away look in her eyes! And perhaps, off in the distance, a whip-poor-will singing!"

James Fitzhubert's silver goblets were really William Fitzhugh's silver bowls, as described in R.B. Davis, *William Fitzhugh and his Chesapeake World*.

Honor goes through a remarkable mixture of good financial fortune and emotional drama, eventually returning to Solomon's Garden to live while writing a successful novel called *The Safe Room*, based on lurid events which were said to have happened in spite of its supposed safety. Eventually she marries her life-long love in the Painted Parlour, and they lived happily ever after.

A DESCRIPTION OF MARMION

We can believe the accuracy of all the above description by Miss Keyes, for at the end of the book she reveals that she wrote parts of it while living at Marmion between April and July, 1935.

H.A.F., 1985.

.oOo.

APPENDIX EIGHT

THE TOWN OF BEDFORD
IN THE SEVETEENTH CENTURY,
THE FITZHUGH PROPERTY,
AND BEDFORD BRIDGE

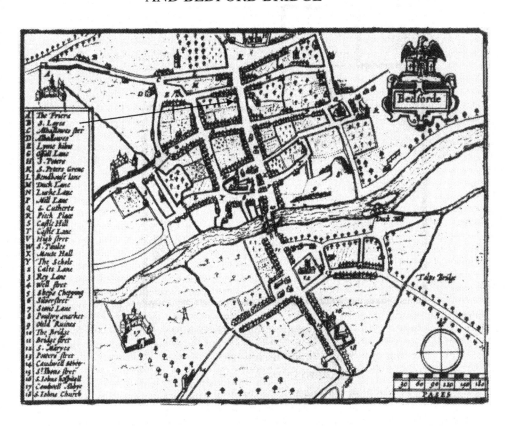

Town Plan of Bedford 1600-1610
Speed's Town Plan of 1610,
Based on Chrostopher Saxton's Plan of 1600
(The arrow points to the location of the Fitzhugh property.)

N

Duck Lane, (now Lime Street)

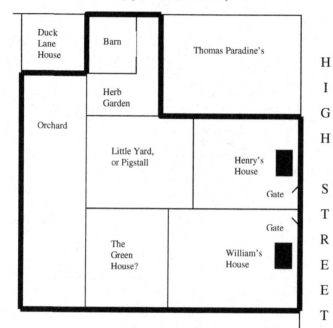

Duck
Lane
House

Barn

Thomas Paradine's

Herb
Garden

Orchard

Little Yard,
or Pigstall

Henry's
House

Gate

The
Green
House?

Gate

William's
House

H
I
G
H

S
T
R
E
E
T

The Fitzhugh Family Properties
in Bedford in 1632,
An approximation based upon
the Will of William Fitzhugh,
who died in 1633
(*Archdeaconry of Bedford Wills*, 1632-3, No. 155)

See Town Plan of Bedford 1600-1610, page
117 Volume One.

To the
High
Bridge

APPENDIX EIGHT

Bedford Bridge in 1660

APPENDIX NINE

My Granny Was A Whore ...,
or,
A Love Story...,
or,
Our Descent From Henry VIII?

By

Henry A. Fitzhugh

*D*EAR READER, before you cringe in horror at such family disloyalty, let me hastily explain that the Lady in question is my great- great- great- great- great- great- great- great- great- great-great-great-grandmother, Mary Boleyn Carey. Time is the universal healer, and when you read this brief summary of the evidence, you will see why I am forgiving, amused, and perhaps just a little bit proud to claim a probable descent from King Henry VIII.

Everyone has heard of Anne Boleyn, the second wife of Henry VIII, for whom he threw over Queen Catherine of Aragon and whom he later beheaded in the Tower of London, for adultery, witchcraft, sorcery, incest, and offending his Dignity. But few know of her sister Mary Boleyn. Both sisters were brought up in the Court of the French King Francis I[1] as part of their

---

1 State Papers of Henry VIII, Volume I, 3348, 9 October 1514; 3357, 12 October 1514; Mary was at first in the Court of the Archduchess of Austria, *Anne Boleyn*, Mary Louise Bruce, Pan Books, London, 1972, British Library Shelfmark X.708.12609.

improvement, which was undoubtedly aimed at raising their value on the marriage market, in order to serve the vaulting social and political ambitions of the Boleyns. Mary certainly took full advantage of the opportunities available and the lax moral tone[1] of the French Court, for King Francis said he had "ridden her" as "my hackney"[2], and twenty years later, when all the tumult of Anne's execution had passed, he referred to Mary as "a great whore, the most infamous of all"[3]. Francis I was arguably the most powerful King in Europe, so he should know. Slightly more tactfully: "Warm hearted and ductile, Mary made the mistake of scattering her favours too widely and making her affairs too public. It was one thing to be the King's Mistress; quite another to be known to be at everyone's disposal. Even at the lascivious French Court there was a code of discretion; Mary had offended it. She was either sent or withdrawn hastily to England."[4]

References to Mary Boleyn having an affair with Henry VIII abound in the footnotes of all references to the Tudor period, but my attention was caught when a historical novel, *The Other Boleyn Girl*, by Philippa Gregory, was published in 2001.[5] The main story line in the novel is that King Henry was attracted to Mary Boleyn just after her marriage to William Carey, and that Henry soon displaced William and took over Mary for an affair of some six years or so, giving her two children into the bargain, namely Catherine Carey and Henry Carey. The point is strongly made that the King would never share the favours of a mistress; he had his

---

1   *Tudor Women, Queens and Commoners,* Alison Plowden, Weidenfeld and Nicolson, 1979, p.42: Referring to the Court of Francis I, "Rarely did any maid or wife leave that court chaste." – Sieur de Brantôme.

2   *The Six Wives of Henry VIII,* Alison Weir, Pimlico, 1997, p.134. Hackney: a common horse.

3   State Papers of Henry VIII, Volume X, 450, 10 March, 1536; *Henry VIII, King & Court,* Alison Weir, Jonathan Cape, 2001, p.221; *The Rise and Fall of Anne Boleyn,* Retha M. Warnicke, Cambridge University Press, 1989, p.46: Francis I's description of Mary Carey was *"una grandissima ribalda et infame sopre tutte",* "a great whore, the most infamous of all."

4   Bruce, *op.cit.,* p.23.

5   *The Other Boleyn Girl,* by Philippa Gregory, Harper Collins, London, 2001. This is not the only historical novel devoted to Mary Boleyn. *The Reluctant Mistress* by Peggy Boynton [BL Shelfmark Nov. 39112] is a very lightweight, and rather inaccurate, romantic novel, probably intended for teenagers.

Royal pride, and he would have to be sure that any child was his, for illegitimate claims abounded in those days.[1] All of this began before but overlapped with the King's growing attachment to Anne Boleyn, who was less beautiful but had more magnetism and cunning than her sister.[2]

The novel covers the rise and fall of the Boleyn family to the day of execution of Queen Anne Boleyn, but from the standpoint of our own family history the central question is this: was Catherine Carey the natural daughter of William Carey or of King Henry? We have a line of descent from Catherine (see family tree following), so we could be illegitimately descended from Henry VIII. The rest of this note weighs up the available evidence.

All of the references following agree that Henry and Mary had an affair, and this is never doubted anywhere. Those that mention dates place it between 1519 and approximately 1525.[3] There is a hint, no more, in some of the references that Mary's marriage to William Carey, who was then one of the King's Gentlemen, was in fact a marriage of convenience for Henry. In other words, the marriage was a useful way to keep Mary accessible, without the risk that he would have to acknowledge her or any children in the way he did for the unmarried Elizabeth Blount and their son Henry FitzRoy.[4] That son had been born in 1519, the same year that Henry started the relationship with Mary. Henry later admitted the affair in 1528, by asking the Pope for a Dispensation to marry Anne Boleyn; he needed this because of his "affinity" and "consanguinity" with Mary.[5] Canon Law made no distinction between a licit and an illicit sexual connection, so Henry's affair with Mary Boleyn made Anne Boleyn his sister-in-law.[6] It is worth noting that in a contested divorce suit, consanguinity could only have been conclusively proven if there

---

1   Indeed the Tudors themselves were descended illegitimately (though later legitimised) through the Beaufort Line.

2   *Henry VIII and His Queens,* David Loades, Sutton, 1994, p.40.

3   For example, see Weir, 1997, p.134, & Loades, 1994, pp.33-4.

4   This point is strongly made in *Anne Boleyn,* E.W. Ives, Basil Blackwell, 1987, p.20.

5   Weir, 2001, p.221; *The Tudor Court,* David Loades, Batsford, 1986.

6   *Tudor Women, Queens & Commoners,* Alison Plowden, Weidenfeld & Nicolson, 1979, p.76.

was a child to show for it. In other words, Henry could have denied that impediment to his marriage if there had been no child.

Mary was married in early 1520, on February 4. King Henry's wedding present was 6s 8d.[1] Bruce is brusque: "It was a sorry match for a Boleyn, but Mary had spoiled her chances for a good one."[2] Catherine Carey was born in 1524, and Henry Carey on March 4, 1526. He was said in his infancy to resemble King Henry.[3] In 1533, Henry Carey, although aged only seven, claimed he was "Our Sovereign Lord the King's son".[4] At this time, his aunt (and stepmother) Anne was on the throne and desperately trying to have a male child of her own, so whoever put the child up to such a statement must have been pretty confident.[5] There are also at least two direct and contemporary references that state that Henry Carey was King Henry's child. In 1535, Sir George Throckmorton accused Henry to his face of "meddling" with Mary Boleyn and her mother. "Never with the mother", replied Henry.[6] Cardinal Reginald Pole also said much the same in a private letter to Henry.[7] And in the same year, John Hale, Vicar of Isleworth, stated that a Monk at St Bridget's Priory Abbey pointed out "yongge Master Care" as the King's bastard son.[8]

Only two references doubt this story.[9] Both simply express doubt and offer no evidence at all. In fact, Fraser's dates are probably incorrect when she says the affair was probably over

---

1   Warnicke, p.36. State Papers of Henry VIII, Volume III, 1539, 11 February, 1520.

2   Bruce, *op. cit.,* p.24.

3   Weir 2001, p.221.

4   Weir, 1997, p.134.

5   It is possible that Anne herself promoted Henry Carey as the King's son. Gregory's thesis is that the reason Anne seized the Wardship of Henry after William Carey's death was that he could then become her own "son" if she failed to produce a natural male heir. She could only have succeeded with this if everyone agreed, at least tacitly, that Henry Carey was the King's son.

6   Weir, 2001, p.126, referring to Letters & Papers of Reign of Henry VIII; also pp. 221, 272, and Weir, 1997, p.134.

7   *The History of England,* John Lingard, 1849, Vol IV. pp. 474-5.

8   *Henry VIII,* J.J. Scarisbrick, Yale English Monarchs, Yale University Press, 1997, p.148; Weir, 2001, p.272; See State Papers, VIII, 567 following for exact quotation.

9   *Henry VIII and His Queens,* David Loades, Sutton, 2000, p.21; *The Six Wives of Henry VIII,* Antonia Fraser, 1988, p.101.

before the children were born;   this is flatly contradicted by Weir.[1]

The Family of Mary Boleyn

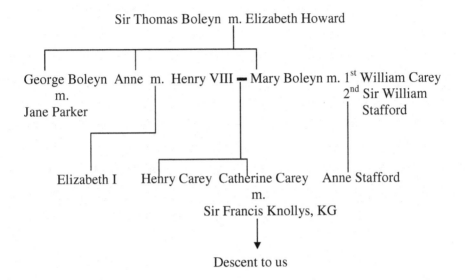

Sir Thomas Boleyn m. Elizabeth Howard

George Boleyn   Anne m. Henry VIII — Mary Boleyn m. 1st William Carey
m.   2nd Sir William
Jane Parker   Stafford

Elizabeth I   Henry Carey Catherine Carey   Anne Stafford
m.
Sir Francis Knollys, KG

Descent to us

The only other point of refutation is most clearly expressed by Fraser, which is that King Henry never showed any special acknowledgement or favour to Henry Carey, although he did acknowledge Henry FitzRoy as his illegitimate child. FitzRoy was the son of Elizabeth Blount, Henry's mistress immediately before Mary. FitzRoy was in a far more favourable position because he was, in fact, the King's first male offspring, and Elizabeth Blount was unmarried, so Chivalry alone would have required an acknowledgement. Having a son proved Henry's potency, a great relief for Henry and an absolute necessity for a fragile dynasty of usurpers like the Tudors, and it did at least place in storage a potential male heir who could be legitimised later if all else failed. FitzRoy was later created Duke of Richmond in 1525[2] when it seemed unlikely that Henry would get a male heir from Catherine of

---

1   Weir, 1997, p.134.
2   Loades, 1994, p.36; Bruce, 1972 points out that Henry gave FitzRoy
        Henry VII's title and a household larger than Princess Mary's.

Aragon. The real point is, though, that King Henry did not <u>need</u> a second illegitimate male heir, and there was no point in acknowledging one. That would have cost the King at least another title and a grant of land and property as well, and the King was notoriously stingy with his mistresses.[1] With this in mind, by itself the offhand treatment of Henry Carey does not really tell us anything as to whether King Henry was his real father or not.

But concerning Royal grants, William Carey was granted his manors and estates in June 1524 and February 1526, dates which coincide with Catherine's and Henry's births.[2] A reward for being a co-operative cuckold?

In any case, for our family history we are not concerned with Henry Carey, but with his sister Catherine Carey, for it is from her that we are descended. She was two years older than her brother and she definitely was born during the time that Henry's and Mary's affair was still very much on. Therefore Catherine's claim to Royal lineage seems circumstantially better than her younger brother's. The evidence in favour of this claim is thus the total of all the evidence in favour of Henry Carey's fathering by King Henry, but with none of the possible detractions relating to her brother Henry. In addition to all of the documentary evidence already cited, it is very clear that it was widely accepted at the time, as shown above by Sir George Throckmorton and Vicar Hale being willing to risk a charge of Treason for saying so in public.

So where does this leave us? With evidence in favour and evidence against. This is the evidence in favour:

- Two contemporary statements – Throckmorton and Hale. To this must be added Henry Carey's assertion of his own lineage, and the confidence of whomever put the child up to saying it.
- Henry's admitting of the affair, admitted in his request for a Papal Dispensation in 1528, and in his Divorce Petition later. He admitted "affinity" and "consanguinity" with Mary Boleyn. This could have been refuted, or might not have been necessary, if there were no child resulting.
- The evidence of dates. Catherine Carey was born well inside the period of the affair. Henry Carey was born just at the end,

---

1   Plowden, 1979, p.45.
2   Warnicke, p.46.

and it is unlikely Henry would have allowed Mary any other lovers at the same time.

- On the evidence of dates, Catherine Carey is even more likely than Henry Carey to be King Henry's child, since she was the firstborn.
- In the manner of the times, one would expect a cuckolded husband to be rewarded for his co-operation with substantial property, and this indeed happened to William Carey at times exactly coinciding with the births of Catherine and Henry Carey.

This is the evidence against:
- Two authors' doubts, but without evidence.
- King Henry's general disregard for Henry Carey, but see the text for reasons why this would be so. In any case, this argument impinges little upon Catherine Carey.
- General lack of primary documents, or hard proof to a high legal standard.

So, then, what do we conclude? What is my own estimation that we are Royal Bastards? I would say 60-80%, but no one will ever know for sure.

Everyone knows that King Henry rarely had a happy time in any of his six marriages, but as far as Mary is concerned, a more romantic ending would be hard to find. William Carey had died suddenly of the 'sweating sickness' in 1528.[1] Bad as that was, there was worse. After William's death, his " … offices reverted 'in the King's gift'. The King generously distributed these sources of income and Mary, his widow, was left destitute. Despite their relationship of several years, Henry felt no lingering affection, no obligation; he scarcely even remembered Mary."[2] Hever Castle passed to King Henry by custom of the widower inheriting his deceased wife's estate.[3] It was later given to Anne of Cleves in

---

1   On June 10. State Papers of King Henry VIII, Volume IV, 23 June, 1528; Volume VIII, 854, 25 April, 1539.
2   Bruce, *op. cit.*, p.101.
3   *The Bullens of Hever*, Gavin Astor, 2nd Baron Astor of Hever, 1972, British Library shelfmark YA1994.a.11548.

1540, as part of her divorce settlement. No one can miss the irony in all that.

But in 1534, Mary sacrificed all – the rewards, the position, the honours, the intrigues – and re-married for love. For nine more years[1] she lived happily ever after. Her letter[2] to Thomas Cromwell comes straight from her heart. Pleading, in vain as it turned out, to be allowed back into Court after marrying William Stafford without family and Court approval, she wrote:

"But one thing, good master Secretary, consider; that he [Stafford] was young, and love overcame reason. And for my part I saw so much honesty in him that I loved him as well as he did me; and was in bondage, and glad I was to be at liberty; so that for my part I saw that all the world did set so little by me, and he so much, that I thought I could take no better way but to take him and forsake all other ways, and to live a poor honest life with him; and so I do put no doubts but we should, if we might once be so happy to recover the King's gracious favor and the Queen's. For well I might a had a greater man of birth and a higher, but I ensure you I could never a had one that should a loved me so well nor a more honest man... But if I were at my liberty and might choose, I ensure you, master Secretary, for my little time, I have tried so much honesty to be in him, that **I had rather beg my bread with him than to be the greatest Queen christened.***"*

That says it all.

---

1   She died on July 19, 1543, Weir, 1997, p.273.

2   State Papers of Henry VIII, Vol. VII, 1655, written in 1534; also 1554, 19 Dec. 1534, Chapuys to the Holy Roman Emperor Charles V. But at least her daughter Catherine Carey, in about 1539, won appointment as Maid of Honour to Anne of Cleves, Henry's fourth wife, Warnicke, 1989, p.237.

Epilogue

Poor Mary and William must have felt like outcasts in 1534, and in 1536, her sister and brother were both beheaded. But, things improved from there on. The Boleyn family was all but wiped out, but on the death of the parents, Mary began to inherit property everywhere, and the State Papers[1] are full of grants, reversions, inheritances and other acquisitions. William Stafford actually made it back into Court circles, being one of the party of Gentlemen who received Anne of Cleves on her arrival in England.[2] One imagines he could not have missed the irony in that.

Henry Carey did extremely well for his position. He was knighted by Queen Elizabeth shortly after her succession and created Baron Hunsdon shortly thereafter (January 13, 1558/9).[3] [He was, after all, the Queen's half-brother, and this may well explain the Queen's affection later in life.] He had a successful political and military career, if minor and unworthy of elevation, always corresponding with the Queen in affectionate terms,[4] and died on July 23, 1596, at Somerset House, the use of which the

---

1   At least a score of separate properties; see list under References, State Papers, following.

2   State Papers of King Henry VIII, Vol. XIV, 572(3), 22 Nov., 1539. With him was his son-in-law to be, Sir Francis Knollys [*DNB*].

3   The story from here on is from the *Dictionary of National Biography*.

4   "'I doubt much, my Harry," wrote Elizabeth to him after his suppression of the Northern Rebellion, "whether that the victory given me more joyed me, or that you were by God appointed the instrument of my glory." And with the bitterness of a true patriot, as well as a true kinsman, he was at times so affected as to be 'almost senseless, considering the time, the necessity Her Majesty hath of assured friends, the needfulness of good and sound counsel, and the small care it seems she hath of either. Either she is bewitched or doomed to destruction."', p.186. Also, p.193: "Queen Elizabeth loved the Knollyses for themselves ... [they] profit at home, continuing constantly at court; and no wonder, if they were the warmest who sate next the fire." - *Historical Memorials of Westminster Abbey*, Arthur Penrhyn Stanley, DD, Seventh Edition, London, 1890, British Library Shelfmark 1609/6090, p. 186, quoting Aiken's *Elizabeth*, i, 243, and Froude, ix, 557.

Queen had given him. She also paid the expenses of his burial in Westminster Abbey. Her Majesty visited him and laid on his deathbed the patent and robes of the Earldom of Wiltshire, last held by Mary Boleyn's father. Her care and consideration, throughout his life, were most unusual; perhaps she knew she was addressing not her cousin but her half-brother? "Madam", he said, "seeing you counted me not worthy of this honour whilst I was living, I count myself unworthy of it now I am dying."[1] On Elizabeth's death, his seventh son, Robert Carey, received the ring prised from the dead Queen's hand and dropped from her window at Richmond Palace, and rode with it in two days to James I in Edinburgh.

Catherine Carey married Sir Francis Knollys (or Knowles), who became Treasurer of the Royal Household.[2] She died on January 15, 1568/9 at Hampton Court while in attendance on the Queen,[3] although it was suggested that her decease was caused by the prolonged absence of her husband in the North of England, where Elizabeth had entrusted him with the custody of Mary Queen of Scots.[4] She was buried at Royal expense[5] in St. Edmund's Chapel, Westminster Abbey. Her memorial there is prominent, and in excellent condition, having obviously been restored in modern times, and is pictured following. An Epitaph was printed in broadside, a copy of which survives[6] and which is reproduced following. Considerable correspondence regarding a dispute over her hearse "fringed in silke and gold cushioned stools" remains in the Westminster Abbey Library.[7]

Catherine left seven sons and four daughters, one of whom, Cecilia, was a Maid of Honour to Queen Elizabeth,[8] and another of whom, Anne, married Thomas West, Lord De La Warr. Of Anne's

---

1   Stanley, *op. cit.*, quoting Fuller's *Worthies*, i, 433.
2   State Papers, Domestic, 1581-1590, p.181, 1584.
3   The Queen keenly felt the loss of Catherine [*DNB*, XI, 278; Hatfield MSS, i, 400].
4   Ballads & Broadsides Chiefly of the Elizabethan Period..., H.L. Collmann, British Library shelfmark C.101.h.10, quoting a letter from Sir N. White to Cecil, Wright's *Queen Elizabeth*, Vol. i, p.308.
5   Hatfield MSS, 415.
6   Epitaph by Thomas Newton dated 1569, published *Bibl. Heber*, Ed. Collmann, p.59. This in now in the Huntington Library, San Marino, California.
7   Knollys, Katherine, 6414-6417.
8   *DNB*, XI, p.278.

marriage, the second but eldest surviving son Thomas West (1577-1618) inherited the title and became a founding member of The Virginia Company,[1] sailing there in 1610 with 150 settlers. One of Anne's younger sons, John West, followed his brother, married a lady named Anne in Virginia, and began a line of Americans leading down to us.[2] So, in one generation, the struggle had changed from Court intrigues to pushing back the Frontier. One wonders if, out in the New World, they ever thought about the old family drama back in the Merrie Court of King Henry VIII.

H.A.F., December, 2001

---

1   A broadside from 1610 advertising this expedition states that "good artificers and persons of good character would now be gladly acccepted" and is preserved; see *A Catalogue of A Collection of Printed Broadsides in the Possession of The Society of Antiquaries of London,* compiled by Robert Lemon, 1866, British Library shelfmark RAR090.941 AN.

2   See Family Tree following.

The Portrait of Mary Boleyn at Hever Castle,
Hans Holbein the Younger

The Signature of
Mary Carey,
February 13, 1534,
from Lisle Papers,
S.P.3/6, 23, P.R.O.

King Henry VIII
Circa 1520, when the affair with Mary Carey began
Unknown Artist, National Portrait Gallery, Catalogue 4690

William Carey, An unfinished portrait

E.W. Ives, [References following] pages 287, note 45, & 288: "Tree ring dating, however, shows that the surviving portrait of William Carey must be a later copy, or even an enlargement of a miniature." He suggests that the artist of the original was Lucas Hornebolte of Ghent; refers to J. Fletcher, *A Portrait of William Carey, and Lord Hunsdon's Long Gallery*, Burlington Magazine, 123, (1981), p.304.

Fletcher [see References at end] makes it clear that this is the original and contemporary miniature, from which a contemporary copy (see next page) was made, and from which a later Elizabethan copy was made in about 1580 (see second page following).

OUR DESCENT FROM KING HENRY VIII

Portrait of William Carey

In *Henry VIII A European Court in England,* Collins & Brown, 1991, David Starkey states, p.57: William Carey (c.1500-1528), a distant cousin through the Beauforts, became keeper of Greenwich Palace in 1526. A gentleman of the Privy Chamber in 1519, he married Mary Boleyn in 1520 and when Anne replaced her sister as the King's mistress, seemed destined for greatness. But in 1528 he died of the sweating sickness.

This painting is identified by an Elizabethan copy [see next page] which includes the sitter's coat of arms. The copy was made after the original [above] had been subjected to overpainting. Instead of a book, the copy shows him holding a pair of gloves and the dress becomes Elizabethan. These changes, removed from the present picture when it was cleaned, were made because (as the cleaning also revealed) the original painting had been left unfinished. Finally the cleaning uncovered an underpainting which resembles Holbein's drawing of 'M Souch' [Zouche], p.101.

This underpainting, and the fact that the date of the sitter's death coincided with Holbein's departure from England at the end of his first visit, must lead to speculation that the painting was his, but despite the sensitive rendering of the face, an unknown French or Flemish artist (though not a Horenbout) cannot be ruled out. Artist Unknown, 16th Cent., Oil on Panel, 790x660, private collection, and quotes J. Fletcher, *A Portrait of William Carey and Lord Hunsdon's Long Gallery,* Burlington Magazine, 123, (1981), p.304; see References at end.

William Carey, An Elizabethan copy painted about 1580, by an unknown artist, oak panel, 460x340, Collection of Hugh Paget. See Fletcher, *Burlington Magazine,* in References following.

OUR DESCENT FROM KING HENRY VIII

Catherine Knollys' Memorial
St Edmund's Chapel,
Westminster Abbey

The Inscription reads:

THE RIGHT HONORABLE LADY KATHERIN KNOLLYS CHEEFE LADY OF THE QUENES MA^TIES BEDDECHAMBER AND WIFFE TO S^R FRANCES KNOLLYS KNIGHT TRESORER OF HER HIGHNES HOWSEHOLDE DEPARTED THIS LYFE THE 15 OF IANUARY 1568 AT HAMPTON COURTE AND WAS HONORABLY BURIED IN THE FLOWER OF THIS CHAPPELL. THIS LADY KNOLLYS AND THE LORD HUNDESDON HER BROTHER WERE THE CHILDEREN OF WILLIAM CAREE ESQUYER AND OF THE LADY MARY HIS WIFFE ONE OF THE DOUGHTERS AND HEIRES TO THOMAS BULLEYNE ERLE OF WYLSHIER AND ORMOND, WHICH LADY MARY WAS SISTER TO ANNE QUENE OF ENGLAND WIFFE TO KINGE HENRY THE EYGHT FATHER AND MOTHER TO ELIZABETH QUENE OF ENGLAND

QUAE FRANCISCE FUIT TIBI CONIUNX EN CATHERINA MORTUA SUB GELIDO MARMORE KNOLLE IACET EXCIDET EX ANIMO TIBI MORTUA SAT SCIO NUNQUAM VIVA TIBI SEMPER AMATA FUIT ILLA TIBI LIBEROS SEX ET BIS QUINQUE MARITO PROTULIT AEQUALIS FAEMINA MASQUE FUIT ILLA TECUM MULTOS UTINAM VIXISSET IN ANNOS ET TUA NUNC CONIUNX FACTA FUISSET ANUS SED DEUS HOC NOLUIT VOLUIT SED SPONSA MARITUM IN COELIS MANEAS, O CATHERINA, TUUM.

Lo! Francis, Catherine Knollys your wife who lies dead under the frozen marble. Dead and removed from your soul she is never forgotten. While she was alive she was always loved. She bore you six and twice five children. Would that she had lived as many years as you and that she had lived to old age as your wife, but God did not want that. He wanted your bride to wait for you in Heaven.

– Tr. Rosemary Jeffreys

The Arms on the Tomb are:[1]

Quarterly of Four, viz. 1st and 4th, Azure Crucilly, a Cross Moline, Or, voided throughout; *Knollys* 2nd and 3rd, Gules on a Chevron Argent three Roses of the Field: *Impaled* Quarterly of Sixteen, viz. 1. Argent on a Bend Sable three Roses of the Field; *Carey.* 2. Sable two Bars Nebule Ermine *Spencer.* 3. Quarterly, *France* and *England,* with a Bordure Gobony, Argent and Azure, *Beauford.* 4. Gules a Fess between six Cross Croslets Or, *Beauchamp.* 5. Chequie Or and Azure a Chevron Ermine, *Warwick.* 6. Gules, a Chevron between ten Crosses Patée Argent, *Berkley.* 7. Gules a Lion passant Argent crowned Or, *Gerard.* 8. Argent a Chevron Gules between three Bulls' Heads, couped, Sable armed Or, *Bulleyne.* 9. Quarterly Sable and Argent, *Hoo.* 10. Or, a Chief indented Azure, *Butler.* 11. Argent a Lion rampant Sable crowned Gules. 12. Asure a Fess between six Cross Croslets Or. 13. Azure three Dexter Hands, couped at the Wrists, Argent, *Malmains.* 14. Ermine on a Chief Sable three Crosses Patée Argent, *Walsingham.* 15. Fretty Argent a Chief Gules. 16. Or, two Bends wavy, Gules *Bruer.* Crests: 1. an Elephant Azure attired Or. 2. a Swan rising, Proper. 3. a Bull's Head couped, Sable, armed, Or. 4, A Maiden's Head, Proper.

Dean Stanley, the authority on monuments in Westminster Abbey[2] says, in a section on Elizabethan Magnates: "…the reign of Elizabeth also brings with it the first distinct recognition of the Abbey as a Temple of Fame. It is a natural consequence of the fact that amongst her favourites so many were heroes and heroines. Their tombs literally verify Gray's description of her court: -

> Girt with many a baron bold,
>   Sublime their starry fronts they rear;
> And gorgeous dames, and statesmen old
>   In bearded majesty, appear.
> What Strings symphonious tremble in the air,
> What remains of vocal transport round her play!"

---

1   *The History and Antiquities of the Abbey Church of St. Peter, Westminster,* Vol. II, Edward Wedlake Brayley, 1823, BL Shelfmark HLL283.42132.

2   *Historical Memorials of Westminster Abbey,* Arthur Penrhyn Stanley, DD, Seventh Edition, London, 1890, British Library Shelfmark 1609/6090.

"The 'gorgeous dames' are for the most part recumbent. But, as we have seen, they have trampled on the ancient altars in their respective chapels." [Page 55 states that Catherine Carey's memorial occupies the space where previously the Altar to St Edmund stood.] "...mural tablets, first of their kind, commemorate ... the cousin of Elizabeth, Catherine Knollys, sister of Lord Hunsdon, who had attended her aunt, Anne Boleyn, to the scaffold."[1] ... "But the most conspicuous monuments of this era are those of Lord Hunsdon... Henry Cary [sic], Baron Hunsdon, the rough honest chamberlain to Queen Elizabeth, brother of Lady Catherine Knollys, has a place and memorial worthy of his confidential relations with the Queen... His interment was signalised by displacing the altar of the Chapel of St. John the Baptist. The monument was remarkable, even in the last century, as 'most magnificent'[2] and is, in fact, the loftiest in the Abbey."

Westmonasterium, Or, The History and Antiquities of the Abbey Church of St. Peter's Westminster, two Volumes, John Dart, London, 1723, British Library Shelfmark 208.i.4.
Volume I, p.112, A Very good engraving of the Monument to Catherine Carey showing the English text clearly. It quotes the full Latin text and then says: "The Verse will make but a bald narrative translation, and signifies only that Catherine, once wife to Francis Knollys, lies dead beneath this cold marble: The Poet tells him, that as he lov'd her living, so he was well assured he could not forget her dead, &c."
Page 187: A very good engraving of the tomb of Henry Cary (*sic*), Lord Hunsdon; pages 188-9 the Inscriptions.

---

1   This has proved impossible to verify, although it is plausible. Anne would have wanted her own supporters who were close to her. Her mother, Lady Boleyn, was in the audience. The State Papers (Henry VIII, Vol. 10, 911, May 19, 1536) say there were four attendants, but does not name them. Anne handed her prayer book to Mary Wyatt, the only name known of the four. [Agnes Strickland, *Lives of the Queens of England*, London, 1842, Vol. 4, pp.290ff, British Library Shelfmark 10805.b.25; also 1895 Abridged Edition.]

2   Fuller's *Worthies*, i, 433.

The Knollys Memorial,
St Nicholas, Rotherfield Greys,
Oxfordshire

According to Pevsner:
In the North chapel a vast and expensive free-standing monument
with the recumbent effigies of Sir Francis Knollys and Lady
Knollys and kneeling children around the sides. On a canopy over
them are Lord William Knollys [a son d. 1632] and his wife before
a prayer desk. The monument is of alabaster and marble with much
original painting and gilding. The effigies recline on fat
embroidered cushions with the exotic heraldic symbols of an
elephant and a swan at their feet. The vault of the canopy is
decorated with pendants and rosettes and stands on six columns. In

the centre are two arched supports with pilasters decorated with gold reliefs of musical instruments. The canopy has urns at the corners, and cherubs in proto-Baroque poses pointing to the kneeling figures. The treatment of the large effigies is stiff and conventional, but the carving of details such as the cherubs and the reliefs on the pilasters of the canopy is polished and accomplished. It is certainly not the work of a local mason and must be by the Southwark school of sculptors.

The Buildings of England, Oxfordshire, Jennifer Sherword & Nikolaus Pevsner, Penguin, 1974.

The chapel was added to the church in 1605 to house a monument of exceptional character and quality. The floor has its original tiles and the west and east facing windows have small inset ovals made up of fragments of early stained glass... The tomb displays reclining effigies of Sir Francis Knollys (1514-1596) and his wife Katherine (née Carey). ... The second of Sir Francis and Lady Knollys' sons, William, who subsequently became the Earl of Banbury, had the chapel built and the monument erected. He himself and his wife are to be seen kneeling at a 'Prie Dieu' on the canopy. Fourteen brothers and sisters kneel on either side of the base of the tomb. The eldest daughter wears the coronet and robes of a peeress. She was married first to Walter, Earl of Essex, and second to Robert, Earl of Leicester. The seven daughters are matched on the opposite side by seven sons. To the right of the mother Lady Knollys lies a sixteenth child that died in infancy.

Guide to the Church of St Nicholas, Rotherfield Greys, 1981.

The Epitaph of Catherine Carey Knollys, 1569, Huntington Library,
California, Call Number 18322; Original size 8 x 13 ¾ inches.
Reproduced with permission

An Epitaphe upon the worthy and
Honorable Lady, the Lady Knowles.

Death with his Darte hath us berefte
  a Gemme of worthy fame,
A Pearle of price, an Ouche of praise
  the Lady Knowles by name.

A Myrroure pure of womanhoode,
  a Bootresse and a stay,
To all that honest were, she was
  I say both locke and kaye.

Among the Troupes of Ladies all,
  and Dames of noble race,
She counted was, (and was in deede)
  in Lady Fortunes grace.

In favoure with our noble Queene,
  above the common sorte,
With whom she was in credit greate,
  and bare a comely porte.

There seemde between our Queene&Death,
  Contencion for to be,
Which of them both more entier love,
  to her could testifie.

The one in state did her advance,
  and place in diginitie,
That men thereby might knowe, to doe,
  what princes able be.

Death made her free from worldly care,
  from sicknes, paine and strife,
And hath ben as a gate, to bringe
  her to eternal life.

By Death therfore she hath receivde,
  a greater boone I knowe:
For she hath made a chaunge, whose blisse,
  no mortall wight can showe.

The vertues all, the Muses nine,
  and Graces three agreed,
To lodge within her noble breast,
  while she in Earth did feede.

A head so straight and beautified,
  with wit and counsaile sounde,
A minde so cleane devoide of guyleds,
  is oneth to be founde.

But gone she is, and left the Stage
  of this most wretched life,
Wherein she plaid a stately part,
  till cruell fates with knife:

Did cut the line of life in twaine,
  who shall not after goe,
When time doth come, we must all hence,
  Experience teacheth so.

Examples daily manifolde,
  before our eyes we see,
Which put us in remembraunce,
  of our fragilitie.

And bid us watch at every tide,
  for Death our lurking foe,
Sith dye we must, most certainely,
  but when, we do not knowe.

Som which to day are lusty Brutes,
  of age and courage ripe,
Tomorrow may be layd full lowe,
  by Death his grevous gripe.

Respect and parcialitie
  of persons is there none,
For King, or Kaiser, rich or poore,
  wise, foolish, all is one.

She here hath loste the companie,
 of Lords and Ladies brave,
Of husband, Children, frendes and kinne,
 and Courtly states full grave.

In Lieu whereof, the gained hath
 the blessed companie
Of Sainetes, Archangels, Patriarches,
 and Angelles in degree.

With all the Troupes Seraphicall,
 which in the heavenly Bower,
Melodiously with one accord,
 Ebuccinate Gods power.

Thus are we sure: for in this world
 she led a life to right,
That ill report could not distaine,
 nor blemish her with spight.

She traced had so cunningly,
 the path of vertues lore,
Prefiring God omnipotent,
 her godly eyes before:

And all her dedes preciselie were,
 so rulde by reasons Squire,
That all and some might her beholde,
 from vice still to retire.

God grant that we here left behinde,
 this Ladies steppes may treade,
To live so well, to die no worse,
 Amen, as I have saide.

Then maugre Death, we shall be sure,
 when corps in earth is closde,
Amonge the ioyes celestiall,
 our Soule shal be reposde.

F I N I S   Tho. Newton.

Imprinted at London in

Fleetestreete, by William How, for Ri
charde Iohnes: and are to be solde at his
Shop under the Lotterie house.

The only text of this ballad in the UK is transcribed in *Ballads & Broadsides, chiefly of the Elizabethan period, and printed in Black-Letter, most of which were formerly in the Heber Collection and are now in the library [of S. R. Christie-Miller] at Britwell Court, Buckinghamshire,* edited with notes and an introduction by *Herbert L. Collmann,* 1912, British Library shelfmark C.101.h.10. These were sold to the Huntington Library in California in 1924. Page 201: "Thomas Newton, poet, physician, and divine, a native of Cheshire, was born about 1512. He studied successively at Oxford and Cambridge. The DNB gives a long list of his miscellaneous publications, which include translations from classical and medical writers, as well as a quantity of contributed verse. He died in 1607. This Ballad was licenced to Richard Jones in 1568/9 (Arber's *Transcript,* i, 385)." The Introduction states: "The Broadside poems ... are ... of an ephemeral character, and may be regarded as a creation of the sixteenth century fostered by the increasing popularity of the printing press, and with the newsletters sowing the seeds of modern journalism. ...by the year 1560 there are said to be as many as seven hundred and ninety-six copies of Ballads stored at the Stationers' Hall. Ballad writing offered an easy livelihood to a number of obscure and not too reputable rhymsters, few of whose names have survived. ... Considerable profit attended the production of ballads, and this soon excited the envy and disgust of the better writers of the day... Their language closely reflects the opinions of nine-tenths of the population of London at the time of their issue."

References & Background Notes
Notes of particular interest are in **bold**.

The historical novel that sparked off this research is *The Other Boleyn Girl,* **by Philippa Gregory**, Harper Collins, London, 2001. Of the references at the end of the book, most of them have been read by myself, and notes from those that refer to Mary's and Henry's affair are summarised below.

Anne Boleyn, Mary Louise Bruce, Pan Books, London, 1972, British Library Shelfmark X.708.12609.
Page 10: Mary Boleyn was born about 1504, George about 1503, and Anne was "the youngest".
Page 15: Mary was initially in the Court of the Archduchess of Austria.
Page 23: "Warm hearted and ductile, Mary made the mistake of scattering her favours too widely and making her affairs too public. It was one thing to be the King's Mistress; quite another to be known to be at everyone's disposal. Even at the lascivious French Court there was a code of discretion; Mary had offended it. She was either sent or withdrawn hastily to England."
Page 24: [Marriage to William Carey] "It was a sorry match for a Boleyn but Mary had spoiled her chances for a good one."
Page 65: "[King Henry] also considered making [FitzRoy, Henry's son by Elizabeth Blount] his heir. Creating him Duke of Richmond in 1525 at the age of six, he gave him Henry VII's title and a household larger than Princess Mary's..."
Page 101: [After Carey's death in 1528] "William Carey's ... offices reverted 'in the King's gift'. The King generously distributed these sources of income and Mary, his widow, was left destitute. Despite their relationship of several years, Henry felt no lingering affection, no obligation; he scarcely even remembered Mary."
Page 105: Eleanor Carey, William Carey's sister, a Nun at a convent, confessed to Wolsey to having two illegitimate children by two priests, as well as an affair with a third man.

Tudor England, John Guy, OUP, 1988.
Page 116: "Henry may have had a child by ... Mary Boleyn".

Page 117: Accepts Henry's consanguinity with Mary Boleyn, in consequence of the relationship with Anne, Mary's sister.

The Tudor Court, David Loades, Batsford, 1986; seen at Richmond Reference Library, November 7, 2001.
Only mention that is useful is: A divorce was prepared against Anne Boleyn based on "consanguinity" with her sister Mary.
My deduction is that consanguinity would have only been provable in court if there had been children attributable to King Henry. In other words, this strongly suggests that it was, or would be, believed and accepted that Mary's children were Henry's.

Henry VIII and His Queens, David Loades, Sutton, 2000.
Page 21: Refers to the affair, but doubts children were Henry's. No reason given.
Page 26: Mary was "probably the elder" [with respect to Anne] by two years.
1994 Edition:
Page 34: **"William Carey received generous Royal grants every year from 1522 to 1525, which is suggestive."**
Pages 33-4: Gives dates of Henry's and Mary's affair as 1519-1525.

Sex In Elizabethan England, Alan Haynes, Sutton, 1997.
Four references to Mary Boleyn, including her affair with Henry.

Anne Boleyn, E.W. Ives, Basil Blackwell, 1987.
Pages 17-20: Long discussion of the relative ages of the Boleyn children, and argues conclusively that Mary was older than Anne, p.20.
Page 20: "Mary... was for a time Henry VIII's mistress. Of this there can be no doubt, *despite efforts to prove to the contrary"* [my italics – HAF]. "Perhaps Henry realised that it was much safer to risk begetting children whose paternity could be denied than bastards who only emphasised his lack of legitimate heirs."
Page 39: Mary Carey at the Field of The Cloth of Gold.
Page 122: Eleanor Carey, sister-in-law of Mary, was a nun who had had two children by priests.
Page 287, note 45: "Tree ring dating, however, shows that the surviving portrait of William Carey must be a later copy, or even

an enlargement of a miniature." Suggests the artist of the original was one of the Horneboltes of Ghent, Gerald the father, or his children Lucas or Susanna; refers to J. Fletcher, *A Portrait of William Carey, and Lord Hunsdon's Long Gallery,* Burlington Magazine, 123, (1981), p.304.

The History of England, John Lingard, Vol. IV, 1849. British Library Shelfmark RB 23 A17107 & 9595.d.1.
Pages 474-475: To Elizabeth Tailbois succeeded in the King's affections Mary Boleyn... She retained for some time the fickle heart of her lover[1], but Henry at length treated her as he had treated so many others[2]... Footnote 1: ...repeated the assertions of Cardinal Pole in his private letter to Henry in 1535: *Didicertat* (Anne Boleyn), *opinor, si nulla alia ex re, vel sororis suae exemplo, quam cito te concubinarum tuarum satietas caperet – Soror ejus est, quam tu violasti primum, et dui postea concubinae loco apud te habuisti - . Ab eodem pontifice magna vi contendebas, ut tibi liceret ducere sororem ejus, quae concubina tua fuisset. –* Pol. f. lxxvi, lxxvii. This is very poor Latin, which translates as follows: Put aside earnestly Anne Boleyn, I say. If for no other reason than for the sake of her sister whom I proclaim a sufficiency of mistresses captured you. She [Anne] is the sister of her [Mary] whom in the first place you violated and secondly you kept [Mary] by you afterwards in the place of mistress. You contended with great force with the Pope so that you would be allowed to marry the sister [Anne] of her [Mary] who had been your mistress. Tr: R. Jeffreys. Footnote 2: There is, however, reason to believe that he provided a husband for Mary Boleyn. At her marriage with William Carey, of the Privy Chamber, the King honoured the ceremony with his presence, and made his offering at the alter. "Saturday (31st January, 1520/21 at the marriage of M. Care and Mare Bulleyn, vi s viii, d". See extract from The Household Book in Sir Frederic Madden's privy purse expenses of Queen Mary, App. p. 282. The date is of importance.

The Earlier Tudors, J.D. Mackie, OUP, 1952, seen at Richmond Reference Library, November 7, 2001.
Page 323: States that Henry had "already possessed" Mary Boleyn and her mother. [Much later, Henry denied possessing Elizabeth

Howard Boleyn, the mother, at the time of Anne of Cleves' divorce. – HAF]

Page 325: Strongly implies that Mary was more important than Henry's other mistresses, and that she was on a par with Elizabeth Blount, whose son Henry FitzRoy was later created Duke of Richmond. [Elizabeth was unmarried, and Henry FitzRoy was King Henry's first male offspring, so it is easier to see why he was acknowledged as the King's son. Henry VIII would have needed Henry FitzRoy much more that Henry Carey, Mary Boleyn Carey's son, because FitzRoy was much older, and later King Henry had a legitimate male heir, Edward, later Edward VI. So Henry Carey was not really needed as an "illegitimate male heir" who could later possibly be legitimised. – HAF]

The Six Wives of Henry VIII, Antonia Fraser, 1988.
Page 101: States categorically that Mary Carey's children were not Henry's, but gives no reason, and only states that the affair was over by the time they were born. Her logic is that Henry would have been just as glad to have an (illegitimate) male heir in Henry Carey as he had been in Henry FitzRoy (Elizabeth's illegitimate son by King Henry). But this is unconvincing; two illegitimate male heirs could have been no more use to Henry than one. [See notes in reference above, J.D. Mackie.]

Tudor Women, Queens and Commoners, Alison Plowden, Weidenfeld and Nicolson, 1979.
Page 42: Referring to the Court of Francis I, "Rarely did any maid or wife leave that court chaste" – Sieur de Brantôme.
Page 45: King "Henry was notoriously stingy towards his mistresses."
Page 76: Canon Law made no distinction between a licit and an illicit sexual connection, so Henry's affair with Mary Boleyn made Anne Boleyn his sister-in-law.

The House of Tudor, Alison Plowden, Sutton, 1998.
Page 263: Mary Boleyn's grandson, Robert Carey, attended Queen Elizabeth on her deathbed in 1603 (at Richmond Palace), and was waiting under the window to receive the Royal Signet taken from the dead Queen's hand, to carry it on wild horseback to the waiting King James in Scotland. [Robert Carey was first cousin to our

ancestor Anne Knowles, who married Thomas West, Lord Delaware.]

Henry VIII, J.J. Scarisbrick, Yale English Monarchs, Yale University Press, 1997.
Page 148: Offers a contemporary eye witness account from a friar that Henry Carey was indeed "the King's Bastard" and quotes in footnote 2: "L.P., viii, 567", which (page 531) is **State Papers of Henry VIII, Folio Volumes (S.P.2), Folio Series L, viii, 567.** Warnicke gives this reference as: **Letters & Papers, Foreign & Domestic of the Reign of Henry VIII, Ed. J. S. Brewer, J. Gairdner, and R. H. Brodie, 21 Volumes, London, 1862-1932.** Available at the PRO.

The Reign of Henry VIII, David Starkey, Collins & Brown, 1991.
Page 71: An unfinished portrait of William Carey; page 6: artist unknown, from a private collection.

Henry VIII A European Court in England, Ed. David Starkey, Collins & Brown, 1991. In an article by David Starkey himself, he states, p.57, under the (second) portrait of William Carey:
William Carey (c.1500-1528), a distant cousin through the Beauforts, became keeper of Greenwich Palace in 1526. A gentleman of the Privy Chamber in 1519, he married Mary Boleyn in 1520 and when Anne replaced her sister as the King's mistress, seemed destined for greatness. But in 1528 he died of the sweating sickness.
This painting is identified by an Elizabethan copy which includes the sitter's coat of arms. The copy was made after the original had been subjected to overpainting. Instead of a book, the copy shows him holding a pair of gloves and the dress becomes Elizabethan. These changes, removed from the present picture when it was cleaned, were made because (as the cleaning also revealed) the original painting had been left unfinished. Finally the cleaning uncovered an underpainting which resembles Holbein's drawing of 'M Souch' [Zouche], p.101.
This underpainting, and the fact that the date of the sitter's death coincided with Holbein's departure from England at the end of his first visit, must lead to speculation that the painting was his, but despite the sensitive rendering of the face, an unknown French or Flemish artist (though not a Horenbout) cannot be ruled out. Artist

Unknown, 16th Cent., Oil on Panel, 790x660, private collection, and quotes the reference J. Fletcher, *A Portrait of William Carey and Lord Hunsdon's Long Gallery,* Burlington Magazine, 123, (1981), p.304.

The Six Wives of Henry VIII, Alison Weir, Pimlico, 1997.
Page 134: Henry Carey, in 1533 (age 7) claimed he was "our Sovereign Lord the King's son". [Clearly he was prompted by someone.]
Page 134: Francis I referred to "riding her" [Mary] as "my hackney". Gives dates of affair of Mary and Henry as 1519 to approximately 1525.
Page 146: Discusses uncertainty over dates of births of the Boleyn siblings, Mary, Anne, and George.
Page 273: Mary died on July 19, 1543. Refers to letter to Thomas Cromwell trying to get back into Court after being banished for marrying Stafford. This is "reproduced" on the back inside cover of the novel. The original manuscript, Howard's Letters, 525, seems unfindable. See notes on State Papers, Henry VIII.
Mary Boleyn was at the Field of the Cloth of Gold, 1520, attending Queen Catherine.

Henry VIII, King & Court, Alison Weir, Jonathan Cape, 2001.
Page 126: In 1535, Sir George Throckmorton accused Henry VIII to his face for "meddling" with Mary Boleyn and her mother. "Never with the mother" replied Henry. Refers to L&P of Reign of Henry VIII.
Page 221: Gives wedding date of Mary and William Carey as February 4, 1520.
There is a portrait of Mary Boleyn at Hever Castle by Hans Holbein the Younger [Warnicke, p.180] (reproduced on the book facing page 416), but it is said to date from the 17th or 18th century. Hans Holbein, 1497-1543, came to England in 1526, returned to Basle in 1528, returned to England in 1532, entered the King's service no later than 1536, and died in England 1543. He is called "The Younger" to differentiate him from his less well known father. – DNB.
Mary Boleyn had affairs at the French Court, including with King Francis I. Twenty years later he described her as "a great whore,

the most infamous of all", "*una grandissima ribalda et infame sopre tutte*", [Warnicke, p.46].

In 1528, Henry admitted to an affair with Mary by asking for a Papal Dispensation in order to marry Anne Boleyn on grounds of "affinity".

Says that Henry did not name a ship after Mary Boleyn, but purchased one of that name, and another named after Anne Boleyn, from her father; refers to L&P of Henry VIII. See Warnicke, pp.267-8, note 42, for a full discussion and list of sources for this.

Catherine Carey was born in 1524; Henry Carey was born on March 4, 1526, and was said to resemble King Henry.

Page 272: In 1535, John Hale, Vicar of Isleworth, stated that a Bridgetine [monk at St. Bridget's, Syon] pointed out "young Master Carey" as the King's bastard son.

Page 286: William Carey died suddenly on June 22, 1528, and the Wardship of Henry Carey was given to Anne Boleyn.

Page 416, facing: There is a portrait of Mary Boleyn at Hever Castle, but it is said to date from the 17th or 18th century.

The Rise and Fall of Anne Boleyn, Retha M. Warnicke, Cambridge University Press, 1989.

Page 36: William Carey was a descendant of Edward III. He was a younger son of Thomas Carey of Wiltshire and Margaret Spencer daughter of Lady Eleanor Beaufort, who herself was a child of Edmund, Third Earl of Somerset.

Page 36: King Henry's wedding present to the Careys was 6s 8d.

Page 46: Francis I's description of Mary Carey was "*una grandissima ribalda et infame sopre tutte*", "a great whore, the most infamous of all."

Page 46: Henry Carey was raised to the Peerage as Lord Hunsdon in the reign of Queen Elizabeth I

Page 46: William Carey was granted his manors and estates in June 1524 and February 1526, dates which coincide exactly with the births of Catherine and Henry Carey.

Page 82: Following William Carey's death on June 23, 1528, the King granted Wardship of Henry Carey to Anne Boleyn, referring to the "extreme necessity" of the widow Mary. At the end of the year, Mary was granted the annuity of £100 that had belonged to William.

Facing page 180: The Hever Castle portrait of Mary Boleyn, by Hans Holbein the Younger.

Page 237: Catherine Carey, at age about 15, won appointment as Maid of Honour to Anne of Cleves, Henry's fourth wife. She married in 1540 Sir Francis Knollys (Knowles) and gave birth to Lettice, the first of many children in 1541. Until she died in 1569, she remained a close friend of her cousin, or more likely half-sister, Queen Elizabeth, and both her husband and brother Henry Carey, later created Lord Hunsdon, served the Queen.

Page 255: Gives reference as: Letters & Papers, Foreign & Domestic of the Reign of Henry VIII, Ed. J. S. Brewer, J. Gairdner, and R. H. Brodie, 21 Volumes, London, 1862-1932.

Page 265, note 13: Catherine Carey died in 1569, married in 1540, gave birth to her first child (Lettice) in 1541.

Page 286 note 43: Mary's letter to Thomas Cromwell is L&P, VII, 1655. This is the letter reconstructed in the book by Gregory.

State Papers of Henry VIII

Volume I, 3348, 9 October 1514.
M. Boleyne "Gentlewoman appointed to have abidden in France with the French Queen."

Volume I, 3357, 12 October 1514.
Names of ... ladies retained by the King [Louis XII] to do service to the Queen ... Madamoyselle Boleyne.

Volume III, 1539, 11 February, 1520, Book of Payments.
The King offered on Saturday (4th February) at the marriage of Mr Care and Mary Bullayn, 6s 8d.

Volume III, 3358, 23 September, 1523.
Expenses of the ship *Mary Boleyn,* 100 tons, Wm. Symonds, Capt., 79 men, £352 8s 6d.

Volume VI, 4409, 23 June, 1528, Brian Tuke to Wolsey.
Mr. Cary ... is dead of the sweat. [See VIII, 453, p.174 below.]

Volume VII, 177, dated 13 February, 1534.
Original is in Lisle Papers, Vol. VI, 23, now filed on microfiche at the Public Record Office as S.P.3/6, 23. Signed by Mary Cary (*sic*) and Sir William Kingston. The footnotes in the State Papers suggest she is the original writer.

Volume VII, 1554, 19 December, 1534.
Chapuys (Ambassador) to the Holy Roman Emperor Charles V (Vienna Archives): Refers to Mary being sent from Court "guilty of misconduct" (*malefice*) where it was not thought proper for her to be seen pregnant (*enciente*).

Volume VII, 1655, Letter from Mary Stafford to Thomas Lord Cromwell, not dated, but calendared as 1534. Original document is "Howard's Lett., 525"; no one at the PRO could identify this. A search of the Historical Manuscript Commission index on the internet revealed 46 Howard family archives in various locations in England. A search of the British Library Online Catalogue was unsuccessful.
The text of the State Paper is as follows:
Desires him [Cromwell] to be good to her poor husband [Sir William Stafford] and herself. He is aware that their marriage, being clandestine, displeases the King and Queen. *"But one thing, good master Secretary, consider; that he was young, and love overcame reason. And for my part I saw so much honesty in him that I loved him as well as he did me; and was in bondage, and glad I was to be at liberty; so that for my part I saw that all the world did set so little by me, and he so much, that I thought I could take no better way but to take him and forsake all other ways, and to live a poor honest life with him; and so I do put no doubts but we should, if we might once be so happy to recover the King's gracious favor and the Queen's. For well I might a had a greater man of birth and a higher, but I ensure you I could never a had one that should a loved me so well nor a more honest man"* Begs him to put her husband *"to the King's grace that he may do his duty as all other gentlemen do;"* and persuade his majesty to speak to the Queen who is rigorous against them. *"And seeing there is no remedy, for God's sake help us; for we have been now a quarter of a year married, I thank God, and too late now to call that again. Wherefore it is the more almons to help [us]. But if I were at my*

liberty and might choose, I ensure you, master Secretary, for my little time, I have tried so much honesty to be in him, that I had rather beg my bread with him than to be the greatest Queen christened." Begs, as he has the name of helping all that need, he will help them; among all his suitors none more require his pity. *"Pray my lord my father* [the Earl of Wiltshire] *and my lady to be good to us,"* and desire *"my lord of Norfolk and my lord my brother"* to do the same. *"I dare not write to them, they are so cruel against us. But if with any pain I could take with my life I might win their good wills, I promise you there is no child living would venture more than I"* – *"And being that I have read in old books that some for as just causes have by kings and queens been pardoned by the suit of good folks, I trust it. shall be our chance, through your good help, to come to the same."* Signed.

To the right worshipful &c., master Secretary.

Mary had married William Stafford secretly and without approval. This letter was an attempt to get them both back into Court, but they were unsuccessful.

Volume VIII, 453, p.174, 29 September, 1538, Windsor Castle Accounts.

William Carey died on 10 June 20 Hen. VIII, 10 June, 1528.

Volume VIII, 567. Calendared 1535, before 20 April.

This is the letter from John Hale, Vicar of Isleworth, to the Council, wherein he states:

"Moreover, Mr Skydmore [a monk at St Bridget's Priory] dyd show to me yongge Master Care, saying that he was our suffren Lord the Kynge's son by our suffren Lady the Qwyen's syster, whom the Qwyen's grace myght not suffer to be yn the Cowrte."

The original of this is in the PRO.

Volume X, 450, 10 March, 1536. Bishop of Faenza to Prothonotary Ambrogio. Refers to Ass. M.S. 8715, f.220b. British Library. This is the original quote regarding Mary's morals in France "… whom the French King knew here in France *"per una grandissima ribalda at imfame sopre tutte."*

Volume X, 909, 19 May, 1536 [day of Anne's execution]
Refers to King Henry's affair with her [Anne's] sister... and this would make Elizabeth a bastard.

Volume X, 911, 19 May, 1536 [day of Anne's execution]
"... four young ladies followed her" [to the scaffold], but are not named.

Volume XIV, 572(3), 22 November, 1539. For the Reception of Anne of Cleves.
Names of those appointed to receive Anne of Cleves: "...young Stafford that married the Lady Cary..."

The following references mention property conveyed and acquired to William and Mary Stafford : Vol. XIV, 236 (p.74), 28 September, 1539, Lady Mary Carie for arrears due from Tynemouth Priory, £66 13s 4d.; Vol. XIV, 854, 25 April, 1539; Vol. XV, 517, 15 April, 1540, 611, April 1540, 31 Hen. VIII, pp.286-7, no.22&23.; Vol. XVI, 779, April 1541, no.22, 1308, October 1541, no.7&12.; Vol. XVII, 258, f.52, April 1542, 362(1), no.1, May 1542.; 1012(58), October 1542 [very large land grant, 1st mention of Catherine Carey & husband].; Vol. XVIII, 623(66), May 1543, I,223(p.123).; Vol. XIX, 80(26), p.40, 141(71) p.84.; Vol. XX, 418(f.86), 21 Sept. 1545.; 496(46) p.226.; Vol. XXI, 643(f.86), 12 Dec. 1544; 1106(72) p.579, June 1546; 717(12) p.355, 1546.

Letters & Papers of Henry VIII

King's grants to William Carey: Vol. III, 317, 1114, 2074, 2297, 2994.
Carey's death: Vol. IV, 4408, 4413; offices at death: 4413.
Wardship of Henry Carey to Anne Boleyn: Vol. V, 11.
Mary's annuity [of £100]: Vol. V, 306.

Lisle Papers

S.P.3/6, 23. PRO.
This is the original of the letter of Volume VII, 177 above, on microfiche. The name of Thomas Hunt begins line 7, and Mary Carey's signature is at the bottom as described above.

The Burlington Magazine

J. Fletcher, *A Portrait of William Carey, and Lord Hunsdon's Long Gallery,* Burlington Magazine, 123, (1981), p.304.
The author reports that tree-ring dating of the frame of the picture under discussion (the one with the Carey Arms displayed) shows that it was painted after 1570. This, with deductive logic, identifies the three pictures of Henry Carey shown in this appendix. The first is the miniature referred to below; the second is the contemporary original discussed by Starkey (1991); and the third is the 1580 Elizabethan copy referred to below. The author continues:
"The account of Brooke House in the Parish of Hackney [London] records that Henry Carey, First Lord Hunsdon (1526-96) added a Long Gallery to that residence ... partially destroyed by bombing in the 1939-45 war, and demolished in 1950. Apart from commissioning portraits of Queen Elizabeth ... [he] would have wished to display likenesses of his mother Mary Boleyn and her husband William Carey. {footnote: Henry Carey's resemblance to Henry VIII is said to support the belief the King was his father.} I [Fletcher] suggest therefore that the portrait of William Carey was painted about 1580 for Lord Hunsdon to hang in his new Long Gallery. The painting could well have been based on a small portrait or miniature painted in 1526 that showed only the head, neck and shirt of the sitter... this would explain the accuracy of the hair style and neckline for 1526 while the shape of the sleeve and the bands on it reflect styles in use c.1550 and c.1570 respectively."

Edward III to Edward & Alexander Fitzhugh

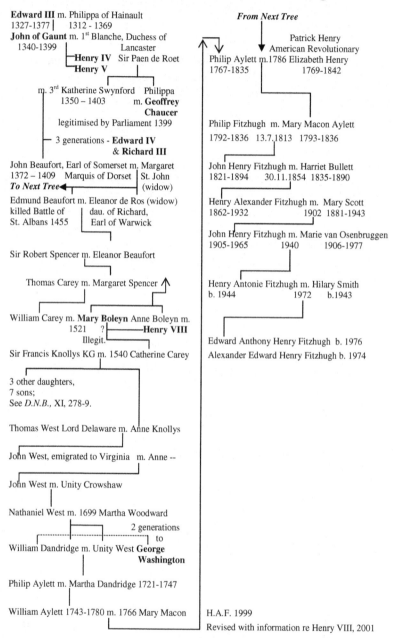

Edward III m. Philippa of Hainault
1327-1377 | 1312 - 1369

John of Gaunt m. 1st Blanche, Duchess of
1340-1399 | Lancaster

─ **Henry IV** Sir Paen de Roet
─ **Henry V**

m. 3rd Katherine Swynford   Philippa
1350 – 1403   m. **Geoffrey**
Chaucer
legitimised by Parliament 1399

─ 3 generations - **Edward IV**
& Richard III

John Beaufort, Earl of Somerset m. Margaret
1372 – 1409   Marquis of Dorset | St. John
To Next Tree ◄─ (widow)

Edmund Beaufort m. Eleanor de Ros (widow)
killed Battle of | dau. of Richard,
St. Albans 1455 | Earl of Warwick

Sir Robert Spencer m. Eleanor Beaufort

Thomas Carey m. Margaret Spencer ↑

William Carey m. **Mary Boleyn** Anne Boleyn m.
1521   ? ├─ **Henry VIII**
Illegit. ─┘

Sir Francis Knollys KG m. 1540 Catherine Carey

3 other daughters,
7 sons;
See *D.N.B.,* XI, 278-9.

Thomas West Lord Delaware m. Anne Knollys

John West, emigrated to Virginia   m. Anne --

John West m. Unity Crowshaw

Nathaniel West m. 1699 Martha Woodward

2 generations
to
William Dandridge m. Unity West **George**
Washington

Philip Aylett m. Martha Dandridge 1721-1747

William Aylett 1743-1780 m. 1766 Mary Macon

From Next Tree

Patrick Henry
American Revolutionary
Philip Aylett m.1786 Elizabeth Henry
1767-1835   1769-1842

Philip Fitzhugh m. Mary Macon Aylett
1792-1836 13.7.1813 1793-1836

John Henry Fitzhugh m. Harriet Bullett
1821-1894   30.11.1854 1835-1890

Henry Alexander Fitzhugh m. Mary Scott
1862-1932   1902 1881-1943

John Henry Fitzhugh m. Marie van Osenbruggen
1905-1965   1940 1906-1977

Henry Antonie Fitzhugh m. Hilary Smith
b. 1944   1972 b.1943

Edward Anthony Henry Fitzhugh b. 1976
Alexander Edward Henry Fitzhugh b. 1974

H.A.F. 1999
Revised with information re Henry VIII, 2001

OUR DESCENT FROM KING HENRY VIII

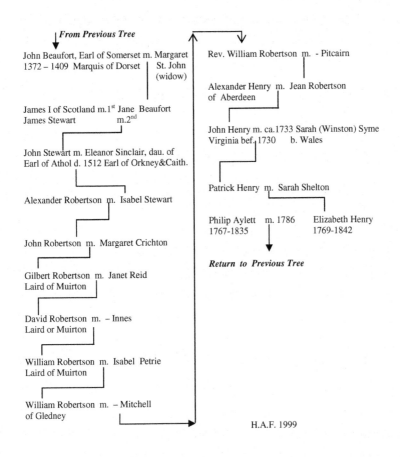

From Previous Tree

John Beaufort, Earl of Somerset m. Margaret
1372 – 1409 Marquis of Dorset | St. John
                                    (widow)

James I of Scotland m.1ˢᵗ Jane Beaufort
James Stewart   m.2ⁿᵈ

John Stewart m. Eleanor Sinclair, dau. of
Earl of Athol d. 1512 Earl of Orkney&Caith.

Alexander Robertson m. Isabel Stewart

John Robertson m. Margaret Crichton

Gilbert Robertson m. Janet Reid
Laird of Muirton

David Robertson m. – Innes
Laird or Muirton

William Robertson m. Isabel Petrie
Laird of Muirton

William Robertson m. – Mitchell
of Gledney

Rev. William Robertson m. - Pitcairn

Alexander Henry m. Jean Robertson
of Aberdeen

John Henry m. ca.1733 Sarah (Winston) Syme
Virginia bef. 1730   b. Wales

Patrick Henry m. Sarah Shelton

Philip Aylett m. 1786   Elizabeth Henry
1767-1835   1769-1842

Return to Previous Tree

H.A.F. 1999

Edward the Confessor to Edward III

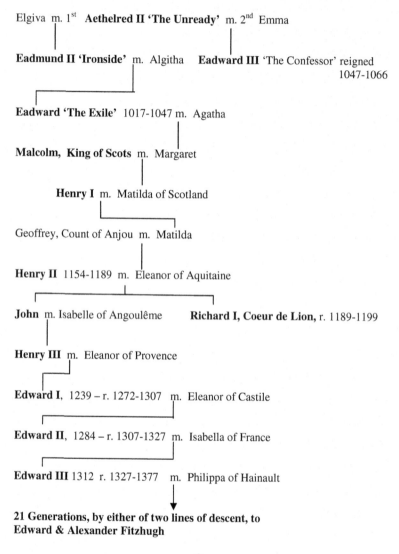

Elgiva m. 1ˢᵗ **Aethelred II 'The Unready'** m. 2ⁿᵈ Emma

Eadmund II 'Ironside' m. Algitha   **Eadward III** 'The Confessor' reigned
1047-1066

Eadward 'The Exile' 1017-1047 m. Agatha

Malcolm, King of Scots m. Margaret

Henry I m. Matilda of Scotland

Geoffrey, Count of Anjou m. Matilda

Henry II 1154-1189 m. Eleanor of Aquitaine

John m. Isabelle of Angoulême   **Richard I, Coeur de Lion,** r. 1189-1199

Henry III m. Eleanor of Provence

Edward I, 1239 – r. 1272-1307 m. Eleanor of Castile

Edward II, 1284 – r. 1307-1327 m. Isabella of France

Edward III 1312 r. 1327-1377   m. Philippa of Hainault

**21 Generations, by either of two lines of descent, to
Edward & Alexander Fitzhugh**

.oOo.

A SHORT SYNOPTIC HISTORY

TIME FRAME	FAMILY MEMBERS Direct Ancestors in *Bold*	EVENTS AND BACKGROUND	CHAPTERS AND PAGES
1223-1358	***Hugh,*** our patronymic forbear, his descendants in order: ***Richard, Roger,*** ***Richard, William***	Our ancestor ***Hugh,*** from whom our surname derives, and his descendants live unnoted lives at Beggary-cum-Goodwick Manor, Bedfordshire, as smallholders tilling the land and raising sheep. The evidence is presented substantiating this part of our ancestry, as well as the early derivation of the Fitzhugh Arms. ***Hugh's*** descendants adopt the Surname Fitzhugh, meaning son of *Hugh*.	Vol. One, Chapter 2, pp. 11-18

TIME FRAME	FAMILY MEMBERS Direct Ancestors in **Bold**	EVENTS AND BACKGROUND	CHAPTERS AND PAGES
Tuesday, July 24, 1358	John Fitzhugh, Elizabeth Fitzhugh, his wife; his brother **Richard**	John and his servant Piers are murdered in hot blood by Richard Stocker, the son of a neighbour, when caught *in flagrante delicto* with Elizabeth. Richard and Elizabeth escape. The family Manor of Beggary passes, after legal difficulties, to **Richard**, John's brother.	Vol. One, Chapter 1, pp. 1-8
15th Century	**Son** of **Richard** (inheritor of murdered John), **William** and his son; **Thomas** who married **Christine Maidbury**, their children, including Thomas and our ancestor **William**	**Thomas** the elder marries Christine Maidbury. His son Thomas, brother of our ancestor **William**, becomes a Barrister at the Middle Temple and has a distinguished career. **William** marries Catherine Bill, perhaps with disapproval of his father.	Vol. One, Chapter 3, p. 27

TIME FRAME	FAMILY MEMBERS Direct Ancestors in **Bold**	EVENTS AND BACKGROUND	CHAPTERS AND PAGES
16th Century, First half	**William Fitzhugh** and his wife **Catherine Bill**; **William's** brother Thomas	**William** and Catherine live at Colmworth and produce 15 or 16 children, of whom 10 survive. They live through and survive the religious upheavals of the Reformation and the Dissolution and a threatened Spanish invasion. **William** is the first in the family to buy a Church property after the Dissolution of the Monasteries. He moves to Wilden, Bedfordshire. Brother Thomas is involved in a near-swindle of a man named Simon Fitz. Thomas dies a wealthy man and leaves much property to his brother, our ancestor **William**.	Vol. One, Chapter 4, p. 40 p. 49 p. 50 Chapter 5

TIME FRAME	FAMILY MEMBERS Direct Ancestors in **Bold**	EVENTS AND BACKGROUND	CHAPTERS AND PAGES
16th Century, Second half, Elizabethan Times	***John Fitzhugh,*** our Ancestor, and Robert, his brother	Our ancestor ***John,*** son of ***William,*** goes into the Malting trade in Barford. He marries Amy Negus about 1566, and she brings a farm as dowry, where he sets up malting. They have a daughter and four sons. The entire family is descended from two of these sons. The Fitzhugh Arms are confirmed in 1566 at the Harleian Visitation of Bedfordshire. Richard Fitzhugh, ***John's*** uncle, sells Beggary-cum-Goodwick, and the family's ancient occupation of the original Fitzhugh manor comes to an end. Robert has trouble marrying off his eldest daughter Mary, but eventually finds her a husband in one William Astry, to whom he offered a complicated land deal as dowry. This was to become the seed of a bitter family dispute, compounded by a strong dislike between father and son-in-law.	Vol. One, Chapter 6 p. 77 p. 80

TIME FRAME	FAMILY MEMBERS Direct Ancestors in **Bold**	EVENTS AND BACKGROUND	CHAPTERS AND PAGES
17th Century, up to 1609	Robert of Paslows, brother of **John**, **John's** son **William**	Robert has four daughters only, but wishes to see his lands, "the ancient inheritance of the Fitzhughs," as he calls them, descend to blood relations of the Fitzhugh surname. He makes a secret Will leaving much to his nephews, including our ancestor **William** of Barford. His obsession is to keep his son-in-law William Astry from inheriting anything not already left to him in his marriage contract to Mary. Astry is bitter at being conned over his wife's dowry, and Robert is certain Astry will try to thwart his wishes. The women on Astry's side of the family persuade Robert, in a weak moment, to tear up his Will. While Robert is so ill as to be near death, Astry gets him to sign a Memorandum signifying a wish to leave his property to Astry and his immediate in-laws. Robert dies shortly after (1609). **William** moves from Barford to Bedford to take over his mother's Malting when her second husband William Negus dies.	Vol. One, Chapter 7 Vol. One, Chapter 8, pp. 115-116

TIME FRAME	FAMILY MEMBERS Direct Ancestors in **Bold**	EVENTS AND BACKGROUND	CHAPTERS AND PAGES
1609-1623	**William Fitzhugh**, his first-cousin-in-law William Astry, Astry's wife Mary, and her sisters Frances and Anne. **William's** brothers Henry and Robert	**William** rapidly establishes himself in Bedford, eventually becoming a Burgess with a Seat on the Common Council. He lives at The Green House.	Vol. One, Chapter 8, p. 116
		Robert's widow Elizabeth tries to administer his Will on the basis of Astry's bogus Memorandum. In order to gain control of the rest of Robert's property, Astry concocts a nuncupative (i.e. oral) will based on vague spoken promises made by Robert to his wife.	pp. 113-114
		William and his brothers unite to take legal action against Astry. The first court case stretches out through 1609-10 in the Star Chamber, but this is inconclusive.	p. 120
		In January 1614, **William** and his brothers again launch a legal attack to establish the validity of Robert's written Will, and the case is heard at Westminster Hall. The Court decrees entirely in their favour. Astry gets into a series of legal and financial scrapes and ends up in the Fleet Prison, London. He dies three months later.	p. 123
		However, Robert's third son-in-law, Richard Saunders, puts in a claim to uphold the nuncupative will on behalf of Robert's widow, even though she is by now dead. Astonishingly, his case is upheld when the Prerogative Court finds in favour of the validity of the nuncupative will. Continued…	p. 125 p. 126

TIME FRAME	FAMILY MEMBERS Direct Ancestors in **Bold**	EVENTS AND BACKGROUND	CHAPTERS AND PAGES
1609-1623	***William Fitzhugh,*** his first-cousin-in-law William Astry, Astry's wife Mary, and her sisters Frances and Anne. ***William's*** brothers Henry and Robert	...A stay of execution is granted to ***William*** and his brothers, but the case drags on into 1617. This time the Court cannot decide and gives Saunders leave to plead his case at Common Law in the Court of Kings Bench. There the written Will is upheld but Saunders is given a stay of execution.	p. 128
		The case comes up two years later in 1619. Saunders submits further arguments and is granted a retrial before a Jury. In May 1621 the Kings Bench Jury finds in favour of ***William*** and his brothers and the written Will, but Saunders is given leave to appeal. This Saunders does successfully, and the entire case goes to a retrial, even though ***William*** has now won the case twice. But in 1622 the Jury reaffirms the nuncupative will, and ***William*** and his brothers have lost, after twelve years of legal struggle and three verdicts in their favour. Seemingly, the Fitzhughs have lost the whole of "the ancient inheritance."	p. 129
		However, an out of Court compromise is reached whereby ***William*** and his brothers pay to Saunders and his descendants certain sums and regain most, but not all, of the property.	p. 129
		Even though ***William*** and his brothers have finally more or less won, the cost proves too great, and they sell up in 1623. "The ancient inheritance of the Fitzhughs," which old Robert had tried so hard to preserve for his descendants of blood and name, is gone forever.	p. 130

TIME FRAME	FAMILY MEMBERS Direct Ancestors in *Bold*	EVENTS AND BACKGROUND	CHAPTERS AND PAGES
1625 onwards	***William***, his sons ***Henry*** and William	***William*** prospers as a Maltster in Bedford, and becomes a Burgess in 1625. ***William*** and Margaret Smith have 8 sons of whom 7 survive. ***William*** apprentices his son ***Henry***, our ancestor, to a Woollen Draper in Bedford. ***William*** builds a new house in Bedford High Street, and survives a lawsuit that he is grinding malt illegally. In his Will of 1633, he leaves his new house to ***Henry***. ***William*** becomes Bridgewarden for Bedford Bridge, but dies in April 1633. His widow successfully defends a lawsuit from her own son William over the terms of the Will. Margaret has 32 grandchildren, of whom 14 are boys. Only one of these, our ancestor ***William the Immigrant***, carries the Fitzhugh surname more than one more generation.	Vol. One, Chapter 9, pp. 142-143 pp. 145-147 p. 148 p. 149 p. 150

TIME FRAME	FAMILY MEMBERS Direct Ancestors in **Bold**	EVENTS AND BACKGROUND	CHAPTERS AND PAGES
17th Century 1614– 1666	**Henry Fitzhugh**	**Henry** is apprenticed to a Woollen Draper in Bedford and marries Mary King. He becomes Mayor of Bedford in 1649. He puts his seal and signature on a document dated 1648, showing that he was using the correct Fitzhugh Arms (*Quarterly, 1 & 4 Ermine, on a Chief Gules, three Martlets Or; 2 & 3 Argent, three Chevrons Sable, each charged with a Bezant*). His father **William** leaves **Henry** a large house in Bedford, of which a complete description remains. In 1653, **Henry** embarks on an investment speculation with a large amount of borrowed money. Some evidence is presented that this may have been to make the River Ouse navigable to Bedford. Henry defaults on the loan repayments and is made bankrupt in 1658. His entire stock in the Drapers trade is inventoried and seized. Continued...	Vol. Two, Chapter 1, p. 6 p. 6 p.8 note 3 Appendix 8 p. 9 p. 12 p.17 note 1

TIME FRAME	FAMILY MEMBERS Direct Ancestors in **Bold**	EVENTS AND BACKGROUND	CHAPTERS AND PAGES
		...Continued	
17th Century 1614-1666	**Henry Fitzhugh**	Trade Tokens of **Henry's** survive from 1655, and he indulges in some property buying and selling at this time. However, he is penniless by 1658. After this, all we know for sure is that he died in Cork, Ireland in 1666, but a long argument, based on available evidence, is presented that he went there sometime after 1659, and became the Clerk of the Powder Store in Cork. His widow Mary is probably destitute, with young children to support, but she remains in the family home. These events probably force his son **William** to emigrate to Virginia Colony.	p.15, p. 16 pp. 19-24 pp. 25-27 p. 27

TIME FRAME	FAMILY MEMBERS Direct Ancestors in **Bold**	EVENTS AND BACKGROUND	CHAPTERS AND PAGES
1651-1701	**William Fitzhugh,** The Immigrant, and Henry, his brother	**William** is born in 1651. He remains in Bedford until 1673, when he sells a property that his father had bought in 1655. He sells it with his wife Elizabeth (whose existence was unknown until the author discovered a crucial document). Less than 8 months later he marries Sarah Tucker in Virginia, who was then aged 11. **William** loses touch completely with his family in England, but settles down to a career of tobacco planting, legal work as a lawyer, and Colonial politics. He enters the Virginia House of Burgesses at age 25 and builds large plantation estates for himself and eventually for all his children. A chance meeting with a traveller in 1685 leads to contact with his cousin William in London, and then to his brother Henry and their mother. **William** pays for his sister Dorothy's passage to Virginia, and begins to subsidise his mother, who is in dire hardship in Bedford. **William** invites Henry to Virginia and offers boundless patronage. An argument surfaces that shows that **William** is using …	Vol. Two, Chapter 1, p.36 pp. 38ff. p.41

TIME FRAME	FAMILY MEMBERS Direct Ancestors in **Bold**	EVENTS AND BACKGROUND	CHAPTERS AND PAGES
1651-1701	**William Fitzhugh,** The Immigrant, and Henry, his brother	...the wrong Coat of Arms (those of the then extinct Barons FitzHugh, *Azure, three Chevrons interlaced in Base Or, a Chief Or*). This has confused all of the American Fitzhughs ever since. Henry proves unreliable and an alcoholic, but this does not diminish **William's** generosity. In 1695, their mother is still in dire circumstances. The correspondence ends in 1698, while mother is still alive. **William** seriously tries to move back to England, but dies in Virginia in 1701. He leaves a total of 54,000 acres in various estates and houses.	pp.42-43 pp.43-44 p.47

TIME FRAME	FAMILY MEMBERS Direct Ancestors in **Bold**	EVENTS AND BACKGROUND	CHAPTERS AND PAGES
1692-1733	*John Fitzhugh*	**John**, the youngest son, is born around 1692. **William** the Immigrant leaves him a relatively small inheritance of 2175 acres, seven Negroes, five pieces of silver, six spoons, and £50. **John** becomes a Justice of the Court in 1720 and a Major in the Militia. **William** installs **John** on an estate called Marmion. He marries Anne Barbara McCarthy in 1719. He helps to found the town of Falmouth as a commercial venture, and seeks a fortune in copper mining, to no avail. He dies on January 22, 1732/3, leaving seven very young children.	Vol. Two, Chapter 1, p.52 p.52

TIME FRAME	FAMILY MEMBERS Direct Ancestors in *Bold*	EVENTS AND BACKGROUND	CHAPTERS AND PAGES
1725-1791	*Col. William Fitzhugh*	*William*, the second son of *John*, is born in 1725 and inherits the Marmion estate. He marries first Ursula Beverley and second Hannah -. He builds a new house on the estate. This house is architecturally and decoratively important. Three photographs of it are displayed in the History, and much background information is given. One of the rooms is subsequently in the 20th Century removed to the Metropolitan Museum in New York. *William* and his wife Hannah lead an exemplary life and play host to Thomas Jefferson. He takes the American side in the Revolution and dies in 1791.	Vol. Two, Chapter 2 pp. 58-60, p.61 note 1 Appendix 4 Appendix 7 pp. 62-63 p. 63

TIME FRAME	FAMILY MEMBERS	EVENTS AND BACKGROUND	CHAPTERS AND PAGES
	Direct Ancestors in *Bold*		
ca 1755-ca 1796	*John Fitzhugh*	*John* is a very shadowy figure in our History. He is the son of *William* and his first wife Ursula Beverley. *John* marries Lucy Redd around 1774. He is a 1st Lieutenant in the 2nd Company of Caroline (County) Men in the Revolution. He lives by planting and commerce and has a respectable holding in movable property. He dies before 1796.	Vol. Two, Chapter 2, p.68 p.69 p.69
1792-1836	*Philip Fitzhugh,* his brother Dennis	*Philip* is born in 1792 in Caroline County, Virginia. He, like many of his near relatives, is the last of his line to live out his life in the old colony. He serves as a Corporal in the War of 1812. He marries in 1813 Mary Macon Aylett. He engages in various forms of mercantile trade, but only sad tales survive. Mary dies on October 6, 1836 and *Philip* follows on December 21, both aged only 44, leaving 8 children, the youngest only 18 months. Dennis sets the pattern for migration by moving to Missouri in the fur trade, before returning to Kentucky to become a Judge.	Vol. Two, Chapter 2, p.74 p.75 p.76 p.77

TIME FRAME	FAMILY MEMBERS Direct Ancestors in **Bold**	EVENTS AND BACKGROUND	CHAPTERS AND PAGES
1821-1894	**John Henry Fitzhugh,** his brothers Patrick Henry, Edwin, and Thaddeus	**John** is born on December 23, 1821 in King & Queen County, Virginia. The fifth of eight children, he enlists in the Army for the Mexican War of 1846. He becomes friends with General Sam Houston, the first President of the Republic of Texas. He is discharged from the Army with a Land Warrant for 160 acres and moves to Kentucky. He marries on November 30, 1854 Harriett Bullitt, and their wedding photograph is shown. **John** sets up as a hardware merchant in Covington, Kentucky. But he develops asthma and for relief goes to visit Sam Houston in 1861 for the dry climate of Texas. The Civil War begins the day his ship docks in Galveston. Meanwhile, George Fitzhugh, a fourth cousin of **John,** plays a significant part in bringing that War about. Brother Patrick Henry, back in Virginia, forms a Company of Volunteers to fight in the Civil War and is elected Captain. In close and furious personal combat he dies on June 17, 1864. John's brother Thaddeus' swashbuckling War exploits are described. **John** enlists in the Confederate Army in Texas, but because of his ill health spends the War running a tanning yard. After the War he returns to Kentucky to find his property confiscated. He returns to Texas and settles in Austin, again in the hardware business. He lives a settled but unprosperous life thereafter, and dies in uncomfortable ill health and poverty in 1894.	Vol. Two, Chapter 3, p.88,92 p.93 p.97 p.102 pp.102-3 pp.104-16 p. 117

.o 304 o.

TIME FRAME	FAMILY MEMBERS Direct Ancestors in **Bold**	EVENTS AND BACKGROUND	CHAPTERS AND PAGES
1862-1932	**Henry Alexander Fitzhugh**	**Henry Alexander** is born on April 1, 1862 in the home of General Sam Houston, during the second year of the Civil War. The family are in financial difficulties. **Henry** has a flair for business adventure and tries his hand and ranch management (when he registers the cattle brand **HA**) and wheat farming. He then tries the oil business but loses control of the company. He moves to New Roads, Louisiana and goes into the cotton seed oil business, but loses all his mills in a price collapse following the end of World War I. In 1902, at age 40, he marries Mary Scott, age 20, a Texas girl and a graduate of Stanford University. They prosper and have six children. He dies in Memphis, Tennessee in 1932, never having seen a grandchild of his.	Vol. Two, Chapter 4 p.135 p.136 p.136

TIME FRAME	FAMILY MEMBERS Direct Ancestors in **Bold**	EVENTS AND BACKGROUND	CHAPTERS AND PAGES
1904- 1965	***John Henry Fitzhugh,*** ***Marie,*** his wife.	***John Henry*** is born in 1904 in Jackson, Mississippi while the family is fleeing a yellow fever epidemic. He is sent to Boarding School in Tennessee. He begins the first serious genealogical work but never makes any contact with the FitzHughs in England or discovers the correct Fitzhugh Arms. He has a serious nervous breakdown around 1926, and marries Eleanor Jeanes, the niece of the Superintendent of the hospital he is in. They have a daughter and are divorced in 1939. ***John*** marries Mrs Marie van O. Halverson, who has three children. Marie is from London, and has had a difficult life including hardship and destitution during the Great Depression and a more or less complete break with her family in England. But she recovers and eventually rises to a top job in the Civil Service. ***John*** and Marie build a large house in San Antonio, Texas. ***John*** indulges in silver and tableware importing, but fails to make it profitable. Together they achieve a reconciliation with the Church, but ***John*** succumbs to an unidentified illness, and dies in 1965. Marie retires to England, devotes herself to charity, travel, and grandchildren and dies in 1977. They are both buried at St. Martha-on-the-Hill near Guildford.	Vol. Two, Chapter 5 p.142 p.142 pp.143-145 p.147 p.146 p.148

TIME FRAME	FAMILY MEMBERS Direct Ancestors in **Bold**	EVENTS AND BACKGROUND	CHAPTERS AND PAGES
1944-	***Henry Antonie Fitzhugh***	***Henry Antonie*** is born in 1944 and grows up in San Antonio, Texas with the older Halverson children. He is expelled from school at age eight for Heresy, but then attends a much better school, where he is given a very strong science education, winning a place on an accelerated programme. With his parents he goes on his first trip to Europe in 1960. He goes to the Massachusetts Institute of Technology (MIT), studies aeronautical engineering, and then to Imperial College, London University to do a PhD. He meets Hilary Smith in 1968 and moves to St. Louis, Missouri to work in the aerospace industry. He narrowly escapes the Vietnam War, moves to England in 1970, and marries Hilary Smith in 1972. They have two sons, Alexander and Edward. He takes a job at London Transport and eventually rises, after many career changes, to become a Director of London Underground in 1986.	Vol. Two, Chapter 6, p.154 p.155 p.156 p.157 p.158 p.159 note 2 p.160-164

.oOo.

.o 307 o.

INDEX TO VOLUMES ONE & TWO

Page numbers in *Italic type* are in Volume One. Page numbers in Roman type are in Volume Two. Page numbers in **bold** in either type are in Family Trees in the respective Volume.

Aylett, Philip, 73, 75, 83

A

Abbey of Bec, *3, 7*
Abbots Ripton, *54*
Alamo, 88, 93
Ale, *76*
Allerton family, 192
Allerton, William, 51, **173**
Allison, Robert, 194
Allison, William, 198
Ampthill, *23, 81, 82, 150*
Amsterdam, 2
Ancient Inheritance of the Fitzhughs, *95, 111, 119, 129, 131*
Anglesey, William, *94*
Anne of Cleves, 257, 284
Appalachian Mountains, 73, 78
Armistead, Major William, 74
Arms, College of, *16*
Arms, Fitzhugh. see Fitzhugh Arms
Ashby-by-Partney, Lincs, *115, 119*
Ashwell, *27*
Aspley Guise, *32, 38, 39, 51, 56, 57, 60, 61, 65, 67, 81, 99, 103, 108*
Aspley Hall, *57, 58, 61*
Astry family, *77, 80*
Astry, Mary, *108, 120, 121, 122, 124*
Astry, Mary Fitzhugh, *93*
Astry, William, *80, 81, 82, 85, **84**, 93, 94, 95, 96, 98, 99, 100, 102, 106, 107, 108, 109, 113, 120, 121, 122, 123, 124, 125, 162, **170**, 182*
Astry, William, character of, *83, 95, 96*
Atkinson, Richard, ***146***
Austin, Texas, 133
Aylesbury, *82*
Aylett family, 198, 211
Aylett, Mary Macon, 73, 81, **174**, 198

B

Baker, John, *21*
Bales, John, 196
Balles, Elizabeth, *82*
Balles, Thomas, *81*
Baltimore, Md, 73
Barford, *11, 13, 49, 50, 75, 79, 86, 87, 88, 93, 99, 111, 114, 115, 116, 118, 119, 122, 123, 133*, 11, 12, 214
Barford Hundred, *4, 21*
Barforth, 214
Barnwell, *39*
Barwick, 214
Basmead, *5, 30*, 179
Beacons, *87*
Beauchamp, Roger de, *6*
Beaumaris Castle, 2
Beckett, Simon, *142, 147*
Bedford, *21, 22, 38, 39, 75, 86, 115, 116, 119*
Bedford Bridge, *116*, 3, 183, 247
Bedford Burgesses, 5
Bedford College of Burgesses, *143*
Bedford Council, 2, 5, 21
Bedford Estate, 39, 44, 47, 79
Bedford High Street, *116, 117, 145*, 4, 9, 245, 246
Bedford, Mayor of, *23, 86, 143, 148*, 2, 3, 4, 5, 8, 14, 20, 34, 184
Bedfordshire, *2, 6, 44*
Bedfordshire, last Fitzhugh, 74
Beer, *76, 142*
Beggary, *2, 3, 4, 6, 7, 11, 12, 13, 14, 17, 18, 21, 23, 32, 38, 79, 155*, 179, 180

.o 309 o.

C

Ouse, River, *2, 24, 55, 85, 116, 149*, 11, 166

T

Y

Z

CPSIA information can be obtained
at www.ICGtesting.com
Printed in the USA
BVOW03*0743231217

503551BV00005B/17/P